NOVI

THE LEGENDARY INDIANAPOLIS RACE CAR

Volume Two
The Granatelli Era (1961 - 1966)

GEORGE PETERS AND HENRI GREUTER

BAR JEAN ENTERPRISES
HAZELWOOD, MISSOURI 63042-0395

Copyright 1998 by George Peters and Henri Greuter

Bar Jean Enterprises
Box 395
Hazelwood, Missouri 63042-0395
U.S.A.

Library of Congress Catalog Card Number 91-75278
I.S.B.N: 0-9630227-1-7

Indianapolis 500 trademark names and photographs used with
permission of the Indianapolis Motor Speedway Corporation.

All Rights Reserved. No Part of This Book May be Reproduced
in Any Form or By Any Electronic Means Including
Informational Storage and Retrieval Systems Without Prior
Written Permission From the Publisher, Except by Reviewers
Who May Quote Brief Passages.

We recognize that some words, model names and designations, for example,
mentioned herein are the property of the trademark holder.
We use them for identification only.

Printed and Bound in the United States.

Front cover photograph courtesy of the Indianapolis Motor Speedway:
    Jim Hurtubise in the #56 Hotel Tropicana Special - 1963.

Back cover photograph courtesy of the Indianapolis Motor Speedway:
    A composed Duane Carter driving the brand new Studebaker-STP Special,
    the Novi-Ferguson at Indianapolis - 1964.

TABLE OF CONTENTS

DEDICATIONS	v
IN MEMORIAM	vi
ACKNOWLEDGEMENTS	vii
PREFACE	x
GALLERY OF NOVI DRIVERS, 1941-1965	xi
CHAPTER 1 - NEW OWNERSHIP	1
CHAPTER 2 - AN EARLY DEPARTURE - 1961	13
CHAPTER 3 - A MIND BOGGLING PROJECT THAT WAS NEVER TO BE	20
CHAPTER 4 - REBIRTH OF NOVI AND DREAMS	23
CHAPTER 5 - TWO NEW NOVIS-YET ANOTHER DISMAL YEAR -1962	26
CHAPTER 6 - GETTING THE ACT TOGETHER	40
CHAPTER 7 - A TRIUMPHAL RETURN - 1963	44
CHAPTER 8 - A CRASH, A BAD CLUTCH AND OIL LEAKS -1963	58
INTERMEZZO - A RADIO CONNECTION	71
CHAPTER 9 - AN OVERVIEW - SOME TECHNICAL CHANGE	72
CHAPTER 10 - EARLIER FOUR WHEEL DRIVE EFFORTS	81
CHAPTER 11 - THE NOVI ARMADA	85
CHAPTER 12 - A TRIO OF NOVIS IN FIELD AGAIN	90
CHAPTER 13 - BEST FINISH IN A TRAGIC RACE - 1964	101
CHAPTER 14 - CHANGES AND MORE CHANGE	111
CHAPTER 15 - THE LAST HURRAH	114
INTERMEZZO - PIT MASTERS, JOHNS GOES NORTH AND HERK IN THE SOUTH	131
CHAPTER 16 - PREPARATIONS FOR ANOTHER 500 - 1966	135
CHAPTER 17 - IS RETIREMENT TEMPORARY?	147
CHAPTER 18 - WHAT MIGHT HAVE BEEN	150
CHAPTER 19 - SOME REFLECTIONS	152
CHAPTER 20 - THE GRANATELLI NOVI YEARS IN PERSPECTIVE	156
INTERMEZZO - A BRIEF GRANATELLI CRITIQUE	160
CHAPTER 21 - ANDY GRANATELLI'S RECOLLECTIONS OF THE NOVI PROJECT	161
CHAPTER 22 - THE EARLY GRANATELLI YEARS	164
CHAPTER 23 - THE KATZENJAMMER KIDS ARRIVE AT INDY	170
CHAPTER 24 - FROM PAXTON TO STUDEBAKER	179
CHAPTER 25 - EARLY STUDEBAKER RACING	184
INTERMEZZO - BONNEVILLE SALT FLATS, PACKARD AND STUDEBAKER	191
CHAPTER 26 - THE BIRTH AND EARLY YEARS OF STP	192
INTERMEZZO - MASTER SALESMAN	202
CHAPTER 27 - THE REMAINING NOVI HARDWARE	204
CHAPTER 28 - THE MAGICAL DRAW OF THE NOVI	208
CHAPTER 29 - THE AFTERMATH	217
CHAPTER 30 - MEMORIES	220
SEVERAL LASTING PHOTO MEMORIES	229
BIBLIOGRAPHY	231
APPENDIX	238
INDEX	259
THE AUTHORS	273

Permission Granted By:

Doubleday, a group division of Benton, Doubleday Dell Publishing to quote material from the Bobby Unser Story by Bobby Unser and Joe Scalzo, ©1979.

Richard Langworth to use quotes from Studebaker, 1946-1966, The Classic Postwar Years which he authored. Dragonwyck Publishing, Ltd. ©1993. Out of print.

Motorbooks International, Osceola, WI, to quote material from Indy Racing Legends by Tony Sakkis, ©1996.

Publications International, Ltd. for use of quotes from "Bold Dollars: The Studebaker Champion of 1939-40" in Collectible Automobiles, June, 1966 issue.

Regnery Publishing, Inc. to quote material from They Call Me Mr. 500 by Anthony Granatelli. Copyright ©1969 by Regnery Publishing, Inc. All rights reserved. Regnery Publishing, Inc., Washington, D.C.

Witness Publishing, Marshall, IN, for the use of several quotes from Hurtubise by Bob Gates, ©1995.

From Parnelli: A Story of Auto Racing by Bill Libby. ©1969 by Bill Libby. Used by permission of Dutton Signet, a division of Penguin Books USA Inc.

Car and Driver for use of quote from "Indianapolis 500" by David E. Davis, Jr. August, 1964.

The authors have taken all possible care to trace any possible copyright holders of material that appears in this book, and to provide acknowledgements of such use.

DEDICATIONS

For the people, alive and gone, who are and were part of the Novi Legend. For the people on both sides of the Atlantic who supported me and helped me to make dreams come true. But foremost for those who allowed me to make these dreams come true Thank You folks.

Voor hen, in Leven en overleden, die deel vitmaakten van de Novi Legende. Voor hen, aan beide zijden van de Oceaan die my hielpen en steunden bij het tot stand brengen van een droom. Maar vooral voor hen die het mogelyk maakten deze droom waar te maken. Bedankt allemaal.

Henri Greuter

For Barbara

This volume would not have reached fruition had it not been for the long and dedicated effort, support and proding rendered by the light of my life, my wife Barbara.

and for

Jared, Alicia and Shianne,
Three jewels in our lives.

George Peters

In Memoriam

Jan Apetz
Duane Carter
Bill Cheesbourg
Neely Connor
Dr. Carl Dunst
James B. "Radio" Gardner
Mike Guglielmucci
Norman Hall
Sam Hanks
Gene Hartley

Roscoe "Pappy" Hough
Jim Hurtubise
Bob Laycock
Louie Meyer
Hal Robson
Bob "Buck" Rogers
Troy Ruttman
Gordon Schroeder
Floyd Trevis
Tom & Lynda Vastine

To those who are gone, but not forgotten as fond memories remain.

How Sweet Must Be The Peace That Heroes Find

ACKNOWLEDGEMENTS

A study of this sort would not be possible without the aid and support of a number of individuals. Some went way beyond the "call of duty" in assisting in our research. To all who helped we are eternally grateful. Thanks to one and all.

Freddie Agabashian *	Walnut Creek CA
Carl W. Alleman	Selma, OR
Mario Andretti	Nazareth, PA
Henry Banks *	Indianapolis, IN
Jack Beckley	Glendale, AZ
Charles Bolton	Anderson, IN
Steve Bonesteel	Clovis, CA
R.J. "Buck" Boudeman	Richland, MI
Johnny Boyd	Fresno, CA
Robert L. Boyer	Bloomington, IN
Clint Brawner *	Phoenix, AZ
Frank Brisko *	Ojibwa, WI
Robert Bruhn	Englewood, CO
Duane Carter Sr. *	Indianapolis, IN
Bill Cheesbourg *	Tucson, AZ
Bob Clidinst	Indianapolis, IN
Randy Christianson	Denison, TX
Jesse I. Cunningham	Schenectady, NY
Donald Davidson	Indianapolis, IN
Mary Ann DeHart	St. Joseph, MO
Louis D'Leia	Pacific Palisades, CA
Harvey Duck	Coral Springs, FL
Ray Erickson	Hudson, FL
Eddie Evans	Bedford, IN
Ryan Falconer	Salinas, CA
Martyn Flower	Ingleby Barbick, Great Britain
James Bell "Radio" Gardner *	Portsmouth, OH
Jim Gardner	Charlotte, NC
Anthony (Andy) Granatelli	Montecito, CA
Vince Granatelli	Santa Monica, CA
Vince Granatelli, Jr.	Phoenix, AZ
Alice Hanks	Pacific Palisades, CA
Sam Hanks *	Pacific Palisades, CA
Joe Henning	Burbank, CA
James Hoggatt	Indianapolis, IN
Ted Hollingsworth	Speedway, IN

John Holthaus	Santa Margarita, CA
Paul Hooft	Zoetermeer, The Netherlands
Deke Houlgate	Redondo Beach, CA
Marvin Jenkins	St. George, UT
Parnelli Jones	Torrance, CA
Bobby Johns	Miami, FL
Jason Koch	Oregon City, OR
Michael J. Kollins	Bloomfield Hills, MI
Thomas Kinney	Speedway, IN
Carel van Kuyk	Zoetermeer, The Netherlands
Bob Laycock *	Indianapolis, IN
C. Dwight Liggett	Zurich, Switzerland
Ralph Liguori	Tampa, FL
Greg Littleton	Columbus, IN
Art Malone	Tampa, FL
Ronald Marinko	Los Angeles, CA
Jim McElreath	Arlington, TX
Louis Meyer*	Searchlight, NV
George Moore	Indianapolis, IN
Dennis "Duke" Nalon	Indianapolis, IN
C. Lee Norquest *	Indianapolis, IN
Lois Norquest	Indianapolis, IN
Lee Pate *	St Joseph, MO
Bruce Peters	Southaven, MS
Dick Rathmann	Melbourne, FL
Jim Rathmann	Melbourne, FL
James A. Reynolds	Pittsboro, IN
Robert Reynolds	Speedway, IN
Bob Rogers *	Tallequah, OK
Bob Russo	Covina, CA
Troy Ruttman *	Lake Havasu City, AZ
Ralph Salvino	Corona, CA
Walt Schaub	Oakville, MO
Gordon Schroeder *	Hollywood, CA
Carmen Schroeder	Hollywood, CA
Don Shepherd	Speedway, IN
Richard Smith	Spring, TX
Al Swenson	Glenview, IL
A. J. Watson	Speedway, IN
Don Woodward	Tucson, AZ
Robert Woodward	Tucson, AZ
Crocky Wright	Speedway, IN
John Zink	Tulsa, OK

* Deceased

We have had correspondence by letter with the following people and organizations:

Ing. Erico Benzing	Milano, Italy
Sir Jack Brabham	Brands Hatch Racing Park, Great Britain
John Cooper	Ferring, Great Britain
Andrew Ferguson *	Team Lotus International Ltd, Norfolk, England
Ferguson Company, FF Development, Ltd.	Coventry, Great Britain
Christopher G. Foster	Gales Ferry, CT
Steve Des Georges	Phoenix, AZ
Franco Gozzi	Ferrari Spa, Modena, Italy
James Hoggatt	Indianapolis, IN
Frank Kurtis *	Glendale, CA
Stirling Moss	London, Great Britain
Rob Wiedenhoff	Leidschendam, The Netherlands
Robert Bosch GmbH	Stuttgart, Federal Republic of Germany

The generous and supportive position taken by the Indianapolis Motor Speedway Photo Shop under the direction of Ron McQueeney, Director of Photography, and his assistant Pat Jones is most deeply appreciated. The personable staff of helpers who also rendered tremendous help were Steve Ellis, Robin Meyers and Sue Jordan. A special thanks to each of you.

One member of the staff stated that while we provided quite a bit of work, dealing with that era and subject, it proved to be a pleasurable experience. The results we saw gave credence to the statement.

The photos with the IMS credit line were supplied by the Indianapolis Motor Speedway. IMS photographs are available from the Photo Office, IMS, 4790 West 16th Street, Indianapolis, IN 46222.

Photographs also supplied by:

Frank "Satan" Brewer	Mesa, AZ
Leroy Byers	Denver, CO
Ken Coles	Pinckney, MI
Bruce Craig	Phillipsburg, NJ
John Darlington	Carmel, IN
Armin Krueger	Davenport, FL
Wim Oude Weernink	Wyen, The Netherlands
Bob Sheldon	Burnham, IL
Bob Tronolone	Burbank, CA
Gerald Walker	Columbus, IN

A tip of the hat is also owed to photographer Tony Sciarrelli of Sciarrelli Photo Lab. of St Louis, MO for his invaluable help in our photographic endeavors.

Sincere thanks to C. Dwight Liggett for his continuing support and encouragement.

Special thanks also goes to George Moore whose excellent <u>Indianapolis Star</u> stories and columns on the Novi have been of extraordinary help during our research.

A sincere thanks to Buck Boudeman for his imput. Not only is Buck a gifted race car restorer, but a mechanical wizard and highly knowledgable auto racing historian as well.

Our deep appreciation is also extended to Eddie Evans, owner of the Antique Auto Race Car Museum of Bedford, IN.

To Jep Cadou - Thanks for his thorough and gratuitous critique of Volume I.

Thanks to Darrol Pierson and John Selch of the Indianapolis State Library Newspaper Dept. for the help they carried out in supplying us with printouts of microfilm of the Indianapolis newspapers of the 1961-1966 period.

Henri Greuter also wishes to thank his collegues at the Dept. of Nuclear Medicine of the Free University Academic Hospital in Amsterdam, The Netherlands, for their support in every meaning of the word.

PREFACE

For those readers who may have missed Volume One of our study of the famed Novi race cars, permit us to briefly recap some of the highlights relating to the years prior to 1961.

The driving force behind the Novis was Lewis Welch who began his working career at the Ford Motor Company's River Rouge plant in Detroit in 1925, at the age of 18. Welch remained there until he formed his own automotive parts factory in nearby Novi, Michigan in 1935. Welch's mechanical expertise and ambition had caught the eye of Henry Ford, who aided Welch in establishing his manufacturing business. Like Ford, Welch also derived pleasure from auto racing. The pair were well aware of the fact that the sport not only helped provide for automobile improvements, but that the resultant publicity could serve as an excellent publicity tactic.

After entering cars in the Indianapolis 500 Mile Race for several years (1938-1940), Welch, in conjunction with noted racing mechanic/designer Bud Winfield, conceived the idea for a new racing powerplant - a supercharged V-8 block that would generate its power through a front wheel drive (FWD).

With input from his more famous brother, the racing genius Ed Winfield, Bud sketched out the basics for such an engine and then had them refined by the Offenhauser Company, the leading producer of Indianapolis racing engines at the time.

The finished product was then placed in a six year old Miller-Ford chassis that had been designed to handle a far less powerful engine, the normally aspirated Ford V-8. However, the new engine would retain the FWD created for the earlier chassis. The new engine entered in the 1941 Indianapolis race proved to be quite successful, its chassis shortcomings notwithstanding. With veteran Indy pilot Ralph Hepburn at the wheel, the car, then identified as a Winfield, finished a very respectable 4th.

As World War II was being concluded, Welch had car builder Frank Kurtis design and construct a new chassis specifically for the powerful blown V-8 engine. With its enormous horsepower the car became an instant favorite to win the racing classic. In several post-war 500s the Novi was the only car not powered by an Offenhauser engine. To add to its uniqueness, there was that banshee sound emitted by the powerful engine.

Yet, during the following years of Welch's ownership the car (some years two entries were submitted) failed to make the dream trip to victory lane. The all-elusive victory was never captured by the car which became known simply as the Novi in 1946. In 1956, Welch commissioned Kurtis to build two rear engine drive cars. The FWD racers and the rear drive creations accomplished some outstanding feats: establishing several new qualifying marks; starting from the pole on several occasions and leading the race on a number of occasions. While a Novi race cars did finish as high as third in 1948 and earned several fourths, a so-called "jinx" label was soon attached to the cars.

Following the establishment of his Novi, Michigan factory, Welch developed other business venues. They included oil field investments, a Ford reconditioning parts factory under the auspices of the Ford Company and a chain of Novi stores that would merchandise a line of automotive products with the lead item being the Novi air conditioner. At the time, air conditioners were some years away from becoming a standard item with most new cars or even a factory option.

By the latter 1950s, Welch's business operations began to sour for various reasons. In order to meet his mounting debt obligations, Welch not only had to dispose of his entire factory operations, but the Novi stores and the oil holdings as well. With such catastrophic business reversals, Welch ultimately found it imperative to dispose of his beloved Novi racing operation. In the latter part of 1960, feelers were sent out into the racing community and a buyer was secured in the early months of 1961. It is at that point that Volume Two resumes the tale of what many racing aficionados consider the most famous and legendary race car(s) to ever compete at the Indianapolis Motor Speedway, notwithstanding the fact that the Novi never achieved a 500 victory.

Editor notes: In an effort to avoid being overly redundant the term Novi is used, though as we have pointed out it was not a single car for on numerous occasions several were present at Indy attempting to make the starting field.

Further, when the proper noun Granatelli is used, it is in reference to Andy (who in his first years of racing was known as Tony). When the plural is used it refers to the three Granatelli brothers: Joe, Andy and Vince.

Finally, our preference for abbreviations when covering front wheel drive is the following: FWD. When four wheel drive is mentioned the identification used is 4WD.

Every possible effort was made to avoid errors or the omission of valued data. Some information obtained was contradictory to other sources. When this occurred we made an exerted effort to clarify the matter.

A dedicated and diligent effort was made to provide as complete a presentation as possible. Some factors are lacking, due to conditions beyond our control. Regrettably, this means that several sources failed to materialize. On the other hand, some long shots resulted in unexpected data that went considerably beyond our expectations.

GALLERY OF NOVI DRIVERS

The Gallery features those drivers who participated in one or more Indianapolis style race car events behind the wheel of a Novi.

Ralph Hepburn   1941 - 4th
1946 - 14th
*1948

Cliff Bergere   1947 - 21st
*1980

*   Denotes year of death

Herb Ardinger   1947 - 4th**
*1973

Duke Nalon   1948 - 3rd   1949 - 29th
1951 - 10th   1952 - 25th
1953 - 11th

Rex Mays   1949 - 25th
*1949

** Cliff Bergere relief driver

Chet Miller   1951 - 25th   1952 - 28th
*1953

Paul Russo   1956 - 33rd   1957 - 4th
1958 - 18th
*1976

Tony Bettenhausen   1957 - 15th
*1961

Bill Cheesbourg   1958 - 10th
*1995

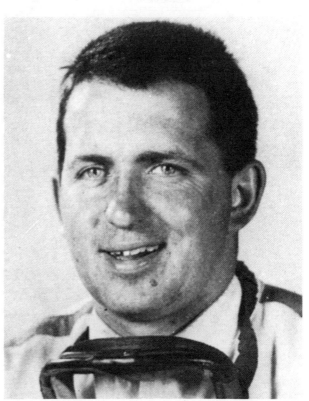

Jim Hurtubise   1963 - 22nd   1965 - 33rd
1965 - Atlanta
*1989

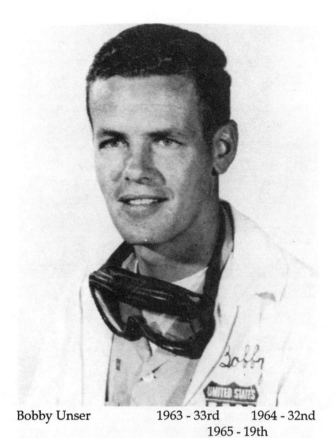

Bobby Unser   1963 - 33rd   1964 - 32nd
1965 - 19th

Art Malone   1963 - 31st   1964 - 11th

Jim McElreath   1964 - 21st

Bud Tingelstad   ***1965 - 14th
Atlanta only
*1981

*** Bobby Unser relief driver

Chapter 1

New Ownership

The famed Novi race cars most certainly had been in the limelight at the Indianapolis Motor Speedway during the years of Lew Welch's ownership. The Welch operation (1941-1960) had enjoyed some glorious moments as well as some dismal disappointments at the Speedway. After experiencing some extraordinary business setbacks in non-racing endeavors, Welch was compelled to sell the entire Novi undertaking in late1960. The failure of his two cars to make the 1960 starting field certainly did not improve his financial position.

Feelers were put out through the racing community in an effort to dispose of the highly touted cars. While some car owners apparently gave consideration to a purchase, the big drawback would be an investment that involved a racing operation centered around a single race each year. There were some reports that California racing innovator Mickey Thompson was interested in such a purchase. One can surmise that Thompson wished to procure the Novi engine in his relentless pursuit of new land speed records or for another of his many creative programs.

However, on March 29, 1961, an announcement was made that the Granatelli brothers had purchased the Novi race cars from Lew Welch. There has been a continuing debate among some members of the Indy racing fraternity as to the actual purchase price of the Novis. In The Kurtis Kraft Story by Ed Hitze, Frank Kurtis is quoted as saying that in late 1960 he received a call from Welch offering all the Novi equipment for $10,000. It is known that Welch had secured a 90 day note for $10,000 and as the expiration date drew close he desperately sought to fulfill the loan obligation. Other reports state that the sale price was in the $30,000 to $40,000 range.

Whatever the price may have been, quite naturally the news of the sale created a stir among the loyal legion of Novi fans. In announcing the sale, the Indianapolis Times headlined the purchase by declaring "Novi's Coming Back to 500." The Times article also stated that dragster Mickey Thompson had been negotiating to purchase the Novis, but for some undisclosed reason, the deal fell through at the last minute.

For the Granatellis, participation in the Indianapolis 500 certainly would not be a new experience as they had cars entered every year from 1946 through 1954. Following the 1954 race, they had backed off from further Indy involvement until the Novi purchase (for the earlier Granatelli record see Chapter 23).

The Granatelli's purchase consisted of two rear drive chassis, three engines and a myriad of spare racing parts. At the time of the acquisition, Andy Granatelli stated that they planned to enter both of the rear drive Novis in the 1961 running of the 500. Frank Kurtis had constructed the two cars for Lew Welch back in 1956. Andy said, "We have quite a job on our hands and I hope the fans in Indianapolis don't condemn us if we fail to set the world on fire our first time back there. But I'll tell you this, and you can quote me, this is the last year for the Offenhauser engine to win. We'll be ready next year." When Granatelli was asked who would be driving the cars, he stated that he had not even had a chance to think about that. In a jovial mood, Granatelli said that they would be looking for "some young eager fellow who thinks he can handle this powerful machine."

When asked about possible changes in the car, he declared that only minor alterations would be made the first year. He asserted that they planned to come back and put themselves in a learning mode with respect to the super-strong Novi engine. Continuing, Granatelli said that he certainly did plan to change the carburetor setup as the cars had missed the last two races because of this malady. Andy seemed unconcerned about potential carburetion problems as he noted that the Granatellis had been manufacturing the Paxton supercharger for several years.

With the sale completed, the Novis and all the accompanying equipment was transferred to the

Granatelli's Paxton manufacturing plant at 929 Olympic Blvd. in Santa Monica, California. The Granatellis also acquired the services of master mechanic Jean Marcenac who had labored on the Novis since 1950. In no time at all, the Granatelli clan beganclamoring about the cars in preparation for entry in that year's 500. Later reports suggest that the Granatellis, along with the assistance of several employees, went through the Novis with a fine tooth comb as they wished to be fully prepared for the race. It has been said that due to the late acquisition of the cars, the Granatellis found it necessary to work around the clock in order to assure themselves the best possible advantage when they arrived at the Speedway. Andy, his brothers and other team members had spent 21 days and nights preparing the car for Indy prior to the departure from California. It was truly a family project for even Andy's young son, Vince, was involved in the car's preparation.

As the Granatellis completed the Novi purchase from Lew Welch, Andy had requested entry blanks for both cars. Yet, at some point it was determined that they would return to Indy with only one car rather than trying to make the show with both racers.

The sole Novi entry arrived at the Speedway on May 2, after a fifty-one hour drive straight through from Santa Monica with "long-time chaperone" Jean Marcenac. The car was the one driven by Paul Russo in the 500s of 1956, 1957 and 1958. It now carried the #75 and was yellow colored with a wide offset black strip that ran from the nosecone on back. The official entry form identified the rear drive car as the Paxton Products Supercharged V-8 Special. No identification markings on the car were made as to the fact that the car contained a Novi engine. To some Novi purists and/or devotees the illustrious heritage of the Novi was gone or at least greatly diminished. Meanwhile, other Novi followers still looked upon this as being a viable Novi entry. For its part, the press consistently referred to the car as the Novi as it was powered by what was basically the heart of the entire Novi legend: the famed supercharged V-8 engine.

The unloading of the car from the flat bed truck in Gasoline Alley created considerable excitement as a group of curious onlookers, including drivers, car owners and mechanics, formed a ring around the truck to view the fabled car now under new ownership. The team arrived with such a vast amount of spare parts, their designated garage space was too small to contain all of the team's equipment. To gain sufficient working space, the crew placed a few packing crates in front of the garage and placed a rope around them. As might be expected, the Novi continued to attract a great deal of attention. One account made reference to the Novi as being the "perennial darling of the fans." Seeing the Novi back once again certainly delighted many fans. Add to that the fact that the car now sported a massive tail fin that could not go unnoticed. One observer described the car as "more distinctive than ever" what with the huge dorsal fin. The tail piece was secured with a stabilizing wire on each side that extended half way up the back of the fin from a nerfing bar positioned around the tail. The enormous fin, constructed of three-eights inch aluminum, had the rear end of the car reaching a height of 52 inches. Some spectators on hand noted that Andy took great pride in the prominent fin, which incidentally was painted black to match the offset black strip. Granatelli alleged that the rudder-like tail was set at 16 degrees off center to the left in anticipation that it would "retain torque coming off the turns and offer 100 pounds of weight to the left side of the car as it enters turns." Later, Joe Granatelli was to assert that the real test for the tail might not be determined on the track but back in Gasoline Alley as "everybody that comes in either wants to lean on it or try to shake it." One observer summed up his judgment of the large fin in a single word: "grotesque!"

Another visual difference compared with the car's appearance in the past was the oil tank. Like many of the Offy powered roadsters, the Novi now carried a teardrop shaped oil tank on the left side of the car, at cockpit level in front of the rear wheel. In the years when Lew Welch owned the 500Fs they never ran with such an oil tank placement.

In discussing the five year old Frank Kurtis built car, Andy said, "It'll either go faster than any other car here or it won't run at all." On the dyno it had reportedly registered approximately 300 horsepower more than any Offy at the track.

With the mad rush to ready the car prior to the team's departure from California, Andy had yet to secure the services of a driver. He was to opt for a chauffeur once the team reached Indianapolis. No sooner was the car at the Speedway than many were asking who would drive the Novi. The Granatellis seemed unconcerned as it was reported that a dozen drivers had made known their desire to pilot the powerful racer. Andy found an interim driver in long-time friend Dick Rathmann. Dick was one of the California hot rod drivers who had journeyed to the Midwest shortly after World War II to compete on the Hurricane Racing circuit that Granatelli had helped form.

Rathmann's racing credentials in the years that followed were certainly impressive. In 1950, he had

(1961) Andy (left) and Joe Granatelli confer with "test pilot" Dick Rathmann. The yellow paint job with the bold black stripe was quite attractive. I.M.S.

made his first 500 appearance driving A.J. Watson's first Indy built chassis. The car, officially known as the City of Glendale Special, was constructed with numerous used parts as the Watson/Rathmann undertaking was truly a shoestring operation. The car was unofficially known as the "Pots and Pans Special." Some railbirds were startled by the mere fact that the car made the show. Dick's race run lasted all of 25 laps before the flywheel, undoubtedly a hand-me-down item, let go.

For the next five years (1951-1955), Dick had switched his attention to National Association for Stock Car Automobile Racing (NASCAR) competition where he racked up 13 Grand National victories. He returned to champ car competition in 1956 and in spite of the five year layoff he finished 5th, completing all 200 laps. For the 1958, race he established a new qualifying record in Lee Elkins McNamara Special to start from the pole. The horrendous first lap crash, instigated by another driver in the front row, put him out of competition for the day. In the 1960 race, driving Jim Robbins' maroon and gold colored #97, Dick again gave every indication that he was a solid qualifier as he posted the 6th fastest qualifying run - 145.5 m.p.h. Unfortunately, his splendid qualifying run was offset by an early departure from the race due to brake failure.

For 1961, Dick once again had agreed to drive for car owner Jim Robbins, although early in the month he did have sufficient time to shakedown the Novi. Andy had invited Dick to test drive the Novi in order to help sort out the recently acquired car. While the engine had considerable dyno time back in Santa Monica, the Granatellis wanted to check out its track performance as qualification approached. Ample time appeared to be at hand as the qualifications would not start until Saturday, May 13. When Andy was repeatedly asked when a permanent driver would be hired, he finally replied that once the crew had the car setup where it could run 150 m.p.h. "then we will go about selecting a driver." The 150 m.p.h. statement seemed somewhat suspect and certainly raised eyebrows as no car had ever qualified with such an average speed. Some were inclined to believe that the Granatellis were overly optimistic on their car's potential and they were not reluctant to be quoted to that affect. This lofty approach appeared to be particularly questionable as the car was new to them.

Dick was more than willing to help with the Novi and in a recent conversation he recalled that his evaluation of the car was very positive. Dick also declared that while Andy took credit for setting up the car, he (Dick) knew how he wanted the car. Rathmann was candid, for he stated that he had learned a good deal about Indy car chassis setups from Rodger Ward and the late Pat O'Connor. Let it be said that Dick was no slouch when it came to race car preparation as he had served as a mechanic on any number of cars that he had driven. This was also the case when he had migrated to NASCAR competition.

On his first outing with the car on May 4, Dick turned in only a handful of laps with the fastest being 140.6 m.p.h. The run came to an end when the blower sneezed as the car roared down the straightaway to end that day's action. In working with the Novi,

The incident aside, a number of railbirds were surprised for few expected the car to reach such a speed so quickly. Among those registering some surprise with the 140 m.p.h. time was Dick Rathmann! Dick felt that his top speed had probably been about 135 m.p.h. When informed of the actual speed Dick said, "It's hard to believe. It was real easy. That car feels real good, super good." As for Andy, he was so delighted and ecstatic he felt that once the wrinkles were ironed out the car would be capable of a speed of at least 155 m.p.h! Andy said, "When a driver tells you he hasn't pushed it hard, yet he runs at a speed higher than expected one has to be quite satisfied. When a driver gets the feel of a car and the thing gets to handling well he can go 155 to 160 m.p.h. just as easily as he can drive a 145-146 m.p.h. lap. The more he gets into it coming out of the turns, the sooner the car comes out and the quicker it will go." Dick has made reference to using the "firewall brake" in driving through the corners at

(1961) Dick Rathmann coming into pits after some practice laps in the Novi. Note the high cowling and wind screen. The tri-winged display on the dorsal fin represents the logo used by the Granatellis' Paxton Products Company.

Rathmann recalled that an engine backfire was rather commonplace and that resulted in the engine compartment hood all but being blown off. Dick said that when this first occurred it "really scared the hell" out of him. Rathmann said he was concerned when the supercharger blew back black smoke on its first outing causing him to shut down the car's power, though he asserted that he was "not frightened by the car's alleged jinxed past." However, conditions quickly improved and Dick gave credit for the improved ignition to the fine tuning by Andy and the crew.

Indy. Dick adds that by firmly planting a foot against the firewall, the temptation to tap the brakes had been lessened. It would be a self-imposed psychological job that some drivers were able to perform.

Up to this point the fastest practice lap had been registered by 1959 winner Rodger Ward. Ward had clicked off a lap at 144.7 m.p.h. in the #2 Sun City Special owned by Bob Wilke. Meanwhile, Granatelli reported that "Dick told me that he could put it (the Novi) on the pole." At the time, the qualifying record was a 149.056 m.p.h.

set by rookie Jim Hurtubise in the Travelon Trailer Special the previous year. Prior to that, the record had been a 145.974 m.p.h. established by none other than Dick Rathmann back in 1958.

The early speed was indeed remarkable for the 140.6 m.p.h. reading was something that had not been turned in by a Novi with any regularity since 1958 and certainly not as easily as what Dick Rathmann had accomplished in a seemingly effortless manner. That first day on the track with a new Novi owner was more than promising to say the least. Some observers now wondered if once again the Novi was going to perform in a spectacular fashion. Was the Novi back on track? Nearly everyone seemed to be hopeful.

The following day it rained to the point of preventing any track activity. Granatelli used the opportunity to talk with the press. He spoke in glowing terms of the car having the possibility of reaching 155 or 160 m.p.h. "with the right man at the wheel."

The next day, Rathmann was back on the track in the #75 Paxton Special and he reached a speed of over 144.2 m.p.h. The only driver to surpass that speed was former Novi pilot, Tony Bettenhausen, who drove the #5 Autolite Special owned by Lindsey Hopkins. The Hopkins' car was one of the so-called lay-over Offys where the engine was tilted to the left. Tony was setting a blistering pace as he quickly had the Autolite car up to 145.5 m.p.h. Tony aptly demonstrated that he was still one of the best drivers in the business and that his mount was one of the hottest ever at the Speedway. When Tony came in after the 145 plus lap, Andy was quick to acknowledge the quick time as he approached Bettenhausen to say, "Nice going Tony."

(1961) Tony Bettenhausen proudly posed with his Autolite Special following a practice session. The Lindsey Hopkins owned car was the fastest during the days preceeding qualifications. Dick Rathmann in the Novi was second fast. I.M.S.

On May 7, Bettenhausen turned a lap at over 147 m.p.h. but to the pure delight of Dick Rathmann and the Granatellis, Dick followed with a lap at over 146 m.p.h. Returning to the pits, Dick Rathmann expressed delight with the car's performance. He said, "Whew, that's a lot of car. It felt like it's got some left." Unfortunately, the caution light had been displayed for another car causing Dick to say, "Except for that I might have cut a real quick one." Others felt that his times were extraordinary considering the limited amount of time the car had been trackside. On its fifth day of track activity it was quite apparent that the Granatellis were headed in the right direction with what many had regarded as a "dead horse" a year earlier.

For the first time in three years the six year old Kurtis-Kraft 500F chassis came close to the fastest speed it had displayed in the past. Some recalled the past glory of the Novi when it was one of the fastest cars at the Speedway what with its phenomenal speeds down the straights. Novi followers had to be delighted and pleasantly surprised at the speeds that were achieved so soon after the car reached Indy.

How had the Novi suddenly become the second fastest car at the track when it could not come close to making the races of the previous two years? The generally accepted solution appears to rest with the Bosch dual magneto system. The background to the Novis using the dual system goes back to 1957. When the Novis had run the high-banked Monza track in Italy, they were able to run at full throttle. Yet, even then occasional misfirings occurred. In consultation with Marcenac, Bosch engineers suggested the use of dual plugs and twin mags. This arrangement had been used with the Mercedes straight eight since the mid 1950s. Marcenac bought the idea. When the Bosch personnel asked what degree advance was planned for the Novi they were told 30. Unbeknownst to Jean, the factory had preset the mags 30 degrees. As a result, when Jean made his setting of 30 degrees, in actuality it was set at a phenomenal 60 degrees! For most engines such a setting would have shattered the powerplant, yet the tremendously strong Novi could handle the extra load to a higher range. With the 60 degree setting, the overloads had been creating the blower problems the previous two years. The whole system bore the brunt of the backfire for as the engine was pushed hard the enormous ignition firing created havoc.

Floyd Wheeler, then General Manager of the Paxton aftermarket business, recalls the discovery this way:

"Joe and I had been upstairs in the engine building clean room, and Joe was discussing with Jean Marcenac why the engine wouldn't turn the 9,000 rpms it was suppose to and was bogging down at six. Joe was the true ignition expert in our group and he said it sounded like the engine had too much timing. When Joe asked Jean how much timing he had told the Bosch engineers he was running in the engine Jean replied 36 degrees, and they put that much into the mags. Then Jean had put another 36 degrees into the engine. So there it was, a total of 72 degrees running in the atomic bomb downstairs with brother Andy sitting three feet from it! Joe ran into the dyno room and shut the engine down. Andy and Ron Falk were sitting no more than three feet from the engine, with no barrier or protection between them or the engine. Andy said, 'What's the big idea?' Joe said, 'Marcenac and Bosch bought a million dollar insurance on you and Falk, Chicago style, and put 72 degrees of timing into the engine. I told them that was okay, but until I was included in the deal, I wasn't going to blow up a perfectly good engine and not collect too!' Joe was an apt trouble-shooter with a fabulous sense of humor. The way he put it, it was very funny at the time although quite sobering after a little reflection."

Dick Rathmann　　　　　　　　　　　I.M.S.

Needless to say an isolation wall was built between the engine and its controls for future testing. [Author's note: While the double 36 degree setting mentioned by Mr. Wheeler exceeds what Andy Granatelli recounts in his autobiography - 30 degrees, one can reasonably assume that whatever the setting, it far surpassed the manufacturer's designated reading.] Andy stated, "It is a wonder that the engine ever ran. An Indy car would be a cinch to at least burn a piston. What we were doing...was firing a piston before it got to the top of the bore."

On May 10, Bettenhausen and Rathmann resumed their struggle as the drama continued to unfold. Both drivers eagerly sought the honor of establishing the unofficial fastest time prior to the opening round of qualifications. Tony laid claim to the honor when he unwound the Autolite to a speed of 149.2 m.p.h. which was just a whisker under the official track speed. As for Rathmann, he followed with a 148.2 m.p.h. clocking. At long last the 146.6 m.p.h. reading by Paul Russo on May 16, 1956, which had been the fastest lap for the 500F Novi at the Indianapolis Motor Speedway (I.M.S.) had been shattered. Remember, this record had been set in the year which saw the debut of the 500F Novi and it had not been approached in the years thereafter. Such an improvement was evidence of what might have been possible in earlier years if the team had not been bothered with one heartbreaking problem after another. This 148.2 reading seemed to convince the Granatellis that a 150 m.p.h. average was then within the realm of possibility. Add to this the fact that Rathmann appeared to be on an even faster lap than the 148.2 m.p.h., but he had to back off when the yellow light was turned on for a minor incident when another driver spun. With the times being turned in by the Novi, obviously the crew was extremely delighted that the car had run without any major sign of weakness. With some nearly flawless performances, Lady Luck seemed to have finally smiled on the Novi. Yet, some people must have been concerned that the familiar "hex" would return. There was some cause for such fears. While Rathmann's hottest lap was possibly terminated because of a yellow, he caused two yellows that same day while driving the Novi. The first was caused by an empty fuel tank and the second because the bypass valve on the fuel pump stuck. So, apart from all the euphoria there were a few minor glitches. A sign of things to come?

With the impressive speeds obtained by the Novi and so early, Rathmann's confidence was such that he decided to leave the Robbins' car on May 11, saying, "I feel confident that I can win in the Novi." He announced his appreciation for everything that Jim Robbins, the Royal Oaks, Michigan car owner, had done in his behalf. Dick then acknowledged that he was at the Speedway to win and that he thought the Novi was the car that could get the job done.

With all of the exhilaration, Andy officially offered Dick the Novi ride for the race. Granatelli said, he "was tickled to death that Rathmann had decided to drive the Paxton car. Dick really sits in the car, knows what he's doing and is a fine driver." He also exalted in the fact that Dick "drove the car boldly and deftly." Dick informed Andy that Jim Robbins had him under contract, yet he assured Andy that he could get out of the contractual obligation in order to drive the Novi. For his part, Dick worked along with Andy as they sought to secure a driver replacement for the Robbins' car. With the assistance of Jim Rathmann, Dick's brother who won the previous year's 500, Andy secured Pat Flaherty, the 1956 Indy 500 winner, to pilot the Robbins' car. Andy went so far as to offer the Robbins' team some assistance in getting their car track ready.

It appears that the Novi camp moved quickly as a press release stipulated that Rathmann was to take over the Novi ride. Yet, such was not to be. On Thursday, May 11, Henry Banks, the United States Auto Club's (USAC) Director of Competition informed Andy Granatelli that in spite of the effort that Andy had undertaken to secure a replacement driver for the Robbins' car it was a futile gesture. Banks reported that Robbins was going to hold Rathmann to his contract and that was that. Robbins was not thrilled with the screaming headlines that his driver had switched to the Novi. For his part, Robbins asserted that he had an iron-clad contract with Rathmann and added, "I gave him a $1,000 advance...I can make him sit here on the pit wall race day if I want to, even if we don't get a car in the race. This contract even keeps him from legally taking a ride in another car." The honeymoon between Dick Rathmann and the Novi was over.

When asked about the deal with Robbins and the attempted switch to the Granatelli team, Dick Rathmann informed us that his Robbins' contract was for something like $3,500 - $4,000. Such an arrangement was the norm for a driver like him in those days. Only a few "hotshots" could attain more up-front money. Andy had offered Dick $5,000 to drive the Novi. Further, Pat Flaherty was more than pleased that his pal, Dick, had secured the Novi ride for it would enable him to obtain the Robbins' ride. That expectation now was not to be realized as a Rathmann move was now invalid. As for Andy, he recalled his feelings about the failure to secure Dick's services with a lot of emotion. He had the #75 Novi reaching a very impressive speed with a good shot at the pole only to see Rathmann's removal from the car. The Granatellis found themselves without a driver and Pole Day less than two days away. Car owner Robbins was so intent on retaining the services of Rathmann that he was reported to have arrived at the Speedway accompanied by a lawyer. A belated attempt to buy Dick's way out of the contract failed for as the discussion was being carried on, the Robbins' car was on the track qualifying!

With Robbins refusal to permit the lead-footed Rathmann to move to the Novi team, Andy was obviously in need of another driver. Driver Ralph Liguori was aware of the Granatelli dilemma and had remained in the area hoping to secure the Novi ride. Ralph was a "third year rookie" in 1961, having passed his rookie test in 1959, although he failed to make the starting field that year and in 1960. Andy agreed to place Ralph in the Novi cockpit.

Ralph well remembers "hanging around the garages" when Andy came up to inquire if he wanted to take a test drive in the Novi. In those days being hired on the spot was not uncommon. In recent years the cockpits have been designed for a particular

Ralph Liguori   *Authors Collection*

driver. Ralph reminds his listener that the cockpits were rather "standard," thus making it far easier for a speedster to hop into any given car. In his autobiography, They Call Me Mister 500, Andy Granatelli recalls that Ralph was carefully instructed by him on how to drive the car. While not recalling all the particulars, Ralph has reiterated that he was not overwhelmed by the fact that he was to be at the wheel of a Novi. He fully realized that Andy wanted the car to get around the track in short order. He was anxious to convince Andy of his driving skills and to prove that he was one who could get the job done. Since Liguori and Rathmann were well acquainted, having raced together on the NASCAR circuit in the 1950s, Dick told Liguori what he could expect when stepping into the Novi. Dick informed Ralph that the Novi felt great and it could "really carry the mail." Liguori went out on the afternoon of May 11, to take the mandatory refresher test as he was still classified as a rookie what with his lack of any actual Indy 500 racing experience. The refresher test consisted of 10 laps at 135 m.p.h.

As the Novi moved down the back straight on its first hot lap with Ralph pushing the pedal deep, the engine wound up and the tach reading soared. Suddenly the supercharged V-8 engine literally blew itself out the bottom of the car causing it to spin, creating one of the longest slides in Speedway history before finally coming to rest in the infield. The engine had shattered as an internal explosion had occurred leaving engine debris scattered for a hundred yards or so. The crankshaft went through the belly pan to tumble down the track with several pistons still intact. As the car finally came to a halt, a badly shaken Liguori abandoned the car on his own power. Luckily, he escaped with only second degree burns on his face and neck as the exploding engine had sprayed hot oil on him. After a brief visit to Methodist Hospital he was released. Liguori's facial burns were so extensive that he was unable to shave for quite some time as the healing occurred.

Liguori told Granatelli that he was halfway down the back straight when it just went "blooey...I don't want you to think it was my fault...A big flame came out of it and it went all to pieces...I didn't stack it up." While being treated in the infield medical center, Ralph reported that when the engine let go it was "like being near a hand grenade when it goes off."

Ralph described the engine explosion in the following manner,

(1961) A wrecker prepares to return the Novi to its garage after the Ralph Liguori incident. The damage appears to be superficial, yet the powerful V-8 was ready for the trash heap. The shiny object under the car is likely a piston, the result of the "hand grenade" explosion.
I.M.S.

"Knowing what I know about superchargers I think that the case overloaded with fuel and ignited. I think that they had the pressure on too high though I am not sure. That is my conviction. When you consider pop-off valves used today it just seems that the pressure was too much and when the crankcase was loaded it ignited and blew the bottom as sometimes happens with a dragster. Because the crankcase with the rods and pistons were still on I ran all over that stuff. The car actually jumped right up into the air when the crank and the pistons came out to lift the car."

Ralph felt the leakage of fuel into the case was a result of the fuel/air mixture leaking between the cylinder walls and pistons because of the high supercharger boost. Liguori remembers that when he ran over the crankshaft it bent the belly pan pushing one of his knees up to hit the steering column. He also recalled that he skidded an estimated two thousand feet down the backstretch due to sliding on his own oil. The severity of the explosion was such that Ralph recalls the bearing webs were still on the crankshaft as it tumbled down the track. One account stated that "the car slid 939 ft., hit the wall, slid 225 ft. hit the wall again, hugged the wall for 113 ft. and then slid 642 ft. more" before coming to rest in the infield. It was generally agreed that the cause for Liguori's car reaching the wall was due to its running over the crankshaft. Driver Bob Veith, in a Peter Schmidt Special a third of the straightaway behind Liguori, informed the press that he saw "something exploded when he (Liguori) was riding right in the middle of the track. It looked like an oil can exploded. The flash was so great, I couldn't see a thing beyond his car. He was in no trouble at all before it happened. He hit the wall pretty good and solid going into the #3 turn and tore the whole underpan out. The pieces flew all over the place." He added that he managed to stay above Liguori as the Novi coasted down to the apron. A photo of the accident scene appearing in the Indianapolis Star carried the caption "Novi Explodes, Rams Wall." Friday's issue of the Indianapolis Times carried an account of the accident under the byline of racing journalist/mechanical authority, George Moore. The account was carried under the headline "Novi Explosion is Major Mystery." Granatelli was later to inquire as to why, when other engines let go, the newspaper references were made to the fact that the engines had blown. Yet, when a Novi let go the press accounts referred to the mishaps as explosions.

Veteran 500 speedster Duke Dinsmore was in the northwest turn at the time of the incident. He stated that the engine exploded when the car was about one-third of the way down the back straightaway. "The car seemed to leapfrog over the debris of the engine, with pieces marking the car's path." Dinsmore added, "I'm proud of the way Ralph Liguori battled the car to hold it after the engine blew."

(1961) Another view of the wounded Novi. From this angle, the car seems to have suffered only minimal damage. Note the guy wire used to stabilize the dorsal fin.   I.M.S.

Driver Bob Christie well remembers the wild episode. Christie recalls that he had passed the Novi several laps earlier as he was warming up his North Electric Special. Then coming off the second turn he noted that the Novi was quite some distance up the track, then "suddenly there was a big explosion like a bomb, with smoke and fire." Bob asserted, "I had tried to avoid hitting many cars in my day but that was the first time I had ever had to dodge a crankshaft." Christie also feels that the Novi hit the wall as the rear end of the Novi ran over its crankshaft. By the time Bob reached the Novi it was down low and Ralph had it under "reasonable control".

Driver Frank Armi who was in the third turn observation post witnessed the entire episode. Frank declared, "It just went poof" and the Novi suddenly disappeared in a ball of fire. Armi further stated that when it smacked the wall, the right front climbed the wall and took a long slide along the wall.

Some Speedway mechanics viewing the car felt that something occurred other than a parts failure. Some believed that fuel had somehow collected in the crankcase and it simply ignited, while others remained bewildered. Some mechanics reported seeing the flywheel and other parts

(1961) With the car repaired, Liguori is ready to return to the track as soon as the hood is fastened. The replacement nose had yet to be painted.
I.M.S.

lying intact in the bottom of the underpan while the crankshaft arrived in Gasoline Alley wrapped in a blanket. Chief Stewart Harlan Fengler said, "Some mechanical failure came up. You can never tell about those things. I was riding with Harry Hartz once and we laid a crank right out on the race track." Fritz Duesenberg, chairman of the tech committee reported, "If you collect the pieces it might be possible to reconstruct the accident. Otherwise you never can tell." While Fengler appeared calm and collect in recounting the episode to the press his temperament had not been even handed.

When the Liguori accident was mentioned to longtime Indy staff veteran Bob Laycock, the track's historian and trackside press representative and his assistant Bill Marvel (currently a USAC vice president), they jokingly recalled the aftermath to the Liguori incident. As was the practice, they headed to the accident scene in the track's press car immediately after the mishap. They then assisted track safety workers in cleaning up the massive amount of Novi debris scattered throughout the area. Harlan Fengler arrived on the scene shortly thereafter and viewing the prompt cleanup went into a rage. His furor was aroused as he believed that the cause of the calamity was more likely to be ascertained if time was taken to study the area. When it was pointed out that the shattered parts were so numerous it would be virtually impossible to determine the cause, Fengler threw his "trademark," a red Alpine hat, on the ground, stomping on it with gusto.

Liguori surmised that possibly the only salvageable parts of the engine might be the camshafts. Ralph reiterated that in spite of the hair raising incident he still wanted to drive the Novi. When driver Chuck Weyant heard this he stated, "There's a man with guts." While Ralph did continue working with the Novi team for a time he failed to retain a firm commitment as the Novi driver.

In reporting on the day's activities, the Indianapolis newspapers stated that Andy Granatelli was quoted as saying that the accident was his fault. Granatelli said that the mishap

"Was no reflection on Ralph but this wouldn't have happened if Rathmann had been running it at 150 m.p.h. We had the car all setup for Rathmann to run a 150-plus and had it tuned and carbureted for 6,400-8,400 revolutions per minute. Ralph punched the throttle down at 4,000 rpm, lugging the engine. In the course of lugging, he just unloaded it. He didn't build up to speed gradually like you have to. He just got on it too quick but I don't blame him because I didn't warn him or tell him. I had no idea that he would punch the throttle through the floor."

In reflecting back on the incident years later

Andy asserted, "Rathmann was the only man in racing history who had ever really mastered the Novi." He went on to add that Liguori was bound and determined to put on a real speed display and simply got caught up in the mishap while working with the high powered blown V-8. The track shut down prematurely that day due to the Novi mishap.

On Friday, May 12, with qualifying just one day off, the competition between the Novi and the Autolite Special tragically came to a sudden end. Tony Bettenhausen was approached by long-time friend Paul Russo who was soliciting some input from Tony regarding his assigned ride; the #24 Stearly Motor Freight Special. This particular car featured a Watson chassis and had been the winning car in the 1959 race. Russo liked it so well that after a practice stint he had said, "Now I know why (Rodger) Ward won so many races in this machine." Yet, he was unable to get the car over 143 m.p.h. and he asked Tony to take the car out for a shakedown as they tried to ascertain what the problem might be. At approximately 2 o'clock in the afternoon, Tony agreed to help Paul try to find more speed though his car owner Lindsey Hopkins and the crew chief Jack Beckley were extremely reluctant to give an okay. However, they finally relented as they were fully aware of Tony's longstanding relationship with Russo. Thus, they certainly understood him wanting to help such a friend. For Tony's, part he felt that he was returning a favor to Russo who had helped on Tony's farm in Tinley Park, Illinois over the winter. Hopkins' agreement with Bettenhausen precluded any test-hopping, yet Hopkins and Beckley reluctantly agreed.

After a few fast laps in the Stearly car, Bettenhausen made a move to return to the pits, but at the last possible moment changed his mind continuing on down the straight. It appeared obvious that he intended to take at least one more lap in the car. As he hustled down the straightaway the

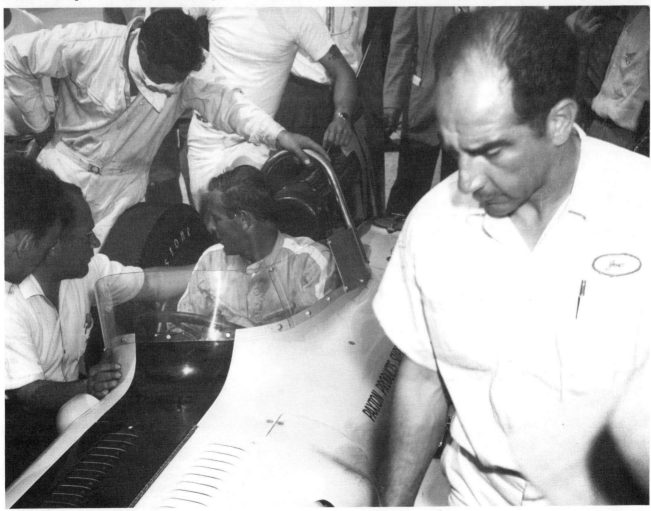

(1961) Russ Congdon prepares to go out in the repaired car. Ralph Liguori (hand on roll bar) listens as Andy converses with the rookie. Ralph wears a bandanna to cover his burned face.   I.M.S.

car appeared to lift as he set up for the corner. Then the car abruptly shot straight to the outside retaining wall to become airborne and then to be hopelessly wrapped in the steel catch fence installed on the top of the concrete wall. The impact of the car hitting the retaining fence took down six steel beams that supported the fencing. Yet, the fence was strong enough to hold the out-of-control roadster. The veteran driver was killed instantly as a result of neck and head injuries.

Bettenhausen had long cherished winning the 500 and now when it appeared that he had the best chance ever of obtaining that goal, his life was snuffed out. Investigations later revealed that a radius rod bolt on the front suspension had worked loose and caused the car to veer out of control when Tony tapped the brake. The nut holding the radius rod in place was found in the northeast turn while the bolt was picked up on the straightaway just past the northwest turn.

The tragic passing of Tony Bettenhausen caused an extraordinarily somber atmosphere to prevail at the Speedway. The 44 year old Bettenhausen was an extremely popular driver who was considered among the very best in the sport. One account reported, "Everybody loves Tony." The so-called "Tinley Park Express" had won the national driving championship twice (1951 and 1958). In the process he had won more 100 mile championship races (21) than any other man who had ever competed in such action. Yet, the Speedway always seemed to provide some nemesis to him, for in 14 previous races he had only managed to go the distance three times. His best finish was achieved in 1955 when he drove the Chapman Special to second place with relief driving provided by none other than Paul Russo. Bettenhausen, a former Novi pilot, had demonstrated his great versatility in establishing a new course record for the high bank Monza track behind the wheel of a Novi when he whipped off a lap in excess of 177 m.p.h. in 1957. Bettenhausen had started his amazing career with the midgets in the Chicagoland area in 1938. His eight victories with the now famous #99 Belanger Special championship car in 1951 will remain a vivid memory for those among us who were fortunate enough to have witnessed the brilliant driving displayed by Tony. Countless fans across the country were to mourn the passing of such a talented and well-liked driver. For many fans the passing of Bettenhausen was very difficult to accept.

The episode recalls the fact that back in 1953, Chet Miller had been killed while practicing in a Novi the day before qualifications were to open. While a somber mood prevailed, the 1961 qualifications went on as scheduled.

Although the Novi crew felt they would not have the car ready for a return to the track for several days, with great determination the Paxton car was ready to return on the first day of qualifications for some practice work. In the crew's rush to repair damage, the car appeared that day with an unpainted nosecone. Ralph Liguori was present and wanted to return to the Novi cockpit and while he did take some shakedown laps with the car no qualifying attempt was made that day. Ralph firmly believes that he would have made the show if given the opportunity. He had enough confidence in himself and the car to get the job done, yet such was not to occur.

Liguori's inability to make the show was intensified when Harlan Fengler berated him for the extraordinary third turn accident in the Novi. An apparently volatile Fengler called Ralph a "grease ball" among other things. Liguori was regarded as among those drivers who tried to present a suitable appearance whenever at the track. Yet, after the amazing accident, Ralph said his face "was like raw hamburger and I could not shave for some time." However, his desire to make the race had kept him at the scene. Ralph had applied a cream to his burned face and he wore a partial face cover of gauze. It was this appearance which inspired Fengler to make his brutal comment which Liguori took as a personal insult. Ralph became so distraught with the entire episode that he then packed his belongings and returned to his Florida home.

Cooler heads prevailed within USAC where some of its members had knowledge of the brutal Fengler confrontation with Liguori. Thus, Liguori has said when he returned to the Speedway the following year he was summoned into the back room of USAC's trackside office. There Fengler privately offered an apology for the tirade of the previous May. As for the luckless Ralph, he continued to return to the Speedway helmet in hand year after year but he was never able to fulfill his dream to compete in the 500 race. On three occasions he qualified for a 500 only to be bumped. The closest he came was that of second alternate.

The prevailing question once again centered around who would drive the repaired Novi. With many drivers already obligated to other teams, this left the Granatellis with few options. According to Granatelli's autobiography and a newspaper account, Andy had an announcement carried over the Gasoline Alley's public address system. He stated that the Novi was ready to run and experienced drivers were invited to come by the garage. In his book, Granatelli also states that three drivers came by but they were "has been or never were to be racer type drivers." When Andy explained the crew's overwhelming desire to see the car on the pole each driver reportedly departed the garage. Thus, on the eve of qualifications the fast Novi was still without a driver.

Chapter 2

An Early Departure - 1961

As the qualifications were about to begin on Saturday, May 13, a "Golden Anniversary" ceremony was held at the start/finish line with a ceremonial ribbon cutting by Speedway owner Tony Hulman. He was joined by that year's 500 Festival Queen and the Hoosier state governor. That year's race was indeed an event to celebrate since it had been fifty years since the first race and with the ribbon cut, the day's qualifications were ready to begin.

Many fans concluded that the magical 150 m.p.h. qualifying mark was a cinch to be broken. The <u>Indianapolis Star</u> headline ask, "Is 150 Lap Next At 500." Some railbirds recalled Tony Bettenhausen having said he was going to "bypass 150 m.p.h. and do 151" after his Quin Epperly built chassis in the Jack Beckley prepared Autolite Special had reached a clocking of 149.2 m.p.h. the day prior to his death. Tony had reminded his listeners that the speed had been obtained while driving in traffic. Although Dick Rathmann was now out of the Novi and tragically Bettenhausen was gone, several other drivers were flirting with speeds in the high 140s and the magical 150 m.p.h. was possibly still within range. Shorty Templeman had reached a 148.7 m.p.h. speed in the Forbes Racing Team car the same day Tony had reached 149.2 m.p.h.

The first qualifier to leave the starting line was Jack Brabham, an Australian driver who had won the Formula One title the previous two years. The officials failed to see his hand signal to start the run and flagged him off the track after the warm-up laps allowed prior to a timed run. Thus, the first driver out was Bill Cheesbourg, the former Novi pilot (1958), who turned in an average speed of 145.8 m.p.h. in one of the Dean Van Lines cars. Thus, Cheesbourg became the first qualifier. The ride had opened when the 1956 Indy victor, Pat Flaherty, who had obtained the ride, made the decision to retire during a practice session.

Then in a show of sportsmanship due to

(1961) Formula One World Champion driver Sir Jack Brabham's qualifying shot. Although a Novi was on hand under new ownership, the diminitive English built, rear engine car drew vast amounts of media and spectator attention. The underpowered car went on to finish 9th. The car inspired others to consider such an engine placement, including the Granatellis.   *I.M.S.*

Brabham's hectic travel schedule, driver Eddie Johnson and his crew permitted Brabham to return to the track for the next run though Johnson's car was slated to be second out. Brabham's average speed in the diminutive rear engine Cooper-Climax was a satisfactory 145.1 m.p.h. In commenting about Brabham's Indy driving style, one driver said, "He makes it look like the car is running on a cable; he never varies the pattern." Long-time Indy mechanic Frenchy Sirois observed that Jack "takes the short way around."

Brabham was scheduled to drive in the Grand Prix of Monaco the following day. He had qualified for that race two days earlier (Thursday) and was in a hurry to leave Indianapolis to rush back to Europe for the Monaco race. The challenging travel demands proved of little value, as he wound up being the second retiree at Monaco, out after 39 of the 100 lap race due to engine failure.

As the Indy qualifications continued through much of the first day, the fastest qualifying run was achieved by Eddie Sachs in Al Dean's primary car. Sachs, the "fast talking Allentown, Pennsylvania pilot" had now obtained the pole for the second consecutive year; this time with a 147.4 m.p.h. The crew chief for Al Dean's team was Clint Brawner, one of the sport's most highly regarded racing mechanics. Filling out the first row were Don Branson in the Hoover Express Special (146.8 m.p.h.) and Jim Hurtubise in the #99 Demler Special (146.3 m.p.h.). A total of 22 cars qualified that day.

While Sachs was the only driver with a 147 m.p.h. reading, seven drivers registered qualifying speeds in the 146 m.p.h. bracket. Don Branson, Jim Hurtubise, Rodger Ward (146.18 m.p.h.), Al Keller (146.08 m.p.h.), Parnelli Jones (146.08 m.p.h.) and Dick Rathmann (146.03 m.p.h.).

Jones, a rookie with an outstanding sprint car record, garnered considerable attention what with his smooth practice runs followed by his posting the quickest qualifying time among the rookies in the field. With his quick time Parnelli started the classic event in the J.C. Agajanian owned Willard Battery Special from the second row between 1959 winner Rodger Ward and Dick Rathmann. Jim Rathmann, the defending champion, was to start eleventh in his Simoniz Special what with his qualifying time of 145.4 m.p.h. The national driving champ A.J. Foyt was to start from 7th in the #1 Bowes Seal Fast Special as a result of a qualifying speed of 145.9 m.p.h.

After qualifying the Jim Robbins' entry, Dick Rathmann, the Novi's temporary pilot, told the fans, "My heart is with the Novi." Dick also reported, "I'd still like to drive that machine, I still think it can win here and certainly there isn't another one around that has the power that baby has." In spite of what might happen in the remaining time trial sessions, the Novi had given every indication of making a fantastic comeback at the hands of Dick Rathmann.

(1961) Dick Rathmann's official qualifying photo. Unfortunately, for Dick and the Novi followers, the run was made in the Jim Robbins Special. Only six drivers posted faster qualification runs. With Dick's skills and bravado, the qualifying time he might have obtained in the Novi will forever remain a mystery. I.M.S.

During that first day of qualifications, Paul Russo came by the Novi garage. He had lost his assigned ride the day before when Tony crashed. "Portly" Paul took the repaired Novi out and moved into the low 140 range during the practice time that day. Paul was delighted with the performance of the repaired Novi and eventually decided to try to qualify the car and had it placed in line after assuring Granatelli that the pole was within his grasp. If Russo could perform in the Novi as he had previously done in 1956 it would certainly delight long-time Novi fans.

Several versions have been cited as to why Paul then failed to make a qualifying run. One account suggests that Paul had a contractual obligation to another party that would make any Novi run impractical for him. When Duke Nalon was asked about Russo's laps in the car, he felt that possibly Granatelli merely wanted to get the former Novi veteran's views on the car's power and handling. Another account, commonly mentioned in newspaper articles suggests that Paul felt a duty to take over the Autolite ride of his fallen friend and to donate his share of any prize money to Val Bettenhausen, Tony's widow. Autolite chief mechanic Jack Beckley had stated that Russo would be one of "two or three drivers" to test the car. Russo did spend a brief period in the Autolite Special, yet nothing came of this undertaking.

The Novi was once again without a driver. Andy has said that he had some second thoughts about Russo driving the car. As Andy remembers it,

"Everybody urged me to put Russo in the car. But, with all respect to Paul, he was beyond his day. It wasn't his time to drive any more. He got in the car and took some twelve laps and when he brought the car in, the disc brakes were all blue. It had been the same old thing, going like hell on the straights and then loading up the brakes, sliding into the turn, stroking and using all the horsepower on the straightaway. He got up to 141 m.p.h. but I could see that wasn't going anywhere. We wouldn't have had enough brakes to run the entire race."

The following day, five additional cars qualified led by "Cactus" Jack Turner of Seattle, Washington. The 41 year old speedster, a former USAC National Midget Champion averaged 144.9 m.p.h. followed by 1952 Indy winner Troy Ruttman with a 144.7 m.p.h. in the Zink car. Turner had an added incentive for setting fast time, for his car owner, Fred Gerhardt, had earlier informed Cactus Jack that if he set fast time for the day with the brand new Kurtis Bardahl Special he could retain all of the money given to the second day's top speedster - $1,200.

With the first weekend of qualifying completed, six spots remained to be filled before any bumping could begin. Unfortunately, the sole Novi still was not in the field. Rookie Russ Congdon came to the Novi garage on the second day of qualifying offering to try the car. Congdon, from Puyallup, Washington, was short on experience in champ cars though he had been in racing since 1945. In 1948, he was the Washington State Midget Champ and by the latter 1950s he had moved into USAC midget competition. In 1958, Congdon had been 11th in USAC's National Midget point standings and 9th in the Midwest point standings. Now the 36 year old driver was given the opportunity to take a few laps in the Paxton Special. Congdon did not appear to be comfortable with the machine. Then on what appeared to be a slow down lap and without any warning Congdon's car spun one and a half times before coming to rest in the infield grass after a long 759 ft. slide. When the Novi was returned to the garage area it was announced that the car's transmission shaft had broken. Russ, who was not hurt in the fray said, "I really have fallen in love with that car. Man, what power." Congdon was also quoted to have said, "I had been climbing steadily, going faster and actually was beginning to get the feel of the car when the transmission went out." Congdon explained, "I'd love to drive it next year. With a little practice, I think I could make 150. Before his spin Congdon had been timed at speeds between 140 and 142 m.p.h.

Prior to the Congdon incident, Andy Granatelli was asked if the famed Novi was still being hounded by its alleged jinx. He replied, "Ridiculous. This car no more has a jinx than any other race machine. So we blew an engine, so what? Are we the first car to ever have that happen? Certainly not. We expect to have some troubles, but they aren't the kind that can't be solved."

With 27 cars in the field, would the Novi make it into the starting field? The front row speeds were certainly below expectations in view of the practice times that had been established by Tony Bettenhausen and Dick Rathmann. The magical 150 m.p.h. barrier had been missed by approximately three and one half miles. Pole sitter Eddie Sachs, while admitting his delight in sitting on the pole, made it known he was disappointed in falling short of Jim Hurtubise's track record of 149.056 m.p.h. set a year earlier. As for Hurtubise's qualifying, the speed was almost three miles below his own record. One can only imagine what the top qualifying speed might have been if Dick Rathmann had been allowed to remain in the Novi or if Tony was able to take a qualification run with the Hopkins Autolite Special.

No second day qualifying attempt was made by the Novi. A short time later Granatelli announced that the team had come to the Speedway to win and "not to play second or to set the car on the wall." Andy cited the fact that he believed that he was in a situation that left him without an acceptable and experienced driver. Further, replacement parts for the broken transmission would not arrive until the following Friday. Thus, Andy felt that this situation would not provide sufficient time for any driver to familiarize himself with the Novi to obtain the desired results. By that time, four drivers had seen action in the powerful car: Dick Rathmann, Ralph Liguori, Paul Russo and Russ Congdon. Granatelli said, "Without practice and a feel for the car a driver might set a record, who knows. But then again he might also get himself killed." He also admitted, "We're just numb. We don't want any further heartbreaks."

Granatelli then announced that he planned to withdraw the car due to the reasons cited and to modify the transmission/driveshaft while building a twin to the present car. He promised to return the following year with every intention of making the race with two Novis. In spite of the set back, Granatelli appeared upbeat when he talked about the following year's race. Perhaps he was putting his best face on a trying and difficult situation. In his autobiography, Granatelli gave the actual circumstance saying, "The transmission shaft wasn't broken, of course. And if it had been broken, we could certainly have fixed it in time for the next weekend...But I knew we couldn't go through that experience of getting bumped again, of finding a driver."

On Tuesday, May 16, the Paxton Special was loaded on its flat bed trailer for the long journey back to Santa Monica. In recalling the incident several years ago, Granatelli again declared that the transmission was not the culprit for withdrawing the car. Granatelli then stated that he simply did not want to see a Novi qualifying time being shaky and the car possibly being bumped. He wanted to protect the mighty Novi from further embarrassment. He also told the press that he had plans to enter the car in Federation Internationale de l'Automobile (F.I.A.) Speed Trials to be held at the Bonneville Salt Flats in August that year. As it turned out, these plans did not materialize.

Granatelli later informed the press that the team's return the following year would be with two *new* cars as he pointed out that the #75 Paxton Special was certainly dated. Andy said, "We'll come back more up-to-date." He reiterated that he wanted to spare the team any further heartaches and that the crew was numbed by the fact that they had burned the midnight oil throughout most of April with a basket case car and the situation was exacerbated when Rathmann, after setting such a torrid pace, was "removed" from the driving assignment. These circumstances were certainly cause for a state of demoralization within the Novi team.

Speaking of the driver situation, Andy asserted that USAC ought to relax its rules and permit "NASCAR drivers to run here or do something at least to have enough drivers to go around." Granatelli startled some when he said he had planned to have Marvin Panch, the winner of that year's Daytona 500, pilot his #75 but he "couldn't get clearance."

In checking with Marv on the idea put forth by Andy, he has no recollection of being approached for any sort of an offer. If in fact such a proposal reached Marv, he asserts that the offer now eludes his mind.

During the second weekend of qualifying (with several bumps having occurred), sophomore driver Lloyd Ruby qualified the attractive Epperly built Autolite car. He was clocked at 146.9 m.p.h. which represented the second fastest time among the 33 starters. He then went on to finish 8th in the race although he had limited practice in the Hopkins' car. The slowest car in the eventual field was that driven by Bobby Grim who qualified at 144.02 m.p.h.

Within barely one month's time, the Granatellis and Marcenac had managed to make the recalci-

Sir Jack Brabham   Authors Collection

trant machine of the two previous years work well enough to live up to the high expectations of the past. In 1959 and 1960 there had been no speeds worthy of mention, yet in 1961 the car had performed in a respectable fashion. Though a non-qualifier, the team could withdraw without embarrassment and leave Indy with their heads held high and with a promise of great strides in the future.

Without question the high finned Paxton Novi was not the only car in the limelight. This was due to the presence of the rear engine Cooper-Climax assigned to reigning Formula One champion Jack Brabham.

(1961) The Brabham car in traffic during the race. The car is dwarfed by the American built front engine cars, but the green mite handled beautifully in the turns. A.J. Shepard, #73, and Gene Hartley, #28, motoring by. Note the Kimberly lettering on the engine bonnet. American sportsman Jim Kimberly had provided financial assistance to the Brabham operation.   I.M.S.

Brabham's fine 145.1 m.p.h. qualifying effort on the first day was certainly impressive. The car, painted a dark green which was the racing color used by English entries in Formula One competition, was a tiny car as its dry weight was only 1,000 lb. which had it weigh in at less than half the weight of the Novi. The car was considered to be heavily underpowered as its horsepower rating was approximately 240 while the Offys were in the 380 horsepower range.

[For the purist, we realize that the engine location in the Cooper was not at the rear as in the VW Beetle, the Porsche 911 or the Chevrolet Corvair model. Technically the powerplant placement was a mid-engine arrangement. However, in the years since 1961, people have referred to the Cooper as being a rear engine car. To avoid any confusion such a reference will be used here though we recognize that this rear engine "revolution" was in fact a mid-engine revolution. Every reference to a rear engine car herein merely refers to any car with the engine placement behind the driver.]

The Climax engine was a slightly enlarged version of the 2.5 liter (152 c.i.) Formula One engine and had a displacement of only 2.7 liters (164 c.i.), so it was eligible for supercharging, yet it was normally aspirated. An American writer suggested that the car possessed "just enough power to go over a cherry pit."

With the power handicap that cost a loss of anything approaching the top speeds on the straightaways, Brabham's qualifying time was quite impressive. The track behavior of the nimble "funny car" as some Americans called it, was far superior to the roadsters which appeared to be rather bulky by comparison. In practice, Jack lost considerable ground on the straightaways, yet through the turns the car ran as if on rails. Interestingly, such a circumstance was just the opposite of what the Novis had faced over the years, particularly with the front wheel drive creations. The Cooper chassis, which was designed for road racing, was far easier to maneuver than the heavy American built cars with their left-side weight bias. The roadsters and lay-downs tried to remain in the corner grooves while Brabham had to continually maneuver his car in the turns to keep from hitting the tails of his front engine competitors. It was the first sign that a finely tuned adjusted rear engine chassis might be able to fully compete with the heavier roadsters.

The Cooper did not fully adhere to the rules as its wheelbase was too short. Nonetheless, Cooper received special dispensation to run the car as the I.M.S. and USAC wanted the extra media attention in Europe and Brabham's participation could help stimulate further foreign participation.

(1961) Lloyd Ruby in the Autolite Special chasing Jack Brabham in the Cooper. Ruby stepped into the #5 Autolite car after the demise of Tony Bettenhausen. "Rube" finished 8th and Brabham 9th.   I.M.S.

USAC's decision was not well received by some American car owners who claimed that the maximum wheelbase rule was installed to prevent them from entering their sprint cars in the race. One team owner had stated that if sprint cars were permitted at the Speedway they could beat the roadster's corner speeds as a short wheelbase sprint car would negotiate the turns much easier. The car owners accepted the waiver for the Cooper on this occasion as they felt it was an isolated exception. It is interesting to note that while the protesters dwelt on the car's short wheelbase, in actuality the greatest advantage was derived from the engine location.

The Cooper had three forward speeds and their ratio was quite close so Brabham would be able to easily move down a gear for quick acceleration when the situation presented itself. It has been reported that Brabham had been less than happy with the transmission used in the Cooper the previous year and that as a consequence a newly designed transmission had been created for use in the Indianapolis 500.

Brabham was the first foreign driver to have any reasonable chance of making the starting field since Alberto Ascari arrived with a Ferrari in 1952. The Cooper project called for transporting two cars from England (one as a backup). The undertaking was financed by Jim Kimberly. Kimberly was a Chicago paper products millionaire (the Kimberly-Clark Corp.), a sports car driving star and former president of the Sports Car Club of America (SCCA). Therefore, the venture was not strictly that of John Cooper, the Cooper Car Company of England and driver Jack Brabham.

The Cooper used English produced Dunlop tires while the engine carried Lodge spark plugs, another English product. The undertaking also had a commitment to use Esso fuel though the fuel would probably be a gasoline/alcohol blend. Some railbirds believed that the Cooper car had several major drawbacks. Not only was the engine completely underpowered, the Dunlop tires were considered questionable following testing at Indy the previous October. Yet, after inspection of the Firestone tires following the October effort, the British felt that they had a suitable tire for the 500.

Quite naturally the diminutive green creation caused a lot of chatter at Indy and some of the American drivers were curious enough to drop by the Cooper garage. Jim Hurtubise, anything but a shrinking violet, quickly appeared and after looking at the Cooper-Climax informed Brabham, "That's quite a little racer you have there." Brabham modestly replied, "We hope so." Jim then inquired, "Are you all tuned up?" "I'll let you know after it runs," replied Brabham. Jim then replied, "I'm not talking about the car. I'm talking about you" as his eyes displayed that familiar twinkle. When Brabham was quizzed about the fact that the Cooper's engine size had been moved from 2.5 liters to 2.7 liters he replied, "An ounce of capacity is worth a ton of theory."

It might be worth pointing out that the two Coopers which were flown to America were not identical in every respect as some believed. The primary car had a slightly modified Formula One chassis for use at Indy while the backup car was a standard Formula One chassis without any modifications.

The "Golden Anniversary 500" was set for Wednesday, May 30. In the early going Jim Hurtubise was the leader until Eddie Sachs and Parnelli Jones swapped the lead. At approximately the quarter point in the race, a gruesome looking accident occurred after Don Davis spun in his own oil on the front straight. The stalled car led to a chain reaction accident involving drivers A.J. Shepherd, Bill Cheesbourg, Roger McCluskey and Jack Turner. Turner became airborne going end over end and for a moment it appeared as if the car was doing a pirouette on its nose before coming to rest against the inside wall. Fortunately, none of the drivers involved received serious injuries.

(1961) A.J. Foyt wins the race in a Bowes Seal Fast Special. It was the first of A.J.s four 500 wins.   I.M.S.

In the latter stages of the contest, a prolonged struggle was set in motion between Sachs and A.J. Foyt. The pair fought a torrid battle that was a bit reminiscent of the stupendous late race lead swapping in 1960 between Rodger Ward and eventual winner Jim Rathmann. When Foyt made his last scheduled pit stop the fueling equipment did not operate properly and he was forced to stop again for fuel on the 184th lap. The late race stop for a splash of fuel seemingly set up a victory for Sachs. Yet, with a mere three laps to go Eddie shocked one and all (none more than his crew chief Cliff Brawner) when he came in for what he judged to be a needed tire change. Sachs' surprise pit stop permitted Foyt to flash by on his way to score his first Indianapolis 500 victory.

(1961) Eddie Sachs - the pole sitter in the Dean Van Line Special. The loquacious Sachs seemingly had the race in hand until he surrendered the lead with only a few laps remaining, believing a tire needed replacement. Foyt inherited the lead and went on to the checkered flag. No shortage of decals on the Clint Brawner prepped Al Dean car. I.M.S.

History was repeating itself, for once again (now three consecutive years) the 500 was contested without a Novi in the starting field. At least it was not one of those years when the entire field consisted of Offy powered racers. Brabham's #17 certainly gave the fans something to talk about - a ninth place finish in the so-called "funny car!" Brabham's placement marked the first time that a rear engine car had ever run the entire 500 miles at Indianapolis.

As for participants in the Novi saga, Dick Rathmann placed 13th as the fuel pump went out on his car on lap 164. Driver Paul Russo qualified the Bryant Heating and Cooling Special the second weekend (143.9 m.p.h.) to serve as first alternate in the car owned by Mari Hulman George, daughter of Speedway President Tony Hulman.

Driver Russ Congdon, ever so willing to drive the Novi, never did secure another such opportunity. He returned to the Speedway the following year with another team, but failed to make the race thus aborting his hopes for an Indy car career.

For the racing community, the tragic loss of Tony Bettenhausen certainly marred the running of the Golden Anniversary race. For the Novi crew that tragic loss was compounded as the Novi dream had suffered another heart wrenching set back, leaving not only the Novi crew, but its legion of fans sadly disappointed. The fact that the Novi supporters were accustomed to such disappointments was hardly a comforting point. While it was the Granatellis initial Novi failure, for mechanic Jean Marcenac it now marked his third straight year of a Novi missing the contest. If there was any sort of consolation at all, it rested with the fact that the Granatellis had promised to return with two Novis the following year. An added comfort for Novi followers was that the sole Novi trackside in 1961 had been one of the fastest cars in practice, thus better times were sure to come.

Chapter 3

A Mind Boggling Project That Was Never To Be

The "pint size" Cooper-Climax that appeared at Indianapolis in 1961 had certainly caused a few American car owners to give some serious thought to the potential threat of rear engine race cars. Among the group was Andy Granatelli. The Granatelli concern came about in spite of the fast times Dick Rathmann recorded while practicing with the Novi. While Andy realized that the Cooper gave away considerable horsepower, especially when compared to the Novi, its performance in the turns was outstanding. While the Novi could storm past other cars on the straights the Cooper was most definitely the car to beat in the turns what with the agility of the rear engine creation. The Granatellis realized that if the Cooper had more power, which translates to higher straightaway speeds, it could become a real threat at the Speedway.

Andy Granatelli was a man who thrived on new challenges and who was not afraid to try engineering concepts that were yet to be fully developed. As a consequence, the notion of having a rear engine chassis powered by a Novi came to mind. Perhaps such was hastened by the stinging failure of the Paxton/Novi to gain entry into the 1961 Indy 500. Whatever the reason, the Granatelli clan began to lay plans for such a rear engine undertaking.

In his autobiography, Andy mentioned the potential for a rear engine car and concluded he had to try such an undertaking. As a consequence he contacted driver Jack Brabham who was preparing to build his own cars having left the John Cooper operation. Andy suggested that Brabham build a rear engine car that would be powered by a Novi. Granatelli further suggested that Brabham consider driving the car. Jack displayed some interest in the proposals and agreed to delve into the plan. According to Granatelli, in the months after the 1961 race the project proceeded. Granatelli asserted that specifications and drawings were completed. At some point, Brabham had serious second thoughts about going back to Indy in 1962 and he then made the decision to pull the plug on this extraordinary plan. His refusal to proceed included not only his unwillingness to drive, but to build such a car as well. The only known reference regarding this project was found in Andy Granatelli's autobiography. Andy stated therein that the plans were cancelled because Brabham was "stung by the criticism by Indy's old timers." Why Brabham gave up the entire project was not made crystal clear beyond the statement regarding the lack of acceptance at Indianapolis.

One source close to Andy said, "For one reason or another we didn't come together with Brabham." The individual also stated that he felt the Novi team was not prepared to take on a rear engine car at the time. Of all the plans concocted for the Novi over the years, this project may well rank among those with the greatest potential. With the powerful Novi engine positioned just in front of the rear wheels, the traction (in theory) would be far better than that available to a front engine roadster due to better weight distribution. No doubt the ultimate chassis would have had to be far more rugged, and as a result, heavier than the 1961 Cooper to withstand the inert weight and the power delivery. However, to make a well-balanced car was not beyond the realm of possibility. As we shall see, the eventual successors of that 1961 Cooper were to create a technical revolution that was to dramatically alter Indy car racing.

If a rear engine Novi had been built and it had worked, there might have been a good chance that American race car builders would have accepted the concept of rear engine technology earlier than what eventually transpired. Such a revolutionary move at that time by the Granatellis would have established them among the pioneers in the transformation to the rear engine cars. One could imagine that the Granatelli owned team might lead the way and conceivably achieved "that" long delayed victory at the Speedway. However, the Granatellis did not fashion a rear engine car for 1962; for as noted, regrettably the entire project was dropped.

Lacking any further solid information, an inquiry was directed to Sir Jack Brabham regarding the matter. Sir Jack confirmed that he had been approached by Andy Granatelli along with John Cooper regarding the prospect of a rear engine Cooper/Novi. Brabham stated that he turned down the offer as the engine was considered entirely too heavy for the lightweight Cooper chassis of that day. The design and creation of a new model was possible, but Cooper did not have a design staff for such a job. Sir Jack also mentioned another factor: there was no gearbox available to handle the Novi power. One must remember that the rear engine cars needed an entirely different gearbox layout than that used in the front engine roadsters. The latter had their two speed transmissions bolted directly against the flywheel with the driveline going to the differential. The rear engine Cooper, however had a transmission-rear end construction placed directly against the powerplant. Brabham pointed out that gearboxes able to withstand the massive torque and power of the Novi were only available for engines situated in the front. A compact gearbox required for a rear engine Novi that would offer any assurance of adequately handling its power simply was not available.

For the record, in 1958 when John Cooper started to built his rear engine Grand Prix challengers, he modified the gearbox of the French Citroen "Traction Avant" passenger cars. This was a front drive car and the gearbox was suitable for racing duties in a rear engine chassis after some modifications. It provided a compact engine gearbox unit without a propshaft. But could a gearbox based on a design which had to cope with some 125 horsepower at its very best also handle the 600+ horsepower of a Novi V-8? Even the power of the early 2 liter Coventry Climax engines, which Cooper used in its early Formula One days before a full 2.5 liter Climax became available, had been hard to handle and the basic gearbox design had been changed and strengthened for use in Formula One competition. With the deep concern regarding a gearbox sufficient for the Climax one can understand why Brabham informed us that strong reservations remained with respect to an adequate gearbox for a rear engine Novi. It has now been suggested that in 1960, Cooper began using a gearbox considered strong enough to handle the power and torque of the 2.5 liter Climax engines. Speculation strongly suggests that this type of gearbox was used on the 2.7 liter Climax powered Cooper that Brabham drove at Indy in 1961.

Sir Jack confirmed that Motor Racing Developments (the company which built Brabham racing cars from 1962 on) was approached by Andy Granatelli to build a rear engine Novi, but this happened either in late 1962 or early 1963. Whatever the date may have been Brabham, Cooper and Granatelli have all stipulated that such an idea had been given some thought. Yet, no rear engine Brabham and/or Novi was designed in late 1961 or early 1962. In an interview several years ago, Andy confirmed that such a car was never built.

Sir Jack informed us "...no drawing was done and no money changed hands with Andy Granatelli. It may have got in the press that a deal was done as it often does. If so it just was not true."

Additional information was uncovered as the investigation to obtain more details concerning this segment of the Novi's history continued. The now-defunct English magazine <u>Competition Car</u> published an interview with John Cooper in its September, 1973 issue. Included therein is an intriguing statement. When Cooper was asked why he did not return to Indianapolis he stated that the problem was the inability to find a suitable engine. A Climax such as that used in 1961 lacked sufficient power while the Offy was too heavy. Going on Cooper stated, "Then there was the Novi. At that time, Andy Granatelli was running the Novis, and they were incredibly quick. When they came off the turns you could see the smoke coming off the rear tyres, as the driver put his foot down. Granatelli came to me and said he wanted to put the Novi engine in our car, but we told him it would be way too heavy. He was also very quick to realize the potential of rear engine cars around Indy."

Presumably, Granatelli first approached car builder Cooper and when the proposal was passed over he then turned to Brabham. While turning down Granatelli's offer, Cooper believed that the failure to reach a mutual agreement did not create any bad feelings. Cooper asserted that he believed that Granatelli fully understood his feelings. Cooper then reported that he met Granatelli on several occasions and that they remained friends. Cooper also reported that in his judgment, Andy Granatelli was a great character and part of the Indianapolis tradition.

When Mr. Cooper was contacted about the possibility of such a car and as to where it would have been built if the project had proceeded, he stated that the car would have been designed and built in England and the engine would have been fitted into the car in the United States.

A final question was put to Mr. Cooper. What were his thoughts regarding the Novi he saw race in 1961? He stated, "I was very impressed when I saw the Novi and at the time I thought there was too much power for the chassis."

It seemed a natural for Andy to approach Cooper and Brabham as the two had worked together on the Formula One circuit. It had been Cooper cars, driven by Brabham, that had spearheaded the end of the front engine Grand Prix cars in the late 1950s and early 1960s. Before closing out the Brabham "story," it behooves us to report that Sir Jack eventually did return to Indianapolis to compete in the 1964, 1969 and 1970 races. In 1964, he drove a rear engine Brabham chassis powered by an Offy placing 20th. By 1969, all of the cars in the field had their engines located in the rear. Again, Sir Jack was in one of his own production chassis. The following year marked Brabham's last Indy appearance. Interestingly, none of the three appearances in a Brabham chassis provided a finish as high as that achieved with a Cooper-Climax in 1961. Of the three 500 rides in a Brabham, the highest placement achieved by Sir Jack was a 13th in 1970.

By the latter 1960s, the starting fields at Indy consisted entirely of 33 rear engine cars. A.J. Foyt's win in 1964 marked the last victory by a front engine car. The evolution recalls a statement made by Jim Kimberly, the benefactor of the 1961 Cooper-Brabham effort. Kimberly recalled that while he was pleased that the Cooper-Climax had finished 9th as the transition to rear drive Indy cars began, "I was a very unpopular guy at Indy. The other car owners told me, `Why you s.o.b., now I'll have to sell everything and start all over.' And they were right." This statement was certainly right on target as time would prove.

The notion of such a dramatic change in race car construction was duly noted by some Indy veterans. Looking down the road they could see the advent of the rear engine car as being the wave of the future. Among the small group was driver Eddie Sachs who told a suburban Indianapolis Kiwanas Club gathering on the eve of the 1962 season "the rear engines may not be a sensation this year or next, but I don't want to have to run against them in the next two or three years." An account of the driver's speech was headlined in a press account as "Offy Living On Borrowed Time-Sachs." The account also pointed out that the Offys had dominated for years while the Novis had "made a splash a few years ago, but they never could get the kinks worked out."

Chapter 4

REBIRTH OF NOVI AND DREAMS

Considering the rush in which preparations for the 1961 Novi project had to be executed by the Granatellis, the results cannot be considered all that bad. In a period of slightly less than two months (which included track time), they had transformed the once powerful Novi to the point where it was again a legitimate challenge for the competition. The extraordinary power of the lone V-8 had once again displayed its potential in a convincing fashion. In the last two years of Lew Welch's ownership, the Novi had failed to make the race having experienced extraordinary mechanical problems. Now the Granatellis felt they were headed in the right direction - particularly with the magneto problem having been resolved.

A main priority involved efforts to improve engine performance prior to the 1962 race. Placing one of the engines on the dyno they came up with just under 500 horsepower at 7,000 rpms at 25 psi of boost. Such a reading was disappointing and certainly below their expectations. More serious, however, was the fact that this engine performance came with a fuel consumption of no less than 142 gallons (551 liters) during one hour of running. Some calculations quickly indicated that with such fuel consumption the power output range should have been between 700 and 800 horsepower. In other words, while it was the most powerful Indy engine at the time, it was also extremely inefficient. In looking over the engines, the Granatellis came to the conclusion that the supercharger had to be the problem for this unacceptable fuel usage. They still had a 10 inch blower that had been used throughout the history of the Novi in order to obtain sufficient breathing. But that large blower blade, rotating at 40,000 rpms had such an exorbitantly high tip speed that the compression of the fuel/air mixture was not efficient. One of the earliest lessons learned with superchargers had been that high rotary tip speeds did not improve blower efficiency. A smaller size blower appeared to be a reasonable alternative.

With this in mind, a new supercharger with an eight inch diameter blade was constructed. Additional changes included new inlet manifolds and ducting. One of the reworked engines was tested on the dyno and the results were astonishing. Power output had climbed to a healthy 640 horsepower at 7,600 rpms on 35 psi boost. In addition, fuel consumption had been reduced by 15 percent to 120 gallons (465.5 liters) an hour. Power consumption for the supercharger at 7,600 rpms was akin to 75 horsepower with the impeller blade rotating at 40,000 rpms.

It will always remain a mystery as to how the Novi might have performed in previous years if this redesigned engine had been on hand. There is good reason to assume that in the past the Novi had given away far too much to its opponents due to lack of efficiency. Yet, who knows how fast the Novi would have gone through tires with this extra surge of power; most particularly with the front wheel drives.

In spite of the credit accorded the Paxton organization for this new blower, a report has stated that the revised blower had some outside help. It has been reported that Andy decided to switch to a cast inducer impeller for the supercharger and contacted a local machine shop in Culver City, California, operated by Lou D'Leia. D'Leia accepted the order asking $250 to complete the necessary tooling. Andy considered the expenditure too high and that ended a possible transaction at the time. Paxton then created a few new impellers which carried blades welded to the center hub. After they were completed the welding spots were dressed down. One of the impellers was mounted onto a dyno prepared engine, but the results were most unsatisfactory. The centrifugal forces completely disintegrated the impeller resulting in pieces being sucked into the engine causing damage that was certainly in excess of $250. A return visit was then made to D'Leia and the tooling for new cast impeller blades was made. Our informant who worked with these inducers commented in the following fashion:

"The tooling consisted of one segment of a corebox. By making eight segments of the corebox and assembling them, it created a mold for a complete impeller. Lou D'Leia's tooling was so accurate that the casting only required that the hub be machined along with the outside of the vanes. The web thickness of the vanes, when measured, varied less than ten thousandths from the low reading to the high reading as cast. The impellers were cast from a high strength patent alloy carrying the trade name of "Ternalloy" and it was made by Apex Metals in Torrance, California. Andy used these cast impellers the rest of the time he worked with the Novi engines."

The engines were reported to have received some major improvements apart from the reworking of the supercharger. The alterations included the addition of a crank vibration damper; the buttons on the piston pins were replaced by snap rings; the flat top valve heads were replaced by Miller type radius cups; new forged pistons were used and some engine parts like the cam covers were made out of magnesium. The changes caused the weight of the engine to drop to a reading of 510 pounds. While still less than impressive, it was a step in the right direction. Another innovation was the use of twin long curving crankcase breathers that came out of the case to ventilated caps that were located just below the underside of the hood.

The compression ratio was set at 8 to 1. According to dyno readings, the Novi was then able to deliver 377 horsepower at 5,800 rpms. This calculation had the Novi coming off the turns producing a little less power than the Offys when the four banger was providing maximum power! Off the turns the Novi was then expected to accelerate up to 8,000 rpms with the engine delivering 645 horsepower. With such, straightaway speeds of approximately 190 m.p.h. could be expected.

A decision was made to give fuel injection another chance. According to Andy, one of the major drawbacks on the Novi engine equipped with fuel injection during the Lew Welch era relates to the extremely slow throttle response. Because of the lagging throttle response it made sense to use a big variable venturi carburetor. But with the engine on the dyno the carburetor also proved to have its problems. Even with the variable venturi to provide sufficient air velocity, the interior of the bulky carburetor was nearly flooded with alcohol. To use Andy's own expression, "There were times when the throttle was hit, it was like standing in a car wash." Thus, it was more than obvious that the carburetion had to be improved. In an effort to achieve this, the Novi team turned to the use of a Bendix fuel injection system. Joe Granatelli said that the team was committed to the use of fuel injection and no consideration was given to a return to carburetors. The feeling prevailed that previous fuel injection problems could be worked out.

Andy also recalled that every time the engines were run the spark plugs had become as black as coal. This caused the team to wonder how the engine managed to run as smoothly as it did. Yet, somehow the blackened plugs did not appear to interfere with the performance.

The reemergence of the Novi went further, for the decision was made to acquire two new chassis. Orders were placed with noted car builder Frank Kurtis, located in nearby Glendale, California, for the construction work. Kurtis reported the cost of each chassis to be $12,500. Incidentally, these two cars were among the last Indy cars to be built by Kurtis-Kraft.

How these new cars came about is a story unto itself. Kurtis described the proceedure in Ed Hitze's, <u>The Kurtis-Kraft Story</u>. According to Frank, Andy had called him shortly after the race of 1961 to draw up plans for a new car. Frank was willing to do so, but asked who was to built it as he had heard rumors that Andy had been talking with about every car builder in the business. When Frank asked to be paid for the drawings, Andy replied he had to see the drawings first. Kurtis then told Andy that there was no deal, thus Andy had to look elsewhere for another constructor. Then in early 1962, Andy and Frank met in a bar and over a drink Andy informed Kurtis about the dramatically altered Novi engines. As a consequence, he wanted to order a new Kurtis chassis like the one driven by "Cactus" Jack Turner in 1961. That car was the attractive 500J Bardahl Special built for car owner Fred Gerhardt. Kurtis then agreed to build such a car and a contract was signed. Two weeks later Granatelli ordered a sister car.

The new cars, identified as 500K, were tub-framed roadsters with rear drive power that had straight axles with conventional suspension all around. The cars also featured cross torsion bars attached to the suspension. The wheelbase was the minimum 96 inches with the left side weight bias much bigger than the older Kurtis 500F cars.

(1961) This Kurtis-Kraft car so impressed the Granatellis that they had Frank Kurtis build two similar cars for their 1962 Indy effort. Jack Turner qualified this Bardahl Special in 1961 finishing 25th due to the spectacular five car crash on the front straightaway. I.M.S.

The new cars had their engines set to the left and installed over seven inches further back within the frame than those in the 500Fs. This was intended to provide better weight distribution. The "left-hand" cylinder block was so situated that it appeared to hang outside of the frame in a fashion reminiscence of a `laydown' or `sidewinder.' Andy has said that the engines were so positioned in order to provide for "better balance, speed and stability in the turns." As was typical with an offset car, the cockpit was positioned slightly to the right. The cars had a pronounced bulge on the left side starting behind the left front wheel. Regarding the weight reduction, the new cars reportedly weighted 1,740 pounds, some 200 pounds less than the 500F. Some of the weight reduction was attributable to the use of magnesium for the blower case, the oil tank and the radiators.

With respect to the delivery date for the cars, two versions have emerged: According to the Novi camp the delivery date was to occur in February, yet the cars were not made available until the end of April. On the other hand, Frank Kurtis was to state that the contract for the construction of the first car was not finalized until January 2, and that the delivery was promised for April 3 or 4. According to Kurtis, the delivery was made one day late. Kurtis' position on this matter was contained in the Hitze book.

The new cars lacked the fin which had been so memorable on the 500Fs in past years. Headrests were incorporated into the bodywork covering the fuel tank, giving the cars a similar appearance to those powered by the Offy. If the cowlings had been lower they might well have been mistaken for a left sided `sidewinder.' However, with its high cowling and the dual exhaust pipes it was obvious that the cars were not Offy powered. The two new cars were to become staples for the Granatelli team for the next few years.

Chapter 5

Two New Novis - Yet Another Dismal Year - 1962

The Indianapolis Motor Speedway opened on April 28, in preparation for the 45th running of the Indianapolis 500. The two new Novis reached the Speedway on May 6, after having made the long journey from California on open trailers in caravan fashion. Reaching the track the cars were housed in garages 50 and 51. The $500 per car entry fee and formal applications were received before the April 15 deadline as the Granatellis most certainly entertained high expectations with the two mint condition Kurtis-Kraft cars. The cars appeared to be among the most creative and streamlined creations that Frank Kurtis had delivered to any customer. One observer in Gasoline Alley commented that they were "real beauties" as a smiling Granatelli stood nearby.

With the lighter and more powerful Novi engines, there was surely reason for worry among the Offy car owners. As if to add insult to injury for the competition, the lone Kurtis 500F was also entered. The opposition would now be faced with whatever challenge the three powerful Novis could offer. While the Novi operation had been somewhat less than fearsome in the past few years (not having made the race since 1958), the old car had displayed impressive speeds just one year earlier and now there were two brand new cars to cope with as well! Previously, there had never been more than two Novis entered in an Indianapolis race. In view of this, the Granatelli camp appeared to represent a formidable foe.

All three cars were entered under the same name, Hotel Tropicana Special, a Las Vegas hotel/casino business entity. Some eyebrows were raised regarding the sponsor's name. Would the Speedway management permit a car bearing a sponsor's name that engaged in gambling, albeit legal (though not widespread across the country at the time), to remain on the cars? Some recall that prior to the untimely airplane crash and death of Speedway President Wilbur Shaw (1946-1954), he had often remarked that sponsors needed to have some <u>direct</u> automotive relationship to the car - that is using a specific part or carrying the owner's name, etc. With changing times, the Tropicana name was to remain on the cars.

The two Kurtis-Kraft beauties had been placed on display at a press conference held in Santa Monica just prior to the departure to Indy. The #75 car was also in the room, but at the back as the Granatellis proudly presented the new cars for public viewing. On hand was a representative from the sponsoring Las Vegas hotel/casino as well as a showgirl from the Tropicana. Chuck Stevenson, assigned to drive one of the new cars, was on hand. He predicted that a 150 m.p.h. speed was obtainable from the cars when they took on the Indy challenge. Joe and Vince proudly posed at one of the new cars that had its hood lifted, thus showing a portion of the "600-hp supercharged V-8 Novi."

No reference to the Novi heritage was placed on the cars though the press continued to refer to them as Novis. The #16 was a gleaming bright

(1962) The mint condition new Kurtis-Krafts arrived in Gasoline Alley following the trip from Santa Monica. Note that #16 sports a black stripe that runs to the end of the headrest. Andy, at the rear of #59, stands by to supervise the unloading. If he only knew what laid ahead for the new creations. I.M.S.

yellow with a black strip running along the top, while the #59 was completely yellow. I.M.S. records indicate that car #16 was to be listed under serial #722 while #59 was #723. The 500F retained its number 75 from the previous year, though it was now painted white with a red stripe. The use of the #59 certainly was not new for the Granatellis as they had been assigned that number with their first Indy entry back in 1946 and it had been used on and off over the years just as a number of the Lew Welch cars, Novis included, had carried the #54.

Andy Granatelli had secured the services of two veteran drivers prior to the arrival of the cars at the Speedway. This was certainly in contrast to the previous year what with the mad scramble that had ensued as they prepared the newly acquired car. As you will recall a year earlier, the #75 had arrived at Indy without a driver assignment having yet to be made.

Although many had expected Dick Rathmann to return to the Novi stable, such did not occur. Under contract this time were Bill Cheesbourg in #59 while the aforementioned Chuck Stevenson was set for service in #16. As veteran Indy campaigners, Chuck had participated in six previous 500s to Bill's four prior appearances. However, the strapping Cheesbourg had Novi experience as he had manhandled a Novi in 1958 going all the way for a 10th place finish. This achievement came in spite of adversity. The car had suffered front end damage as Cheesbourg had to take to the infield in the third turn of the race's first lap due to the massive accident among a number of the cars up front. Cheesbourg still managed the splendid finish.

The 34 year old driver was a long-time veteran of racing as he had started competing with stock cars and midgets in the Southwest operating from his hometown of Tucson, Arizona. Bill's first 500 participation came in 1957, when he entered with the urging and support of close friend Jimmy Bryan. Though his qualified car was bumped, he returned to make the race in another car, the Seal Line Special, finishing 26th due to a split fuel tank. In the 1961 race, Cheesbourg had fallen victim to the aforementioned five car crash as Don Davis' car came to a halt on the front straightaway. Drivers following had to play bumper car and the ensuing melee eliminated four other cars including Bill's Dean Van Lines Special. The mishap at the quarter mark of the race saw him finish 28th.

Arriving at Indy in 1962, Bill's best finish had been the 10th place he had earned in his earlier Novi outing. Bill was initially offered a ride in the Konstant Hot Special for 1962 - at a reported sum of $1,500. The agreement also called for "Cheez" to drive a Konstant Hot Special on the Championship Trail that year. Outstanding racing mechanic Jud Phillips was to handle the wrenches on the Konstant Hot cars. When Granatelli called Cheesbourg to inquire about Bill's possible interest in driving the Novi, Cheesbourg told him that he was already committed. However, according to Bill, "When the Konstant Hot money didn't arrive," he visited the Granatellis in Santa Monica and was instantly hired, receiving the agreed upon money on the spot. With hindsight, however, Bill considered his departure from the Konstant Hot ride a major mistake.

Stevenson, who hailed from Newport Beach, California at the time, had an Indy record that predated Cheesbourg as he had made his first 500 appearance in 1951 driving the Bardahl Special owned by Carl Marchese. He finished 20th that year after the car caught fire. He returned to the Speedway the next three years. His best finish was a 12th in 1954 in a J.C. Agajanian car. Stevenson's sparkling record was further enhanced by virtue of his victories in the stock car classification in the 1952 and 1953 Pan American Road Race (La Carrera Pan Americana). He raced

Chuck Stevenson - the A.A.A. National Driving Champion in 1952. His best Indianapolis finish came in 1961 - 6th place. The following year he was unable to make the field with an ineffective Novi.   I.M.S.

in the death-defying charge across Mexico in a Bill Stroppe-Clay Smith prepared Lincoln Capri. Above and beyond that, Stevenson had captured the highly coveted National Driving Championship in 1952 piloting Bessie Lee Paoli's Springfield Welding Special. He edged out that year's Indy winner Troy Ruttman and Sam Hanks for the crown. Chuck's point total (1,440) topped Ruttman by 30 markers and Hanks by 50. Stevenson's racing credentials were impressive as he ran well on both dirt and pavement. In fact, he won the last dirt race run at the Milwaukee Mile, a 200 lap affair in August, 1953, and then the first pavement race held there in June, 1954.

Following his 1954 competition, Chuck was absent from the championship cars for five years. The absence was due in large measure to the tragic passing of his very close friend, Clay Smith, considered by many to be the best racing mechanic on the circuit. Smith was killed in a freak accident during a championship car race held at the one mile dirt oval at Du Quoin, Illinois in September, 1954. Chuck said, "I had no desire to race on the Championship Trail anymore." For the next few years he did test driving for Ford and when the memory of Smith's sudden, tragic passing was not a constant reminder, he returned to active competition in 1960. His best Indianapolis finish had been achieved the year prior to joining forces with the Novi squad when he earned 6th place in 1961, going the 200 laps in the Metal-Cal Special, a Quin Epperly produced car powered by an Offy.

The track surface at the Indianapolis Motor Speedway had changed considerably from the previous year as the front stretch was now paved except for one yard of symbolic bricks that remained at the start-finish line. This was a sentimental gesture, for at one time the entire surface was brick, thus the nickname often applied to the racing plant - "The Brickyard." With the entire track paved, it seemed more than logical to assume that average lap speeds would climb. Some observers felt that paving the front straightaway would add at least one or two miles per hour in circling the oval during qualification runs. For the Novis this certainly seemed beneficial, as the straights were the track locations where they were to gain their advantage. Now, with both long straightaways paved, it appeared reasonable to assume that the cars could more aptly demonstrate their superior top speeds.

As the track opened for practice, the tempo picked up rapidly, for by May 3, the previous year's fastest rookie, Parnelli Jones, was up to 148.5 m.p.h. in the Agajanian Willard Battery Special. The next day he topped 149 m.p.h. as he began flirting with the magical 150 m.p.h. mark. On May 5, he was up to 149.7 m.p.h. The Novis took to the new racing surface for the first time on May 8. Granatelli seemed satisfied with the Novi's first outing, for "fresh out of the box" Cheesbourg did 136 m.p.h. on the 1st lap followed by 137 m.p.h. before he pulled in. One observer stated, "There was no doubt that the cars could go fast what with their 645 horsepower." For his part Andy was quite enthusiastic saying, "They're capable of 155 to 160 m.p.h. if the driver and everything else is right. There is nothing that could touch them if everything is going right." This enthusiasm bore a striking similarity to his positive oratory of the previous year.

However, within a short time the two new Novis experienced their first problem of the year as they began spewing oil on the track. Was the old Novi jinx returning, and if so, this quickly? When the cars were examined it was discovered that the liquid was coming out through the breathers with some of the oil dripping onto the exhaust to create smoking rooster tails. Andy Granatelli explained, "In putting the motor in the new chassis we had to move the location of the oil breathers." As you may recall, when the powerplants were placed in the new chassis the breathers were located on each side of the engine. The twin crankcase breathers consisted of long curving tubes that came up virtually to the underside of the hoods. By working throughout the night of May 8 on the #16 car the problem was solved. They had resorted to the installation of a single breather positioned at the front center of the V-8 "valley." Once that work was completed the crew then performed the same alteration on the #59 car.

As the Novis had experienced the oil problem during their early track appearances, attention was focused on several other cars that had reached significant speeds. Shorty Templeman was clocked at 148.2 m.p.h. in the Forbes Racing Team Special while rookie Jim McElreath, in Ollie Prather's Schulz Fueling Equipment Special, surprised the railbirds when he cut loose with a 147.5 m.p.h. for the third highest speed run achieved on May 8. That represented the fastest lap ever turned in by a rookie driver.

As for the two new Novis, no sooner had the oiling problem seemingly been resolved before another problem surfaced. It was the same old bug-a-boo. The fuel injection system was creating havoc with the cars, just as had been the case in the late 1950s when the Novi operation was still under the control of Lew Welch. The team did a

(1962) The layover concept can be seen in this shot. The revamped engines retained the twin Bosch magnetos used by the Novis since the late 1950s. The blower quill can be seen at the front of the engine. Note the breather cap located on the left front of the V-8.   I.M.S.

great deal of adjustment work and Cheesbourg would return to the track for a few laps only to reenter the pit area to report that the car was not performing properly. Bill recalled that every time he "went out that was to be `the magic run' for somehow the difficulties had been straightened out." Andy would rush to the car as it pitted, leaning close to the driver, only to receive the bad news. Bill asserts that Granatelli felt that the drivers were not standing on the gas, although they assured him that they were moving as fast as their cars' setups would allow. When Andy informed Cheesbourg that he was balloon footing it, Bill became rather disgusted as he felt that he was going into the corners at a clip that all but had the back end swapping places with the front.

In an attempt to determine where the mechanical problems might rest, a camera was eventually mounted at the back of the #59 cockpit. The camera was activatived with a micro switch to obtain photos of the gauge readings (the tach, oil pressure, blower pressure, etc.). The film was then rushed downtown for developing. Returning the processed film to the garage, the Granatellis would pour over the illustrations in order to determine if they could locate the problem(s). The camera was a bone of contention with Bill! The tension was exacerbated as Cheesbourg and Stevenson were not permitted to view the film.

With the Novis not taking to the two and one-half mile oval until the 8th and with the ensuing problems, the team was in a real bind as the first weekend of qualifications was set for the 12th and 13th. The cars continued to lag in speed. With but one day remaining before the time trials opened, Stevenson was only able to reach 141.6 m.p.h. While the weather was less than desirable at the time, what with high winds, such a speed average was a keen disappointment. On the eve of the first qualifying session, the crew started working on the chassis and managed to iron out some of the handling wrinkles. However, during the weekend the Novi squad came to realize fueling was also giving problems.

(1962) Driver Bill Cheesbourg in one of the new Novis - a Hotel Tropicana Special inspired by the Kurtis Kraft model.
Gerald Walker Photo

(1962) Bill Cheesbourg, standing at the right rear tire, chats with fellow driver Paul Goldsmith, while his chariot is being examined. Problems continually plagued both Novis that year as the new cars failed to make the 500.   I.M.S.

On the opening day of qualifications, a great deal of excitement abounded at the famed track, yet none of it had any direct relationship to the Granatelli team as they were busily engaged in the garage with the troublesome Novis. While they failed to make any qualification attempts, Parnelli Jones established a new one lap (150.729 m.p.h.) record as well as a new four lap record (150.370 m.p.h.). The Illustrated Speedway News front page headline proclaimed, "Jones Breaks 150 mph Speed Barrier." No other driver was able to exceed the magical 150 m.p.h. standard as second fast time was set by Rodger Ward when he qualified Bob Wilke's Leader Card Special at 149.371 m.p.h. Third fast time was the 149.349 m.p.h. reached by Bobby Marshman in the Bryant Heating and Cooling Special. In all 19, cars qualified on opening day. Among the group were two rookies, Jim McElreath (149.025 m.p.h.) and Dan Gurney (147.886 m.p.h.). Gurney was at the wheel of a Mickey Thompson owned rear engine Buick. Dan had originally been tied in with a John Zink entry, a very unconventional car as it contained a rear engine gas turbine. With its failure to adequately perform, Gurney had then joined forces with Thompson to put the low profile Buick, a Harvey Aluminum Special, into the starting field.

Dan's qualifying run was sparkling as he was the seventh fastest qualifier in the field.

As noted earlier, the entry of a rear engine car at the Indianapolis Motor Speedway did not materialize for the Granatellis in 1962. However, such a car was in the field under the direction of Mickey Thompson. Though Brabham and Cooper were absent, Thompson's Buicks provided for the continued participation of a rear engine car.

West Coast Land Speed Record car constructer, driver and racing entrepreneur Mickey Thompson (1928-1988) was thinking in terms similar to the Granatellis - going to a rear engine car. Mickey, who had established a new LSR of 406.6 m.p.h. in his Challenger on the Utah Salt Flats in September of 1960, had now turned his attention to Indianapolis race car competition. In his autobiography, Challenger: Mickey Thompson's Own Story of His Life of Speed, Thompson pointed out that while many costly attempts had been made to enter modified production engines at the Speedway "to challenge the domination of the heavy, ancient Offenhauser 4-banger, but everyone had failed. So, naturally, whenever I spoke of my own production engine plans for Indy the usual reaction (was) that there are fools in this world that just refuse to learn." He then pointed out that Buick had recently introduced an "all aluminum" V-8 that was exceptionally light and that it might well be the powerplant needed for a truly modern Indy car. He had acquired several Buick aluminum engines and put them to work on the dyno. Mickey pointed out that "there was no point in taking steps to design and build a chassis until I had a thoroughly developed and proven engine." By early February, 1962, Mickey had a 255 c.i. engine to the point it was capable of putting out a steady 330 horsepower "for hours on end." Pleased with the dyno performance, work then began on a chassis design. Thompson believed that the car needed to be much smaller and lighter in every way. This included replacement of the solid axle, wagon-spring roadsters with independent suspension on all four wheels. Mickey had taken note of the recent revolution of the rear engine Formula One cars, so why not take advantage of that lesson? Thompson referred to the Indy roadsters as being "old sleds."

Thompson car, Gurney quickly departed for The Netherlands as he was due to drive a Porsche in the upcoming Grand Prix of Holland at Zandvoort. Gurney had competed in Formula One racing for several years where rear engine cars were the norm rather than the exception and Dan would play a vital role in future Indy competition.

The Indy qualifying field was expanded by

(1962) Driver Dan Gurney in a Mickey Thompson creation. The ever resourceful Thompson had picked up on the rear engine concept used with modest success in 1961. Thompson and Gurney served as major links between the Brabham car of 1961 and what was to follow.
I.M.S.

At about this time, he had the good fortune to learn that John Crosthwaite was residing in America. Crosthwaite had previously worked with Cooper and Lotus in England and was considered an authority on road racing chassis. Thompson was able to convince Crosthwaite to join forces with him and from this merger came the construction of three Thompson rear engine cars. Before construction was even completed, Jim Kimberly bought one that he intended to have English driver Jack Fairman race at Indy. Mickey was to use Americans Chuck Daigh and Dan Gurney as his 500 drivers. Chuck Daigh experienced seemingly endless problems as he could not move his Thompson car to a competitive speed, nor did he enjoy any success with the so-called Zink Trackburner turbine. Thompson had observed Gurney for several years as he established a reputation as one of the leading road racing drivers. Thus, he was able to secure Gurney's services after the John Zink Trackburner failed to achieve satisfactory results. Therefore, rookie Gurney secured a ride in Thompson's Harvey Aluminum Special for the 1962 race.

Following his qualification success in the

only two cars on the second day of time trials as Eddie Johnson and Bob Veith qualified. There were several surprises when one looked at the qualified field for not only were the two sleek looking mint condition Novis not yet in the field, several of the hot shoe drivers were also missing. These drivers included Eddie Sachs, Troy Ruttman, Jim Rathmann and Jim Hurtubise. Hurtubise, the former track record holder, had seen his #99 Demler Special seriously damaged when he hit the wall during the last day of practice prior to the opening round of qualifications. Sachs who had started on the pole the previous two years was experiencing difficulties with his Dean Autolite car, a situation to which the Granatellis could relate.

As the Novi crew attempted to get on top of the mechanical difficulties, they most certainly had their work cut out for them. More than half of the 21 qualified cars had lap speeds that were in the 146 - 147 m.p.h. bracket. Realizing the mammoth task confronting the Novi undertaking, the #75 Novi was parked in front of the team's garages with a sign taped on the high dorsal fin that proclaimed "FOR SALE - CHASSIS ONLY."

With the fuel injection system continuing to be a nagging problem, the Novis were presented with a new innovation as an accelerator pump was hooked up to the supercharger. The hope was that the abrupt loss of fuel experienced as the drivers momentarily backed off in the corners would then be overcome. Yet, by May 14 (the day after the first round of qualifying), the decision was made to remove the fuel injectors replacing them with carburetors with the expectation that the switch would increase speed. Marcenac was dispatched to Santa Monica in order to secure carburetors for the replacement work. Jean was to return by Wednesday morning and the team's plans called for the installation of the carburetors to be completed by late that afternoon. Granatelli explained that if one experienced trouble with an Offy, getting parts for it was like getting pieces for a family car "but we can't have that luxury. We can't buy anything. We have to make everything we have. We can't copy. Everything is original with us and we have to work everything out and de-bug it." Andy went on to explain that the day prior to the first qualifications was the first good day the crew had experienced and "we started working on the chassis and got it pretty well straight. Then on Saturday and Sunday we started realizing the fuel injection was giving us trouble. We hadn't been up fast enough before to know." He explained that the team had opted for a fuel injection setup because of the unit's lightness and compact size, but the crew simply did not have sufficient time to make all the necessary adjustments. He pointed out that neither Stevenson or Cheesbourg had been able to get their rides to the ragged edge. He also called attention to the time lost when the cars experienced the oiling problem, for the Novis had been forced to run under the white line. This caused the air scoops to funnel in dust like a vacuum to a point that both engines had to be gone over in a

(1962) Bill Cheesbourg seated in a Novi while conversing with Andy Granatelli. Note a cigar in Bill's mouth. He would light up a stoogy as soon as he stopped in the pits and as Andy leaned into the cockpit Bill would unleash a puff of smoke that greatly agitated Andy. Bill and his fellow racer from Arizona, the late Jimmy Bryan, not only smoked cigars, but were pranksters of the first order.   I.M.S.

meticulous fashion. To add to the woes a clutch release bearing had let go in the Stevenson ride early in the week while the mechanics awaited Marcenac's return.

Still exuding confidence while detailing the uphill struggle, Andy stated, "We feel both cars are capable of running well over Parnelli's record." On Wednesday the 16th, Cheesbourg moved close to the 147 m.p.h. mark, but such occurred while he was test hopping one of Mickey Thompson's Buick powered cars! As it turned out Cheesbourg would do considerable test driving before the month was out. With his impressive mechanical background he was probably the most sought after test pilot since driver Freddie Agabashian had performed such services back in the 1950s. Cheesbourg aptly demonstrated his versatility for he was the only driver to take rides in all six of the different type cars at the Speedway that year. They consisted of the conventional Offy, the rear engine Thompson car, John Zink's turbine powered Trackburner, the Novi, the sole Chevrolet powered entry and a somewhat modified English race car - the de Villiers. With all the car hopping during the month, Cheez seemed to be in more cars than a parking lot attendant. When Cheesbourg, who was reported to have a "rather lucrative contract" with Andy Granatelli, was asked about the possibility of switching rides he declined comment. However on Thursday the 17th, Bill was again out in one of the three rear engine Buicks when the car spun and hit the wall almost head on after a 480 foot slide. Luckily, he escaped injury. The car, owned by sportsman Jim Kimberly, had been assigned to Jack Fairman who hailed from Worth, Sussex, England. The road racer had been unable to get the car up to speed. Cheesbourg's driving performance was such that it was stated that Daigh and Fairman were not able "to show the same results" in the Thompson cars.

On Saturday, ten more entries qualified to bring the field up to 31 cars. The fastest qualifier on the third day was Gene Hartley driving the Drewry's Special (who picked up $1,200 for the feat) as the day's fastest qualifier. Hartley's speed was 146.969 m.p.h. Among those who qualified was Eddie Sachs who would now start the race from the ninth row. The 1960 winner Jim Rathmann finally managed to get his qualifying run completed in the Simoniz Special owned by Smokey Yunick (146.6 m.p.h.). The eye-appealing A.J. Watson built car carried Smokey's traditional colors, black and gold.

Once again the Novis were not included within the starting field. During the third day of the time trials, Cheesbourg escaped injury when the

(1962) A speedy Novi moving down the front straight during a practice run. I.M.S.

As the second weekend of qualifying approached, the weather abruptly changed. On May 17, a record high of 90 degrees was reported at the local weather bureau. The Novi team spent the day waiting for a cool down before attempting to set the carburetion on the temperamental Novis. They worked feverishly as they tried to get the carburetors to provide a richer mixture so as not to lean out and run extremely hot. When the team discovered that there was not enough time to adjust the Holley carburetors properly they once again returned to the use of fuel injection!

On the eve of the second round of qualifications, Andy reported that the team would try to qualify Cheesbourg's #59 on Saturday and then wait until Sunday to put Stevenson's car into the field. Some observers along pit lane had reported no clockings of over 144 m.p.h. for the cars.

throttle linkage broke and his car locked up due to fuel starvation. The incident occurred as he roared down the backstretch. Fortunately, no contact was made with the wall, although the ride was a wild one for Bill. All four tires were flat spotted. In the ensuing slide, an indentation (referred to as a heel cup), that Bill had hammered into the belly pan, was sheered off by its contact with the track. This allowed one of Bill's shoes to be worn completely down to the sock. Before the car came to a halt, going into the third turn, the sock was being shredded, although Bill was endeavoring to get his feet up out of danger. Bill later stated that his adrenaline was pumping so fast that he had no time to be concerned about his personal well-being.

Granatelli said that with the damage incurred to the engine the crew would turn their attention to getting Stevenson's #16 car ready for the last day of qualifying. The engine damage to #59 certainly was sad news for the crew as they had been laboring night and day trying to tweak enough speed out of the Novis to assure starting spots in the Memorial Day race. Andy told the press that when the fueling arm broke with the throttle open "the engine was sucking in air and getting no fuel. The temperature goes sky high when you lean down the mixture. It shows what a small thing can do to you. It could've happened to anybody."

While the crew was understandably disappointed, Cheesbourg was dismayed over the fact that Granatelli informed him that the broken linkage was due to driver error. Bill recalls that when Andy made such an assertion "that kind of ended it" between him and the Novi team.

Cheesbourg was not the only driver experiencing problems, for Jim Hurtubise hit the southwest turn on his second qualifying lap after putting in a 147.5 m.p.h. on the opening lap in the #99 Demler Special. Assessing the front end damage, car owner Norm Demler of Niagara Falls, New York, said there was no way the car could be repaired in time for the next day's last round of qualifying. Fortunately, Hurtubise was able to jump into a Jim Robbins roadster and qualified at 146.9 m.p.h. during the last hour of Sunday's time trials.

On the last day of qualifying, the starting field was filled with four cars actually being bumped. The day's fastest qualifier was Johnny Boyd in the Metal Cal Special at 147.04 m.p.h. The slowest car in the field had registered a time of 146.09 m.p.h., which was two miles over the slowest qualifying speed of the previous year. During the day, Cheesbourg was out in a Mickey Thompson Buick powered car when it blew an engine and caught fire on the back straight. The driver escaped without injury. By late afternoon, after a Herculean struggle with the #59 Novi engine, the team had Cheesbourg ready to roll once again. Thus, while Bill had been freed by Andy on Saturday to seek out another ride, on Sunday the pair was reunited in a last desperate attempt to make the show with a Novi.

A grim faced Andy and Joe stood by the repaired #59 as a dejected Cheesbourg sat in the cockpit - helmet and gloves on ready to move onto the track. Reportedly, Andy had offered another driver a cash settlement if he would move out of line - all to no avail. When the 6 P.M. closing gun sounded the Novi was first in line! Once again the Novi would be absent from the 500 - for the fourth straight year. The torment had been intensified by the fact that the enormously powerful Novis were contained within brand new Kurtis chassis.

In the Gasoline Alley column of the <u>Indianapolis News,</u> co-authored by Wayne Fuson and Angelo Angelopolous, Wayne spoke of the episode thusly:

"That 6 P.M. pistol shot hit every heart of the Novi lovers. Engine running in a hope against hope, one of the most popular prospective rides in the history of the Indianapolis Speedway was left waiting at the church. The Grantellis, those patient paisans, a sleepless crew battling a destiny that seemed not to want to relent, stood around their powerful yellow Tropicana with the stoicism of men who have known the rough route... Bill Cheesbourg, a big man with a large measure of guts who goes from spin-

(1962) An excellent frontal shot of the car assigned to Chuck Stevenson. The extended left side hood resulted from the engine layover. The expression on crew member Wally Garabedian's face says it all. The inability to get the two new Kurtis-Kraft cars up to competitive speed weighed heavily on the crew.
Bruce Craig Photos

ning race car to other race cars he's never been in, sat in the cockpit. A miserable, hot afternoon for the race fan had been a back-aching, nerve torturing night-and-day race with the clock, the most remorseless enemy of all. At one point in the afternoon toil, with the weary crew moving robot-like one member seated in the cockpit for wheel-weight checks couldn't keep his head from falling back on the rest in a search for sleep."

As for Cheesbourg, one newspaper account describes his month of May as doing "everything but qualifying. His various cars spun, crunched, burned, seized, roared in protest, but not one carried him into the field."

(1962) Andy and Joe Granatelli in an intense conversation with Chuck Stevenson. Chuck and Bill carried out some car swapping that was to determine if one driver could squeeze additional speed out of his teammate's mount.   I.M.S.

In discussing his misfortunes, teammate Chuck Stevenson had said, "I'm running good...but we're not going any place. I'm driving the socks off it, and getting 144 m.p.h."

Holding a meeting with his team in the Novi garage after qualifications closed, a distraught Andy, obviously under great pressure and with much disappointment, chastised the crew for the inability to make the race. He informed them that if they had taken fewer coffee breaks and less nap time the team might well have been successful. Marcenac was unable to accept this posture as he exited the team's garage area.

The pressures were so great that on one occasion that year Andy and Joe were seen battling it out in a free-for-all in Gasoline Alley (perhaps it was Katzenjammer Kids playtime - see Chapter 23). Following the fisticuffs they would head back to the garage to roll up their sleeves as they resumed their efforts in preparing the cars!

During the practice sessions with the Novis, Cheesbourg had reported that the chassis setup was at least "half way decent." Yet, in looking back it is noted that the problems of the cars were twofold: the fuel injector vs. carburetor setup plus the handling.

Following the closure of qualifying, a full week remained before the traditional Carburetion Day, Monday, May 28. It was reported that Granatelli placed primary blame on the chassis setup and according to one source, such was due to the "steering and poor handling, etc." For his part, Cheez believes that the ignition was the primary culprit. According to one source, when the front suspension had come off the jig, hardened spacers of an inch or slightly more had been placed at each corner. They were to remain in position until the front end was installed. The oversight of not removing them was belatedly discovered.

In his autobiography, Andy mentioned a steering snafu. He asserted that Kurtis had provided the cars with a different steering setup than what Andy supposedly had in mind. In an interview, Andy stated that when they finally measured the steering arrangement the crew discovered that one wheel toed in much further than the other. Andy said one wheel turned in 22 degrees while the other turned in 18 degrees. As a result, one wheel wanted the car to make a sharper corner than the other! Because of this situation the tire wear was tremendous, and it also explained the bad handling of the car. Before all of this was discovered and settled a good deal of time had been wasted. If true, little wonder that Cheesbourg and Stevenson had experienced challenging problems in the corners. For his part Frank Kurtis charged that Granatelli blamed him for "lousy steering and poor handling, etc." Continuing, Frank said, "I was so sick when I read these reports in the papers that I went back to California and didn't go back to Indy." One Novi crew member recalls having to drill new frame holes one inch away from the original setting to compensate for the alleged handling malfunction. Thus, we have the builder and the owner in conflict as to the car problems - at least in regard to the handling. Long-time Speedway Bear Alignment specialist, Marcel Periat, informed us that front end alignment at the rack was not mandatory.

Wanting to validate this finding as the cause for the handling struggle and to test hop the altered steering setup, Andy approached Chief Steward Harlan Fengler in an attempt to secure approval for one of the Novis to run a few laps to check out the corrected front end. Fengler allowed the run to be held on Carburetion Day. Andy then asked Jim Hurtubise to drive #16 for some shakedown laps. Jim accepted the proposal. He took the car out and demonstrated to the Granatellis that #16 was at least capable of times unattainable earlier. He drove four laps with the fastest being 146.8 m.p.h. That was enough to make the field if the time could be sustained and it had been an official attempt. That fastest practice lap was approximately seven-tenths of a mile more than the slowest in the field. A slim margin but acceptable. Whether he could have maintained that speed for four official laps to ensure a starting position is a moot question. Yet, it certainly demonstrated the cars had more speed than they had previously been able to demonstrate. Time had simply run out. The Granatellis now had confirmation that they had unscrambled the front end malaise, but it was obviously too late for the 1962 race. When questioned as to the reasoning behind Jim Hurtubise taking the car out for a few laps instead of the assigned drivers, Cheesbourg or Stevenson, Andy replied that he thought that he would give another driver a chance since the pair had difficulties in getting the cars much over 140 m.p.h. In his autobiography, Andy asserted that Chuck and Bill had done "a magnificent job fighting along with us." According to Bob Gates in his book, Hurtubise, an elated Granatelli quickly offered Jim a Novi ride for the following year after the Carburetion Day run.

Jim, who had acquired several nicknames "Herk" or "Hercules," had been a sensation in qualifying in 1960, when on the final day of qualifications the rookie demolished the track qualifying records then held by Dick Rathmann. Herk had been at the wheel of the Ernie Ruiz Travelon Trailer Special wrenched by top-notch racing mechanic Danny Oakes. Records are made to be broken, but it was even more remarkable when an Indy record was shattered by a rookie! From that point on, Jim was to become well-known as one of the hardest charging drivers in Indy car competition. Herk was gaining a reputation as a driver who could wrestle any type of car to its utmost limits.

As a footnote, it might be pointed out that since Jim had made the race qualifying the Robbins' Special (at 146.963 m.p.h.), Jim Robbins had assumedly given his permission for the test hopping ride. If so, the owner who had prevented Dick Rathmann from moving to the Novi a year earlier had now relented or could it be penitence? The matter is a bit murky as the owner of the Robbins' car was listed as another Michigan resident, John Marco Puslio of Wynadotte, Michigan.

The superhuman effort of the Granatellis and the crew showed great determination to make the best of an obstacle filled situation. Time was far too short and the failure to qualify the Novis could be anticipated when all the problems that befell the cars were considered. It is also a somewhat sad circumstance that once again fuel injection did not properly function. To have a normally aspirated engine work with this equipment usually represented minimal problems. Meanwhile, one must consider that the high boost supercharged Novi presented an entirely different set of circumstances. In Vince Granatelli's opinion the main problem during their Novi years was that the cars were never campaigned elsewhere while many of the Offy entries competed at other tracks. Thus, teams often would exchange information to resolve a particular mechanical difficulty at one track or another. In expanding on his statement, Vince said that in working with the engine in the earlier days, they constantly found several cylinders would be running dead rich while others would be running dead lean. He suggested that with the blower pressure reaching 65 to 70 pounds there was a continuing problem with equal fuel distribution as port injectors were still in the future.

Several days after qualifications closed, Andy informed Indianapolis Star writer George Moore that the team's problems resulted from several factors. Granatelli stated that the crew "was mislead in thinking that the carburetion was their problem when in effect the car wouldn't handle in the corners and subsequently the engine rpms would drop too low." Continuing, Granatelli also stated, "The front torque bar arms were binding, causing the weight to load into the front end on the turns." Andy also asserted that the "steering ratio was too slow and the front end geometry was wrong. By freeing up the front torque bar arms and changing the steering ratio" he believed that the corner speeds would be up and that a higher rpm level could have been maintained coming off the curves.

The inability of the two new Novis to make the starting field added a very dismal footnote to the history of the famed Novis. On only one previous occasion had a Novi failed to make the race the year it was unveiled at the Speedway - the #31 roadster back in 1956. In fact, the failure of the 1962 Kurtis-Kraft Novi to make the field is most definitely in stark contrast to the introduction of previous new Novis. For example, the first chassis constructed for a Novi engine in 1946 established a new track record that year. Ralph Hepburn burned up the track qualifying the front drive

(1962) Novi crew members working on the high finned #75 that had been so fast the previous year. It sat in the garage area in 1962 with no known track time. One can only wonder what the car might have achieved if some shakedown work had been undertaken. I.M.S.

Novi Governor Special at 133.9 m.p.h. breaking the existing record by over three and one-half miles per hour. And in its first year at the Speedway, the 500F rear drive roadster driven by Paul Russo set the unofficial track record during practice with a speed average that was not surpassed by anyone else that year in either practice, qualifications or during the race.

What might have happened if the team had prepared the lone 500F chassis for driving duties? The year before the car had not experienced handling problems in any form similar to that in the new chassis and it had been very impressive. In fact, the previous year the #75 had been driven even faster than what Hurtubise finally managed to do with the new car in 1962 after it was presumedly sorted out. Dick Rathmann had been over 148 m.p.h. officially the year before and he had been unofficially timed at over 149 m.p.h. while Hurtubise did not reach 147 m.p.h. Perhaps if the 500F had run there might have been a chance that at least one Novi would have run fast enough to make the show. Presumedly, there may have been a good chance of qualifying the old war horse. On the other hand, if the team had insufficient time to solve the problems on the two new cars, how could they have found the time to get a third car running as well? Perhaps "Old 500F" would have suffered from the fuel injection malady. But at least the team had learned something about the setup in order to obtain additional speed. Beyond that, it is not unlikely that the team would run short on parts to construct another running engine in addition to the ones already in use in the newer cars. All of this is certainly a case of wishful thinking but then again what if...?

When asked about this, Andy informed us that if they had worked on #75 it is likely that they could have made the race. Then when asked why he did not give it a shot, he replied, "We worked so hard on the other cars and we were always hoping the next thing we were going to do was going to be okay." As for the #75 car, even when it had been offered for sale, sans a Novi powerplant, there were no takers. It certainly appears that the problems for the Granatelli Novi operation ran deep.

The depth of Andy Granatelli's distress was described by Sid Collins, the radio announcer for the annual race. Sid was so much a part of the classic race that he was deemed the "Voice of the 500." In a book detailing Sid's life, <u>Stay Tuned For The Greatest Spectacle in Racing</u>, Collins reported that some hours after the last day of qualifying he made a late trip through Gasoline Alley and noticed that a door to the Granatelli garages was still unlocked. He went in to take a look and noted a dejected Andy sitting on an empty Coke case. Andy invited Sid to come on in and have a seat. Sid remained for some time talking to Andy. From this late night encounter, Sid reports that a strong relationship grew. Andy promised Collins that one day he would repay Sid for the kind attention and concerns he displayed that evening. Andy remained true to his word and in later years he hired Collins to do some radio commercials for products being made by a firm headed by Andy. One can well imagine the disenchantment of Andy after the heartbreaking month. He certainly had reason enough to feel lowly. Yet, while he was mentally whipped the spirit was not broken.

Other members of the team also felt saddened beyond belief. The team's adrenaline had been so high as they had worked on the cars. The long tedious hours of labor were seemingly endless, but they were still able to cope until the very end. When the cars failed to qualify and the 6 o'clock signal denoting the close of time trials arrived, the adrenaline drained, leaving an exhausted and dejected crew. One crew member made reference to the fact that they were to return to California "with their tails tucked between their legs." Envision the distressed state of Jean Marcenac who had labored for four consecutive years (Welch's last two years at the Speedway and now the first two with the

(1962) Rodger Ward the 1962 winner. Teammate Len Sutton finished 2nd. Such a feat was not achieved again until 1997 when Arie Luyendyk beat out teammate Scott Goodyear in capturing his second 500 victory.   I.M.S.

Granatellis) to secure a starting position in the 500 for at least one Novi only to wind up with broken dreams on each and every occasion.

In looking at the events that transpired at the track in May of 1962, perhaps the most memorable circumstance was the fact that the "magical" 150 m.p.h. barrier for qualifying had been broken by Parnelli Jones and that no other driver was able to top the 150 mark. The honor was most deservedly earned by Parnelli. A handful of Novi loyalists pointed out that the elusive mark simply was not destined for a Novi, although the #75 had come so close the previous year in practice when Dick Rathmann was at the wheel. But then, Tony Bettenhausen had come even closer to breaking the magic barrier driving Lindsey Hopkins' Autolite car.

In 1962, Rodger Ward captured his second Indy 500 victory, once again driving a Leader Card Special owned by Bob Wilke with A.J. Watson as chief mechanic. The Leader Card team pulled off a real coup as the team's other driver, Len Sutton of Portland, Oregon, finished second. Such a feat has not been accomplished since 1948 when Mauri Rose and Bill Holland finished one-two in Lou Moore's Blue Crown Specials. Eddie Sachs finished third behind the Wilke cars after having started the race from the 27th position. The previous year's winner, A.J. Foyt, was 23rd after his Bowes Seal Fast car lost a wheel on lap 70. Parnelli was the early leader in the contest, but at approximately 175 miles his brakes gave out. In one observer's view, it was like driving a "fired bullet, which he can turn, but can not stop." Jones eventually lost the lead but valiantly struggled to finish an amazing 8th. It turned out that the exhaust pipe, lacking clearance, dropped slightly making contact with the brake line. The resulting friction created a leak in the brake line.

The Rookie of the Year was Texan Jim McElreath who finished a solid 7th. Paul Russo, who had performed so spectacularly in 1956 and 1957 in a Novi, made his Indy finale in the 1962 race. His last ride was

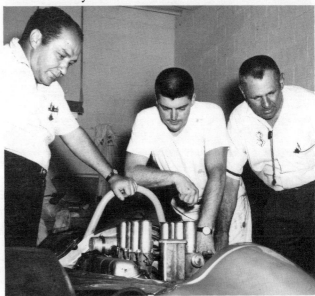

(1962) A studious trio indeed. Andy left, Mickey Thompson and three-time 500 winner Louie Meyer check out the rear engine used with Mickey's entry. The power was supplied by an aluminum Buick block.   I.M.S.

aboard the Denver Chicago Trucking Company Special owned by Myron Osborn that finished 28th. Paul went a mere 21 laps due to a piston problem though he later saw action in the race as a relief driver.

The 1962 race field consisted of 32 front engine Offenhausers and the sole rear engine stock block Buick in the Thompson/Crosthwaite chassis driven by Gurney.

The lone Buick did not seem to attract nearly the press attention rendered the Brabham driven car the previous year. No doubt this was due to several factors: it was not the first rear engine car and while Brabham had finished 9th, Dan Gurney finished 20th due to a broken rear end transaxle seal. With the presence of even a single rear engine car in the field, some folks were convinced that the rear engine car would be the way to go in the future. The concept must have certainly been on the minds of a number of the Indy car competitors. While Mickey Thompson was the only interloper at the "Playground of the (Offy) Roadsters," the Establishment was being challenged and among the watchful, thinking observers were the Granatellis.

An interesting sidenote having a direct relationship to the Novi operation occurred in 1962. The designated pace car was to be the newly introduced Studebaker Avanti. The sporty looking car had been unveiled to Studebaker dealers and stockholders at the annual stockholders meeting in South Bend, Indiana on April 26. However, the company was unable to have an Avanti fully prepared to lead the starting field at the offset of the race. As a consequence, pace car driver Sam Hanks, the Speedway's Director of Competitions (at the wheel of the pace car for the 5th consecutive year), had to use a Studebaker Lark. The Novi connection came about as a result of the auto company's board of directors approving the purchase of Granatelli's Paxton Products company on March 9 of that year for a reported $275,000 of which $125,000 consisted of stock in the firm. The acquisition also included the services of Paxton executives including Andy Granatelli.

Studebaker's involvement in racing in years gone by was showcased as former Novi chauffeur, Cliff Bergere, made a parade lap the second weekend of qualifying in the #22 Studebaker Special; the car he had driven to 3rd place in the Indy 500 thirty years earlier (1932).

Yet, as the curtain came down on the 1962 Indianapolis 500 mile race, the month had not been good for the Granatelli undertaking, nor for Studebaker. There was no Novi in the show and for the Studebaker folks the valuable opportunity to properly display the designated Avanti pace car had to be scrapped.

(1962) An Avanti parked on pit lane. While the car featured a streamlined silhouette, for many it appears to be stark and forlorn, perhaps the failures generated by it inability to fulfill its designated role as the official pace car. It was a bad year for the Novis as well as the Avanti. Speedway President Tony Hulman and the track's Director of Competition, Sam Hanks (1957 Indy winner) stand behind the Studebaker.

I.M.S.

Chapter 6

GETTING THE ACT TOGETHER

For four long years, the Novi had missed the starting field for the Indy 500. Obviously, such a circumstance created considerable disappointment for the legion of long-suffering fans of the cars. All sort of mistakes, bitter failures and unusual bad luck (or might we say the Novi's usual bad luck?) had prevented any chance for the Novi to aptly and fully demonstrate its prowess during the prolonged dry spell. Yet, in spite of all the disappointments and failures, the future appeared brighter. The two 1962 cars had been in the Granatelli's hands for a year. Sufficient time certainly had allowed the cars to be properly prepared for a successful return to the Speedway. Engineering improvements had been made and renewed promise was prevalent. Testing had taken place with the cars at the Indy track during the summer of 1962, with Bill Cheesbourg behind the wheel. He did so after Andy's strong urging. The inducement included the payment of $1,500 and a new Paxton supercharger for Bill's truck. During the summer of 1962, Bill had maintained a shop at Indianapolis for his USAC stock car operation. Jim Hurtubise was also reported to have put in time shaking down the Novis that summer.

Bill recalled some of his tire test experiences with the Novi that summer. One day, when running late in the afternoon with a low amount of fuel, he approached 150 m.p.h. and remembering the 142 m.p.h. averages during May, Bill was elated. The chassis was now working properly and happily he reported, "We're there." Bill drove approximately 1,800 miles at the Speedway that summer and spent evenings busily working on his stock car. On weekends, it was off to another USAC stock car race.

Another driver at the wheel of the Novi that summer was Parnelli Jones, the current track record holder. Andy Granatelli informed a member of the press about this outing.

"I just asked him as a friend if he would take it out and then tell me if it was me, the car or the driver was wrong. In four laps he's doing 148.5. Nobody does that! It was sensational! He was driving absolutely smooth and capably. He doesn't drive like a crazy man. He doesn't have to. He has a feel for a race car."

A disheartened Granatelli described how the team had spend most of two weeks modifying the car according to the suggestions of other drivers.

"One day I put it back to the way I had it originally and told a driver how to run the track, shutting off at certain point and getting back on it at others. He ran three laps at almost 147, then had some suggestions. It took us three days and we were back down to 143."

Andy continued by summing up his feelings about the entire episode as follows:

"I get sick when I think of it. Here I am, practically killing myself for two weeks trying to get this thing running this way for a certain driver and that way for another. Then to have a guy jump into the car cold and run so fast so quickly, it's just too much. Why, did you know that Parnelli didn't even fit in the car right? He's so small he was looking through the steering wheel and just over the cowl."

Some years later when we talked with Andy, he gave us the following comment about Parnelli's stint in the Novi:

"He (Parnelli Jones) tried one of my Novis for me once. In a few laps he was going six miles an hour faster than anyone else had gone in that car. If he had driven one in the 500, I'm sure he would have won in it. With that special handling, the Novi could have won. I wanted him to and he wanted to. But he was loyal to Agajanian and he wasn't going to leave him."

Parnelli's comment about this stint in the Novi can be extracted from a statement he rendered about Granatelli a few years later. "I felt he'd (Granatelli) given the Novis a helluva go. I ran one once. I admired what Andy had done for the car." According to Parnelli, Andy hounded him to compete in a Novi. However, Jones declined, saying that the "reliability and history of the Novi were not too great, thus I was not anxious to drive it."

In a talk with Parnelli Jones that included some discussion regarding his Novi outing, he recalled being asked by Andy to drive one of the cars during a tire test. He accepted and drove it enough to impress Andy.

When Parnelli was asked how he felt about the car he replied, "I found it quite impressive. Actually, it had so much power on the straightaway that it was a relatively easy car to drive. I thought it was one of the easier cars I've ever driven." With respect to the much quoted weak performances in the turns, Parnelli informed us that he felt that the weight of the car was not the most serious problem. He thought the problem was related more to the throttle lag because of the supercharger and its behavior of losing and then having to build up boost again. However, the driver had better be ready when the boost kicked in!

In addition to all this, a member of the Novi team recalled that when J.C. Agajanian learned that his driver was on the track in a Novi, he almost blew his stack. He immediately had Parnelli called in off the course.

Apart from working on the chassis, the Granatellis once again went over the V-8 engines and made a number of changes. New cylinder blocks were cast, but with smaller ports than those used in the older blocks. This was in contrast with what would be normal (greater ports and valve area means a smoother flow into the cylinders), but the aim was to obtain more power in the mid-rpm range. The port passages had been downsized from one and one-eight to five-eighths inch, then widening before entry into the combustion chamber. The results of this construction was that the fuel/air mixture created a greater velocity flow. Because of the narrow ports the valves were one-eights of an inch smaller than those previously used.

The new cylinder blocks were reported to be 40 pounds lighter than the previous powerplants. The blocks were stiffened by additional webbing at the end, instead of only two coolant outlets, four were now in place directly above the cylinders. Thus the new block provided more water area around the cylinders and the valves. The blocks were also equipped with newly designed Winfield cams.

New connecting rods were designed and used as were new intake manifolds in order to offer greater low end torque. This was believed to offer a more flexible engine range. The blower drive ratio was set at 4.5 to 1 and quoted as delivering 27 pounds of boost at 8,000 rpm and a still impressive 15 pounds at 6,000 rpm.

A new exhaust arrangement was developed by Hedman Hedders. The exhaust setup on each side of the engine had the outlets joined, thus forming a single large exhaust stack. All three cars had a three speed gearbox.

As might be expected, the Granatellis had opted to continue trying to reduce weight in the cars whenever possible. For the blocks, a shell mold process to cut weight was used. New water and oil radiators were made of a lightweight aluminum, while dual Airheart braking systems with calipers on both sides of the rotor disc were introduced. With Parnelli Jones' car incurring brake failure in 1962, the Granatellis, ever mindful of ways to upgrade their cars, had fittings that permitted backup brakes to take over if the primary set failed. The dual mags and dual spark plugs were retained.

Andy Granatelli and his brothers remained strong believers in the use of a fuel injection system for the Novi. Therefore, Andy contacted the Bendix Company and with their assistance the Novi team reworked a Bendix aircraft engine fuel injection system for use on the supercharged V-8. The system eventually called for the fuel supply coming from a spray ring located in the "eye" of the supercharger. The ring contained 164 holes for fuel atomization that would create a fine spray before entering the blower.

The maximum power output of the 1963 engines was a reported 741 horsepower which placed them way above other cars entered in the 1963 race. Even when coming off a turn, the Novi V-8 was said to deliver 420 horsepower, which was about the maximum power figure for the Offy.

The two 1962 chassis had to be reworked to accept the new powerplants. Obviously, this consisted primarily of work with the body shell. All the developments on the mechanical parts of the cars necessitated the construction of a new hood. The new hood/nosecone assembly had a massive bulge to permit all mechanical parts to be out of sight under the bodywork. The bulge was placed on the left side starting at the left front tire axle.

It continued, after reaching its apex, to slope back to the cockpit. The Novis represented two of the most fearsome looking cars ever entered in the race.

The rear part of the bodywork was also changed. The rather conventional tail piece with an enclosed headrest, so familiar with Offy roadsters and "sidewinders," was now gone. Instead, a separate streamlined headrest was installed under the roll bar. The headrest had an appearance of the nose of a bullet with the pointed end naturally trailing to the rear.

The strangest aspect of this 1963 version of the 1962 chassis is that from a certain angle the car looked very nimble, but at other angles it offered a more familiar bulky impression. Overall, they presented an attractive appearance and some observers considered them to be among the most beautiful of all the Novis.

The Granatellis decided that the old 500F, not having been sold, should be returned to action for 1963. The seven year old chassis also contained one of the reworked engines. The 500F, however, did not need the massive rebuilding of the bodywork like its "younger sisters." It remained in nearly the same configuration as in 1962 when it sat in its garage without an engine. While the newer cars needed the big bulges on top of the nosecone, the old 500F only needed a small extra blister near the left front wheel, far less prominent than those required on the newer cars. Entries were filed for the three cars with high hopes of making the race. By all accounts, the Novi team appeared to be far more of a force to be reckon with than a year earlier.

Since 1962, the Novi was not the only V-8 engine that was competing against the seemingly invincible Offys. That year saw the arrival of several rear engine cars, inspired by the Cooper design of 1961 and the modified aluminum Buick V-8 powered cars entered by Mickey Thompson in 1962. Such was reminiscent of the years when the only competition offered to the Offys came from the Novi entries in the field.

Thompson was to return to the Speedway in 1963 with new cars nicknamed by others as the "roller skates." Such was derived from the fact that they were very wide and flat. They ran on the smallest tires ever used at Indy, having a diameter of 12 inches (30.5 cm). The radical entries were only 21 1/2 inches high from the track surface to the base of the windscreen. Mickey also entered several of his older cars. This time all five cars entered were powered by aluminum Chevrolet V-8 255 c.i. engines. The total weight of a roller skate was said to be only 1,050 pounds.

After driving the Thompson car in 1962, Dan Gurney began an even more ambitious plan for the following year's race. During the remainder of the 1962 season, Dan had raced a Porsche in Formula One. It was obvious to him that the outstanding car of that year was the Lotus 25, a revolutionary design because of its monocoque chassis construction. Some observers judged the Lotus 25 of 1962 to be the first decent Formula One monocoque car. Undoubtedly, Gurney must have been impressed when he first saw the Lotus 25. The Chapman car ran its initial race on May 20, 1962, in the Dutch Grand Prix at Zandvoort. Dan suggested to Colin Chapman, the Lotus designer, that he should look at the possibility of entering a rear engine monocoque car prepared to meet the challenge of the Indy 500. Gurney was able to persuade Chapman to cross the ocean and have a look at the Indy race, although that event was held only days after the Dutch contest. To encourage Chapman, Dan offered to cover Chapman's expenses in attending the 500 mile race of 1962. The invitation was accepted by Chapman.

Chapman was shocked to see the near "prehistoric" Indy cars. Front engine cars had disappeared in Formula One during 1961. Beyond this, Chapman with his own advanced technology, must have felt as if he had gone back in time when he saw the "old fashioned" technology of the tub frame roadsters with their solid axles.

Colin Chapman re-introduced the so-called monocoque chassis. Such constructions had been used briefly in the past, but without any major success. Yet, Colin was convinced that a lightweight monocoque car with a suitable engine was more than capable of displacing the roadsters. If such a scheme worked, the roadsters were bound for automobile museums, unless the existing chassis remained in action as modified race cars or in other similar racing venues.

A monocoque is simply a box construction, open on the upper side to make the cockpit accessible. The engine suspension and other parts that makes a race car complete would be attached. It has the same function of a tub frame, but is generally far lighter and stronger, thus enabling it to withstand more torsion than a tub frame. As mentioned above, monocoque cars had been built earlier, but no one had fully realized the potential of the design until Chapman came up with his first model.

In June, 1957, the American automobile manufacturers had unanimously agreed that its members would "disassociate" themselves completely from racing. The move was prompted by a growing concern after members of the U.S. Congress had raised questions regarding the methods by which the manufacturers promoted sales. Members of Congress felt that the corporate approach stressed speed and horsepower that could be detrimental to the motoring public. While the agreed abstention existed, within a few years manufacturers began some covert assistance in an attempt to enhance sales. Such an application had a greater relationship to stock car racing than to Indy car competition. As the restriction continued, the factories made available the services of consulting engineers and provided funding and automotive parts. With the passage of time the agreed upon regulations was virtually ignored by Detroit.

In June of 1962, the Ford Motor Company terminated its moratorium when Henry Ford, II asserted that the ban "no longer had either purpose or effect." Within weeks, the Chrysler Corporation declared that it would also return to participate in racing. General Motors did not make such an announcement at the time, for after all, there were the Thompson Buicks at Indy in 1962. To what degree General Motors may have assisted is unknown. It appears as if the Big Three were all becoming involved at one level or another. Ford made the bold decision to go racing world-wide. While Indy and Formula One cars did not have the marque recognition associated with NASCAR competition, involvement in such racing would offer a splashy image that could prove to be most beneficial to sales.

In view of such a supposition, Dan Gurney managed to arrange a July 23 meeting between Ford Motor Company officials and Colin Chapman. According to Doug Nye in his volume, Theme Lotus, 1956-1986, Ford hedged on full racing participation until Jimmy Clark won that year's US Grand Prix and some test driving was carried out at Indy. Although Clark's Indy testing was carried out with a 91.5 c.i. unblown engine and without a chassis set precisely for the Indiana track, Jimmy had recorded laps at 144 m.p.h.

Ford then decided to cooperate by fielding a two car Indy team for 1963 that would use redesigned versions of the Lotus monocoque powered, of course, by Ford V-8 engines. The deal was finalized and as a result the Indy fans were to be confronted with the "Lotus Powered by Ford" cars. One car was to be entered for Lotus Formula One driver Jim Clark, while Dan Gurney was assigned the second car as a reward for his assistance in helping to put together the arrangement. Gurney remained extraordinarily busy that summer, for not only was he active at Indy, he also spent considerable time at Stuttgart, Germany, working with the Porsche racing operation while also involved with Chapman in a Ford deal. As noted, Gurney was a key player in the rear engine revolution that was to reach American shores.

These first Indy Ford V-8s were alloy versions of the Fairlane V-8 engines, slightly destroked, but still employing two valve pushrod heads. The Lotus cars were to be the successors of the lone 1961 Cooper which offered a slight clue as to the forthcoming revolution at Indy. The Cooper had taken the initial step, Thompson had further nurtured the seed with his 1962 rear engine endeavor. Then the 1963 Lotus would give a strong indication of offering a monumental impact. Such was the situation as the 1963 running of the Indianapolis 500 approached.

Chapter 7

A Triumphal Return - 1963

As the 1963 race approached the Novis were once again considered among the cars that might well capture newspaper copy. With eleven rear engine cars entered for the 1963 race (out of 66 entries), practice began with keen anticipation of high speeds and fierce competition.

The two 1962 Kurtis-Kraft chassis were again entered under the name Hotel Tropicana Special. A photo of a Novi on the front cover of National Speed Sport News correctly reflected the feelings of diehard Novi followers as a headline above the photo stated, "The New Novi...Ooops, Tropicana Special." The picture caption proclaimed that despite the Hotel Tropicana name, "The famous V-8 racers at Indianapolis will always be known as the Novi."

The pair were no longer identical in color. One of the cars had retained the yellow and black color scheme used in 1962, but it now carried #6. The other car was painted fluorescent red and white with a gold trim and was #56. The sister cars were identical in virtually every technical aspect. However, the #6 had a new 8 inch supercharger while the #56 used a 10 inch blower.

The old 500F Kurtis (built in 1956) retained its familiar #75; yet, it was entered under a different name. It was now identified as the STP Special, the first of many famous and illustrious cars entered under this name. STP was a company that produced an oil treatment additive for automotive use. Andy Granatelli had become president of the company in August, 1962. The company, officially known as the Chemical Compounds Division, was a recent acquisition by Studebaker (see Chapter 24). The STP Special 500F was painted white and red and retained the giant tailfin it had carried since 1961.

The Granatellis also had the support of another business entity as the Ashland Oil Company of Lexington, Kentucky, signed on for the 1963 Indy race. Ashland's Valvoline Division had agreed to provide the lubricants and fuel to be used by the Novis that year. Andy Granatelli had brought Valvoline into "big time racing." He had noticed that Valvoline was seriously supporting drag racing operations on the West Coast. James A. Reynolds, who has served as Manager of Racing Services for Valvoline, has stated that Andy, aware of this Valvoline involvement, approached the West Coast representatives of the company regarding a possible Indy hookup. Under the arrangement, the Novis would carry Valvoline SAE 50 motor oil while using an Ashland fuel blend of alcohol and aviation gasoline.

The entry of Valvoline was to represent a giant step in the company's long-term involvement with the many facets of racing. This was to eventually include dragsters, champ cars, stock cars, sprinters, etc. The involvement of the Valvoline organization has remained strong at the Speedway and Indy Car racing in general. A pinnacle for Valvoline Oil was achieved in the 1992 Indy 500 when Al Unser, Jr. won while driving a Valvoline Special. The company remains active in auto racing and at this writing, it also sponsors cars in other racing venues such as the Valvoline Ford Special driven by Mark Martin in NASCAR's Winston Cup competition.

The Novi team had signed three drivers for their 1963 entries. Tragically, one did not arrive at Indy to take his place in the assigned #6 car. Andy had signed a contract with a promising 23 year old rookie, Bobby Marvin. Marvin, a Columbus, Ohio resident, never had an opportunity to prove his skills in the Novi. On April 7, 1963, he lost his life in a sprint car crash at Langhorne, Pennsylvania. That day's racing consisted of twin 50s at the famed one mile dirt track. Marvin had finished 4th in the first contest behind winner A.J. Foyt, Roger McCluskey and Bobby Marshman. Marvin was then running in 3rd place in the second 50 when his Chevy powered sprinter hit the outside fence and bounced off the top of another car to roll about 175 ft. down the track before coming to a stop. Although Marvin had to complete the rookie test at the Indianapolis Motor Speedway, he had participated in seven USAC 100 mile races in 1962. For the Granatellis, this tragedy was the first of a number of setbacks that year.

(1963) Jim Hurtubise in a state of concentration. The goggles are partical taped to ward off glare and to reduce distractions in order for Jim to be afforded unimpaired vision. Full face helmets had yet to appear. I.M.S.

The Granatellis had signed Jim Hurtubise for the #56 car. You will recall that the gregarious driver had handled the #16 a year earlier during the Carburetion Day activities. Obviously, the Granatellis had been impressed with Jim and Herk's expressed desire to compete with a Novi was then fulfilled. Jim had seen his track record broken in 1962 by pal Parnelli Jones who won the pole that year. But Jim was considered quite capable of regaining the record behind the wheel of a Novi if all went well. Jim was a crowd favorite and his popularity with the fans had increased in 1963, as he was then at the wheel of one of the crowd pleasing Novis.

After two dismal years, some of the loyal Novi fans had lost faith in the Granatellis guidance. Further, the Novis had failed to make the 500 while still in Lew Welch's ownership in 1959 and 1960. With Hurtubise's legion of fans added to whatever popularity that remained with the Novis, undoubtedly, there would be greater fan support than that witnessed in several years.

The third scheduled driver within the Novi team was rookie Art Malone, a Tampa, Florida resident. Art carried the nickname "Colonel," although some referred to him as "Art the Dart." Malone was possibly one of the best qualified candidates to turn a wheel in a Novi considering his racing background. Malone had a great deal of experience in controlling overpowered cars as he was one of the top performers within the dragster ranks. It was felt that Art would not be overwhelmed with the handling (launching) of a Novi on the straights! Malone had some oval experience as he had begun his driving career in the Tampa area with stock cars in the early 1950s before moving on to enjoy great success with dragsters. Although Art's racing background was largely relegated to dragsters, he had aptly demonstrated his capabilities in high speed oval course work.

The "Mad Dog" car in which Art Malone broke the 180 m.p.h. barrier at Daytona. Art Malone

Many recalled that Art was the driver who had established a track record at the relatively new Daytona International Speedway. In 1961, NASCAR President Bill France had a standing offer of $10,000 prize money to the first car that could break the 180 m.p.h. barrier at the two and one-half mile, high banked tri-oval. Driving the Bob Osiecki owned "Mad Dog IV" car, a Kurtis-Kraft chassis, the "Colonel" was able to reach a speed of 181.561 m.p.h. The daring ride was made with a 413 c.i. (6768 cc) Chrysler hemi V-8 engine sporting a 671 Roots supercharger. The car used an Iskenderian cam and an "Isky" decal was placed on the car. In fact, the engine had been setup and dyno tested by Ed "Isky" Iskenderian employees. As a matter of fact, it was Isky who had nicknamed Malone, a southerner, as the "Colonel." The Kurtis-Kraft body had been reworked and the alterations included small side wings for additional downforce and a large dorsal fin as the tail. After several other drivers left Osiecki's car, Art was offered an opportunity to make an attempt to surpass 180 m.p.h. by Osiecki, an entrepreneur with several Charlotte businesses: a speed shop and a drag strip. Bob had promised Art $2,500 from the prize money if he could break the 180 m.p.h. barrier. Accepting the offer, Art began working the car up to speed. It was said that "at first he almost drowned in his own perspiration." After working with the car for some days, on August 28, 1961, he managed to collect the $10,000 for Osiecki.

(1961) NASCAR President Bill France, Sr. hands over the $10,000 check offered to those responsible for the first lap over 180 m.p.h. at the Daytona International Speedway. In the center is car owner Bob Osiecki and on the right one very happy speedster, driver Art Malone.   Art Malone Collection

Eventually, Malone decided to take a shot at the Indy 500. With such in mind, he travelled to Indianapolis in 1962, hoping to somehow obtain a ride. His biggest problem rested with the fact that he was not acquainted with members of the racing fraternity working the Indy car series. All his dragster experiences and the "Mad Dog" adventure had gained Malone some fame, but naturally it was far from enough to have champ car owners pleading with him to sign a driving contract. The situation was such that Art was still waiting around when he happened to come across old friend Wally Parks, founder of the National Hot Rod Association (NHRA), at the Holiday Inn across 16th Street from the IMS. Wally knew some of the people in Gasoline Alley and when Art informed him of his Indy aspirations Parks offered to introduce him to Andy Granatelli.

Obviously, Parks had kept his word. The following day when Art went into Gasoline Alley he saw Andy Granatelli sitting on one of the golf carts. As Art approached Andy, Granatelli asked if he was Art Malone. Art confirmed the fact and Andy asked if he would care to try to make the 500 in one of the Novis. Art answered with a firm, "Yes sir." To his utter surprise, Granatelli replied, "You've got yourself a ride." Art stated that he had obtained a ride with Granatelli even before they shook hands! Although the teaming was easily consummated, Art lacked the necessary experience to take a champ car out onto the track. USAC stipulated that an individual had to have experience in at least three other champ car events before he would be allowed to participate in the Indy rookie test.

Granatelli had sufficient confidence in Malone and secured a dirt car for Art in 1962 in order to provide him with the opportunity to get the three required events under his belt. Art recalled that the three races were quite an experience for him. Under the guidance and watchful eyes of the Granatellis (who worked with him at the events), Malone gained the required experience to have a go at Indy for 1963. During this time, he had signed a three year contract that ensured him future rides with the Granatelli team.

Many years later, one observer stated that though there was nothing personally wrong with Art, his inclusion on the Novi team was an injustice. The theory put forth asserted that other drivers with Indy experience were available, thus offering some advantage over Art on oval tracks. Yet, according to conjecture, Art was acceptable to the Granatellis as he could serve as an excellent source for marketing the STP product as the company attempted to make further inroads into drag racing. Taking in one of the famous drag racers and introducing him to Indy certainly would enhance interest among the drag racing fans coast-to-coast. On the other hand, the Daytona record smashing run had obviously demonstrated Malone's oval track racing skills.

Malone arrived at Indianapolis after having captured the 1963 United States Fuel Champion title that spring at the Bakersfield, California drag strip in what was considered the biggest and most important independent show at the time. Art gained the title with a 183.88 m.p.h. clocking and his victory was described "as a perfect example of cool, consistent driving." Art publicly revealed at the time that he was destined to try for a spot in the Indianapolis 500 field later that year.

With Hurtubise and Malone, the Novi operation seemed to offer great promise. It appeared to be one of the more formidable teams after years of disappointment for Novi followers.

The Granatellis had opted for a "youth movement" as they had planned to assign rookies Bobby Marvin and Art Malone to two of the cars. Only Jim Hurtubise offered any previous Indianapolis 500 experience (three races 1960-1962). Compare this with the driver selections made by the first Novi car owner Lew Welch. When Ralph Hepburn drove the first Novi powered car in 1941, he had already participated in 13 previous 500s; when Cliff Bergere drove a Novi Mobil Special in 1947 he was a veteran of 15 races and when Chet Miller first drove the Novi in competition in 1951 he had 14 Indy races to his credit.

The following day, Jim went out for his first warmup laps and by his second, he was up to 145 m.p.h. With his delight in being on the track in a Novi, he made as many shakedown laps as he possibly could. The run included several in the 146 m.p.h. bracket. Jim diced for a while with Jim Clark who was at the wheel of one of the rear engine Lotus-Fords. Hurtubise's fastest lap that day was an encouraging 148.6 m.p.h.

Granatelli said he was quite pleased with the car's performance. The #6 car previously assigned to Marvin would not be made available to a rookie as Andy said, "We know what the car can do and we want an experienced driver." Granatelli was making reference to the fact that the #6 car was

(1963) Duane Carter in Mickey Thompson's 1963 chassis offering. Cynics referred to the unusual design as a roller skate and the tires as donuts. Most importantly, the rear engine concept gained additional consideration and respect by competitors. Duane finished 23rd due to a connecting rod problem. I.M.S.

In 1963, unusual opposition for the American cars came in the form of the British built, rear engine Lotus cars of which three were entered, largely due to Dan Gurney's efforts. The Lotus-Fords were judged to be modified Ford Fairlane V-8s. With their V-8 engines, they had now "joined" in the Novi V-8 versus the Offy battle. Another "member" of the "V-8 Club" would be the Chevrolets entered by Mickey Thompson as his five rear engine cars, the Harvey Aluminum Specials were designed and built in America. The majority of the American champ car builders still believed that the tried and proven front engine Offy was the way to go.

The track opened for practice on May 1. The #56 was the last of the three Novis to arrive, doing so on May 5. Driver Jim Hurtubise was anxious to get on the track with his #56 as soon as possible.

quite similar to the #56 car. The Novi team assumed that in large measure whatever potential was demonstrated in the #56 could be recreated in the untested #6 car. If the Granatellis had been interested in obtaining the services of a rookie, a sizable number was on hand, although some already had assigned rides. The rookies present included Bobby Unser, Johnny Rutherford, Curtis Turner, Bob Harkey, Bob Wente, Bruce Jacobi, Pedro Rodriguez, Masten Gregory, Al Miller, Graham Hill and Jimmy Clark.

On May 7, fans were a bit surprised to see veteran Jim Hurtubise on the track with rookie stripes on the tail of a Novi ! As it turned out, it was the #75 STP Special that he was shaking down before rookie Art Malone began his driver's test in the machine. Malone went through the 120 m.p.h. phase and part of the 125 m.p.h. phase handily before the track closed. Malone passed the 135 m.p.h. phase of his rookie test on May 9, thus completing the mandatory rookie orientation program. Remember, Dick Rathmann had driven over 148 m.p.h. with the same car two years earlier. Art later said he was originally scheduled to drive one of the newer cars, but for some unspecified reason, he ended up in the old #75.

Malone recalled that after he had passed the driver test, "Andy wanted me to hold the rpm to 8,000 and to roll out the throttle early like at the start-finish line. Then apply very little brake or no brake and pick up the throttle again while still going down the straightaway, just about where you go into the turn. The Novi had always had a stumble if you drove it like an Offy and Andy felt you would loose very little at the end of the straightaway and pick up a lot of corner speed his way, because you would be pulling going in and it would be smoother. Andy had a camera above the driver to look at the gauges during my runs. I was a student as I promised and did exactly as Andy asked. I felt I owed that to him since he gave me a chance...Everybody else was driving all the way down into the corner as hard as they could before tapping the brakes, then getting back on the throttle as quick and as hard as they could. This could abuse the car badly, but it was not an ecomony run."

To become better acquainted with driving at the Speedway, he received a good deal of assistance from Jim Rathmann, the 1960 Indy 500 winner and a fellow Floridian. An unabashed Malone has also said that he received a great deal of help from several other drivers, including Eddie Sachs and Bobby Marshman. The same day that Malone passed his rookie test, the Novi team had a visitor of special importance; Elmer Haase, the designer of the Bendix fuel injection system. Haase assisted in optimizing the setup of the injection systems now fitted with aircraft injector heads to provide even more power.

Eddie Sachs, one of the most popular of the Indy drivers and one of the better drivers of the period, had a different opinion about what the Granatellis needed to do to improve their cars. Eddie, in a new Watson-Offy, had been dicing with Jim Hurtubise for a while and he described how he could easily gain ground on the Novi in the turns, although the Novi left him far behind as the cars came out of the turns onto the straights. Sachs felt that the Novi team could gain more speed if they could somehow sort out their car's handling through the turns. A familiar story for the Novis.

The following days were quiet for the Novi team. Meanwhile, a strong concern had developed with some of the teams regarding the racing tires. On May 11, Parnelli Jones became the prime candidate for the pole while registering a speed of 152.027 m.p.h. using 15 inch tires. Parnelli attributed his speed primarily to the smaller tires stating, "You can run quicker like the Lotus-Fords have done on 15 inch tires." Parnelli's burst of speed added fuel to a brewing tire controversy.

Firestone had supplied a new low-profile 15 inch tire which was not available to all teams. The fabrication of the 15 inch tires was a result of the fact that the Lotus cars were using them with an obvious amount of success. To give the smaller tires enough total "footprint" area, the tire width was increased. As a result, the four tires had more track contact, thereby enhancing the gripping power to enable greater speeds. When such tires were tried on the American built roadsters, the drivers informed their crews that the cars handled better, thus they were able to go faster. This resulted in a great demand for Firestone to produce more 15 inch tires. Some competitors, without the 15 inch Firestones, requested that the tire be withdrawn as they felt it offered a greater advantage to the lighter rear engine cars. Firestone, however, informed the entrants that they were committed to the program and would not withdraw the tire in question. A Firestone spokesman declared that his company produced different type tires for different cars just as they did with passenger cars. He made the point that the Firestone 15 inch tires had been designed for lightweight cars just as it had 12 inch rubber for the Mickey Thompson cars. He asserted such tires were not approved for use on the heavier Offys. Yet, such a circumstance did change things. Driver Don Branson carried out some "successful testing" with the 15 inch tires on the Leader Card Special. Firestone then relented, approving the unrestricted use of the 15 inch tires. It was at that juncture that other roadster car owners tried the 15 inch tires.

With the introduction of the 15 inch tires, parts manufacturer Ted Halibrand made it known that his company had received over $14,000 in cancellations for 16 and 18 inch wheels while at the same time he could not meet the demand for the suddenly popular 15 inch wheels.

Another indirect participant in the 1963 tire struggle was the Goodyear Tire Company. Some drivers who had used Goodyear stock car tires now tried the 15 inch Goodyear tires on their Indy cars. However, it turned out that these stock car Goodyears were not suitable for use at Indy.

The Novis remained with the 18 inch tire, although Granatelli set up #6 for runs on 15 inch tires. Yet, as fate would have it the car never did take to the track and perform with the 15 inch Firestones. Wheels were available but tires were not, thus the car was converted back to the 18 inch tire setup. This was a pity as the Novis always lacked grip and when an improved method arrived, they could not benefit from it. It is intriguing to imagine what sort of performance the Novis might have achieved in 1963 if they had been able to run on the wider 15 inch tires.

(1963) Jim "Herk" Hurtubise in the #56 Hotel Tropicana Novi. Herk and the car made for an excellent combination due to the popularity of both driver and car.
I.M.S.

Meanwhile, speeds rose considerably and a few 150+ m.p.h. averages were recorded. Jim Hurtubise performed the trick on May 15. He was able to top that speed as he soon had his Novi thundering past the 151 m.p.h. mark. This made Jim one of the favorites for the pole which would be contested on May 18. Parnelli Jones, however, was the man to beat: he had already gone over 153 m.p.h!

With the excellent times achieved by Hurtubise, an unexpected twist occurred as several drivers actually dropped by the Novi garages to inquire as to the possible availability of the #6 ride! Granatelli stated that he did not want to sign a driver who was still under a contract to pilot another car. He well remembered the unpleasant experience of trying to obtain the services of Dick Rathmann in 1961. Therefore, the Granatellis held firm and the #6 remained without a driver.

On May 16, the Novi operation suffered a setback as the engine in Malone's #75 let go. The incident sprayed water and oil on the track. Rookie Curtis Turner, driving Smokey Yunick's Fiberglas Special, lost control due to the liquids dumped by the Novi and crashed heavily into the wall. Curtis emerged from the wreck with some minor injuries, but the car was a write-off. As Malone arrived in the pits, he was met by a Novi chieftain with a "request" that he inform the press that a radiator hose had let go. Malone rejected the idea that he would join in on a fabrication as to the actual cause of the mishap.

Turner, who had won countless stock car races in the South, described the transition from racing stock cars to racing Indy cars saying, "You can drive a stock car there (down South), but everybody can't drive a race car here." Curtis was a fearsome competitor and on the NASCAR circuit he was always a threat. Meanwhile, a resilient Yunick stated, "I'll be back next year if I can find a sponsor," as he went about cleaning out his garage. Two other NASCAR drivers were on the Indy scene that year. They were Junior Johnson and DeWayne "Tiny" Lund, that year's Daytona 500 winner. However, Lund failed to connect with a car owner.

With the Turner crash, the so-called Novi Jinx had victimized another car. While the Yunick car was a total wipe out, the Novi had only incurred internal damage due to the blown engine. There was some fear that Malone could not qualify for the race two days later because of the blown engine, but it was suggested that quite possibly he would take the #6 car out.

Another Turner, Jack Turner experienced a horrific crash coming off the fourth corner during practice. The vicious roll-overs left Jack hospitalized and from his bed "Cactus" Jack announced his retirement from racing. Jack, who had won the A.A.A. midget championship in 1954 and 1955, had competed in six 500s.

On the Friday just prior to Pole Day, nine drivers surpassed the once magical 150 m.p.h. barrier. These hotshoe drivers were: Parnelli Jones,

49

Rodger Ward, A.J. Foyt, Len Sutton, Bobby Marshman, Jim McElreath, Dan Gurney, rookie Jimmy Clark and Novi driver Jim Hurtubise. It was felt that the pole sitter would emerge from this group.

On the eve of the chase for the pole position, <u>Indianapolis Star</u> writer George Moore, in commenting about the Novis, asserted that they were "somewhat an enigma. Being supercharged, these brutes are very complicated and very unpredictable. If atmospheric conditions are just right, the carburetor right on the nose...this thing is liable to fly. However, it can also go the other way, in which case nothing seems to work." Andy Granatelli declared that he had some apprehension regarding Herk's driving as he said, "I honestly think he's going too darn quick. But, Jim's capable. He knows that he has to drive different in this car and he's working on it."

On Pole Day, May 18, in front of some 200,000+ spectators, Parnelli Jones claimed the coveted first starting position with a sparkling 151.153 m.p.h. average for the four laps, thus breaking his own record of 150.370 m.p.h. set a year earlier. In recognizing his record smashing run, Jones acknowledged the work rendered by the Agajanian crew headed up by chief mechanic Johnny Pouelsen. But to the delight of many Novi fans, he came close to losing the pole to Jim Hurtubise who placed his #56 Novi next to Parnelli's car in the front row. Jim's lap speeds were 151.261, 150.779, 150.401 and 148.613 m.p.h., giving a four lap average of 150.257 m.p.h.

The crowd in the grandstands went wild, as did the Novi crew. Track announcer Tom Carnegie, in describing the tumultous reaction of the fans seated on the front straightaway, spoke of this excitement and jubilation - "A Novi powered beauty is once again in the front row." One long-time observer stated he had not witnessed such an overwhelming ovation since Duke Nalon captured the pole in 1951 in a Novi after his life threatening crash during the 1949 race.

Hurtubise earned his front row starting spot in his second qualifying attempt, the first had been waved off as he was averaging "only" 147.6 m.p.h. for three laps. After Herk had completed his second run he said, "That was a scary one." As Hurtubise came into the pit area he received "one of the most thunderous ovations in (the track's) history." Speaking with the press he altered his statement slightly saying, "I'll never do that again." Such a statement was caused by not only the speed mark, but by several other factors: a very slippery track and persistent, gusty winds. Unbelievably, conditions that day were such that

(1963) A happy pair! Andy and Herk celebrate the splendid run that placed a Novi in the front row at Indy for the first time since 1951. Further, the Granatellis had finally made a return to the race after two years of frustration with the Novis. I.M.S.

only seven drivers braved the elements and were able to reach speeds that were considered solid enough to make the starting field. Eleven other attempts at qualifying were aborted.

Following Herk's great qualifying run, Louie Meyer, a three-time Indy 500 winner and builder of the famed Offenhauser, said that the Novi crew "appeared to have solved their fueling problems. The engines are running better than I'd ever heard them and they must be considered a contender."

One writer noted that in celebration, the "Brothers Granatelli did an impromptu dance while Jean Marcenac sat on the pit wall." In short order, Andy spontaneously ran to the pit wall and brought an elated but reserved Jean forward to share in the moment. At one point Marcenac reached under his glasses to wipe away a tear. In an exuberant state, several of the Novi crew members hoisted a modest, but emotional Jean Marcenac on their shoulders and proudly marched down pit lane celebrating the return of a Novi into an Indy 500 starting field. Finally, "Jean was so overcome with emotion that he removed his glasses to wipe the tears away." The carrying of Marcenac down pit lane by Novi crew members was a moving scene that would remain a strong memory with many for years to come as it denoted Jean's years of laboring love for the mercury fast, but tempermental cars. Although Marcenac's influence within the team was not as prominent as in years past, he remained a respected and much beloved individual who had devoted his life to auto racing. Art Malone remembered that the amiable Frenchman was always on

(1963) The Novi appears to have a case of the mumps. The blister is a result of the desire to lay over weight to the left and to have all engine components under the hood.   *Gerald Walker Photo*

hand, but it was largely the Granatellis and their crew who took care of the car's preparation. Marcenac's role had been altered as he was viewed as serving in some form of "consultant" role.

Imagine, a Novi was not only in the field for the first time in five years, but it would start from front row! The last front row starting position for a Novi had been in 1951 when Duke Nalon had captured the pole. Additionally, for the first time since 1952, an all - Offy powered front row was prevented.

Indianapolis sports writer Bob Collins put a twist on the highly impressive run when he said the Novi, though operating under the alias of Hotel Tropicana Special, "is back in business. So, in the closing lines of the old mellerdramers, 'come home daughter, all is forgiven'." The 20 year romance between the multitude and this machine was on again. Collins then went on to identify Jim as "one of the brave ones. You always figure he will try a little harder, drive a little deeper into the turns, chase that extra fraction of a second. Yesterday he had the Novi wound so tight it was screaming like a wounded rhinoceros."

Jones and Hurtubise were joined in row one by Don Branson who had averaged 151.188 m.p.h. in his Bob Wilke owned Leader Card Special. The second row consisted of defending champion Rodger Ward, Jimmy Clark and Jim McElreath, while Bobby Marshman was the sole qualifier for the third row at 149.458 m.p.h. As it turned out, only the three front row starters were in the field after opening day with times over 150 m.p.h. Remarkedly, only two other drivers who qualified after opening day were to register times that surpassed 150 m.p.h. They were A.J. Foyt who qualified at 150.615 m.p.h. and started 8th, while Paul Goldsmith qualified at 150.163 m.p.h. and started 9th.

It is customary for formal photographs to be

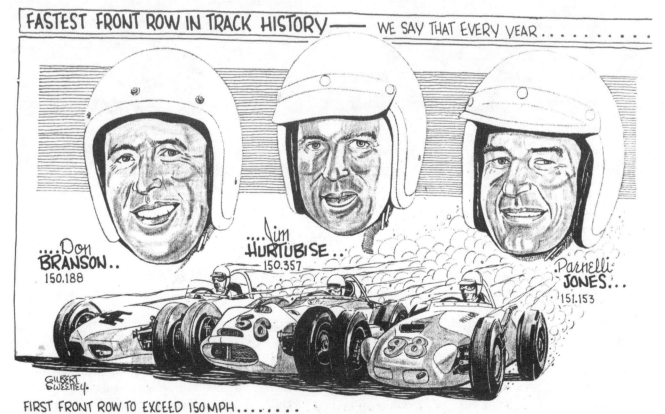

(1963) Indianapolis Star artist Gilbert Sweeney highlighted the trio of swift drivers who would start the race from the front row. They represented the first front row to ever exceed 150 m.p.h. at the Speedway.   *Courtesy of Indianapolis Star*

taken of the front row once the positions have been locked in. At the announced time for the photo session, the three cars were pushed out to the track and placed in their respective starting positions. Drivers Jones and Branson were on hand and ready, but Hurtubise was no where to be seen. As time lagged on and the Granatellis prepared to panic, Jim's brother, Pete, was summoned to the scene and placed in the Novi. With the three drivers sitting in the cars and wearing helmets, it would be difficult for one to differentiate between Jim and Pete as there was a facial similarity between the brothers. Had Jim overslept, forgotten about the photo session or was he merely playing another one of his frequent pranks? As the photo shoot was in progress, Jim was spotted beaming as he stood among the onlookers off to the side and behind the photographers.

#75. Further, the #6 was still without an assigned driver. As a consequence, there was only one Novi in the field after Pole Day, but a week of practice remained in which to alter the situation.

Art recalls that he was seldom allowed to enter the garage that housed his car. Granatelli believed that Art needed to concentrate on driving while the team's responsibility was to care for the car. For this reason, Art could not tell if his car had undergone any adjustments between the practice sessions. Still, Malone stated that the car handled properly as all Novis he drove handled "really well." When the interviewer mentioned that the cars were rather bulky, Malone replied, "As bulky as they were, they always had a little push to them and that's why I liked them."

Art also stated that he felt a little out of place at Indy as he was a drag racer and not accustomed

(1963) The traditional front row photo with chief mechanics requested to stand behind their drivers. They are Johnny Pouelsen, chief wrench for Parnelli; Andy and Vince Granatelli, and crew member Mel Cahill who helped to fine tune the Don Branson Leader Card Special. Seated in the Novi is Jim Hurtubise's brother Pete. Herk had failed to arrive at the appointed time. *Armin Krueger Photo*

Well aware that Pete was serving in a substitute role, photographer Armin Krueger moved around and took several side shots of the trio. Pete, perhaps aware that a profile shot taken at close range might betray his identify, looked straight down as if studying his shoes. As the Branson and Hurtubise cars were pushed away, Hurtubise stepped forward and the trio had shots taken around Jones' Willard Battery Special.

Meanwhile, Art Malone was not ready to qualify as repair work continued on the engine in

to being with the well-known drivers on the Championship Trail. It was simply a situation to which Art would have to adjust.

In the meantime, #6 had been test driven by several drivers, some of whom were already assigned to other cars. The group included Parnelli Jones and one wonders if he wanted to get a handle on the caliber of car Hurtubise would have in challenging him on race day. Parnelli did not feel his laps in #6 offered any advantage or knowledge that could help him in meeting any challenge encountered by the Novis. He felt that any good driver would be able to get a handle on the Novi. As for Herk racing at his side, Parnelli was quite familiar with this circumstance as he and Jim had been competing on the same tracks since the late 1950s; first starting with sprint cars on the West Coast.

(1960) The "Chevy Twins." A familiar scene of off track buddies turn adversaries on the track. Parnelli Jones in the famed Fike Plumbing Special behind Jim Hurtubise in his equally renowned #56 Sterling Plumbing Special. The pair competed in sprint car activities for some years before they made their way to the champ car trail and the 500. The scene is Heidelberg, PA.   Ken Coles Photo

Other drivers who tried the #6 on Sunday, May 19, were Cliff Griffith and a Novi veteran of the Welch Era, Paul Russo. Another Welch Novi Era veteran, Dempsey Wilson took the car out for some laps on Monday, May 20. However, no driver/car hookup was made for #6.

On Monday, May 20, Parnelli Jones suggested to Andy that he give rookie Bobby Unser an opportunity to try the car. Unser had completed his rookie test, but Jones, among others, did not feel that the assigned car was really a promising ride. Although a rookie at the Brickyard, the 29 year old Unser had been around racing seemingly all of his life as his dad and two uncles had raced. In 1949 at the age of fifteen, Bobby began driving stock cars around his home town of Albuquerque, New Mexico. Within a year the teenager had won the state's modified stock car championship. He repeated the feat the following year before turning to sprinters. A wiry six footer, Bobby seemed in his element whenever behind the wheel of a race car.

In 1956, continuing a family tradition, he began competing in the annual Pike's Peak Hill Climb winning the championship division. The next year he was fifth before putting together six consecutive wins (1958-1963) over the twisting mountainous road to become the undisputed "King of the Hill." Away from the annual 4th of July Pike's Peak Hill Climb, Bobby competed with the California Racing Association (CRA) sprinters and then the International Motor Contest Association (IMCA) sprint chargers before moving into USAC late in 1962. Although he failed to qualify in his first USAC champ car attempt at Sacramento in late 1962, he was not to be deterred.

Unser was the second of the Unser brothers to try his hand at Indy. His brother Jerry had raced at Indy in 1958. In that contest, he crashed on the first lap when his car catapulted over the tail of Paul Goldsmith's car. This contact carried Unser's car over the outer wall. This incident was part of the totally wild scramble on the disastrous first lap. Amazingly, Jerry suffered only a dislocated shoulder in the wild escapade that involved virtually every car in the field. The following year, Jerry was to lose his life while practicing for the 1959 Indy 500.

(1963) Several of the stars from NASCAR were on the scene in 1963. Seen here is Junior Johnson in the last roadster built by Frank Kurtis. Junior preferred a roof over his head, but had to settle for a roll cage. His comfort level was such that he wisely returned to action down south.   I.M.S.

Upon Bobby's arrival at the Indianapolis Motor Speedway as a rookie, things did not go too well. Chief Steward Harlan Fengler had initially denied Bobby a chance to take to the track in his assigned ride; the American Rubber and Plastics Special, an Offy layover (tilted to the left) owned by La Porte, Indiana businessman John Chalik. Chalik had several other cars entered for the race. Interestingly, one had been assigned to NASCAR speedster Junior Johnson. Junior had stated that he really preferred to drive cars with a top on them and as something of a compromise, Chalik had a roll cage installed on the Kurtis chassis, however, the stock car ace remained at the Speedway for only a short time. While Indy cars did not seem to be of Junior's liking. He returned South and won

53

seven of the 33 NASCAR events he entered that year.

With old friend Parnelli Jones' continuing effort, Unser ultimately secured permission to take the layover Chalik car out for a shakedown. Unfortunately, Bobby was not able to obtain a satisfactory speed with the car and on one occasion he fell victim to a spin as he lost control of the car coming off the second turn. The car slid 1,080 feet, spun again and then hit the inside retaining wall. The impact bent the front of the car, though it was believed that the car could be repaired in time to qualify.

(1963) Bobby Unser in the John Chalik owned car in which he passed his rookie test. When the offer came to drive a Novi, Bobby bolted to the Novi ride. Bobby's relationship with Chalik had not been overly strong and amiable.   I.M.S.

With Unser reportedly going through tires at a rapid pace, several sources have stated that Chalik reached the point where he insisted that Bobby would have to pay the cost for the next set of tires. The proposal was completely unacceptable to Bobby. He then quit the ride and when Jones heard about the situation he offered to introduce Bobby to Andy Granatelli in an effort to obtain the ride in the still unassigned #6 Novi. Parnelli asserts to this day that he was merely returning a favor as Bobby had rendered him valuable assistance during his attempt to compete in the 1962 Pike's Peak run. Further, the pair had run together in sprint car action. Parnelli had also competed with Bobby's brother Louie for several years in California Racing Association sprint car action. Bobby accepted Parnelli's offer of an introduction and Jones approached Granatelli urging him to give Unser a chance to drive #6.

According to Bobby, his father, Jerry Unser, Sr., had been the first to suggest that Parnelli attempt to arrange a contact with Granatelli as he felt that Bobby would be well suited for the Novi. Initially, Granatelli was not too keen on trying the New Mexico driver, but with the tenacity displayed by Jones and Unser, he finally agreed. Once Andy acquiesced, Bobby took his first ride in the car that same day (May 20). Bobby stated that the car did not quite fit him and cockpit adjustments were needed. Yet, Unser went out after receiving the "basic" instructions regarding the piloting of a blown V-8 Novi. When he returned to pit lane, Granatelli informed him that #6 was available for him to qualify the following Saturday! Unser had turned in three laps of over 149 m.p.h. which was enough to convince Andy that Bobby was man enough to control the powerful car.

Bobby had finally nailed down a suitable ride, yet in no time, Granatelli seemed on the verge of losing him. Such a circumstance came about as Jones, with his continuing apprehension regarding the reliability and endurance capacity of the Novi, had continued to make his way about Gasoline Alley looking for a suitable car for Bobby. Discovering that car owner Gordon Van Liew still had a driver opening in his #29 Vita Fresh Orange Juice Special, Parnelli gave some thought to trying to obtain the ride for Unser. He considered the car superior to even his own #98 "Old Calhoun" in which he had captured the pole. Parnelli was able to make a deal with Van Liew, although Gordon requested that Jones first set up the car. When Parnelli informed Unser about the "better ride," Unser said he preferred to stay with Granatelli and drive a Novi. Bobby had his ride and that was it.

Granatelli reported to the press just how and why he had assigned the ride to Bobby. According to Andy, he was not willing to change the setup on #6 since Hurtubise had dialed it in. A number of drivers then drove the car, but none of them could reach the high 140s. Then Bobby drove it and he reached a speed of 147.3 m.p.h. on his sixth lap with the car. Bobby's demonstration of

(1963) Rookie Bobby Unser shifts to the Novi. Andy offers assistance as his son, Vince, listens.   I.M.S.

three 149 m.p.h. laps had fully convinced Granatelli that he had found the right man. Andy also proclaimed, "I am glad Unser is a rookie with little experience. Driving a Novi is like driving nothing else and this way Unser won't have to break a lot of bad habits." Bobby reported, "That Novi was one screaming fast race car. It was heavy, and with its skinny tires, sometimes all I could do was point it, and even then it slid its tires for a long way before I could catch it and put them straight...but somehow that big Novi had almost been made for me, and nobody but Daddy had known it."

In the following days, both Malone and Unser were on the track on numerous occasions to become completely familiar with their mounts and trackside observers were highly impressed. One source asserted that on one of the days, the Granatelli cars were seen sporting Goodyear rubber. Andy was said to have informed the press that he was evaluating the tires in order to secure whatever rubber was best for the Novi cars. Another account stated that Andy was only "timing the Goodyear equipped cars through the corners."

On Friday, May 24, the last day before the second weekend of qualifications, Malone broke the 150 m.p.h. barrier in the #75 500F. Malone recalls that the day prior to qualifying, Andy had finally agreed to let him run further into the corners before lifting. Art was in a state of joy for he had been "cruising" on the straights at only 7,000 rpms, while the red line was set at 8,500. Art believed he would be able to do 152 m.p.h. if everything came together. Many railbirds felt that Malone had done a great job with the "old hack" which was the heaviest car entered in the race. At that time, Art's car carried a new engine and the new mill had proven to be a dandy.

The #75 Novi was ultimately to carry a nickname painted on the side of the car - "Tired Iron." The name was based on the fact that the car had such a long history with its many rebuilding jobs since its construction in 1956. In his autobiography, Andy said that the two rookies "did a fantastic job. And I don't think they got to show off the full potential of what they really could do."

As qualifying closed on its third day Saturday, May 25, the Novi-STP crew were certainly happy campers. Such resulted from the fact that both Unser and Malone had make the starting field. As Unser took to the oval, track announcer Tom Carnegie informed the crowd that Bobby was piloting the "famed Novi engine and that we wish the young fellow here at the Speedway a lot of luck." Announcer Chuck Bailey then talked the crowd through the laps. Unser's first and second laps were outstanding for a rookie - in the 149 m.p.h. bracket. He inched the speed up to 149.676 m.p.h. to average 149.421 m.p.h. for his four laps. This placed him in the 16th starting position, although his time was to be the 12th fastest in the entire field. Rookie Unser had the fastest run of the 17 cars that qualified that day.

As Bobby's lap speeds proved to be more than sufficient, an elated Andy relinquished the yellow flag used by the crew if they wished to abort a qualifying run. He then turned, giving mechanic Jean Marcenac a bear hug before dashing off to greet and congratulate Unser.

Art Malone captured the 23th spot with his average of 148.343 m.p.h. As Malone and the crew posed for the official qualifying picture with "The Tired Iron," they were as proud as peacocks over the run by the old car. Malone's time was good for 25th fastest overall when the field was filled the following day.

(1963) Rookie Art Malone having qualified for the 500, is surrounded by STP "big guns" Joe, Jean Marcenac and Andy. The dragster star had made the prestigious race in his first year at the Speedway. I.M.S.

Recalling his qualification effort, Art stated that, "On my first time out after 10 laps I was running the same or better than most. But it took me 10 laps to work up to that qualifying speed. Andy said okay put it in the qualifying line up. Let's get the car qualified. I said, Andy, let me go out one more time to get use to what I am doing. I need some additional running time at that speed with these shut-off points. I think I can run faster. Andy said no, put it in the qualifying line. For a car that had not competed in years and that was probably 800 to a 1,000 pounds heavier than the other team cars Tired Iron had done well."

Only A.J. Foyt, who started 8th after qualifying on the second day at 150.615 m.p.h., surpassed the average of Hurtubise. This made Jim the third fastest in the 33 car field. For the long suffering Novi sentimentalists, this certainly had to be a red letter day. Never before had three Novis begun the world famous auto racing event.

After Unser and Malone had qualified, Jean Marcenac said, "It's wonderful. Out of this world." Jean heaped credit on the drivers saying the two rookies had taken the powerful cars onto the track and had handled them in a splendid fashion. He assigned 80 percent of the cars' excellent performances to the drivers saying the Novi team had the strongest and most powerful cars at the track. Jean had nothing but praise for the newly designed Novi engine.

In a gesture of sportsmanship and cordiality, former Novi car owner Lew Welch had a telegram dispatched from Los Angeles to friend Jean Marcenac, the long-time chief Novi mechanic, stating "Congratulations on getting all of your cars in the race. Praying this will be your year to win."

The #6 did not make the field without some

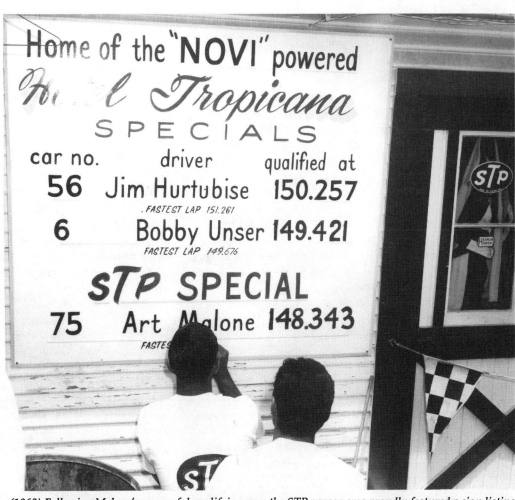

(1963) Following Malone's successful qualifying run, the STP garage area proudly featured a sign listing the qualifying speeds of the trio of cars. No low profile for this team.   I.M.S.

difficulty. When the engine was being examined the night before its qualification run, a mechanic accidentally dropped a penlight into the engine. A bent valve was the result and the repairs consumed all night. And if all this was not enough, when the car was being removed from the Bear wheel alignment rack it fell abruptly off the stand. This necessitated the replacement of a radiator. Had the Novi jinx struck again? Fortunately, when it really mattered, the #6 did not let Bobby Unser down, nor did it disappoint the many diehard Novi fans in the grandstands.

While the Granatellis certainly had reason to rejoice with their trio of entries in the field, they most certainly had additional cause for jubilation. In fact, several insiders felt they were fortunate in still being permitted on the grounds of the Speedway as there was sufficient cause for their removal. As the Granatellis realized that their cars had to make at least three pit stops, they felt it advantageous to practice pit stops. Such an activity was carried on in Gasoline Alley at their assigned garage area, although such a practice with fuel was forbidden by track regulations.

(1963) Bobby Unser at speed in the #6 I.M.S.

In his autobiography, Andy relates how track superintendent Clarence Cagle was on the phone to verify a report that practice refueling was taking place. As they conversed, the fuel hose ruptured and the pressurized tank commenced spraying fuel.

The crew member at the shut off valve was so terrified that he took off in a run. Another crew member realizing the potential danger dashed to the release valve to stop the flow of the highly inflammable fuel. Having avoided a possible disaster, the crewman then went to the shower as he was soaked by the fuel, but even more remained on the ground in Gasoline Alley. Returning to the Novi garage, the crew member was startled to see that several members wanted to plug in a fan before all of the spilled alcohol had been cleaned up!

As it turned out, the fuel line was the culprit as a crew member had bought a lightweight hose that was of questionable quality. As it took a mere twelve seconds to refuel a car with 73 gallons of fuel, this placed tremendous pressure on the fuel hose.

Recalling the potentially dangerous incident, Cagle recently stated, "We allowed pit practice fuel stops in the garage area, but we didn't allow them to have any fuel. Well, this particular time they had a drum of 55 gallons and it turns out that they were practicing in the center isle and the 55 gallons of methanol flowed right down the center isle of the garage area which could have set everything on fire if somebody had dropped a match or cigarette. It was quite frightening and I really bite on him (Andy) pretty hard."

After the third day of qualifications, the starting field had been filled with two drivers having been bumped; Pedro Rodriguez of Mexico and Chuck Rodee of Speedway, Indiana. Rodriguez was in a six cylinder Aston-Martin Cooper that averaged 146.687 m.p.h. It was the same Cooper chassis that Jack Brabham had driven back in 1961, although the engine bay had been lengthened to accommodate the longer six inline Aston-Martin engine. Though there was little consolation, the 23 year old Mexican driver had broken one of the oldest records in the book as his time set a new record for a six cylinder engine. The experimental car bested the mark of 130.138 m.p.h. set by Jimmy Snyder prior to World War II. Even Rodee's 147.197 m.p.h. was insufficient to remain in the field. Three drivers were under extreme pressure as they were on their third and last attempt to make the starting grid. The trio consisted of Len Sutton in the Leader Card Autolite Special, Dick Rathmann in the Chapman Special and Bob Christie in the Travelon Trailer Special. Fortunately, all were successful in their last allowable attempt to make the field.

On the last day of qualifications, two cars bumped their way into the field; Al Miller in one of Mickey Thompson's Harvey Aluminum Specials and Troy Ruttman in the Autocrat Seatbelt Special. Ebb Rose also joined the field; actually, rejoined the field for he had been bumped, but regained entry in another car - a Sheraton Thompson Special from the garages of fellow Texan A.J. Foyt.

A total of four rear engine cars made the field. Duane Carter and Al Miller would be at the wheel of Mickey Thompson's Harvey Aluminum Specials. Thompson had managed to place two of his five rear engine cars in the field. It had been rough going for Mickey as three of the cars had crashed during the month. One of the cars had been qualified by Masten Gregory only to be bumped by Ralph Liguori who later fell victim to bumping as well. Other rear engine cars making the field were the Lotus-Ford entries driven by Jimmy Clark and Dan Gurney.

It might be noted that the year marked the third attempt by the Novi team to eliminate carburetors by replacing them with fuel injectors. Some believed that they were the last of the cars using carburetors at Indy. When they had last qualified for the race in 1958, the Novis were among the few cars still using carburetors. However, while they were among the last to make use of this type of fueling procedure, they were not the last cars to use carbs at the Speedway. In 1963, the two Lotus-Fords of Clark and Gurney ran with 56 mm Weber carburetors, making them the last Indy cars to qualify for the race using carbs.

As a final footnote, the Van Liew car, built by Eddie Kuzma, made the race with Dempsey Wilson who secured the ride late in the month. Wilson had worked long and hard in an effort to put a Novi into the 1959 and 1960 races, but to no avail.

After four years of non-qualifying, the Novis were in the field and not with merely one car that barely made it, but with three. After the third day of qualifications, the Novi camp was in a state of ecstasy as were the many Novi followers. Such an accomplishment had never been attempted by a Novi team. Now the big question was could one of the Novis handle the demands imposed by the 500 to finally capture that all-elusive victory?

Chapter 8

A Crash, A Bad Clutch and Oil Leaks - 1963

During the drivers meeting held prior to the 1963 race, Chief Steward Harlan Fengler warned front row starters Jim Hurtubise and Don Branson not to "jump start" pole sitter Parnelli Jones. Fengler said to Jim, "Don't use the long nose of that Novi as an excuse." Another significant warning was given by Fritz Duesenberg, the chairman of the USAC Technical Committee. Duesenberg stated that any car leaking oil or fuel would be black flagged. Fengler underscored the statement with a similar comment. During the meeting Eddie Sachs addressed the group as he offered congratulatory comments to Andy Granatelli for bringing the Novis back into the starting field. The loquacious Sachs said, "We are proud you have brought the three Novis back and made them the great cars they were in the past." He also offered compliments to Englishman Colin Chapman for his strong and successful efforts in placing the Lotus cars, to be driven by Jim Clark and Dan Gurney, in the race.

Acknowledging Sachs' remarks, Granatelli announced future Novi plans by stating that he intended to return the following year with at least one rear engine Novi powered car. Such a car would be designed around the engine instead of merely being placed in one of the current rear engine designs. Andy went so far as to promise a 160 m.p.h. average for such a car. He quipped that if a Lotus was to win an Indy 500 they had better do it now for the following year the Lotus team would most certainly be running behind a rear engine Novi. Andy's confidence in a rear

(1963) Race Day and some last minute work on Herk's car. Andy (back to camera) supervises the undertaking. Authors Collection

engine Novi was based upon the knowledge that the Novi still managed to spin the rear tires in their quest for traction. Andy believed that with the Novi powerplant positioned at the back, rear wheel spin would no longer be a major concern.

When Hurtubise was asked about his racing strategy, he replied, "I'll just go like hell. This car is built to race and that's what I'm going to do. We got into the front row to lead the race and that's what we'll try to do. I don't know where I'll be running at the first turn or after the first lap - but I'll be going for the front. That's why we're in the front row." Such a commentary certainly helps explain why Jim was sometimes referred to as a "racing daredevil."

Racing photographer Ken Truitt vividly recalls an incident at a favorite watering hole for members of the 500 racing fraternity, Mates White Front located several blocks east of the track on 16th Street. Qualifying was over and the race was several days away. Hurtubise was in attendance and when a remark was made as to the undependability of the Novi, Jim's hair fairly bristled at the expressed notion. Beyond asserting he would lead the first lap, Herk announced, "The hell it won't last...and I'm going to win the damn race." Without question, Herk's convictions regarding the Novi were strong.

Then it was on to the Memorial Day race. The 47th annual race was paced by a Chrysler 300 Convertible driven by Sam Hanks, Director of Competition at the Speedway since his 1957 Indy victory and his retirement that immediately fol-

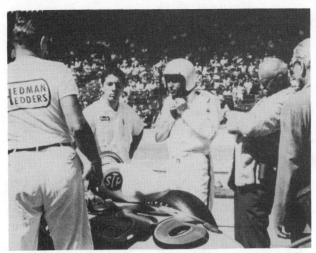

(1963) Herk getting ready for the start of the 1963 race as he buckles his helmet. At his right is young Vince.   Authors Collection

lowed. This was Sam's sixth consecutive drive as pace car pilot, a record that remains intact to this today. Riding with Sam was Speedway President Tony Hulman.

The start of the race was to become a near disaster for two of the Novis. The Novis' transmissions were not properly geared to drive at the speeds set by the pace car and then by pole sitter Jones. According to Andy, the Novis' first gear was too high while the racing gear was too low for the fast start of the race. Such a condition was said to cause them to bog down. Hurtubise lost power as the field was flagged away and fell back to about seventh place during the first two turns. On the back stretch, the V-8 came to life and Jim roared around the cars that had passed him. Picking up the tempo, he came off the fourth turn with only pole sitter Jones in front of him. To the delight of many in the stands he then shot around Jones to lead the first lap. The Novi was not just back in the race and starting from the front row, it had now lead the first lap as well! For the first time since 1957, a Novi once again was in the lead at Indy!

Granatelli recently described the first lap with much of the same emotions he had displayed at the time, which included hand waving, great gesturing, raised voice and enormous enthusiasm. He remembered looking up the front straight waiting for the cars to come off the fourth turn to complete the first lap when he noticed Herk holding down second spot behind Parnelli. But then, in the wink of an eye, Jim had charged past Parnelli to take the lead. It all happened so fast that as one observer noted "it was as if the cars had changed positions in a split second." Jim later stated rather matter of factly, "All the fans expected me to lead that first lap. I just couldn't let 'em down!" Herk's speed was such, 143.312 m.p.h., that he established a new opening lap record. Folklore has it that Herk and Parnelli had made a $5.00 wager going to the leader at the completion of the first

(1963) The cars on a parade lap. Branson and Hurtubise are slightly out in front of pole sitter Parnelli Jones in J.C. Agajanian's #98. Note Don looking over his shoulder, perhaps wondering when Parnelli will make his move.   Bruce Craig Photos

59

(1963) A promise fulfilled! Jim Hurtubise leading Parnelli Jones on the first lap. Note the crowd on their feet.   I.M.S.

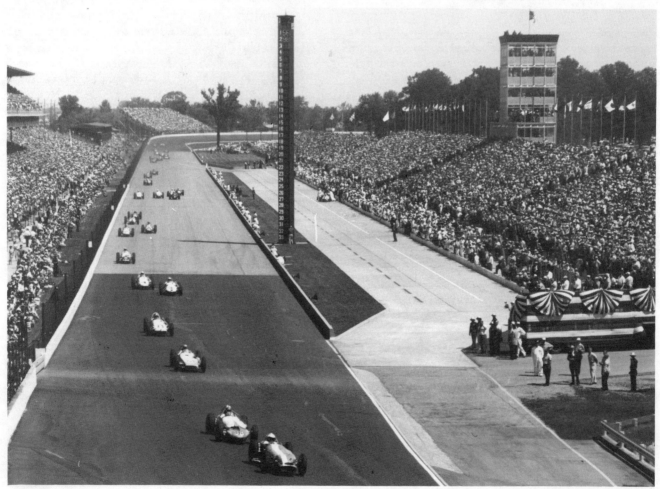

(1963) A beautiful shot as the race's second lap unfolds. Herk has pulled in front of Parnelli having crossed the start/finish line first in completing the opening lap. Meanwhile, Malone's car is already in the pits!   I.M.S.

(1963) Herk holding the lead though the adventure was short-lived as Parnelli reeled him in on the back straight during the second lap.
Bruce Craig Photos

lap. The bet was alleged to have been made on the quiet side as the car owners had heavy investments plus prestige riding on the outcome of the event - not the first lap results.

In talking with Parnelli Jones, he clearly expressed being surprised when he had seen Hurtubise falling back at the start. He remembers thinking this was due to Herk's car possibly jumping out of gear. Yet, before the lap was over it was now Hurtubise in front of him! After this fabulous start by Hurtubise things looked up, although Jones was able to surge back in front as lap two was completed.

While all of this excitement was taking place on the track, Art Malone came into the pits after only a lap as his car's transmission was not functioning properly. As it turned out, while the car was to be equipped with three gears, second was inoperative. The problem was compounded by the fact that the pre-race parade and pace laps were too slow for this Novi. Consequently, Art stayed super busy shifting gears and slipping the clutch. Art has said, "I had to keep slipping or buzzing the clutch dragging the car along in low gear." Art was fully aware that if he rode the clutch repeatedly it would most certainly fry the plates. If he had moved into high gear he would have run over the cars out in front. In running the

(1963) Bobby Unser loses it early (lap 2) to finish last.
John Darlington Photo

low gear, he would be virtually creeping at 60 m.p.h. Art reports, "I'm a savvy guy as mechanical things go," and he immediately recognized that he had to nurse the car until the green was displayed. When the race did start Malone was instantly confronted with an uncooperative transfer of power through the transmission to the driveline. Pulling into his pit after one circuit, Malone informed Andy that the transmission was locked in first. Granatelli advised him to return to the race saying that possibly the gearbox would "break lose" and he could then obtain the necessary running gear. Art said, "We shut off the motor and put the transmission in high gear, jacked up the rear end of the car. I raced the motor up to 7,000 rpms and they dropped the car down making a smoky drag race type start. That worked until the back straightaway where it started slipping again. I could race the motor from 10 to 12,000 grand and weld the clutch together." As it turned out the errant behavior of the transmission-clutch created havoc with the engine, bending valves and causing other mechanical woes. Rather than cruise around without any chance of rectifying the situation, Malone pulled in on lap 18 in order to stay out of harms way what with his car limping around the track. Thus, he was classified as the 31st finisher in the STP Special.

Unbelievably, Art was not the first Novi pilot to retire from the race. Bobby Unser's luck ran out before Malone, as he was classified 33rd finisher - dead last! Unser had also experienced trouble on the race's opening lap as he fell back in the field when his engine lost power in a fashion similar to what had confronted Hurtubise's #56. The engine finally came alive on the back straight and Bobby rapidly made up lost ground. Then going into the first turn on the second lap, Bobby closed in too quickly on a car in front of him, thus he had to choose between the wall or the car in front. Unser opted for the wall. Fortunately, the field was able to get around him without further mishaps. The car was damaged to the point that it could not continue as the rear end of the car had hit the wall rupturing the fuel tank. Thankfully, there was no fire, for with the amount of fuel still in the car a fire could have created a precarious situation. Bobby was very lucky as he emerged with no physical injuries, only shattered pride and disappointment. As he climbed from the cockpit, Unser

(1963) After hitting the wall in the first turn, Unser quickly evacuated. The tail has taken part of the punch, thus the leaking fuel.
Bruce Craig Photos

hit the hood of the car with his fist in disgust. Then, helmet in hand, Bobby made the long, lonely walk back to the pits. In recalling the withdrawal of Unser's car from the race, Vince Granatelli made reference to the Indy rookie getting in over his head as he attempted to move up with the leaders in the very first laps of the race.

In The Bobby Unser Story, Bobby described his rookie year mishap thusly, "I was picking up positions as quickly as I could and I went into a corner in a pack of cars that blocked the groove." He then stated that one driver got on his brakes too hard and "loaded with fuel as it was, the Novi weighed 2,300 pounds, when I hit on my brakes we just kept whistling. I pitched sideways...and slammed into the outside wall. It was a pretty minor wreck compared to the hell of a mess that could have happened" if the other car had been nailed in the rear end.

So with the race's first two laps completed, one Novi was out and another was malfunctioning and apparently hopelessly out of contention. In Granatelli's words, "There I was, I had one car in the lead, one car in the wall and one car in the pits!"

One healthy Novi was left and it remained in second place following Parnelli. Jim trailed as best he could, but it was not an easy task as Parnelli was much faster in the turns and he slowly but steadily widened the gap. Granatelli informed us that Jim might have become worried after seeing Bobby Unser putting the sister car into the wall. According to Andy, Jim had always been concerned about his car's front end push. Andy went on to say that this may well have been Jim's own fault as Herk had a habit of constantly making adjustments on the cars he drove. According to Andy, Hurtubise was the kind of fellow you never left alone in the garage when the crew retired for the evening as he might completely alter the setup. Andy firmly believed that Jim preferred to slightly curtail his pace after seeing Bobby's car following the wall smacking incident. To possibly add to Jim's woes, he was followed by a group of cars that were also faster in the turns and only by smoking them on the straights when the V-8's power "spoke clearly" was he able to retain second spot. Finally on lap 38, Roger McCluskey in the Konstant Hot Special managed to overtake Herk. Then several other drivers, including Jimmy Clark, were able to slip around the big brute, but Jim managed to hold on to a spot in the top ten.

Hurtubise made his first pit stop for fuel and fresh rubber (the rear tires and right front) after 48 laps before returning to the race. The pit stop had consumed just under 30 seconds so he was still in contention for a solid finish. After some 80 laps, Jim begin to charge again moving up into 7th position as he began to average speeds slightly over 149 m.p.h. Slowly but surely, he continued to move forward until he ultimately engaged in a

(1963) A dejected Unser, helmet in hand, on the long walk back to the pits.   Bruce Craig Photos

duel with A.J. Foyt for third position. The #56 Hotel Tropicana was definitely on the move. Novi watchers thrilled at the sight and may well have thought of what might follow. Even if Herk could not overtake front runners Parnelli and Clark, some thought the Novi would be in the top five at the end of the race. Such a notion surely would stir many as they witnessed the Novi resurgence by the unflappable Hurtubise.

After 101 laps while in third place behind Jones and Clark, it was time to come in for fuel, thus Herk's second pit stop. Jim was in a super hurry as he came down pit lane, turning left toward the pit wall before abruptly turning right. In so doing, he slightly overshot his pit and #56 ended up halfway in the next pit - that of teammate Bobby Unser. The crew had to push the car back in order to engage the fueling hose. Again, the right front and two rear tires were changed during the stop which consumed 48 seconds. Then the sad drama began.

One home movie shows a slight trail of smoke emerging from the car as the Novi came down pit lane to stop. The #56 Hotel Tropicana Special was smoking slightly as it returned to the track. Officials in the pits noted a splash of oil at the spot where the Novi had stopped. This led to the logical conclusion that the Novi was losing oil. And rules being rules, this meant that the Novi had to be black flagged. Jim was waved back into the pits with smoke trailing from the car. USAC tech officials looked under the car then ordered its removal as they determined that it was indeed leaking oil. With such a judgment by the officials, Jim slowly extricated himself from the cockpit. Then with hands on hips, a disgusted Hurtubise stood alone for several minutes staring at the front end of his car before moving behind the pit wall. Dejectedly, Hurtubise walked down pit lane receiving a tremendous ovation from the fans in the immediate area. The last of the three Novis was now out of the chase. Hurtubise was credited with 102 laps and 22nd place in the final standings.

In the movie, "Design for a Winner," produced by Mobil Oil, the narrator states that Hurtubise's ride left the race due to "a serious oil leak." It was also said that "the Novi team knew it was all over for another year."

(1963) Malone remained in his disabled car as it was pushed back to Gasoline Alley having finished 31st.
I.M.S.

Further disappointment came after the race as it was "discovered" in the Hurtubise garage that the engine was in fine shape. The account rendered by Granatelli was that he had the engine run at over 8,000 rpms for three minutes and the engine did not miss a beat nor leak any oil. One version had it that the oil spillage was due to the abrupt stop made by Hurtubise during that less than perfect second pit stop. Some oil had sluiced through the front mounted breather due to mass inertia. The officials, seeing the oil slick, made the call as the rules required. According to Andy, the oil spillage story was as follows: located under the fuel injector was a catch can for any fuel spillage, i.e. overflow. Thus, when Herk made the pit stop revving the engine, some of the fuel splashed over into the catch reservoir. This is what caused the spot that was left on pit lane; not oil but alcohol.

Therefore, the Novi was eliminated on what some considered to be a questionable decision. In a post-race newspaper account it was reported that in examining the Novi engine it was discovered that the breather tube had suffered metal fatigue that "resulted in a nasty leak." After the race, Joe Granatelli made a rather interesting and apparently revealing remark as he said that if Hurtubise had been able to continue "he had a 50-50 chance, but part of that chance was on his life." In an effort to pinpoint the car's retirement, a USAC source was recently asked about the organization's pit side tech observers. The hope was that the official responsible for the Hurtubise pit might be able to shed some light on the situation. Unfortunately, we were informed that USAC officials only signed the final technical inspection sheets and not pit side reports.

black flag! About the time Chief Steward Harlan Fengler apparently was preparing to have flagman Pat Vidan display the black banner, he was approached by J.C. Agajanian. Aggie pointed out to Fengler that the leaking had stopped as the split in the external oil tank was vertical (in line with the two bolt hangers) and the oil level was now below the crack line. Therefore, the car was in no position to spill additional oil. He requested that Fengler verify this assertion before allowing the black flag to be dropped. As the discussion between Fengler and Agajanian continued, a quiet Colin Chapman stood several feet away listening to the discussion. Further, "one of Clark's crew talked with Fengler briefly and then returned to his pit area." Jones was allowed to continue the race. If Fengler had been consistent one would presume that he would have black flagged Parnelli earlier to be checked as had been the case with Hurtubise. The difference appeared to be timing as Parnelli was in the closing laps of the rich race and a black flag most certainly meant losing the world famous event.

(1963) Ganging up on the Hurtubise Novi. Lloyd Ruby in #52, A.J. Foyt #2 and Eddie Sachs #9.
Armin Krueger Photo

In the closing laps, Clark who had been closing the gap on Jones, backed off, possibly sensing that Jones was to be black flagged. When this failed to occur, Clark played it safe and accepted a sure second instead of losing in a late bid for a victory with a possible spin out. With 25 laps to go, Clark was a mere five seconds back. At the close of the race he was 21 seconds behind the winner. Following the race, Clark was to say, "I could see that (the oil) up ahead and I didn't want to take any chances of getting into that and spinning out." The unwillingness to sideline Parnelli at any point remains one of the most controversial decisions ever made by a chief steward in the history of the 500.

In a somewhat ironic twist, the race's second retiree Johnny Boyd was brought in after 12 laps. Following an inspection, his Bowes Seal Fast Special was ordered from the race due to an oil leak. It was stated that oil from the breather was blowing onto a rear tire.

The duel for victory came down to a battle between Parnelli Jones, "The Torrance Torpedo," in his J.C. Agajanian owned Willard Battery Special/Offy and Jimmy Clark, "The Flying Scot," in the surprisingly well-behaved Lotus Powered by Ford Special of Colin Chapman. In the late stage of the race, it became quite obvious that Jones' car had been leaking oil. But this time there was no

Considering the fact that the Novi was black flagged immediately and Jones was allowed to continue, it cannot be denied that Fengler seemed to use different standards for the same mishap.

(1963) The big, heavy Novi was quite a handful. Note the serious expression on Jim's face while working his brute through the corner. The right hand is high on the steering wheel, a Hurtubise trademark. Attempting to overtake Herk is Roger McCluskey in the Konstant Hot Special.
I.M.S.

For Granatelli and the Novi team, Fengler's point of view appeared to represent a rather unfair situation. The unhappiness was heightened with the knowledge that Fengler had warned drivers and car owners in the pre-race briefing that oil spillage would automatically result in a black flag. Fengler was quoted as having said, "The two things that will get you off this race course right now are if you lose brakes or oil. If you don't believe me, just test me!" Seemingly from case to case interpretations of the rules were subject to change.

One of the local newspapers carried an enticing statement made by one of the biggest names in Speedway racing who wished to remain anonymous. The individual vented his disgust about the fact that it seemed that new rules had to be written all the time because of Agajanian. It was mentioned that the previous year Jones had lost his brakes and in order to stop the car in the pits, tires had to be laid down for him to run over as crew members grabbed the car in an attempt to bring it to a halt. Agajanian claimed he was sure that if he had not protested Fengler would have black flagged Parnelli. Aggie pointed out that Parnelli was not the only driver who had been leaking oil and they were not causing that much trouble. One USAC trackside official, positioned in an observers stand, has remarked that he did not realize the magnitude of the track oiling until he returned to his Indianapolis home that evening. As he removed his wearing apparel, he became aware of the extent of the oil and grit that had been present during the race.

Fengler stated that he could not take a race away from a man on snap judgment. One may wonder how Hurtubise and the Granatellis felt about this statement. To make the inconsistent behavior of Fengler even more clear he also stated, "If Parnelli's car had not stopped leaking I would have black flagged him." Such a statement is an admission that Fengler knew Parnelli had been leaking oil and perhaps still was doing so. In spite of this knowledge, he did not have Parnelli flagged in for an inspection.

In further defense for his action or inaction, the chief steward said, "Hurtubise was dumping oil on the track and Parnelli was only dripping oil and then the leak stopped." This at its best is another questionable excuse by Fengler. Hurtubise may have dropped oil but it appears that he did so only in the pits. It appears there were no reports about the Novi dropping oil on the track before Herk's pit stop. Fengler was so quick in displaying the black flag without solid

(1963) Hurtubise leaving the pits after a fuel stop. Crew members assist in getting the heavy car rolling once again. The side panel was removed prior to the race, therefore venting off additional heat from the engine compartment.   I.M.S.

confirmation that Hurtubise did not have the time to prove that he was not leaking oil on the track. When Fengler was asked about the possible black flagging of Jones he said, "Sure we considered it. But you must consider the time in the race. Lots of cars had spilled oil and parts on the track by then." The chief steward also stated, "If I had thought Parnelli was creating hazardous conditions, I would have black flagged him." To further support his position, Fengler stated that the oil tank on Aggie's car was still half full while a number of cars were about two-thirds full. One can only wonder about the oil level in the Novi tank when it was forced from the race. As it were, the warnings issued during the drivers meeting certainly seemed to have been forgotten once the race was underway.

In a <u>Sports Illustrated</u> magazine article detailing the race it was suggested that perhaps the loss of oil from #98 continued to the close of the speed contest. The story included a photo displaying a black substance on the oil tank implying a continuing leakage. The article also contained a photo showing a smiling Parnelli as he motored down pit lane at the conclusion of the race. The photo caption includes the following statement: "The nearside of the car is oil-grimed and the oil appears still to be seeping from one of the circular bolts attaching the tank to the car's frame." Accentuating the statement, the photo has a boxed in border of the questionable part of the oil tank. The photo caption was entitled, BRING IN A GUSHER. No regard was apparently given to the possibility that this may have been residue from an earlier "self-cured" leak.

While Jimmy Clark had seen fit to back off a bit behind Jones for safety reasons, Roger McCluskey and Eddie Sachs were not as fortunate. In the closing laps of the race they spun. Roger was running 3rd at the time and only two laps remained when his mishap occurred. The spin caused him to finish 15th. Sachs had crashed with 18 laps remaining to finish 17th. With respect to Fengler's challenge to "test me," one of Sachs' car owners, Dick Sommers, asserted in <u>Eddie Called Me Boss</u>, "The chief steward had been right: oil had gotten Sachs and McCluskey off the race course." Sommers statement obviously displayed not only a bit of humor but some bitter irony as well.

(1963) Having made his pit stop, Herk had departed leaving several wet spots on the pavement. Fuel, water or oil? Andy (standing on pit lane) and crew members looking eagerly toward the 4th turn as #56 was black flagged - the command to return for a tech inspection. At the moment, the misspelling of Hurtubise's name on the pit wall was of no consequence.   I.M.S.

Some drivers were quite outspoken in their disgust about Parnelli not receiving the black flag. The animosity spilled over to an incident the following day at the nearby Holiday Inn when Parnelli and Sachs were involved in a brief scuffle.

(1963) With USAC officials declaring the car out of the race due to oil spillage, an obviously forlorn Hurtubise gets out of the car.   I.M.S.

(1963) The Novi effort is over for another year. With Hurtubise's car being pushed to the garage area, all three Granatelli entries were out of the classic contest.
I.M.S.

The <u>Indianapolis Times</u> headlined the controversy with "Parnelli's Oil Ignites Slick Feud at the 500" and the subtitle read, "Fengler tells why he stopped Hurtubise and not Jones' car." The chief steward responded to questioners saying that some cars other than Parnelli's were throwing oil. Gentleman Jimmy Clark, the man who had the most at stake, made only a few public statements about the entire oiling situation accepting things as they were. He did say, "I had enough rubber and petrol to go the distance. But I was getting sideways in Parnelli Jones' oil. I thought I'd try to keep my car on the island. I would much rather be second than dead." Being such a gallant loser certainly enhanced Clark's popularity. In fact, Clark seemed to be the most liked and respected foreigner at Indy during the 1960s. It should be noted that no protest was filed within the allotted time the morning after the race.

In the Hungness <u>1995 Indianapolis 500 Yearbook</u>, Parnelli is quoted as saying that while he still had most of the oil in the tank several other cars had run completely out of oil. He specifically mentioned Dempsey Wilson and Jim Hurtubise. Yet, he stated that everybody appeared to place sole blame on his car. It might be pointed out that Dempsey went the full 200 laps in a Vita Fresh Special, although several other cars did experience severe oiling problems.

The race's 1961 winner, A.J. Foyt finished 3rd while Rodger Ward, the 1959 and 1962 winner, was 4th. The first six finishers all beat Ward's existing record of 140.293 m.p.h. Jones was to finish with a 143.637 m.p.h. average. Second place finisher Clark was clocked at 142.752 m.p.h. Costa Mesa, California driver Dan Gurney in the companion car to Clark's Lotus finished a creditable 7th.

(1963) Defending champion Rodger Ward leads eventual winner Parnelli Jones. Note the oil behind the left rear tire of Jones' car. The tail of Ward's car also sports evidence of oil grim.
Armin Krueger Photo

According to one account, the Fords won the hearts of the fans after the Novis went out and the low slung chassis was sensational in its debut. Al Miller of Roseville, Michigan was ninth in one of the Thompson rear engine Chevys. As for Duane Carter, his Chevy was eliminated at the halfway point with a bad rod. While Jones prevailed with the front engine Watson's roadster, as Bill Oursler has pointed out in a <u>National Speed Sport News</u> article, it was a case of a front engine car winning the battle, yet going on to lose the war.

Remarks about Jones' victory and being allowed to remain in the race may be harsh, but it cannot be ignored that Parnelli's victory was controversial in view of what happened to his car and Hurtubise's Novi. But to say that Jones was a lucky winner, thanks only to Harlan Fengler, does not appear to be appropriate. Parnelli certainly had been the outstanding driver all month, in practice, qualifications and having driven a fantastic race. Parnelli had lead 167 of the 200 laps. Oily track aside, his speed set a new track record. The pole sitting winner, the first to do so from that position since Pat Flaherty in 1956, had won two USAC champ car contest to this point - the Phoenix 100 in 1961 and the Hoosier 100 of 1962. In the future (1967), Parnelli was destined to lose a 500 victory which was in the palm of his hands when "destiny" sidelined his Granatelli ride a mere 4 laps from the checkered flag.

Parnelli's splendid win notwithstanding, Jimmy Clark's second place finish in the tiny Lotus caused more than a few car owners to think about the future. The rear engine cars, the so-called detested "funny cars," could no longer be ignored. Some members of the American racing fraternity took the challenge seriously. The rear engine cars of Jack Brabham in 1961 and that driven by Dan Gurney in 1962 did not set the world on fire. The situation would now change what with Clark's very strong second place showing. There was much food for thought with respect to engine location as well as to chassis construction.

Another major influence from the 1963 race was the fact that several drivers had requested the Goodyear Company to consider the development of a tire for Indy competition.

The overall results for the Novi team were more than disappointing. Losing a car within two laps, having a second in the pits early and then the black flagging of the third was a very difficult pill to swallow. Still, Hurtubise had made a good impression and demonstrated that a Novi could be truly competitive. With a little more luck, there was still a chance a Novi could win the prestigicus Indianapolis 500.

With no protest filed by the Granatelli camp, they presumedly appeared at the Victory Banquet at the Murat Temple the following evening. The only reported absentee drivers were Dan Gurney (who had departed for a Canadian road race), Roger McCluskey and Eddie Sachs. When questioned about the Jones episode at the banquet, Hurtubise replied, he is a "personal friend of mine," but then observed "that other drivers have won this race and have lost oil."

In many of the reports emanating from the

Speedway that year regarding the race, much has been written about Jim Hurtubise leading the first lap in his Hotel Tropicana Novi. In a memorial tribute to Hurtubise following his death in January, 1989, Indianapolis Star writer Robin Miller penned, "When Jim muscled the Novi into the lead at the start of the 1963 Indianapolis 500 I don't think I ever yelled any louder." Undoubtedly, Robin's reaction was shared by countless others in attendance that day.

The year was indeed the best yet for the Granatellis and their Novi team. The outfit seemingly had finally picked up some momentum. The Granatellis decided to keep that momentum alive and improve on the cars and engines for the following year. An element was to be added to the Novi camp in an attempt to afford the powerful V-8 and an even better chance of winning. In keeping with this notion, Andy said following the race that he hoped to build a "dream car from the ground up" and that it would be one he felt capable of establishing new track records. The comments were similar to those uttered at the drivers meeting and gave many cause for reflection as to what might lie ahead for the Novi team. Andy certainly could not be charged with a lack of exuberance or optimism.

With respect to Clark's fine second place showing and with other rear engine cars having placed 7th and 9th quite possibly the black flag was out for an entire era of racing at Indianapolis.

(1963) The 1963 winning car and driver - Parnelli Jones in the Agajanian Willard Battery Special. The race's outcome swirled with controversy for some time.
                                                                    I.M.S.

Intermezzo

A RADIO CONNECTION

A solid connection can be made between the original Novi racing team created by car owner Lew Welch and some 1960's action at the Speedway. The colorful James "Radio" Gardner was the only crew member who served with the Welch Novi team from its inception in 1941 until its demise after the 1960 Indianapolis race.

Radio's son, Jim, served on the Novi crew for several years prior to the sale to the Granatellis. Radio continued to maintain an extremely strong interest in the classic race for years thereafter. In 1963 when the Chapman/Clark team arrived at the world famous racing oval for "a go at it," they were long on experience but short on a complete pit crew. Radio approached Chapman, suggesting that his son was quite capable in assisting in the team's one planned pit stop. A brief discussion with driver Jimmy Clark was the clincher. Jim's assignment was that of changing the right rear tire. Jim's previous track side experience was helpful and his size was certainly no deterrent. Jim, a former guard on the Duke University football team, was 6 foot 1 inch and tipped the scale at 250 pounds.

The Ford Motor Company was quite satisfied with the arrangement and they brought in two more pros for tire changers - there was no plan to change the left rear Firestone. One of the pair was veteran Ford mechanic Bill Stroppe while the other fellow was a member of the Holman-Moody Ford team then extremely active in NASCAR competition.

The sole pit stop so impressed <u>Sports Illustrated</u> that in their issue of June 13, 1963, a four picture sequence of the stop was shown with a clock in the corner of each photo. The third shot shows Jim at his assigned position - the right rear tire changer. His arms are raised indicating he had completed his task. While his job was completed in 20 seconds, unfortunately, the right front tire exchanger (from Holman Moody) bobbled causing a delay and the total time in the pit amounted to 32.3 seconds. One source calculated that if all three tires had been changed in the 20 seconds achieved by Gardner, "Clark would have won with 1.3 seconds to spare." Such a hypothesis apparently presumes that Clark would have moved out in front of Parnelli before oil spillage became a paramount concern.

While leading Jimmy had to make the scheduled stop. The stop was a memorable one for Clark, due to what followed as he roared out of his pit. He described the action in his book, <u>Jimmy Clark at the Wheel</u>. Clark recalled Jim Gardner's nickname as being "Big Jim," and that he was a master at the technique of changing race tires. When Clark pitted, Big Jim completed his assigned right rear tire change in rapid fire order then signaled to the jack man by raising his arms. Indy cars Jim had worked up to that time on carried only two gears and therefore several crew members would often provide a push as the car departed the pits in the lower gear which could be slightly sluggish. Jim thus prepared to shove the car off, positioning his hand at the back of the racer. Unbeknowst to Jim, the foreign built Lotus used a four speed transmission. Thus, when the jacks were lowered Clark dropped the clutch and took off post haste. The sudden speedy departure by the Lotus caused Jim to take an involuntary multi-sommersault. As Clark checked his mirrors to see if the path was clear to rejoin the race, he was surprised and horrified to see Gardner tumbling down pit lane. Clark was momentarily distraught, thinking he had somehow run over Big Jim in his charge out of the pits. But Clark then realized what must have occurred and he continued on his way. In recently recalling the incident, Jim chuckled as he described his acrobatic display in the pits as the Lotus pulled away.

Jim remains active in the sport to this day with his wife Judi. They own and operate a stock car team that competes on the Automobile Racing Club of America (ARCA) circuit. Their home is conveniently located near the Charlotte Motor Speedway.

Chapter 9

An Overview - Some Technical Changes

Significant changes at the Indianapolis Motor Speedway had occurred in racing technology by the latter 1960s. The changes included the introduction of turbocharged engines; changes in tire sizes and durability as well as a choice of brands (Firestone or Goodyear) and a complete movement to rear engine cars. Other changes also occurred, though of a lesser scale. However, a dramatic change did occur within the Novi camp. While the Granatellis saw fit to adopt such a significant alteration other teams did not to follow suit.

As Andy Granatelli and the Novi team were working on their new "weapon," a good deal of attention was still focused on the remaining roadsters. The Granatelli team apparently was unwilling to put all of their eggs in one basket. Thus, the two 1962 Kurtis-Kraft cars were retained. They were now considered somewhat akin to backup cars if by chance some failure should arise with the new car. Meanwhile, "Tired Iron," the old 500F, was finally retired. Yet, in qualifying for the 1963 race it helped provide the Granatellis with evidence that they were moving in the right direction in the continuing development of the Novi engine, as was the case with Herk's #56.

Early in the spring of 1963 following four consecutive years of unqualified Novis, Andy Granatelli had a meeting with Stirling Moss in the United States. Moss was one of the top Formula One drivers during the late 1950s and the early 1960s. His career had come to an abrupt end after he crashed a Formula One Lotus on the English Goodwood Circuit in April of 1962. According to Granatelli's autobiography, the meeting with Moss was an aftermath of the brief, defunct Brabham-Granatelli alliance.

Stirling had driven a very unique car in the early 1960s. It was the Ferguson P99, a front engine car. According to Formula One specifications, it was fitted with a 91 c.i. (1.5 liters) Coventry Climax straight 4 engine. It had also raced with a 152 c.i. (2.5 liter) engine. The car's primary feature was its 4 wheel drive (4WD) and it had been built by the British firm of Harry Ferguson Engineering, Ltd. in Coventry. The model was to demonstrate the potential of the 4WD system they had developed and were offering for sale. Moss had driven the car on several occasions in 1961 and it had performed remarkably well under challenging hill climb situations. However, overall the car was not much of a match for the more conventional Formula One cars. Yet, in its third competitive appearance, the P99 was very successful as Moss won a race at Oulton Park in September, 1961. Admittedly, it was a wet track, but conversely it faced only rear engine opposition as Formula One had already made the switch to rear engine cars.

An interesting comment regarding the P99 was made by Stirling in 1991 during a social event covered by writer Eoin Young that appeared in the October 31 issue of the British magazine Autosport. Young recounted that Stirling had said the P99 "with its 4 Wheel Drive, it went where you steered it and that wasn't always what you wanted with a race car. You couldn't steer it on the throttle." Young also reported that Graham Hill, who drove the car in the New Zealand based Tasman Series, had asserted that the engine produced a tremendous amount of heat that would flow back into the cockpit turning it into an oven. But other front engine cars were also known for this trait.

Whatever one might say about the P99, it did become a legend among cars raced in Europe. Though the Oulton Park Gold Cup race was not an official Grand Prix event, in winning that race the P99 became the only 4WD Grand Prix car to ever win a race. In addition, the race marked the last victory for a front engine Grand Prix car in an event slated for Formula One.

As a result, Moss suggested to Granatelli that a 4WD setup could be a possible solution in transmitting the massive power to the Novi V-8 engine at the Indianapolis Motor Speedway. Traction and tire wear would most assuredly improve with 4WD. When we asked Stirling about the meeting with Granatelli, he could not recall the particulars other than to confirm that he had made such a suggestion to Andy. Granatelli's recollection regarding the meeting is rather cloudy, although he recalled stating that the suggestion was worthy of serious thought and that due consideration would be given to the proposal.

While first hand information on the conversation was not obtained, one source highlighted what transpired after Andy heard of the idea of employing 4WD technology. A British publication, Motoring News, carried an article entitled "The Ferguson-Novi Four Wheel Drive Indianapolis Car." According to the article, Moss traveled to the United States of America several months after his victory at Oulton Park. The account asserts that in conversation with Andy Granatelli, "Stirling recommended that he (Granatelli) use the 4WD principle for the Novis." Moss then informed Major Tony Rolt of this conversation and Rolt wrote to Granatelli in March of 1962, but received no reply.

Rolt was a former European driver of some note. His racing accomplishments included winning the 1953 LeMans 24 Hours race with co-driver Duncan Hamilton in a C-Type Jaguar beating out Ferraris, Alfa-Romeos and the American Briggs Cunningham team. The following year, the pair finished 2nd in a D-Type Jag. Rolt was now employed by the Ferguson Company. Possibly, Granatelli's failure to immediately reply was due to the fact that the Granatelli's Paxton firm was in the process of being sold to the Studebaker Corporation. Then rather unexpectedly, Rolt received a letter from Granatelli regarding the possibility of a 4WD drive in Indy car competition.

With Major Rolt's suggestion coming as the 1963 Indianapolis race was rapidly approaching, time did not permit the Granatellis to give any immediate thought to a 4WD at the Speedway. Any serious consideration regarding a 4WD had to be temporarily placed on the back burner. Yet, Andy, Vince and Joe decided to investigate the prospects of a 4WD Novi later that year.

As noted earlier, Andy was still contemplating the possibility of building a rear engine Novi. This notion was retained as the traction of a rear engine car was judged to be improved, what with the weight closer to the power driven wheels. Poor traction had remained a nagging problem for the over-powered Novis. Since Andy and his brothers had taken over the Novi operation, they had reportedly committed a sum in excess of $200,000 during the previous two years to the Novi project.

The 4WD plan was selected to receive priority attention following the 1963 race. When we asked Andy about why he opted for the 4WD approach, he replied, "We couldn't get the traction with two wheel drive. So obviously it didn't take much to figure that we needed 4WD."

However, before making a full and final commitment, the Granatellis wished to see the P99 in action at Indy to determine how such a 4WD car would perform on this particular oval. With that in mind, Andy contacted the Ferguson Company in June of 1963, informing the firm of his interest and plans for a possible 4WD run. The folks at Ferguson fully understood the situation with respect to Granatelli and the prospects for the company as well. Using a 4WD system on a Speedway car such as the Novi certainly would offer tremendous potential in sales if successful. With this in mind, Ferguson was willing to assist in the shakedown of their 4WD at Indy. The P99 was made ready for shipment to Indianapolis and it was to arrive late in the summer to participate in a test session organized for the Granatelli team. Reportedly, the Granatelli operation was to pay the cost of having the car flown to Indianapolis for the testing project.

Meanwhile, in late July of 1963, the Firestone Tire Company conducted testing of their 500 racing tires at the Speedway. The Granatellis had the #56 Hotel Tropicana on hand with driver Jim McElreath scheduled to carry out the driving duties. Over a 12 lap run, McElreath was clocked at over 152.820 m.p.h. on two laps and he drove four laps in excess of 152.5 m.p.h. using the standard 8.00 x 18 rear tires and 7.60 x 16 front tires. It had been suggested that if the new and wider 15 inch tires had been used the speed range could have moved up even higher. Andy was elated with the performance of the car, claiming that during the sessions a total of over 300 miles with averages above 151 m.p.h. had been reached. Imagine what this time could have done in qualifications only two months earlier when Parnelli Jones had set a new track record at 151.153 m.p.h. Jones' best time during May's practice had been a 153.557 m.p.h. in the Agajanian Willard Battery Special Offy. Thus, a McElreath run in a Novi had established the second fastest non-qualifying test run recorded at the Speedway.

The Granatellis had to be impressed with McElreath beyond the speeds obtained. Only days prior to the sparkling practice runs, Jim had flipped a sprinter at the Hatfield Speedway in Pennsylvania suffering several injuries. They consisted of a shoulder separation, bruised ribs and a burn under his right arm. As the Arlington, Texas driver prepared for a run, Steve Petrasek, Firestone's racing development chief, asked Jim if he felt like running. The laconic Texan replied, "Not much, but we might as well get finished." Petrasek then told McElreath not to push too hard. A tough as

(1963) The Ferguson P99 Formula One car, built in 1961 when the rear engine revolution was in vogue in F-1. Yet, the 4WD surprised a number of fans when Stirling Moss won the rain plagued Oulton Gold Cup race driving the 99. In winning, the car left it's rivals at some distance. Here we see it at Indy for testing in the summer of 1963 as the Granatellis considered a move to a 4WD car. I.M.S.

nails McElreath replied, "It doesn't hurt any more to go fast than to go slow." Granatelli was impressed with McElreath's handling of the car, while Jim was delighted with the Novi. As a result, the pair agreed to see it they might work out a driving assignment for the 1964 running of the 500.

Following the Firestone testing, the Goodyear Company had been allotted ten days for tire testing at the track with A.J. Foyt, the 1961 Indy winner, present to carry out the primary driving duties. On July 31, as the Goodyear cars took to the track, the Granatellis were present with Bobby Marshman. The young Pennsylvania driver was to test drive the #6 Novi on Goodyears. Bobby drove on 15 inch Goodyears and during 12 laps he reached a top speed of 151 m.p.h. Marshman then had the misfortune of having an engine blow when a connecting rod let go. The Granatellis then made the decision to stop testing in view of the fact that their engines had not been overhauled for more than 2,000 miles and they did not wish to risk further engine failures.

Goodyear had made plans to debut at Indy since the firm had been approached by several drivers. Leo Mehl, a Goodyear employee who would ultimately become its long-time director of racing, recently stated that Goodyear's foray into Indy car racing had occurred in 1963 after "prompting from A.J. Foyt and they went to Indy with their stock car tires." Leo went on to state that, unfortunately, the tires were not suitable, yet the Akron, Ohio firm made the decision to back off and to return in 1964. As noted, Firestone had run into problems in attempting to supply all 1963 participants with the faster 15 inch tires and this had seemed like the perfect opportunity for Goodyear to step in and claim a share of the market. This explains why Goodyear had organized its testing session using Novis as part of the experiment. Incidentally, it has been reported that this was the first testing of the Goodyears at Indy by the Novi, but that has been challenged. According to Lee Norquest's The Fabulous Novi Story, one of the Novis had used Goodyears at least briefly during practice in May of 1963.

In August, during the tire testing session, the P99 arrived at the famed track. The appearance of the 4WD caught members of the Indy racing community by surprise. The Ferguson organization had sent drivers Jack Fairman and Major Tony Rolt from England to pilot the car. Some may recall that Fairman had driven for Jaguar in many sport car outings. He had also participated in the Race of Two Worlds at Monza, Italy, in 1957 and 1958 competing with the Indy car contingent while at the wheel of a Jaguar. Further, Fairman had been on the Indy scene in 1962 as he was assigned to drive a rear engine Mickey Thompson car. However, no qualification attempt was made.

On August 9, Fairman drove the P99 which was still powered by a 152 c.i. (2.5 liter) four cylinder Climax. It was a far cry from being a fresh and healthy engine, yet it was strong enough to allow Fairman to lap the two and one-half mile oval at speeds of over 141 m.p.h. Bear in mind, that the car had not been constructed for Indianapolis competition. Granatelli remained somewhat skeptical as he wanted Marshman to drive the car to see what a driver with Indy experience could do. Bobby took the P99 out and within a short time he was lapping at over 141 m.p.h. On the straights, the car was not outstanding but Marshman assured Andy that he could drive the car flat out all the way around the oval without lifting. This statement by Marshman impressed Granatelli, thus Andy became more enthusiastic about the use of 4WD with the Novi. Shortly thereafter, Anthony Granatelli issued a statement that he planned to have a 4WD Novi ready for Indy in 1964. Yet, he made no commitment at the time as to who was to build it and whether or not it was to be a rear engine creation.

the one auto manufacturer committed to the use of a supercharged V-8 as a passenger car powerplant. The alliance with the Novi team was quite a natural as Andy was serving as president of STP, a subsidiary of Studebaker. As a consequence, the 1964 entries were to be identified as Studebaker-STP Specials.

According to a statement released by Studebaker, the Novi team was to have a front engine 4WD chassis using independent suspension at all corners with the chassis being built by Ferguson. Further, the two 1962 Kurtis cars were to be included as part of the Studebaker-STP team. One of the cars was to have a wide track conversion while the other was to use the 1963 spec tires. The 1963 #6 Hotel Tropicana had already been converted into the aforementioned wide track setup.

At the time of the announcement, Granatelli said he expected to field two newly designed cars and to use the car which Jim Hurtubise had started from the front row as a practice machine. Andy felt the Ferguson 4WD would enable the car to go much deeper into the

(1964) When the Studebaker Corporation announced its direct involvement with the Novi-Ferguson project, the press release included several futuristic sketches of the forthcoming product. In this illustration the car appears to be virtually missile shape in design. Authors Collection

Granatelli talked with the Ferguson firm with respect to possible assistance and eventually they agreed to join in the effort. A stipend was paid to Ferguson in September to initiate a design study for a 4WD Novi powered car. On October 31, the Studebaker Company informed the public that they were going to sponsor the Novi team the following year. Studebaker President Sherwood Egbert told a press conference held in Detroit that "we will run in Indianapolis and we intend to win at Indianapolis." Egbert further announced, "We believe racing is an excellent way to improve the engineering and design of our automotive products and we feel motorsports is one very good way to improve the public image of our product." He went on to point out that the Novi engines already had a correlation with Studebaker as it was

turns at high speeds and to power out at a higher throttle setting. The reference to the two new cars dealt with the Ferguson and a second car to be built at the Granatelli's Santa Monica shop. Andy said that the entry would be the widest ever seen at Indianapolis, measuring six feet from the outer edge of one tire to the outer edge of the other. The wheels at the front and rear axle were set further apart, making the car wider, thus providing it with a wider track. Coincidentally, the cars also started using wider tires, although the main modification with respect to the chassis dealt with a new suspension which provided for expanded breath. Studebaker's entry followed the spectacular success enjoyed by the Ford Motor Company in the previous 500 when the rear engine Lotuses finished 2nd (Clark) and 7th (Gurney).

A week after the Studebaker-STP press announcement, a top Ford official, Vice President Lee A. Iacocca said that the company planned a strong racing program for the following year. Iacocca said, "We expect to gain important product knowledge not only from the oval tracks of the U.S. stock car races, from Indianapolis and from the sports car races in which the Ford powered Cobras are setting the pace, but also from LeMans and some of the other top competitive events of Europe." Continuing, Iacocca said that preliminary tests of a new double overhead cam racing engine at the Indianapolis Speedway were successful and the development of these engines was proceeding. With the press announcements coming forth from Studebaker and Ford, one could well envision a car manufacturer's battle in the next 500 run.

It appeared obvious that Studebaker was seeking a larger share of the American passenger car market. In so doing, it would risk its name in the hazardous sport of auto racing for publicity benefits. By virtue of returning to auto racing, the firm was breaking the industry's self-imposed ban on factory sponsored racing. It took little imagination to realize that Ford and Studebaker officials hoped the racing results would pay off with increased sales. Beyond offering fans a chance to identify with car sponsorship by a major producer such would likely do more than just increase engineering advancements. That success could hopefully translate into generating greater passenger car sales.

The #6 car was back at the Speedway in early November for some additional Goodyear testing. During this appearance a Novi was to create a bit of historical lore in Indy history for on November 7, the wide track car, already wearing the Studebaker-STP identification, was driven by Studebaker test driver Paula Louise Murphy. Therefore, she became the first woman known to drive a championship car at the Speedway. It has been reported that on several occasions in the 1920s and 1930s several women had been driven around the track in the riding mechanic's seat of race cars. Among those who reportedly took such a ride was the famed aviatrix Amelia Earhart.

The 28 year old Murphy had earlier been involved in several LSR attempts with Studebakers equipped with Paxton superchargers. Running a Studebaker Avanti on a two way run at Bonneville, she had been clocked (by USAC timers) at 161.29 m.p.h., the fastest speed ever obtained by a female driver. With reporters and photographers present at Indy, Murphy's travels around the track consisted of three laps with her reaching a top speed of 90 m.p.h. After the three laps she was flagged off the track as officials seemed to have a case of the jitters. Indy track officials ordered the car to return to the pits. Years later, Vince Granatelli was to say that the run was primarily a promotional arrangement. It certainly worked, for the brief run did attract substantial press coverage from coast-to-coast.

The media certainly had a different angle what with a woman driver. Paula willingly posed for shots in the cockpit of the Novi. She was an extremely cooperative participant as photos were taken of her checking her appearance via a hand held compact mirror and then applying lipstick. Among those on hand were Andy Granatelli and Novi driver Jim Hurtubise. Andy flippantly said to Jim, "Herk, I never have this much trouble with you. I don't have to hand you a purse, comb and lipstick. But this driver sure beats you on looks." Driver Eddie Sachs, also on hand, complimented Paula for being able to get out of the pits without killing the engine. The effort was something that a number of novice male drivers at the track had not been able to quickly accom-

(1964) During the November testing of the Novi/Ferguson, Andy had Paula Murphy on hand. It provided an outstanding opportunity for publicity shots and a new angle for the media. The small "NOVI POWERED" lettering was the only visible identification to the Novi heritage.   I.M.S.

plish. Paula later stated that she had kept telling herself there was no way she was going to stall the car after hearing several Goodyear technicians in a heated discussion regarding her chances of even getting out of the pits. Murphy admitted that she had to press down with all available energy to get the car into gear. Granatelli conceded that he was not prepared to nominate Paula to drive a Novi, but that she was the best female prospect to race at the track some day.

(1964) Several closeup shots of the intricate detail involved in the construction of the Novi-Ferguson. The cockpit had quite an array of gauges. In the wheel photo the brake rotor appears to be all but swallowed by the puck. *Authors Collection*

Paula had driven sport cars competitively for six years in addition to having credentials with the Sports Car Club of America. She also possessed a USAC license for record trial runs. For her part, Murphy said that when she first saw female sport car drivers, "I thought those women must be crazy." She continued by saying that after moving to California she caught the racing bug and finally started driving an MG in competition.

Meanwhile in England, the Ferguson Company had started to build the 4WD car in late November of 1963. This was a rather optimistic approach as the final agreement with Studebaker/Granatelli to actually build the car was not finalized until December. Even with the early start, Ferguson was left with little time to complete its work. Some knowledge gained from the P99 run during the previous summer could be used, but in many ways the project was somewhat similar to approaching the drawing board for the first time. The new car was to be officially identified as the P104.

The project was guided by engineer Derrick Gardner who would gain considerable fame some years later when he designed the Tyrrell Formula One cars. The Tyrrells were leading racers from 1970 until 1977 and were used by Jackie Stewart in his runs in Formula One in 1971 and 1973 that propelled him into the World Championship. The highly remarkable Tyrrell P34 Formula One six wheeler car used in 1976 and 1977 was also Gardner's brain child. The P34 did not have four wheels at the rear like the long remembered Pat Clancy Special that raced at Indy in 1948 and 1949, but four small wheels at the front.

Some English magazines contained articles about the P104 project asserting that it was hoped that the car would be completed in time for testing at the Speedway in late March. Otherwise an alternative car would be used on the one mile Phoenix, Arizona track. As it turned out, the company's work on the car was completed by March, having consumed just five months of labor. It was immediately dispatched to the United States for testing at Indianapolis. It goes without saying, that the testing of the Ferguson was contemplated with tremendous exhileration within the Novi camp.

Tire testing, in preparation for the 1964 Indy 500, was also scheduled during March. No less than four different tire manufacturers were on hand to test their products during separate weeks. The group consisted of Firestone, Goodyear, Dunlop and Sears.

The blower used on the Novi-Ferguson. On the lower left edge of the blower housing is the plug to remove condensed fuel that may have remained within the unit after switching off the engine. The draining was performed prior to restarting the engine.
Authors Collection

77

The Novis were on hand to participate in these tests. Bobby Unser drove the wide track Goodyear shod Kurtis-Kraft chassis; the same chassis he had used in the 1963 race. However, in 1963 it was the original narrow track layout that carried the #6 identification. For the 1964 race it had been renumbered as #28.

(1964) Bobby Unser was on hand to lend assistance in the early adjustment work in order to have the Ferguson 4WD in top form come May. It was a cold March day as the crew continued to worked on the car.   I.M.S.

While the Ferguson was on its way to America, Bobby Unser set a new straightaway speed in the #28 Novi as he reached a straightaway trap speed of 194.38 m.p.h. This demonstration of power (averaging over 152 m.p.h. for the entire lap) was not enough to surpass the speeds achieved by Bobby Marshman and A.J. Foyt in their rear engine cars. Marshman drove an updated 1963 Lotus with a brand new Quadcam Ford V-8 while Foyt drove a Joe Huffaker-Offy which featured a 'Hydragas' suspension system developed by the British Leyand firm. The car was identified as the MG Liquid Suspension Special.

A.J. Foyt also took a ride in the #28 Kurtis-Kraft Novi and was over 149 m.p.h. on his first hot lap. On his third hot lap A.J. averaged over 151 m.p.h. According to Andy, coming into the pits Foyt "told at least ten people including (George) Bignotti that the engine was four times stronger than the best Offy he ever drove and if the car handled through the corners it would be a whole new deal." Foyt offered a considerable amount of praise for the Novi, especially noting its acceleration and the power of the car. Yet, he considered the behavior of the car in the turns to be subpar.

One Novi crewman vividly recalled Foyt's outing in the Novi. The car had been fitted with a new front axle and the right front wheel was nine or ten inches further away from the bodywork. The concept dealt with the chassis being set further out to increase stability. With the car ready for test driving, Andy managed to convince Foyt to take a ride in the car. The crewman reported, "Foyt got in and in two laps he went faster than the car had ever been driven! Instantly!" The crewman also recalled that when Foyt returned to the pits he had a hand up before his mouth. This caused some concern as crew members thought he might have been hit in the face by some flying object since full face helmets were not yet in vogue. As Foyt lowered his hand, they saw that he was smiling from ear to ear. He told Andy that he (Foyt) hoped that Granatelli would never figure out how to make the car handle properly. When Andy inquired about the statement, Foyt replied, "Because I have to race against you." According to one source, Andy spent the evening urging Foyt to drive a Novi offering a substantial amount of money for his services. Yet, Foyt refused to accept any such proposal.

(1964) As work continued to properly adjust the 4WD Novi, additional time was spent at the Speedway sorting out problems. Among the chauffeurs was A.J. Foyt. The latest approach had the right side wheels extended beyond the norm. Foyt was less than enthralled with this arrangement.   I.M.S.

According to Foyt, if the cornering problem could be resolved he felt that nothing could stop the Novi. Foyt also turned down a request by Granatelli to help setup a Novi by saying that he would be unable to touch the Novi during a race by doing so.

All of this leaves a tantalizing thought. What might have happened to the Novi's level of performance if men such as A.J. Foyt and/or Parnelli

Jones had accepted the offers of Granatelli to drive for him? The pair were considered not only the outstanding drivers of the era, but they were also well versed in chassis setups. The Novis always seemed to come up short with respect to decent handling and Foyt's reaction suggested that they were still far removed from a proper setup. Foyt was asked about his thoughts on the front suspension setup with its "extended" right wheel. A.J. was very outspoken in his belief that such a setup was causing him to experience a handling problem. Therefore, he could not get the car to the speed it was capable as the condition caused him to drive slower.

When further discussion about the Novi was attempted with A.J., he was unable to draw upon his memory for any pertinent information. A.J. has driven so many cars during his 35 years of Indy competition it is understandable that a brief test hop could be quickly forgotten. The now defunct Indianapolis Times (3/31/1964) reported that both Bobby Unser and A.J. Foyt reached speeds in excess of 150 m.p.h. during Goodyear testing. In addition, C. Lee Norquest also mentioned Foyt's ride in the car in his The Fabulous Novi Story. Correspondence between Norquest and Granatelli regarding the tire testing further reveals that Foyt did drive the blown V-8.

(1964) During the spring shakedown effort, a fire erupted in the Novi garage. Cinders rest on the hood while it appears that other parts were completely free of any remnants of the blaze.

I.M.S.

Nevertheless, the Novi car that could presumably solve the cornering problem made its first lap. The long awaited appearance of the Novi-Ferguson 4WD was at hand. It might be pointed out that some time expired before the car was truly ready to take to the oval as the water pump had to be removed as it was airlocked when the engine was initially cranked. Therefore, the first appearance was far from exhilarating to say the least. Later that afternoon, the engine did start and Andy took the Ferguson out for its first shakedown laps around the track. There were some slow warm up laps, but Andy returned quite impressed with his new "toy." Even though it was raining, Andy claimed he had been clocked at 128 m.p.h. reaching some 7,000 rpms in third gear using Dunlop tires. The temptation to drive this new Novi had been understandably quite strong and irresistible for Andy. While he was duly impressed by the car's handling, he was certainly less than enthralled with a developing oil leak. When the car was examined it was discovered that the Ferguson Company had set the oil tank for right hand cornering as they were accustomed to doing for the European cars prepared for road courses. The problem was temporarily fixed in order to continue testing for several more days. According to correspondence between Granatelli and Norquest, Andy asserted that the oil leak was not from the Novi engine but through a vent line as a result of the oil tank being set up for right hand cornering. A day of rest was observed on Easter, March 29, but the following day Bobby Unser moved out from the pits in the Ferguson for some additional shakedown laps. With the prevalence of cold weather, he completed only 23 laps reaching a top speed of 145 m.p.h. while in third gear.

It has been reported that the following incident occurred during one of the first runs with the car. On that occasion, Vince Granatelli and A.J. Foyt allegedly drove a pace car as they followed the Ferguson out on the track to see how it reacted. Foyt told Vince that he did not like to view the car from the rear. Vince then told A.J.

(1964) The greatest damage may well have been incurred on the garage and most particularly to the roof.

I.M.S.

A publicity shot of the Novi-Ferguson. The Fergie 4WD is ready to go.   Authors Collection

that he had better get use to it because that was all Foyt was going to see during the race. Little did they realize what the future had in store for the Ferguson-Novi.

During the evening of March 31, a fire broke out in one of the garages (#52) used by the Granatellis damaging the Ferguson and the #28 roadster. The Novi team was fortunate that the fire was discovered early by Barney Larkin, a senior research technician with the Ford Motor Company. Thanks to Ford crew members, Superintendent of Grounds Clarence Cagle, the fire department and the early discovery of the blaze, it did not reach disastrous proportions. The Novi crew did lose some of their equipment such as tools and spare parts, but in large measure, the Novis emerged unscathed. Cagle stated that the cause of the fire was most likely due to a short in an electric heater situated on a work bench in the garage that had been used to knock off the chill of the cool March weather. Cagle estimated the damage in the garage area to be approximately $10,000. Surveying the damage Andy commented, "If something like this had to happen I wish the whole outfit would have burned up. Then I would have had an excuse to get out of this business and live like a human being." Years later Clarence recalled, "They had a heater in there...We didn't allow it but they found a way. They were like the Katzenjammer Kids, they found a way."

Andy and the crew then gathered up their remaining equipment and prepared to return to California. Andy then stated that he now had every intention of entering all three Novis in the upcoming race. There was no way the Novis were not going to be back at the Speedway in May.

To some veteran railbirds the fire brought to mind the Gasoline Alley conflagration that occurred on the morning of the 1941 race. Fortunately, only one qualified car was prevented from participating in the race, that of driver George Barringer.

On May 1, the three Novis were once again parked in Gasoline Alley. The Novi team had again performed some tidy work in preparing their cars for the rapidly approaching race.

Chapter 10

EARLIER FOUR WHEEL DRIVE EFFORTS

The Novi-Ferguson 4WD was not the first Indy car entered using such an arrangement. There had been several cars in earlier 500s that had raced with such a driveline. Five different types of 4WD had been entered over the years (if one excludes the Clancy 6-wheeler which delivered power to all four rear wheels) and three of them had raced at least once. The results had not impressed the racing fraternity, otherwise most definitely, a large contingency of such cars would have been built. With the Novi 4WD destined to take its place in Indy history, permit a brief look at the earlier Indy 4WD cars.

The 4WD concept had been around for a longtime, yet little attention had been rendered to this automotive arrangement. Some American automotive historians claim that the first 4WD car had an American heritage due to the existence of the Twyford. This vehicle had a very complicated and crude 4WD layout. Designer Robert Twyford came up with a prototype (circa 1898) and a patent was granted in 1900. However, his car had no differentials which must have limited the practical use of the vehicle. The steering mechanism of the chassis was said to be inconvenient for mechanical work. If the questionable designing was not enough, all sorts of problems manifested themselves with the few Twyfords that were built.

(1906) The "clothed" 4WD. The signage indicates that the car is "Driven On Four Wheels." Courtesy of Win Oude Weernink

It is generally believed that the very first practical 4WD ever built was of Dutch heritage. The car was built by the Spijker brothers in 1903. They gave their car the name Spyker, possibly for some "international flavor." The 4WD Spyker, dubbed 60/80 HP was also the first six cylinder engine car to ever appear on the road. The Spyker Company went out of business in 1925. However, the aforementioned car still exists and is on permanent display in the Autotron Museum at Rosmalen, The Netherlands. By coincidence, the town is the community where future Indy 500 winner Arie Luyendyk spent part of his early years.

In general, the use of a modern high tech differential is the difference between the Twyford, the Spyker and modern day 4WD. Items such as the limited slip differential, visco-differentials, the Torsen Gleason differential and the X-TRAC to name a few, did not exist at that time. Yet, the Spyker 4WD basically had everything an adequate 4WD needed. It had a center differential to split torque and power to the axles. To obtain a decent handling 4WD chassis, no matter if it was for a truck, an off-road vehicle, a passenger car or a purebred competition machine, a driveline containing three differentials provided the best solution and the Spijker brothers recognized such back in 1906.

(1906) The world's first practical 4WD, a six cylinder Spyker. The construction was performed by the Spijker brothers of Holland. Courtesy of Win Oude Weernink

81

As for the competitiveness of the 4WD Spyker, Jacobus Spijker raced the car in the 1906 Birmingham Hill Climb and won handsomely in a pouring rain. But like early supercharged engines, the 4WD principle did not gain wide spread use within racing circles and it took many years before it reappeared. Bugatti was one of the first to do so when it introduced a 4WD Bugati T53 in the 1930s. That was the time the first 4WDs appeared at Indy.

In considering the Indy 4WDs, we begin with a failure. A 4WD appeared at Indianapolis in 1932 identified as a Coleman Four Wheel Special. The car, to be driven by rookie Fred Merzney, was to be powered by an unspecified Miller, but it failed to qualify. The very first 4WD car to make the race at the Brickyard was built by famed racing engineer/builder Harry Miller. Two such cars were built in 1932 and one of them was sold to the Four Wheel Drive Company of Clintonville, Wisconsin. The firm had been building 4WD trucks for many years, then saw great potential in becoming engaged in promotion by participating in the famed Indianapolis Sweepstakes race. Miller was interested in trying the 4WD layout to combine the advantages of both front and rear drive in a single car, for after all, he had constructed cars in the past that had power trains in either the front or the rear. In their first two years, the Miller built 4WDs ran with a 300 horsepower Miller V-8. This V-8 engine had an unusual block angle of 45 degrees with a single plane crankshaft. Both cars were driven in the 1932 race, but they were the second and third cars to retire from the contest. Outstanding sprint car ace Gus Schrader wrecked the Miller factory owned car after 7 laps and was classified as 39th finisher in the 40 car field. The Four Wheel Drive Company owned car retired after 17 laps due to a broken oil line to finish 38th. Driver Bob McDonough had shown some great promise in qualifying (113.275 m.p.h.) which gave the car the tenth fastest qualifying speed, although he had to start the race from the 38th position.

The following year the 4WD owned by the Wisconsin company was driven by Frank Brisko, but the V-8 had an oiling problem that caused the bearings to fail. Such a calamity caused the car to finish 36th in a field of 42 starters. Unhappy with the Millers performance, Brisko worked on the engine over the winter and drove the car again the following year (1934). He was rewarded with a 9th place with relief help provided by driver Rex Mays. However, in reminiscing about his Indy driving career, that consisted of twelve races, Frank Brisko said that during his two years with the 4WD he was not overly impressed with its performance. One point of interest with this particular 4WD rests with the fact that the transfer case could be set to use only one set of wheels if so desired.

In 1935, Mauri Rose drove the car to a 20th place finish, pulling off after 103 laps due to some sort of mechanical failure with the 4WD. The following year, he lead the race for some

(1933) Driver Frank Brisko along with riding mechanic Johnny Hughes in the FWD Special. The car was entered by the Four Wheel Drive Company of Clintonville, WI as a means of publicizing its 4WD vehicles - trucks, fire engines and the like. Frank finished a lowly 36th in the 42 car field, the result of an oiling problem that created havoc on the engine bearings. Over the winter Frank redesigned the engine and the car finished 9th as he went the entire 500 miles. Mauri Rose then drove the car several years before Tony Willman had a go at it in 1937. Rose had the best finish, a 4th in 1936. Some drivers facetiously referred to FWD as meaning "Flirting With Death." I.M.S.

time before eventually finishing 4th after starting 30th in what was to prove to be the last year for this car at the Speedway. The sister car never qualified after the 1932 contest, although it was entered in 1934 with Pete DePaolo, the 1925 Indianapolis winner listed as the driver. However, the entry was eventually withdrawn.

The next year there was an absence of any 4WDs, although a single rear engine entry was made. While the concept may have caused some interest, it was far from being competitive. As a consequence, no qualification was even attempted. The odd appearing car was equipped with a 183 c.i. straight 6 Marmon.

The 1938 race witnessed the entry of several remarkable cars constructed by Harry Miller. He had worked with the Gulf Oil Company to create a 4WD car that would be a potent competitor. The supercharged Miller 4WDs were also unique in that the engine placement was behind the driver.

As it were, several of the constructed cars succumbed to tragic endings. While the cars did not qualify in 1938, one made the starting field in 1939. Driver George Bailey experienced a valve spring problem that forced the Miller-Gulf car to the sidelines early to finish 26th. Only eight cars had qualified faster than Bailey. The situation appeared to be similar to what was to face the Novis shortly thereafter; fast in qualifying but often falling from the field long before the checkered flag appeared. While Bailey had made the race (125.821 m.p.h.), two other Miller 4WDs failed to achieve starting spots. Zeke Miller was unhappy with the performance of his car while Johnny Seymour wrecked his 4WD in practice.

The following year, Bailey's car went out of control during a practice session and he was fatally injured. The remaining cars were back in 1941 with two qualifying for the race. The drivers were George Barringer and Al Miller. Even before the race began hard times befell the Miller-Gulf team. As mentioned earlier, on the morning of the race a blaze surged through some of the garages. When the fire was extinguished only one of the destroyed cars was among those that had qualified for the race - Barringer's! As for Miller, his car lasted 22 laps before it was forced out due to a transmission failure. The result: a 28th place finish. After World War II, Barringer drove one of the 4WDs (1946), but it was an early departure as he finished 26th due to a gear problem. One last charge was made by Al Miller in the 1947 contest driving a car sponsored by Preston Tucker (of Tucker Torpedo automobile fame) only to finish 25th. None of the quartet of Miller-Gulf 4WDs survived the full 500 miles or even finished reasonably well in the results. It has been stated that the cars handled well as a result of the 4WD. The bad performances by the Miller cars was due in part to the Gulf Company insisting that the cars use regular pump fuel instead of any type of blended fuel mixture suitable for supercharged engines. The type of gas that the Gulf Company demanded for use was the same type of fuel as sold at Gulf gas stations. Such a power disadvantage certainly did little to help the cars. Ease in handling was of little consequence if the speed was not there.

For the 1946 race, Ohio bus manufacturer Lou Fageol entered a unique 4WD car - the Fageol Twin Coach Special. The car's power was derived from two supercharged Offy midget engines, one

(1941) George Barringer in one of the 4WD cars built by Harry Miller for the Gulf Oil Company. A fire on race morning in the garage area destroyed the qualified car.   I.M.S.

employed at each axle. Paul Russo's qualifying time was 126.183 m.p.h. The extraordinary speed displayed on the first day of the time trials had him start the first post-war race from second place, sandwiched between pole sitter Cliff Bergere (who would drive a Novi in the 1947 race) and Sam Hanks in Gordon Schroeder's 16-cylinder Sampson Spike Jones Special. Qualifying later, Ralph Hepburn shattered the existing qualifying record with his time of 134.449 m.p.h. The sizzling run in the Novi Governor's Special was such that it deservedly overshadowed the times of Bergere (126.471 m.p.h.), Rex Mays (128.861 m.p.h.) and Russo: the only drivers over 126 m.p.h. The Fageol car's run was impressive early on, yet Russo crashed on lap 16 to finish last. No further 4WD efforts were made at Indy until the arrival of the Ferguson car in 1964.

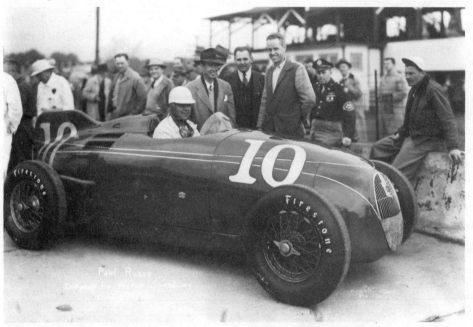

(1946) Driver Paul Russo at the wheel of a unique racer. It was a 4WD creation as each axle was driven by an Offy midget engine. The Fageol Twin Coach Special finished last as Paul crashed on lap 16. Ohio industrialist, Lou Fageol, a builder of school busses, chose not to enter the car in any future 500s.   I.M.S.

Although the Indy car designers had completely turned away from 4WD, European car constructors were enticed by the idea. The group included the Porsche firm that produced a mid-engine 4WD with a 91 c.i. (1.5 liter), Roots blown flat 12 cylinder engine. While it set one world speed record, the project was set aside as the appropriated funds were depleted.

There was also some talk about Mercedes moving to 4WD with their nearly invincible W196 Grand Prix cars in the mid-1950s, though these plans never came to fruition. About the same time, Alfa Romeo was giving some thought to a 4WD Formula One car; however the project never got off the ground. Then in 1961, the Ferguson P99 made its appearance and the car's performance was sufficient to provide food for thought. The concept then fell victim to the rear engine revolution which had started earlier in Formula One.

We have referred to the stillborn 1961 Novi rear engine car as being one of the more mysterious aspects of the Novi legend. A second project has received even less exposure. Bud Winfield had considered building a 4WD front engine Novi in the late 1940s shortly before his death. The only information we have acquired was related by former Novi driver Duke Nalon. He has mentioned that Winfield came up with such a plan to build a 4WD Novi due to the extraordinary tire wear and the lack of gripping power during acceleration. The plans were never executed, and with Winfield's untimely death, in late 1950, the concept was put aside. What might have happened if Winfield had lived we will never know. Duke also mentioned that Andy Granatelli had contacted him about the 4WD plans of Bud Winfield. While no 4WD Novi appeared in the 1950s it seems that a bit of thought was being considered for such an undertaking.

Former 4WD driver Frank Brisko said that Andy Granatelli had also asked for his input as the American group sought to evaluate the possibilities of a 4WD race car. Brisko informed us that he "passed on to Andy Granatelli all the things that I had tried when using a 4WD." His departing remark to Granatelli was "now you go from there."

As has been pointed out, the primary problem with the earlier 4WD cars was that each of the wheels was traveling at a different rate of speed in the turns. Thus, in a sense they were "fighting" each other. The result: tricky handling. The Novi Ferguson was reported to have largely overcome the problem as each wheel received a different amount of power. Only time would tell if the design was suitable.

Chapter 11

THE NOVI ARMADA - 1964

The Studebaker-STP team "armada" that Andy Granatelli intended to use in 1964 consisted of the three cars as noted in a press release made available late in 1963. A good deal of detailed technical specifications regarding the Novis was supplied in the promotional literature. While the three cars were basically of two different chassis types, the supposedly twin Novis differed from one another in some detail. Before we provide coverage regarding the cars, permit us to deal with the one "standard" piece of equipment. All three cars contained the Novi V-8 engine.

Apart from having developed one new chassis and two up-dated versions of the existing cars, the Granatellis had carried out some changes with the engines. The main priority had been given to the relocation of the fuel injection units and the oil coolers in order to provide for a smoother body line silhouette. The Bendix fuel system which had been perfected for use with the Novi engine had been retained.

The bore of the engines was reported to be 3.2 inches (81.28 mm) and the stroke 2.6 inches (66.04 mm), giving a capacity of 168 c.i. (2753 cc). The power output of the engines had dropped slightly from the previous year as the Novi produced 700 horsepower. The reduction notwithstanding, the Novi remained well above all other entries in the horsepower department. It was anticipated that there would be increased reliability due to the use of benzol - i.e., better fuel consumption.

The power was supplied to the flywheel and transferred to the gearbox with the use of a 9 plate clutch measuring 9 inches (22.86 cm). The weight of the engine was cited at 470 pounds (231 kg), a considerable reduction compared to the 575 pounds in previous years. Yet, the Novi was still the heaviest of all engines entered for the race. All the Novi engines were reported to be identical with no listed differences between the Ferguson and the roadsters.

The two rear drive roadsters were to be entered under number 3 and 28. The #3 was the #56 Hurtubise car of 1963 and the #28 had carried the #6 when driven by Bobby Unser a year earlier. The frame weight was reduced by extensive drilling in the units at all points where it seemed likely that the drilling would not cause undue stress. The frame weight of #28 was listed as 170 pounds. The weight of the cars with engine, fuel, fluids and driver was listed as 2,200 pounds (998 kg). Compared with 1963, both cars had new nosecones which lacked the previous bulges. They also lacked the secondary air scoop on top of the upper surface giving the front end of the cars a much smoother profile. For the purists: the air intakes within the cones differed slightly for the two cars. It shall be noted that during May the #28 was further altered in appearance regarding the nosecone.

The Granatellis, having learned an all-important lesson regarding the gearing as a result of the start of the 1963 race (the low gear was too shallow and the top gear too high to allow for a proper running engine), the Kurtis-Krafts were now fitted with "functioning" three speed gearboxes, designed and built at Paxton.

Paxton also made the radiators and oil coolers with a seven gallon (22.2 liters) capacity. The oil coolers on the cars were located on the left side below the cockpit and just above the exhaust manifold. The oil cooler for the Ferguson was different in that it was not teardrop shape, but fashioned to the configuration of the side of the car. The air that passed through the coolers was to be vented off by a side mounted exhaust ducting in the bodywork.

The air filters were located just in front of the injectors and were inclined at a 45 degree angle. All bodywork was made out of magnesium and aluminum panels.

The #3 used Airheart disc brakes while #28 used Halibrand binders, but both systems utilized Raybestos linings. The tires were also dif-

Studebaker at Indianapolis 1933-1964

(1964) This Joe Henning drawing appeared in the <u>1964 Clymer Indianapolis 500 Mile Race Yearbook</u>. It denotes the fact that the Studebaker Corporation, which had entered several cars in the 1933 race, was once again active in Indianapolis competition. Shown are Zeke Meyer and his riding mechanic Walter Mitchell in the #9 Studebaker entry of 1933 and Bobby Unser in the 1964 4WD Novi financed by Studebaker through its STP Division.
Courtesy of Joe Henning

ferent for the two cars as the #3 was to run on Firestone tires, while the #28 was scheduled to use Goodyears. Both cars were to use Halibrand magnesium wheels with size 15 inch x 8½ inch at the front and 15 inch x 9½ inch on the rear.

With the bullet shaped headrest used on the cars a year earlier removed, and apart from the roll bar and fuel tank fillers the rear deck was almost flat. The outer skin of the fuel tank served as the bodywork for the tail.

Some facts and figures: the wheelbase of both cars was 96 inches (243.8 cm), both cars used the wide track setup which measured 53 inches (134.6 cm) and 51 inches (129.5 cm). Contrary to the late 1963 press release, there was no narrow track car.

Of course, the most interesting of the three Novis was the 4WD Ferguson. The entire chassis, as noted earlier, had been built in England, while the engine and the gearbox were American products. The construction of the P104 chassis called for a semi-monocoque center section and it was built of square chrome-moly tubing. The monocoque side sections and the cockpit shell were made of an aluminum alloy with the frame listed at a weight of 95 pounds.

The suspension used on the car was of a special wishbone arrangement, fully independent all around. The springs were mounted inboard with Armstrong type AT10 adjustable shocks. At the front, the shocks were located before the axle, while the rear shocks were behind its axle.

The Fergie's wheelbase was 100 inches (254 cm), the tracks at front and rear were 60 inches (152.4 cm) with an overall width of 72 inches. The overall length was 166 inches (421.6 cm); thus four inches longer than that of the roadsters. The maximum height of the car was 28 inches (71.1 cm) with a ground clearance of three and three-fourths inches (9.5 cm). Dunlop 7.5 x 15 Indy designed tires were to be used on all corners, so

(1964) An excellent photograph of the Novi supercharged engine and the elaborate front wheel driveline and suspension. Authors Collection

the three Novis would all ran on different brands of tires. The Dunlop tires were mounted on Dunlop mag alloy rims and the brakes for the car were activated by twin master cylinders.

Unquestionably, the most interesting feature of the car was the power application to all four wheels. Ferguson had promoted their 4WD system for all types of vehicles; from luxury sport cars to off-road duty vehicles and a Formula One car; this being the Project 99. The system had worked very well under most circumstances. The driveline installed in the Novi-Ferguson had undergone enormous testing beyond that provided for any so-called "standard" Ferguson 4WD. No doubt the Ferguson 4WD system now faced the ultimate test; coping with the tremendous power and torque of a Novi V-8 engine.

The transmission housing was composed of a magnesium casting. The axles received their power via the following route: the power was transmitted into a four speed gearbox with a constant dog mesh engagement. The gearbox was fully designed for lubrication, although it lacked a reverse. From there the power was carried to a special version of the Ferguson center differential, then to the four wheel drive control unit. This unit was specially constructed for use with the powerful Novi engine. It was reported to have a variable torque splitting capacity of between 30:70 and 60:40 over the front/rear axles. No figures were made available on the actual torque split ratio beyond the suggestion that it very likely used the standard 50:50. However, a source within the Granatelli organization stated that 30:70 turned out to be the best setup.

From the 4WD control unit, the power went to the differentials within the two axles via propshafts. The final drive units were identical at front and rear. The gearbox was so constructed that it laid to the left, thus enabling the two drive shafts to the front and rear axles to be situated on the left side of the engine, giving left weight bias in the process. The engine itself was not mounted offset in the chassis.

The drive shafts and universal joints were Dunlop-Bendix CVs and were situated at each wheel. Because of the offset driveline, the final drive units at the axles utilized extending parts at

(1964) Andy and several crew members laboring on the Novi-Ferguson. The complex layout appears to be a nightmare for the non-mechanical souls among us.
Authors Collection

88

the right side which enabled the use of identical CVs all around the car. The team had a range of primary reduction gears available to gear the car to reach top straightaway speeds from approximately 150 m.p.h. on up toward 200 m.p.h.

The bodywork of the car was constructed out of an aluminum based alloy. The primary fuel tanks, saddle mounted, were of the flexible bag type made by Marston Excelcior. A reserve tank was located in the tail of the car. It was hoped that the fuel capacity would be sufficient to require only one pit stop for fuel and tires. Of course, such a strategy was dependent on the fuel consumption and tire wear. A combined oil tank and oil cooler was mounted outside of the bodywork of the car on the left side just below the cockpit. The large chrome plated tank made it highly visible. This exterior tank had not been on the car during the March testing.

But there were more visual differences to the car. The car had appeared for the first test runs in March with a slightly different body work than that used in May. During the early test the air intake was wide but had a low slot-like opening. After the March 31, Gasoline Alley fire, the rebuilt car ran without such an air intake on the upper deck of the nosecone. The tail section had also been changed. The car was originally delivered with a tail that curved to a point. The P104 appeared at Indy in May with a more square, box-like tail.

The cockpit panel contained gauges for the engine's oil temperature, water temperature, oil pressure and the fuel pressure. There was also a Smith's rev counter with a maximum of 9,000 rpm.

According to specifications released by STP, the Ferguson weighed in at 2,000 pounds (905 kg), with all fluids, fuel and driver on board. This would make it 10 percent lighter than the two roadsters despite the extra weight for the more complex driveline system. Andy Granatelli has recounted a different view regarding the car following delivery in respect to weight. In recalling his years with the Novi, Granatelli stated that after having made the decision to go for 4WD: "I flew over to England, talked to Major Rolt and commissioned the building of a car. They built me a tank instead of a car! They built me a 2,400 pound race car while the rules were for 1,500 pound cars!" Vince Granatelli sadly recalls that the Ferguson weighed as much as some sport cars. The 1,500 pound rule was the minimum weight for Indy race cars. So the figures released regarding the car were likely to be quite optimistic. Whatever the weight, Andy's comment about it being a tank is not far off target. Indeed, its very appearance was that of a bulky car. The weight distribution over the front and rear axle was a reported 46-54 with full tanks and changing to 54-46 when empty. Although the car had its engine positioned up front, some people felt that it was not a roadster in the true sense of the word as the engine was not offset to the left. The V-8 was located in the middle of the chassis with the cockpit offset somewhat to the right. Without question, the car was one of the most expensive creations to reach the Speedway up to that time and technically one of the most interesting.

(1964) An on-going task with any racing team - working with engine installation and/or removal. Such endeavors sometimes seem to be a daily chore. Instruments on the dash include (left to right) the on/off switch, oil temperature, a large tach, oil pressure, water temperature and fuel pressure. The oil tank/cooler is neatly placed at the left of the cockpit as it fits the contour of the body shell.   *Authors Collection*

Chapter 12

A Trio of Novis in Field Again

As May arrived, one familiar face on the Novi team was missing. Jean Marenac had retired and left the Novi organization after a tenure of 14 years. The affable Marcenac had joined the Novi operation in 1949 as car owner Lew Welch hired him when he added a second Novi to the team. Jean's participation in Indy car competition had started in 1920 when he served as a riding mechanic. (Marcenac's racing career is contained in Chapter 23 of Volume I). With Jean's departure, a longtime love affair with his beloved Novi had come to an end. His departure, at age 69, did not create the great void one might have expected. The Granatellis now had a "good handle" on the Novi engine though Jean's absence did not go unnoticed. The amiable and well-respected Marcenac certainly would be missed by a legion of friends.

Not only was Marcenac absent from the scene; other changes had quite naturally occurred. Certainly one of the most formidable was Ford's introduction of its V-8 Quadcam Indy engine. The debut heralded the arrival of a powerful racing version of the Ford Fairlane. The powerplant contained four valves per cylinder and DOHC cylinder heads. The valve angle was altered to fit the Hilborn injectors between the camshafts. This arrangement had the exhaust manifolds running down the center of the engine, giving the top of the engine's powerplant the appearance of a "plumber's nightmare." Ford's backing on this project was massive to say the least.

The year was certainly to prove very interesting. Would the front engine roadster be able to withstand the attack of the rear engine machinery to say nothing of the new 4WD creation offered by the Novi camp? Several of the top teams were heavily financed by Ford with its advanced experimental engines. No less than 24 of the cars entered contained rear engines. To add to the interest, some Offy powered rear engine cars were also on hand. Surprisingly, among the rear engine entries was Australian driver Jack Brabham, who had left Indy after the 1961 race somewhat in disgust, his ninth place showing notwithstand-

(1964) Bobby Unser and the Novi are back together for a second year. C. Lee Norquest, author of <u>The Fabulous Novi Story</u> booklet welcomes Andy upon the team's return to Indianapolis. Note the Goodyear tires.
I.M.S.

ing. In spite of his earlier unhappiness, he was once again on the scene to do battle; this time with his own rear engine creation. As for the Novi camp, they felt extremely confident, particularly in regard to the 4WD. An indication as to how strongly Andy felt about the unrelenting challenges by the Novi was demonstrated via a remark accorded to him. In the volume, Parnelli, author Bill Libby quoted Andy as saying, "The Novi is a virgin with the habits of a harlot, I just can't give up on it until I make it with her."

The three cars were all entered under the name of Studebaker-STP Special with each having its own color scheme. The #3 was painted dark blue with a striking pink used for the number. The #28 was white and red and the numerals on the hood and nosecone were filled with small STP decals, thus giving the appearance of the number being made up entirely of decals. The numbers on the tail, however, were without the decals. The Ferguson was painted red, except for the chrome plated side mounted oil tank, while the car's numeral 9 was silver.

Two drivers were under contract by early February. Bobby Unser was back and assigned to the #28, the same car he had driven the previous year. Meanwhile, Jim McElreath, who had finished in 6th place in the two previous races, was assigned to handle the chores with the #3 Novi. Both men had driven Novis in tire tests at the Speedway since the previous 500. You may recall McElreath's splendid runs in a Novi the previous summer when he reached speeds in excess of 150 m.p.h.

Jim, a soft spoken taciturn Texan who let his driving do much of the talking, had gained a reputation as a steady driver with nerves of steel. He had begun his career shortly after World War II driving modified stocks in the Dallas, Texas area. After racing in the Lone Star state through the Fifties, Jim stepped up to the tough IMCA sprint circuit where in 1961 he had established himself as a top contender. His sharp driving skills were aptly displayed when he won the 1961 running of the Little 500 at the Sun Valley Speedway (now known as the Anderson Speedway) in Anderson, Indiana. Imagine the stamina needed to drive a 500 lap sprint car contest over a quarter mile track. With the stellar performances, the seemingly imperturbable McElreath was offered a ride in that fall's Hoosier Hundred at the Indianapolis State Fairgrounds. He showcased his abilities by finishing third behind winner A.J. Foyt and Bobby Marshman. In 1962, he made the starting field in the Indy 500 in Ollie Prather's car. His 6th place finish earned him Rookie of the Year honors. The following year he brought Bill Forbes' car home for a second consecutive 6th place showing. During the remainder of the year, he finished 8th or better in all champ car races except the Milwaukee 200. After his departure from the Novi operation, Jim was to have some additional stunning performances at Indy: he was 3rd in 1966; 5th twice -1967, 1970; and 6th in 1974. Further, Jim was the winner of the inaugural champ car race held at the Ontario Speedway in California in 1970.

When the Speedway opened for practice on May 1 for the 1964 classic race, all three of the Novis were on hand and the crew was ready to begin shakedown work. Yet, the Ferguson car was still without a driver. It was made clear that an assignment would be announced at a later date, although there seemed to be a general understanding that McElreath could take over the 4WD if he so desired. Missing from the Novi driver lineup was Art Malone. Malone reports that after checking out the 4WD he was not ready to commit to the ride. Several factors came into place regarding his decision. Art was distressed that the driveline lacked an adequate protective cover. It consisted of only 600 aluminum sheeting and the line was virtually at his

(1964) Two of the Novi drivers, Jim McElreath and Bobby Unser. There is no shortage of the STP logo.   I.M.S.

91

side. Beyond that, Malone noted that the frame was brazed; which was not much different from a soldering job.

Art's fine performance the previous year had attracted the attention of long-time car owner Jim Robbins. As a consequence, Malone was able to take over the driving duties in Robbins' Auto-Crat Seatbelt Special. To Art's surprise Granatelli made no effort to prevent the move over to Robbins. There were no hard feelings and Andy came up with an even greater surprise. He informed Malone that he could rejoin the Novi organization if he so desired. If conditions did not work out favorably with Robbins a ride would be waiting for Art. Andy Granatelli certainly displayed a bit of sportsmanship in regard to Malone's departure.

Therefore, as practice began, the STP team had only two drivers - at least for the time being. Both Unser and McElreath drove the Ferguson in the first days of May. Jim was at the wheel first, as he went out on opening day. He cruised around the track at speeds that reached 145.2 m.p.h. which turned out to be the fastest lap for any driver during the day. Following that driving stint, Jim reported that the car felt "heavy like a Cadillac or Lincoln." McElreath had only one mechanical problem during practice and it involved a wheel hub difficulty, although no damage was incurred. However, another minor mishap did transpire as McElreath's goggles were blown off his face when he reached the high speeds as the result of an improperly shaped windscreen. In discussing his experiences with the Ferguson racer years later, McElreath said that after his early runs in the car he backed away as he considered it still in the experimental stage and he preferred to drive a proven car. As previously noted, several other Indy veterans saw fit to avoid a Novi ride over the years for the same reason.

Also on hand early in the month were the two Lotus cars receiving direct help from the Ford Motor Company. The driver assignments had been given to Jimmy Clark and Bobby Marshman. On hand to assist with the Lotus operation was car owner/builder Colin Chapman. The Ferguson Company was not to be "left in the dust" as they were quite involved with the performance of "their" car. The invaluable services of Tony Rolt, the technical director at Ferguson, were available as he was present throughout the month to provide assistance to the Novi operation.

In the days that followed, McElreath spent considerable time in his assigned mount, the dark blue #3. On May 4, he had the car over 150 m.p.h. and caused some concern when the racer began to leak fuel. Fortunately, nothing came of it as Jim was able to drive the car safely back to the pits. Both McElreath and Unser clocked in with an average of 151.5 m.p.h. in their rear drive cars. Bobby Unser seemed to be keeping a low profile in the #28 roadster. However, this changed when he finally moved into the Ferguson on what appeared to be a permanent basis. On May 6, he had the car up to 148 m.p.h. while McElreath was once again up to 151.5 m.p.h. in "his" Studebaker-STP

(1964) Veteran pilot Duane Carter shakes down the Novi-Ferguson. Carter had previously participated in eleven 500 runnings with his best finish being a 4th in a Murrell Belanger car. Carter and Andy were unable to work out a driving assignment in 1964 due to contractual conflicts.
I.M.S.

Special. A day earlier the Ferguson escaped a potential problem when Jim Hurtubise's car, the Tombstone Life Special owned by DVS (an Indianapolis trio of partners George Deeb, Jr., Robert Voigt and Richard Sommers), hit the wall literally seconds after he had overtaken Unser who was at the wheel of the Ferguson. While the Tombstone Special was badly shattered Herk emerged unscathed.

On May 8, driver Duane Carter took to the cockpit of the Ferguson. The veteran toured the oval for 20 laps, reaching a top speed of 151.210 m.p.h. Returning to the pits the 50 year old Carter said that he "hoped to work out a deal" for he was pleased with the speed after only a brief stint with the car. Carter had considerable experience in handling different equipment over the years and his versatility had once again been displayed. Duane was later to report that the car was the most predictable of all the Speedway cars he had driven in his eleven 500 races. Carter publicly stated that of the many cars he had driven that year he felt the 4WD Novi was the best. Carter was quoted as saying,

> "It gets you through the turns very quickly. The engine has always put out the horsepower, but they have never been able to control it. Now they can control it and take advantage of the horsepower in the turns. For my money the engine has finally found a home. The only disadvantage is that another two sets of differential gears could go out. But generally speaking you have very little transmission trouble."

At about this time, some reports began to circulate that the Ferguson did not handle all that well as both Unser and McElreath seemed to prefer their assigned roadsters. In talking about his time in the 4WD, Duane was to inform us that the ride was offered due to the fact that Jim and Bobby were not too keen on running the Ferguson. Eventually, Carter surrendered the ride as he and Granatelli could not come to an agreement regarding the spark plugs to be used in the car. The two had differing commitments with regard to the brand of spark plugs to be used. Away from the track, Carter worked for the Champion Spark Plug Company and Granatelli had a contract to use only Autolite Plugs. This prevented Carter from taking over the ride on a permanent basis. Incidentally, this would not have been the first time for Duane to drive for the Granatellis. With his extensive experience he could recall driving for the Granatellis as early as 1950 in the A.A.A. inaugural race at the new Darlington, South Carolina, mile and a quarter oval. Carter informed us that he always had a cordial relationship with Granatelli. When Duane was asked about an offer to drive the Ferguson, he informed us: "He (Granatelli) ask me to shake it down and try to get it ready for Bobby Unser." Carter recalled he drove the car four or five times over a period of probably a week. About the car itself he said, "I liked it, it handled very good." In fact, Carter was so comfortable that he did not offer any suggestions with respect to chassis changes. Duane said that both McElreath and Unser told Granatelli that "they didn't like the car." Carter revealed that the fact that he reached 152 m.p.h. in the car helped him secure other rides, although he failed to make the field. Carter felt that the car was "very secure" thanks to the four wheel drive. Yet, regarding the acceleration, Duane said that it was far better than what the two wheel drive Novis had ever achieved. Carter felt that the previously used six inch wide tires had been a problem for the Novis. The tires were simply too small and the tire compound too hard to transfer all the available power.

On May 8, while driving the #3 STP, McElreath engaged in a duel with Pennsylvania hot shoe Bobby Marshman in a Lotus Ford. The Novi proved to be more than able to uphold its end in the "contest." Jim set a fast lap of 153.296 m.p.h., proving that the Novi roadsters were not antiquated. One day later, Unser was second fast to Marshman averaging over 150 m.p.h. in the #28 car.

(1964) Duane Carter (right) observes some wheel work being attended to on #9. Having driven for Mickey Thompson the previous year, his uniform bears the name Mickey Thompson Special.   Bruce Craig Photos

On May 10, Jim McElreath once again demonstrated that the Novi roadsters still had a bit of speed left in them as he was clocked at 153+ m.p.h. for five laps. This made him one of the fastest drivers of the month. Other drivers receiving considerable press coverage for their quick times were Marshman and Clark in their Lotus Fords, while Parnelli Jones and A.J. Foyt were the fastest drivers using front engine cars. A change in the bodywork of #28 had aluminum blisters added on both sides of the nosecone in an attempt to streamline the front suspension. Something similar had been done on Parnelli Jones' "Old Calhoun" roadster.

per joined in with a photo displaying a crew member wearing the outfit with the caption, "Dig those pajamas." Another observer referred to the apparel as "clown suits." Years later, one STP crew member said he had never felt so humiliated as when he arrived on pit lane on race day to be viewed by over 200,000 fans on the front straightaway. Another crew member has said his objection to wearing the outfit was so adamant that he was finally promised one percent of the car's purse winnings provided he donned the STP covered outfit.

Andy's outfit, also containing the STP decals, was a tailor made suit while the crew uniforms

(1964) Let the "Pajama Party" begin. When the crew appeared in such garb, some fans found the outfits amusing while others judged them to be outlandish and ridiculous.
Armin Krueger Photo

Another noteworthy event on the 10th dealt not with speed, but of all things, a crew's wearing apparel. It seems that fifteen members of the STP contingency came out onto pit lane wearing uniforms covered with the STP logo. They instantly became the subject of countless jibes, jokes and considerable laughter. The atmosphere was one of lightheartedness. This appearance caused one observer to note that the crew members "certainly seemed embarrassed." Some onlookers referred to the outfits as pajama suits. One newspa-

were in the form of mechanic's coveralls. Perhaps it was impressive to the point that it played a part in a profile story by noted sports commentary writer Jim Murray (later to win a Pulitzer Prize for his journalistic endeavors relating to sports) to refer to Andy in print several years later as looking "like a cross between Diamond Jim Brady and a department store Santa Claus...Criticism rolls off Andy Granatelli's back like olive oil off his lasagna. Andy is a big lovable Italian bursting with life. He's as extraverted as an otter. On race day, he's down in the pits like a downed barrage balloon in a costume that looks like a combination of the aurora borealis in a gangster's funeral wreath. It does everything but give off sparks. It's dangerous to stare too long into it with the naked eye." Yet, if the purpose was not merely a new uniform but to promote the STP product the gimmick worked magnificently.

(1964) Though the crew wore the (infamous?) STP coveralls, the boss, "Mr. STP," sported a tailored suit. Hideous or not, the apparel garnered a tremendous amount of publicity for the product.
I.M.S.

With respect to identification, the STP crew members were easily recognizable due to their logo laden uniforms, but the driving apparel for the Novi drivers was spartan by contrast. The uniforms of Unser and McElreath carried a single decal over the right breast, the familiar STP patch. That was it except for a STP decal on the helmet and a smaller decal on each side.

On May 11, Bobby Unser was in the Ferguson and reached a clocking of 153 m.p.h. For a brief time this made him the second fastest driver at the Speedway. This glory was rather short-lived, for shortly thereafter, Marshman had his Lotus over 156.1 m.p.h. Only Parnelli Jones who had driven 156.223 m.p.h. several days earlier in his Offy roadster was faster than the two Bobbys. The general impression had it that the Ferguson was showing more corner speed that day and onlookers felt that it still had a bit more speed at its disposal.

In his volume <u>Tire Wars, Racing With Goodyear</u>, former Goodyear publicist William Neely delves into the impressive 156.223 m.p.h. clocking registered by Jones. Neely states that Firestone, with its growing concern over Goodyear's arrival and performance, offered to reimburse the Jones' team any expenses incurred if they would run a Firestone shod car with approximately a 50 percent nitro mix. Details were worked out between a Firestone representative and Parnelli's chief wrench, Johnny Pouelsen. A nitro-methane mixture added to fuel can dramatically increase a car's speed. Yet, a heavy concentration will rapidly cause the engine to expire. Therefore, the psych-job was to consist of only a few laps at high speed before returning the car to the garage.

Returning to the Ferguson, it can be stated that the exact cause as to why the car had not been all that popular with McElreath and Unser is difficult to say. One story circulated that the steering geometry had not been properly set. Yet, in spite of its weight and experimental status, Bobby Unser began to take a liking to the new creation. When he surpassed 153 m.p.h. he said that he didn't think the car was capable of such some days earlier "but Andy and my dad did." Bobby also related that "I kind of imagined I'll stay with it. I still think the other one (the #28 roadster) will go just as fast." One story has it that Bobby's father reminded him that brother Al hoped to be at Indy to make the race the following year and Bobby had better get with it now if he did not want his brother, as a rookie, to outrun him.

Bobby Marshman broke the 157 m.p.h. barrier on May 12 and he appeared to be the man to beat as Pole Day (Saturday, May 16) approached. The fastest time registered by the Novis had been Unser's run in the Ferguson at 153.8 m.p.h. May 13 went by with some casualties among a few of the participants, but the Novi came through without any damage. Up until that time, the Granatelli team had had a relatively easy time when one considers the notoriously bad luck experienced by the Novis in the past. To this point, the only difficulties suffered by the Novi team had been the leaking fuel tank, the hub difficulty and McElreath's lost goggles. Two days prior to Pole Day, Unser reached a speed of 154.8 m.p.h. in the Ferguson demonstrating anew the great potential the car had for a solid qualifying speed.

But then on the last day before qualifying, a mechanical problem of massive proportion struck the cars of both McElreath and Unser. The decision had been made to install sodium filled exhaust valves for the qualification runs. Such valves had a reputation of being able to withstand more internal heat within the combustion chambers. When put in use on Friday, the sodium filled valves barely survived a single lap at speed! McElreath hit a fast lap of 154.6 m.p.h. but he had to promptly return to the pits. The valves were from Porsche and a source asserted that the "valves and guides were not compatible for some reason." It was reported that the valve guides had lacked proper clearance causing the valves to gall or hang up in the guides. Of course, this meant an overhaul of the engines, thus denying Bobby and Jim any chance of qualifying during the first weekend of time trials.

Pole Day became a Lotus-Ford affair as Jimmy Clark captured the coveted pole with an average speed of 158.828 m.p.h. for his four lap run. The time represented a new track record. History was made once again, for as in 1963, the field would not start with an all Offy front row. With Clark's record breaking run being made on Dunlop tires, consternation must have prevailed that evening in Akron, Ohio headquarters of the Firestone Tire Company. Clark's use of the English made Dunlops ended Firestone's "strangle hold" at the Speedway. Track official Bill Marvel, tongue-in-cheek, said that Akron has "just been declared a disaster area."

To add insult to injury, the Offy powered domination was further reduced as second fast time was set by Bobby Marshman in his Pure Oil Firebird Special, another Lotus-Ford creation. The remaining spot in the front row also went to Ford as Rodger Ward placed a rear engine Watson-Ford up front. Thus, the front row was without a single Offenhauser.

The second row did have Offys with Parnelli Jones and next to him A.J. Foyt, while Dan Gurney was in another Lotus-Ford on the outside. In all, sixteen cars qualified the first day. The slowest of the sixteen was Ronnie Duman at 149.744 m.p.h.

Burning the midnight oil (an old story for the Novi crew), the mechanics had Jim McElreath's car ready to run on the second day of qualifying, but he was waved off. While the sodium filled valves had been replaced it was now reported that a piece of the fuel injector had worked loose and made its way into the engine causing the powerplant to sour. Therefore, another overhaul job was in order. During a warm up lap, McElreath was officially clocked at 153.689 m.p.h. Such a speed, if it had held over a four lap qualifying period, would have given him the honor of being the fastest second day qualifier.

During the second day of qualifications, five cars qualified with Eddie Sachs being the fastest of the lot at 151.439 m.p.h. A day earlier, Sachs had hit the wall in his American Red Ball Special and the repair work was not only challenging but also time consuming as the Halibrand Shrike chassis needed parts from the Halibrand plant in California. Ted Halibrand eased the difficulties as he had parts flown in from his plant in his private plane. This allowed Wally Meskowski, chief mechanic on the car, and the crew (with Halibrand pitching in) to hustle and make the show in fine order. As a result of his second day qualification, Sachs would start directly behind rookie Dave MacDonald.

On Monday, Bobby Unser turned in a few laps in the Ferguson which by then had "regular" valves (non-sodium) installed. The following day he was back on the track, but this time the ride ended rather abruptly and spectacularly. The car went into a 600 foot spin as he tried to pull off the track believing something had gone wrong in the engine. Bobby was fearful that the engine would blow and had wisely decided to cut power, but he then lost control of the racer. Once back in the garage, it was discovered that the car's engine was fine and that a malfunctioning mag had been the culprit. Bobby had driven up to 151 m.p.h. before the mishap. On May 20, McElreath was the fastest driver on the track as he reached a creditable 153.5 m.p.h. On the last practice day before the second qualification go around, Andy Granatelli said that Bobby had driven 42 consecutive laps without any major problems and that he had set a fast lap at over 154 m.p.h. during this stint. That day Bobby was second fastest with an average of 154.374 m.p.h.

Former Novi driver Paul Russo, a veteran of 15 races, took some laps during the week in the #28 Novi. Word then circulated that he was assured of getting the ride in that car. When the news of the presumptive ride reached Granatelli, he responded, "He must be suffering from hallucinations." Another Indianapolis paper had quoted Russo as saying that he would get a chance to drive the #28 car. Russo had originally been scheduled to drive Wally Weir's Mobilgas Special. However, after two unsuccessful qualification attempts, he parted company with Weir. Driver Bob Harkey was to eventually put the Mobilgas car into the show with a 151.573 m.p.h. clocking and to finish the contest in 8th place. Russo, who had brought such glory to the first rear engine Novis in the late 1950s, was, at age 51, winding down his career as a driver. He would make no additional Indy races, yet he remained on the scene as a manufacturer's representative for Per-

(1964) An overhead shot of the Novi-Ferguson. With the exhaust outlets situated in front of the driver, the noise must have been deafening. Earlier Granatelli Novis had the exhaust funnel out beyond the cockpit.   *Bruce Craig Collection*

fect Circle piston rings. Paul was to remain active in the sport until his passing. The tough and pugnacious driver was to die in his sleep at Daytona Beach while on hand to attend the Daytona 500 race in 1976. Russo's best finish at the Brickyard had been a second in 1955 when he drove relief for his long-time friend Tony Bettenhausen. Paul's highest finish without relief had been the 4th place achieved with a Novi in 1957.

As for Mickey Thompson's so-called roller skate cars, driver Eddie Johnson escaped injury when his Sears Allstate Special went out of control in the third turn skidding 930 feet to hit the wall head on. Although teammate Dave MacDonald had qualified on the first day, he expressed some concern saying his Allstate car did not feel just right. Others felt that his reservations were probably due to the fact that his background was that of a sports car driver who simply had not grown accustomed to the Speedway. Teammate Johnson was to qualify at 152.905 m.p.h. Eddie was a veteran of ten Indy 500s.

As the second round of qualifications began, the Novi team was ready. Both Unser and McElreath qualified on Saturday with Bobby posting a most impressive 154.865 m.p.h. clocking at the wheel of the Ferguson. Such a time had him secure the fifth fastest time for the entire field as well as fastest for all qualifiers that day. The "Big Red #9" 4WD had certainly demonstrated to one and all its ability in getting around the Speedway. The elated Novi followers now wished that a first weekend qualification run had been made. Such would have permitted a much higher starting place on the grid. As it was, Bobby started from the 22nd position. The 4WD might well have created a sizzling run for the lead during the opening laps of the race if he had not needed to work his way through the field. Bobby's speed average of 154.865 m.p.h. was surpassed only by the front row: Clark, Marshman, Ward and Parnelli Jones the second row pole sitter.

Jim McElreath was ready for his run when the #28 Studebaker-STP suddenly developed a blower problem. Thus, another qualifying attempt (the second for this car) had to be waved off after only one lap. The car was exceedingly fast when working properly as Jim was over 153 m.p.h. during the one completed lap before the run was aborted.

Later in the day, the Novi crew once again rolled out the #28 which had become the backup car since Unser had moved over to the Ferguson cockpit. Jim did a solid job in qualifying the car, averaging 152.381 m.p.h. with the fastest lap all but at the doorstep of 153 - 152.905 m.p.h. He became the 16th fastest driver in the field, although he would start from the 26th position. There were now two Novis in the field. Andy Granatelli created some hilarity after McElreath qualified the #28. Running down pit lane to the car, Andy inadvertently ran into one of the little tractors that was used to pull cars from the garage area to the pits and visa versa. This caused him to tumble to the ground, but he wasn't seriously hurt. After this incident, one wag observed that he could envision a newspaper headline: Andy Granatelli killed on pit lane by a tractor. This was not the only time that Andy, in his exuberance, would take a tumble.

(1964) An elated Andy losing his footing as he dashes down pit lane to congratulate one of his newly qualified drivers. Andy took a tumble and two crew members found the sight rather amusing.   I.M.S.

One important note of interest bears mentioning at this point. The #28 was reported to be running on Goodyears while the Ferguson was to carry Dunlop tires. However, both cars used Firestones during their qualification attempts. Andy Granatelli informed us that although the original plans called for use of Dunlop rubber on the Ferguson, he changed his mind as he lost faith in the Dunlop's durability for long runs at high speeds. The decision was to prove correct as the Lotus team was to find out later; much to their chagrin.

During qualifying, #28 used its third different type nosecone. The original cone with the red painted 28 filled with STP decals had been modified by adding streamline blisters. This modified cone, however, had been replaced with a new white cone, carrying a blue 28 'sans' STP decals. It lacked any front suspension streamlining and compared with the original cone and the one used on car #3, the radiator opening was much smaller.

On the last day of qualifying, four spots still remained in the starting field and once again it was a day in which a Novi turned in an impressive performance. The #3 car retained one more allowable attempt to make the field after the difficulties McElreath had encountered with it before moving over to the #28 speedster. Art Malone, still working for car owner Jim Robbins, had been experiencing some tough going. Art recalls that the Robbins' car, fresh out of the box promptly turned in a 150 m.p.h., but then the speeds instantly seemed to drop after the crew had worked on the car. Art said that unfortunately, notations on the original setup had not been retained and the crew was unable to get the car dialed in properly. With Malone's chances to make the field very slim, Robbins had met with Granatelli on Saturday to ask if the promise offered by Andy was still valid. Granatelli assured him that the offer remained open.

On Sunday, Art walked up pit lane toward Andy to inquire about the still vacant Novi ride. Andy was fully aware of Malone's situation and beating Art to the punch, he asked Malone to take over the ride for a final attempt. Malone gladly obliged and without time for any significant shakedown laps the Floridian placed the Novi in the show.

Years later, Art stated that he had some reservations about moving behind the wheel of a powerful Novi once again. It had been a year since he had driven a Novi, and compared to the Offy powered Robbins' car that he had driven during the month, the Novi was much faster with its blistering top speeds on the straights. Further, the car was far heavier than the Robbins' Offy, making for a very different handling situation. The Novi was not a car you could simply slow down by lifting the throttle. One had to be attuned to the throttle response or face dire consequences. The driver had to know how to lift. This was all due to the characteristic of supercharged engines, whereas a very different approach was necessary when running with a normally aspirated engine. To his relief, Malone was able to quickly regain his "touch" with the Novi with only four practice laps!

On Sunday, he was the fifteenth car in the qualifying line. Somewhat miraculously, Art was in the first car to make the field that day! Art had his work cut out for him since the car was down to its third and last allowable attempt. Further, gusting winds prevailed at the time and he was in a car after only a very brief acclimation period. Though he still retained some trepidation what with the limited practice time in the Novi, the car was placed in the qualifying line. Art asserts, "I was not about to tell people how to do things." It was definitely pressure cooker time. With fairly stout winds, many drivers were concerned about crosswinds on the track and decided to wait until late afternoon. When his turn arrived, Art and the crew selected to go for it and he turned in an average time of 151.222 m.p.h. for the four laps. Art and the Novi rose to the task as its speed average was 25th fastest which was enough to place it in the 30th starting position. Vince Granatelli recalls that "the rings hadn't even been seated in yet" when the refurbished car took to the oval for its last time trial assault. Malone's splendid performance under such pressure certainly would serve to silence those who had labeled him "a hot rodder" who was out of his element behind the wheel of a champ car. Making the field on the last permitted attempt for the three year old #3 car under such enormous pressure was an extraordinary display. The feat certainly

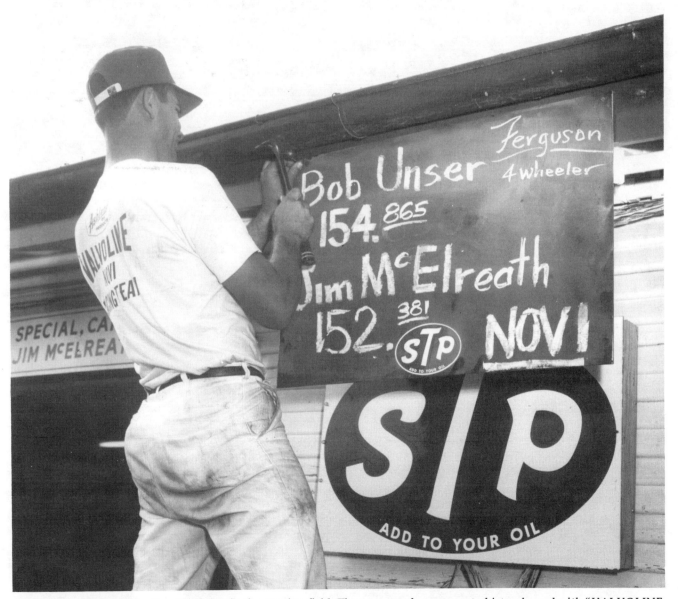

(1964) The results are in: Two Novis are in the starting field. The crew member wears a t-shirt embossed with "VALVOLINE NOVI RACING TEAM." Valvoline was involved as it provided support to the Novi undertaking. Such participation was Valvoline's first at the Speedway.
I.M.S.

had to rank as one of the proudest moments during the Granatelli Novi period.

While the STP team was decal sticker happy, the drivers' uniforms were rather spartan by comparison. Then with Malone's late qualifying run and having been with the Robbins' crew, he qualified the #3 Novi wearing a uniform devoid of even one STP patch. Only his helmet displayed the famed decals. What a lost opportunity for the STP team.

Other last day qualifiers were Bob Wente, Norm Hall and Bill Cheesbourg. Each last day entry had its own intriguing tale. Norm Hall, driving his Nothing Special, had blown two engines during the month. Now with a downsized sprint car powerplant borrowed from good friend A.J. Watson, he made the field. By race day, he had secured some sponsorship funding from an automotive firm, the Hurst Company.

Rookie Wente, the prevailing USAC midget champ, offered high praise to his chief mechanic Bob Higman for putting him into the show. Incidentally, Wente's run bumped Paul Russo who became the race's first alternate. Russo's car had been entered by Mari George, daughter of Speedway President Tony Hulman, but was then sold to Richard Kemerly to run as the Kemerly Chevy and Olds Special. Paul had made the race, at least temporarily on the third day of qualifying (on the car's third attempt) with a time of 148.644 m.p.h.

Bill Cheesbourg was at the wheel of the Apache Airline Special that featured a layover engine. He was to start the race from last place. Cheesbourg's last day qualifying run reminded some of his dramatic last minute qualifying of a Novi in the 1958 contest. That year, Bill had started last, yet finished 10th, going the distance in a Novi.

As with the other two Novis, the Malone car

(1964) The view the Granatellis wanted other teams to have during the race - Novis from the rear. The car's tire pressure is being checked by a Firestone staffer before taking to the track.
Gerald Walker Photo

was also shod with Firestones. The tire count had the two Thompson cars equipped with Sears rubber, an equal number with Dunlops (the Lotus-Fords) and 29 with the Firestone compound. Further, there were 23 Offys and ten V-8s, three of which were the Novis. Altogether, it had been a reasonably "normal" practice and qualifying effort for the Granatelli camp. All three cars were in the field and if it had not been for the faulty exhaust valves two of the cars might well have started much higher in the starting field. But at that point, they were in the race and that was what really mattered.

Following the success in placing two Novis in the show, the Novi team's pride and joy was such that they displayed a chalk board at the Novi garage area. It proclaimed "Bob Unser - Ferguson 4 wheeler - 154.865 / Jim McElreath - 152.381 STP NOVI." Now they had proudly added to the sign "& Malone." With the lineup finalized, a Novi was to start from the 22nd position (Unser), one from the 26th spot (McElreath) and the third from the 30th position (Malone).

Chapter 13

Best Finish in a Tragic Race - 1964

On race morning the Novi team had a surprise, for as their cars emerged from the garages, observers immediately noticed a change. The left side tires had been painted white in a manner similar to whitewall tires on passenger cars. This approach certainly lead to some raised eyebrows. The undertaking was an effort to make it easier for the crew to quickly identify their cars, particularily as they came out of fourth turn. If it was not helpful, at least it offered an unusual appearance! Some considered the overnight paint job to be rather outlandish and ugly.

The pace car was a model recently unveiled by Ford, a 1964 and a half Mustang with driver Benson Ford at the wheel. Interestingly, a Ford Fairlane had initially been selected for the pace car duties. Yet, the promotional opportunities offered with the new pony car was simply too great to be by-passed by the Ford executives.

Following standard operating procedures, the field was away as the pace car pulled off of the course onto pit lane. The race's start went smoothly as pole sitter Jimmy Clark quickly assumed the lead with Bobby Marshman following the Scotsman. The tightly packed field of cars moved through the first lap without any apparent problems. Clark began to put some space on others as the leaders moved into the second lap. Yet, that second lap would always be remembered. A horrendous incident unfolded as the drivers in

(1964) The field is away as the crowd stands to take in the action. Several of the Novis can be easily spotted what with the left side tires painted white.
Armin Krueger Photo

the middle of the field began making their way through the fourth turn on the second lap. Starting positions are important in a race, but this time the positions proved to be of extraordinary importance - even in human cost.

Rookie Dave MacDonald, driving one of the

(1964) Another view of the first turn, first lap drama. Unser is on the apron in the #9 STP, while fellow Novi chauffeur Jim McElreath, in #28, is virtually surrounded by other cars. The so-called "roller skate" ride on the outside is Eddie Johnson in #84. His teammate, Dave MacDonald in #83, is up front and thus out of the picture. MacDonald started from the 14th place while Eddie was back in the 24th starting position. I.M.S.

(1964) Dave MacDonald in the Sears Allstate Special that triggered the accident that claimed his life and that of Eddie Sachs. The Ford powered Mickey Thompson car carried Sears Allstate tires. Note the front wheel wing deflectors. I.M.S.

two rear engine Fords built by Mickey Thompson, a Sears Allstate Special (a 1964 version of the 1963 so-called Thompson "roller skate") lost control, skidding to the inside retaining wall as he exited the fourth turn. A fuel tank split as MacDonald's car ricocheted back onto the track. A massive fireball developed, followed by a huge black cloud. The cars running close to MacDonald attempted to take evasive action as all hell broke loose. Eddie Sachs, running behind MacDonald, was left without any room to maneuver around the burning car. He broadsided the out-of-control Sears Allstate car, ripping a second tank in the MacDonald mount. Meanwhile, other cars were attempting to snake their way through the inferno. Dave had started the race from the middle of the fifth row while Eddie started from the middle of the sixth row - immediately behind MacDonald. Sachs died immediately from the impact. MacDonald was removed from the wreckage, still alive, but he was to die a few hours later due to smoke inhalation. As good fortune would have it, no other cars were trapped in the conflagration.

In one account detailing the race, Bobby Unser described the carnage as follows: "I got hung up where the fire was. I knew it was going to get hot and I just jammed down on the pedal and tried to push my way. Johnny Rutherford went over the top of my car." Unser also stated that he had already passed a few cars and was side-by-side with Rutherford. Elaborating further Bobby stated in The Bobby Unser Story:

"I looked for an opening and suddenly saw a car slide across the race track in front of me. There was a big explosion and fire. And then I saw that the whole race track was blocked with fire. Once again I couldn't stop in time. I was coming upon the fire very quickly and instinct told me that there were race cars in there, burning race cars that were causing the fire. I didn't know if it was one burning car or ten; it looked like ten. I couldn't go around them, so I had to go through them. And I had two or three seconds to figure out how I was going to do it. I lowered my head and stood on the gas harder because the only thing I knew was that I didn't want to stop in the fire. I'd rather come out of the fire trailing wreckage or with my car all torn apart - anything - but I did not want to

(1964) The Novi-Ferguson at the wall following Bobby Unser's brush with death. In less than two laps, the highly touted 4WD is out of the race. A dream shattered with the race barely underway. Fans in the area are focusing on the calamity that transpired near the fourth turn.
Armin Krueger Photo

catch on fire. I put the pedal to the metal, closed my eyes, and hoped I'd come out. I hit Ronnie Duman, but I came out of the fire still going straight and so I thought that maybe I was all right. What I didn't realize was that I had a complete wheel and tire gone plus no steering or brakes; I had no control at all. Just then Rutherford sashayed out of the fire behind me and his burning roadster jumped over my hood. His wheels almost came through my cockpit. My Novi sat parked along the front straightaway wall where I left it, junk. If I hadn't gone blasting through the fire and hit Duman and knocked his car clear, he'd have been as dead as Eddie Sachs and Dave MacDonald were. He still got burned very severely, but at least he was alive."

In recalling the incident years later, driver Johnny Rutherford stated in the Bob Gates' book, Hurtubise:

"I was starting outside on the fifth row alongside MacDonald. When the green dropped, he was loose and practically out of control going into Turns 1 and 3. I decided to let him go. Coming off four on the second lap, there was still a lot of dirt and dust but I could see a car get sideways and smash into the inside wall. It was like you pulled a black and orange curtain across the track. I knew Sachs was an old pro and could get through the wall of flame if anyone could so I decided to try and follow him. My most vivid recollection is Eddie's Day-Glo orange helmet darting side-to-side searching for a hole in the smoke screen. I was on the brakes so hard my car began chattering as we plowed into MacDonald. If I hadn't been sitting upright in a big front engine roadster I surely would have burned with Eddie and Dave. Somehow, I went over the top of both cars. I managed to get the car out of gear when Bobby Unser's Novi slammed me into the outside wall so hard it ripped my uniform seams and broke my seat. Somehow I found low gear and drove away."

Emerging from the conflagration, Rutherford moved on down the front straightaway as driver

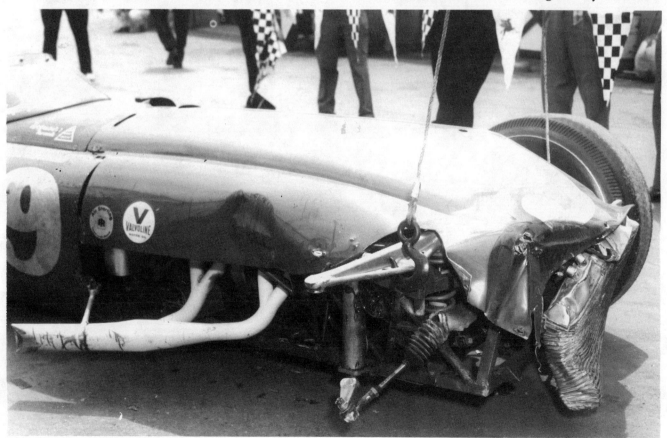

(1964) A view of the right front reveals significantly more damage than what was observed on the left side. I.M.S.

Bob Veith pulled alongside of him. Johnny said that Veith was "wildly gesturing for me to pull into the infield. Entering into turn one, MacDonald's fuel injector horns broke loose from my rear axle where they had become wedged." Johnny stated that he could still see sparks flickering in his cockpit. He stopped on the backstretch motioning a fireman to come over, asking if any fire remained about the car. The safety worker said he did not think so; thus, Rutherford shifted into low and drove on around. Another driver stated that MacDonald had appeared to be driving in somewhat of an erratic fashion as the race got underway.

Sadly, Bobby and the Ferguson-Novi were out of the race. He had moved up, climbing from 22nd to 14th in less than two laps prior to the accident. He could not completely avoid the MacDonald/Sachs wreckage making contact with Ronnie Duman, who had started 16th on the inside of row six next to Sachs. The Ferguson had the right front

Life magazine published several vivid colored photographs of the tragedy in its June 26 issue. One of the pictures shows Unser's Novi virtually covered in flames. Miraculously, Bobby's 4WD did not burst into flames. For the second consecutive year, Unser was again out of the race after only one full lap of competition. Small consolation that it was at the time, he had improved his finish by one position over the previous year since he was now declared 32nd in the final standings!

Photos of the disaster also show Jim McElreath's car emerging from the inferno. He was the last driver reaching the scene without any opportunity to stop in time. Miraculously, he came through without any bodily injury or car damage before the track was completely blocked with the carnage. Some of the drivers at the rear of the field, Bob Wente, Bob Harkey, Bill Cheesbourg, Bob Mathouser, Chuck Stevenson, Norm Hall and Art Malone in the remaining Novi, were able to stop in time.

(1964) Jim McElreath in his Novi was the last car to make it through the blaze. With his disabled Novi at the outer wall, Bobby Unser stands on the top of the wall immediately behind the Novi-Ferguson. I.M.S.

wheel completely ripped off with the highly publicized 4WD creation coming to rest near the outside wall. Such a circumstance palls in light of the catastrophe that caused his forced withdrawal. With the calamity, the most promising of the three Novis was now eliminated from competition. Had Bobby Unser qualified the first day with the time he eventually posted he would have started the contest from the middle of the second row. If that were the case he would have been well out in front of the horrific accident.

In talking with Art, he vividly recalled that he had come close to being involved in the disaster. While working the short chute between three and four, he saw the explosion resulting from the accident out of the corner of his eye. Art lifted the throttle, wondering what could have happened, "All of a sudden cars were going everywhere. Then I saw this large fire with smoke to the heavens. Cars completely blocked the track. I have never seen anything like it. I decided to try to stop as I had no chance of finding a hole. It looked bad." To avoid the pile up, he applied his brakes. To his utter amazement, he found himself in a real pickle as the car's braking power was weak and the car did not come to a complete stop until it was no more than eight or ten car lengths from the blazing fire.

The cars out front of the conflagration were indeed fortunate. Furthermore, the tragedy might well have been intensified if the fuel cells on Sachs' car had ruptured. An inspection indicated that they had not split, thanks to the sturdiness of the car's Shrike chassis - a product of Ted Halibrand's racing plant.

For the first time in its history, the race was red flagged because of an accident. Even during the 1958 first lap melee that had cars scattered through the third turn, the north short chute and in the grass, the race went on under a caution while the track was cleared of debris and to remove the seven cars eliminated from the race.

The 1964 accident eliminated not only the two drivers directly involved in the accident, but Rutherford, Chuck Stevenson, Ronnie Duman, Unser and Norm Hall. Norm reported that with the race never having been previously stopped, he tried to work his way through. When he realized that this was not possible, he abruptly applied the binders, stopping short of the accident scene like Malone, though damage was inflicted to the tail of his car as it made contact with the wall.

While the engines were cooling down waiting for the restart of the race, the surviving Novis ran into a new problem. The fuel within the manifolds was condensing. As a semblance of calm returned, USAC officials circulated among the teams to inform them that no repair work could be performed on any of the cars prior to the restart. This meant that the Novi crew could not repeat the standard procedure of using cold spark plugs to start the Novi engines before a change to hot plugs prior to the resumption of racing. Malone and McElreath were thus forced to run the engines on the hot plugs and hope that the engines could survive the rough treatment. Before the restart, Andy complained to the officials that the #28 Novi should have been placed higher in the single file start as it had managed to come through the fire before the race was red flagged. The protest was denied.

When the racing resumed, the first departure was made by Eddie Johnson in the Ford V-8 Sears Allstate car, the sister car to MacDonald's. Johnson went out after six laps with a reported fuel pump problem. As for the Novis, both cars were

(1964) Art Malone's #3 STP being pushed from the area of the multi-car crash. The episode marked the first time in the history of the Speedway that the event had been red flagged for any reason other than inclement weather. The #18 ride is the Bill Forbes Special, driven by Lloyd Ruby.   I.M.S.

immediately down on power. Then after 77 laps, McElreath's racing for the day was over. While several versions have been cited for the retirement (including a bad magneto), the commonly accepted cause was a blown piston. McElreath's finishing position was listed as 21st.

Thus, it all came down to the one remaining Novi to carry the team "honors" - the #3 Kurtis-Kraft built car with dragster star Art Malone at the wheel. Malone was the last driver to join the team and the last to qualify. On the 35th lap, Malone spun the car going off the track, but he managed to regain control and return to the oval. The spin did toss some dirt onto the track and for this reason the yellow was briefly displayed during the cleanup period. Malone soldiered on, making two stops for fuel (on his 72nd and 149th laps), although no tires were changed.

Malone, having discovered the fading brakes on his car during the abrupt stoppage on the second lap, had to alter his driving style when the race resumed. The soft brakes forced him to take it a little easier moving through the turns. With respect to his first pit stop, Art knew that he could come to a stop in time by pumping the brake pedal as he moved toward his pit. By the second stop, the braking power had been drastically reduced causing him to start backing off the throttle on the back stretch in order to avoid overshooting his assigned pit. The pit crew was fully aware of the loss of braking power after that. Thus, when

Art returned to the pits they had to grab the tires to aid in stopping the Novi. It is not clear if the Novi crew had given any consideration to possibly correcting Art's braking problem during the race.

(1964) Art Malone leaving the pits after a fuel stop. With brakes fading, Art had to start slowing down on the back straightaway when preparing to pit. I.M.S.

The fading brakes may well have cost him at least several positions. Malone recalled dicing for quite some time with Johnny Boyd who was in the Vita Fresh Orange Juice Special. Malone would lose ground as the pair moved into the corners, but he then regained the lost ground on the straights. However, with brake efficiency disappearing, Malone had to back off from the cat and mouse chase. To his credit, Malone was able to remain on the track and to be somewhat competitive with the lame Novi. Art stated that he did what he had to do given the circumstances. The problem was serious enough that he had to back off in order to achieve some degree of success by remaining in the race, holding the car together to finish. At the close of the race, he was flagged off after having completed 194 laps. He was the next to last participant still running at the time. The top five finishers had managed to finish the full 200 laps before the race was stopped. Malone's Studebaker-STP Special was to be accorded 11th place honors. Such a performance by Malone fully demonstrated that the dragster was not out of his "element" as a few observers had suggested. His fine run with the crippled car served to solidify his oval track skills.

When asked about the dicing with Malone, Johnny Boyd simply could not recall the episode. He said that he had been having his own problems with handling and had no time to worry about others. The Vita Fresh car was setup to go the distance with only one pit stop for fuel. This meant that Johnny had to work with a drastic transition with the car's handling characteristics. He stated that it was like driving three different cars as the fuel load diminished. As a consequence, he had his hands full and the dicing incident was lost in the total concentration he had to give to his car and what was in front of him.

After his departure from the race, Bobby Unser offered his services to Vita Fresh car owner Gordon Van Liew in case Boyd did not feel he wanted to continue after the stoppage. Johnny would have no part of it, going on to complete the race, with a splendid 5th place showing in spite of all that had transpired during the day. Several of the drivers competing that day have said that restarting the race was one of the toughest encounters that they were ever involved in during their racing careers. None had ever witnessed such a horrific fire and the carnage that followed.

With his services as a relief driver not needed, Bobby then assisted the Novi crew on a job which unnerved the crew members. After the fiery fourth turn inferno, a number of crewmen were reluctant to refuel their team's cars. Only Novi crewman Ryan Falconer, who admitted to being uneasy, was willing to refuel the two Novis remaining in the race. Unser volunteered to be Falconer's assistant by keeping an eye out for possible fires, with a fire extinguisher readily available.

When the race was finally resumed, after nearly a two hour delay, Bobby Marshman driving the Pure Oil Firebird Special owned by Lindsey Hopkins, managed to wrestle the lead from Clark. He then began moving away from the front runners as he built up a minute and a half lead with the rear engine Ford powered car. A beleaguered Hopkins then saw his car eliminated on lap 39, for as Marshman went below the white line in the southwest turn, the car bottomed out causing a break in the oiling system. Some sources suggest that the oil plug was sheared off. At this point Jimmy Clark moved back into first with his Lotus Powered by Ford Special, but his front running position did not last long. On lap 48 as Clark came down the front straight, the left rear Dunlop tire began chunking with a portion breaking the left rear suspension. He managed to maintain control down the straightaway, then pulled off the course in the first corner.

(1964) These photos might well be referred to as before and after shots. A fresh smiling Art Malone and then a grimmy, tired driver after the disasterous 1964 race. Art's running most of the race with little or no braking power certainly was no picnic.   Authors Collection

During this period, action was thick and heavy as another one of the top contenders, Parnelli Jones experienced his own difficulty on lap 55. While in the pits, Parnelli's Agajanian-Bowes Special caught fire and Parnelli saved himself by leaping from the car to suffer only minor burns. In a promotional film ("Way of a Champion") that concentrates on the Novi efforts in 1964, the viewer may note that during a Malone pit stop after Parnelli's fire, the Novi team sprayed CO_2 over the tail section of the car. There was no fire but the action was taken as a precautionary safety measure. The high expectations of the Colin Chapman/Ford endeavor was completely dashed as Dan Gurney's Lotus left the race on lap 110 due to "tire failure" with its Dunlops. It is generally agreed that the powers that be within the Lotus team made the decision to bring Dan in, fearing a repeat of Jimmy's misfortune. Safety outweighed any desire to win.

At this point, the race became a battle between A.J. Foyt and Rodger Ward. Foyt prevailed to score his second 500 victory in three years. The fine performance was achieved with a Sheraton-Thompson Special, a front engine roadster. In spite of Foyt's victory, many realized that the

(1964) Malone in action. He was being pursued by Bud Tingelstad in the #15 Federal Engineering Special that used a Floyd Trevis chassis in finishing 6th.
Armin Krueger Photo

days of the heavier, front engine cars at Indy were definitely numbered. Despite the horror created by one of the rear engine Fords, it was evident that the lighter, rear engine cars represented the wave of the future. The days of the normally aspirated Offy powered front engine cars were rapidly coming to a close. Even winner A.J. made reference to the front engine cars as being dinosaurs. Some went so far as to predict that a rear engine car would win the race by 1966.

An assessment of the race finish indicated that the top ten finishers were all Offy front engine cars with the exception of second place finisher Rodger Ward in a Bob Wilke rear engine Ford. The race field contained twelve rear engine cars; five Offys and seven Fords. The remaining Fords were those run by Lotus (Clark and Gurney); Lindsey Hopkins' car (Bobby Marshman), the DVS car (Eddie Sachs) and Mickey Thompson's two cars (Eddie Johnson and Dave MacDonald). After running Buicks in 1962 and then Chevys in 1963, the ever resilient Thompson had then moved to Ford power.

The Foyt triumph, beyond being something of a phyrric victory, was also an indication that the days of the layover engine were soon to be just a memory as only one managed to qualify. The duel between the roadster and the layover had been decided, but in the long run such was of little consequence. The roadster concept had enjoyed success, but it now appeared to many observers to be on the way to extinction.

In evaluating the race, the Novi team did not fair all that well. The end result was the elimination of one car after only one full lap while the other two apparently lost any chance of victory as a result of the second lap disaster and the prolonged delay. There was one positive note - a Novi was running at the close of the contest. Such had not occurred since a Novi salvaged 10th place in 1958 when Bill Cheesbourg went the distance for Lew Welch, the former Novi car owner.

In discussing the fatalities, Andy Granatelli quickly laid the blame on lightweight cars and the use of gasoline. All of the Ford V-8s, except Rodger Ward's car, used gasoline while his carried alcohol. AUTOCAR magazine published a statement attributed to Granatelli in its June 19 issue. In the

(1964) Jim McElreath's Novi being passed by eventual race winner A.J. Foyt. Jim was forced to park his Novi after 77 laps with "engine trouble."
Armin Krueger Photo

perodical, Andy declared that the calamity was "due to the lightweight cars: its due to the slow start of the race and its due to the fact that these cars ran on gasoline. Gasoline is highly inflammable. Gasoline explodes. You can light it with a match. You can't light methanol with a match and how can you put a fuel tank all around the driver and engine? You can't seat a driver in a death seat with gas all around him. What chance does he have? And both of these drivers were in that kind of car."

Car and Driver replied to Granatelli's statement in an article published that August. "Granatelli's Novis weigh as much as an average bulldozer and they suffer as many structural failures than anything on the race track. Mr. Granatelli knows that he will never be able to get any publicity by winning the 500 so he must do what he can to keep himself in the public eye." Such strong statements were heard as emotions ran extremely high following the double tragedy.

A rather moot question at this juncture relates to whether the MacDonald crash would have set off the same sort of inferno had methanol been carried in the tanks of his car rather than gasoline. As is so often the case there was much speculation as to what might have been or what should have been.

It seems a bit odd that Andy Granatelli blamed the lighter rear engine cars for the early race disaster as three years earlier he had attempted to be one of the first American Indy car owners to possess one! And it has to be admitted that the heavy Novis did have their shortcomings. In Andy's defense, it has to be said that running the complex supercharged Novi engine was a far cry from using an Offy or even a Ford Quadcam V-8.

Whether the swift but heavy 4WD Ferguson would have been able to overcome the so-called jinx and gone the distance that year we will never know. Perhaps if the car returned to the Speedway the following year one would be in a better position to not only analyze possible virtues of the car, but to assess the chances of it lasting the distance.

The possible merits of the 4WD Ferguson certainly could not be elaborated on with its departure from the race before the completion of two laps. As it were, a Novi had managed to run until the race was completed. The 11th place finish by Malone was the best achieved by any Novi car during the Granatelli years - yet, whatever luster may have been created by this accomplishment, such was far outweighed by the tragic nature of the race.

Chapter 14

CHANGES AND MORE CHANGES

When the 1964 Indianapolis 500 nightmare was over, it was clear to many racing participants that changes would be necessary before the next 500. A repeat of the tragedy had to be prevented irrespective of the cost. As a consequence, new regulations regarding fuel tanks and refueling were announced. The new rules included a prohibition on pressurized fueling; a maximum fuel capacity of 75 gallons (291 liters); the installation of any fuel tanks in front of the driver was now forbidden and "standard" pump gasoline was all but outlawed. Two mandatory pit stops were initiated with the expectation of eliminating the need to carry excessive fuel. Additionally, with the increased concern for fuel safety, a no smoking ban was imposed in Gasoline Alley. Another new rule stipulated that the maximum capacity for normally aspirated engines would be reduced to 183.06 c.i. (3 liter) and 122.04 c.i. (2 liter) for blown powerplants. This requirement was to take affect in 1968. This represented an ominous sign on the horizon for the supercharged Novi V-8.

The technical revolution in the USAC National Championship Series was almost complete. For the traditional dirt track events in the series (Springfield, Du Quoin, Indiana Fairgrounds, etc.) the front engine car was still the way to go, but for the paved ovals (Indianapolis, Milwaukee, Trenton, etc.) the front engine car was now considered to be passé.

Nearly every top-rated driver, including A.J. Foyt and Parnelli Jones, now made the switch to rear engine cars. Not all drivers were happy with the transition, but to remain competitive it seemed vital to run a rear engine car. The Granatellis decision to stay with the front engine Novis for another year is something that is not fully understood. One possibility: it would keep them active while dramatic changes was being worked on behind the scene. Yet, it must be said that the Novi team did not have to rely on just front engine cars what with the 4WD in their stable.

Improved engines were apparently available for the Novi cars as it was claimed that the latest version was capable of developing approximately 762 horsepower. Such a circumstance was somewhat unbelievable, when one considers that after 25 years the big V-8 seemingly was still obtaining additional power. It also seemed that the end had not been reached for the Novi. The changes in the engines appeared to stress weight reduction. The Granatellis managed to shave some engine weight by employing a magnesium crankcase and aluminum bearing webs which saved approximately 40 pounds. It was reported that the Novi engine then weighted in at 430 pounds. The block still retained only three main bearings and the redline was at an impressive mark - 9,800 rpms. It has often been mentioned that the design at the bottom end of the Novi V-8 with only three bearings was questionable. However, with the engines allegedly being able to rev close to 12,000 rpms, one can not deny that it was a more formidable powerplant than some believed.

When the Granatellis pondered the bulky nature and weight of the Ferguson, they made a rather dramatic decision. They would build a new front engine, 4WD chassis under the guidance of Vince Granatelli at their Santa Monica shop over the winter of 1964-1965. The car was to be lighter and smaller than the Ferguson used in the 1964 race. The driveline was to consist of the same design as used in the Ferguson P104. According to supplied literature, the car was never assigned any official type of registration other than being identified as an STP Special or STP Division Studebaker. Perhaps a suitable identification would have been Granatelli-Novi or Paxton-Novi.

A few of the specifications regarding the car are available. The new creation was reported to weigh in at 1,500 pounds. Andy Granatelli, however mentioned a figure of 1,700 to 1,800 pounds for the new car. In referring to the new car, Andy

(1965) A publicity shot from the STP press kit made available to the media. Vince and Andy posed with the rebuilt Novi-Ferguson and the brand new car constructed over the winter by Vince. The new 4WD was designed as an improved version. Unfortunately, #6 crashed on the eve of qualifying and was finished.   Authors Collection

later said, "All the faults we had in the Ferguson were corrected in this car. It was a jewel." The fuel tanks, capable of carrying 75 gallons, were installed on the left side of the car's tail. The seven gallon (27.2 liter) oil tank was also installed on the left side with an auxiliary oil tank and cooler mounted in a fashion similar to the Ferguson.

Despite being longer than the Ferguson (166 inches), the new car provided a more nimble impression than the earlier 4WD. Possibly this was due to a reduced wheelbase of 96 inches as opposed to 100 inches with the Ferguson. While the Granatelli 4WD chassis appeared bulky when compared to its rivals, it offered trimmer lines than the Ferguson P104. The efforts put forth in this project suggest that the Granatellis may still have harbored a strong belief in the potential virtues of a 4WD Novi. As for the Ferguson, it was only slightly altered from the shape it had presented a year earlier. The main difference was a new exhaust setup and the shape of the nosecone with its radiator opening. It was a bit smaller than the 1964 nose and more oval in shape. The car's two fuel tanks had capacities as follows: 50 gallons in the tail and 25 gallons in the left tank. Both were flex bag tanks with polyurethane baffling made by Firestone with the expectation of eliminating fuel sloshing in the tanks and more importantly, to dramatically reduce chances of any gas tank splitting. The new Jones' tach installed had a maximum 10,000 rpm reading. With respect to rpms, Joe Granatelli said that the car would be on the mark if it could consistently crank out 7,500 rpms. He felt, at that speed, the engine would be putting out sufficient power to avoid lugging as the Novi went through the corners. Further, the cars now carried gauges for the oil temperature and oil pressure at the transmission. It is possible that there were other differences between the 1964 and the 1965 specifications of the Ferguson, though research failed to unearth other alterations.

At the same time, any number of people in champ car racing realized that the roadster, or for that matter, any other front engine car concept was now obsolete. Foyt had won the 1964 race with a front engine, but this transpired after the faster rear engine Fords had been sidelined. A rear engine car was obviously the way to go in the future. Most of the car builders realized this fact as new fabrications were being carried out in their workshops in 1964 in order to have new cars available for USAC champ car races on paved tracks later in the year.

A major factor in all of this was the tremendous change after years of domination by the Offenhauser. It now was on the chopping block due to its apparent obsolescence. While some teams would stand firm with Offy power, the majority of the teams appeared ready to opt for a rear engine powered Ford. The fact that the two fastest qualifiers, Jimmy Clark (158.8 m.p.h.) and Bobby Marshman (157.8 m.p.h.), had been at the wheel of rear engine Fords was not lost on their competition. Clark's qualifying speed was slightly more than 4 m.p.h. faster than that of A.J. Foyt, the race winner. In fact, Bobby Unser's qualifying run in the Ferguson surpassed A.J.'s time trial run by approximately two-tenths of a mile. Among the dozen drivers in rear engine cars was the individual who had fully put the concept into motion - Sir Jack Brabham. The 1964 race marked his first appearance since the initial Brabham run in the Cooper-Climax in 1961. For 1964, Sir Jack drove the Zink Urschel Track Burner Special, a rear engine Offy housed in a Brabham chassis. He placed 20th due to a split fuel tank. Another change dealt with the growing tire war between Firestone and Goodyear. Wider tires were now most definitely the way to go. A.J. Foyt won the 1964 500 using Goodyear rubber, thus breaking Firestone's reign of 40 consecutive Indianapolis 500 victories.

As stated, the Granatellis decided to hold fast with their Novi engines for the coming year, continuing with a mix of the two 4WDs along with the two rear drives. Although the 1964 racing season was over for the Novis, they remained active as they were pressed into duty for several tire tests. The Ferguson and the #3 roadster were used for this activity. September, 1964, was a busy month for the cars and the Novis participation did not go unnoticed. On September 22, Jim McElreath reached a straightaway trap speed of 199.93 m.p.h. at the Indianapolis Speedway using Firestone rubber while at the wheel of the #3 Novi that Malone had driven in May. Jim's fastest lap in a Novi was recorded eight days later when he obtained a lap speed of 155.8 m.p.h. The following day, Jim averaged 159.1 m.p.h. in a rear engine Brabham Offy! In October, Bobby Unser drove the Ferguson at IMS with the fastest lap being 156.7 m.p.h. The car used the Firestone's 1964 spec tires. Then in November, Bobby lapped the Phoenix one mile oval with a time of 30.46 seconds. This was an outstanding performance, but one week later Parnelli Jones set a new one mile closed track record with a time of 30.41 seconds in a Lotus-Ford. The Phoenix track was not without its downside for in December Bobby Marshman died at the track while testing. With his passing, the champ car trail lost one of its brightest rising stars.

The Granatelli crew stayed busy from May to May updating the Ferguson while working at designing and building the lighter 4WD car for 1965. Yet, at the same time the Granatellis continued to render considerable time and serious planning for another potent Indy car. Work on this new project was to start within a short time. It was a project that was to have some dramatic implications for the Novi and the Speedway's venerable history as well. But as long as the new "super weapon" was not ready, the Granatellis would continue their Novi efforts. But it would be difficult for even the new lightweight 4WD to fully challenge the stellar new rear engine cars.

Chapter 15

The Last Hurrah - 1965

The Novi team entered three cars for the 1965 Indianapolis race. They consisted of the two FWDs and one of the Kurtis-Kraft roadsters. The Studebaker name was now missing from the cars and the company's subsidiary, STP, had assumed sponsorship of the team. The Studebaker Company had been experiencing fiscal difficulties and had moved its auto manufacturing operations from South Bend, Indiana to Canada in 1963.

year. It was now to carry #59. (That number had been used off and on by the Granatellis since their first Speedway entry in 1946, although such a numbered car had failed to qualify in 1948, 1949 and 1954.) The primary color remained blue, although the nosecone was a bright yellow. This car seemed to be a totally separate entry when compared to the 4WDs as it differed in color and entry name. The Kurtis was entered under the name of

(1965) Bobby Unser at the wheel of the new 4WD built under Vince Granatelli's supervision. The 4WD Granatelli-Novi was not as bulky as the Ferguson. Mounted behind Bobby's head is the often present camera to take shots of the gauges for crew viewing and interpretation.
Bob Tronolone Photo

For the 1965 race, the Ferguson retained the number 9 and it was fluorescent red with some white having been worked into the color scheme. The silver #9 on the nosecone had been replaced with a conventional black number on a white circle. The entry bore the name STP Gasoline Treatment Special. The new 4WD car that the Granatellis designed and built was identified as the #6 STP Oil Treatment Special. The Kurtis roadster that was brought to Indy was the car driven by Art Malone to eleventh place the previous

Chemical Compounds Division, the official business moniker for the STP arm of the Studebaker business. Apart from the colors and a different exhaust system, the car looked identical to the shape it had displayed in 1964. The Novis were reported to develop 750 horsepower from their 167.8 c.i. with 10,000 the maximum rpm reading. Joe Granatelli said he preferred "to quote the power figure as 742 horsepower at 7,400 rpms."

It was expected that the 4WDs were to be the major weapons in the Novi camp. The Kurtis roadster could be held in reserve to be used in case of some unforeseen problem(s). Andy Granatelli then said the Ferguson had only been entered in order to allow the crew additional garage space and the new 4WD was to be the primary ride. It appeared obvious to the Granatellis that the newer car was a better package than the Fergie. One STP account put it thusly: "The team will have the new car and two older reserve cars" (the Ferguson and a Kurtis-Kraft).

Again, the famous Novi name was not mentioned on the official entry forms much to the chagrin of true Novi fans. For the dyed-in-the-wool Novi supporters, the year had already started out on a sad note as the legendary chief mechanic for the Novis, Jean Marcenac had passed away on February 14. The man who had labored so long and hard on the beloved Novis for almost two decades was finally at rest without a 500 victory for the highly touted but beleaguered Novis. However, many recall that the likeable Frenchman had wrenched four 500 winners before World War II. A fitting tribute to the quiet and yet highly personable French born mechanical wizard was authored by 1925 Indy winner's Pete DePaolo. The touching tribute appeared in that year's Floyd Clymer's Indianapolis 500 Mile Race Yearbook under the title "A Legend of the Speedway."

Although the Granatellis had entered three cars, surprisingly, STP had signed only one driver. Despite the unlucky outings he had experienced in the previous two 500 races, Bobby Unser was provided another opportunity to improve on his record with the Novi team. Hopefully, this would not be too difficult as he finished dead last in 1963 and then 32nd the following year in the brand new Ferguson as the result of the deadly MacDonald-Sachs crash. Therefore, he had accumulated only three laps of 500 race experience in two years. Bobby certainly was showing a dogged determination to succeed in returning to the team once again. It might be pointed out that as a rookie he finished last, the only 500 winner who has ever done so. Signing up one driver might well indicate that the team was prepared to initially concentrate on placing one solid entry into the field and to make the very best of this one car/one driver combination. The results of such an effort would then dictate the action that might be undertaken by the team.

The track opened on May 1 for the 49th annual 500 mile race. A total of 68 cars were entered in what one source referred to as "A Month Long Carnival of Speed." Chief Steward Harlan Fengler was again in charge of the USAC crew that oversaw the technical inspection of the cars, officiating, scoring and various other track responsibilities.

The Novi team arrived at Indy on May 4. Bobby Unser made his first appearance on the track on May 7, behind the wheel of the brand new 4WD #6. As Unser took to the track for the initial shakedown, the car did not make it to the backstretch as a brake locked up as he was coming through turn two. The car spun 180 feet before Bobby was able to bring it to a halt in the infield. Even with a new car, perhaps the old Novi jinx remained steadfast. The car was returned to the garage area and the necessary repair work completed. That afternoon Bobby was back out on the track. Unfortunately, a second mishap once again sent him back to Gasoline Alley. An oil line had broken and Unser spun off the track in the car's oil, traveling 600 feet before the

(1965) Unser watches as several mechanics inspect the damage incurred in his first mishap of the month. I.M.S.

spin was concluded. Fortunately, no contact was made with the unforgiving wall on either occasion. One wag described the day's activities as getting the Novis "off to a typical Novi start." With regard to his second spin, the Albuquerque, New Mexico driver said:

"I saw a puff of smoke coming out of the side as I went into that first turn. But I didn't think it was anything serious. Then I felt it slide a little bit and I thought I had a little more trouble. Then it really started to move on me and I knew I must be loosing a heck of a lot of oil and I knew I couldn't drive out of this one."

When one of the small lawn type tractors attempted to pull the #6 into the garage area it stalled! Another tractor than had to be used for the task. This caused one fan to call down to the STP crew, "This just isn't your day." Following his two spectacular slides, one observer asked Unser about his pay with the Novi team. After a bit of thought Unser replied, "Well, today it seemed like I was working on a sliding scale." The debut of the new "dream" car had been somewhat less than auspicious.

On May 8, things improved as Bobby had the #6 up to a speed of 150.8 m.p.h. The following day, with Unser on the track, Andy Granatelli took a tumble as he dashed down pit lane to alert Chief Steward Fengler to have the yellow caution lights switched on. As Unser was practicing, the crew noticed that the car's belly pan appeared to be ready to drop from the car. The car came to a safe halt, although Andy suffered a cut knee and bruised ankle in the dash. Granatelli later said, "My spirit is still willing but my flesh is getting weak." When A.J. Foyt later saw a wounded Granatelli he asked what his problem was and Andy quipped, "Unser tried to run me down, that's what."

As conditions returned to a semblance of normalcy, Unser continued to move his speed upward. He was able to reach 154 m.p.h. and then on May 11, he surpassed the 155 m.p.h. barrier in the 4WD beauty constructed under the supervision of Vince and Joe. On May 12, another mishap befell the Novi team after Art Malone was allowed to try out the #59 Chemical Compound Special roadster. The run ended abruptly with the car against the southwest wall, although the damage to the front end was minor as the contact with the wall had been little more than a slight brush. Malone asserted, "I just swiped it (the wall) with the nose." Fortunately, Art emerged unscathed. He reported that the car had been "pushing just a little bit and I got on it just a little bit and it got out." The car slide 300 feet below the white line before going into a 240 foot slide sideways, then it straightened up to a one-half spin for another 100 feet before a struggling Art saved the Novi. Malone thought that he could power drive the car out of trouble but obviously it did not work.

(1965) A shattered front end on the newly built Granatelli 4WD Novi. The car was said to have several mechanical improvements and a weight reduction over the Ferguson. All was for naught as the Rose-Unser crash put the car out of action on the day prior to the opening of qualifications. I.M.S.

If the Granatellis had any notion that these minor set backs would be all that would confront them during the month, they would have been badly mistaken. On the 14th of May, the last day of practice prior to the opening round of qualifications, driver Ebb Rose of Houston, Texas a veteran of three 500s, lost control of his rear engine Offy #79 Racing Associates Special coming off the 4th turn. The driver following Rose could not avoid the spinning car and the two cars tangled in t-bone fashion with contact occurring at Ebb's side pod fuel tank. The collision caused the second car to veer off to smash into the wall. The car tangling with Rose was the brand new 4WD #6 STP Oil Treatment Special with Bobby Unser at the wheel! Unser's car slamming into the side of Rose's car was one of great impact. While Rose emerged unhurt, Unser suffered a badly bruised arm and shoulder and some lacerations on his face, but he was able to get out of his disabled mount and walk without aid to the nearby ambulance for the compulsory medical checkup at the infield medical center. Novi crew member Mike Garabedian recalls seeing an "ashened faced" Unser following the episode. A brief visit was then made to a nearby hospital before Unser was formally released and cleared to drive again.

Regarding the Rose-Unser incident: you may recall that following the 1964 inferno, USAC had mandated new rules concerning fuel storage. This included self-sealing fuel cells and stronger outside tank covers. The self-sealing tanks were a product from the Firestone Tire and Rubber Company. It has been agreed that the introduction of this fuel cell averted disaster. For his part Rose said, "There were plenty of sparks flying around and it had all the makings for a fire. That fuel tank and cell saved me. I got maybe a half teaspoon of fuel sprayed in my face on impact. I knew it was fuel 'cause I could smell it...They can pass all the safety rules they want from here on in and I'll vote for them 100%."

In discussing the crash with Ebb prior to the 1996 Indy 500 race, he reinterated what he had said at the time of the episode. Going further, he said that Unser's hitting him was a blessing in that it had kept his car from darting up to the outside wall. While Bobby's car was scuffing off power prior to hitting the wall, Rose had apparently gone over an oil slick causing his ride to become ballistic.

(1965) The external damage to Ebb Rose's Racing Associates Special following the unwanted meeting with the new 4WD Novi. One report asserted that #79 "got out of shape" moving through the 4th turn and that Bobby Unser had no option - thus the t-bone.   I.M.S.

The severely damaged Novi was in need of heavy repair work and the first weekend of qualifying was less than 24 hours away! Andy Granatelli was to conclude that the car damage was too serious to be repaired and/or replaced within one week's time so the entry was scratched. Bear in mind that replacement parts for the Novis could not be ordered "off the shelf" as was the case with most other cars. One account asserted that the mishap "wiped out #6." A winter's work had gone into the construction of a one of a kind 4WD only to be eliminated in not much more than the blink of an eye on the eve of qualifications. Andy was quick to point out that the #6 had been a very fast car and he claimed that Unser had unofficially broken the 160 m.p.h. barrier during practice. The "dream" car was now just a memory. Instead of having a top contender ready to roll,

117

Andy had one "old" car and the Ferguson "tank" which had yet to be driven a single lap that year. Even with the bruised shoulder, Bobby was able to drive the following day as the team had the Ferguson car setup for its first shakedown laps. One can only speculate as to the extent of work that must have been undertaken to prepare the car which originally was not destined to be pressed into action.

(1965) Young Vince, Andy's son, talking with Bobby as he and several other crew members moved the Ferguson out of its garage. With the continuing support from Valvoline note their decal. It is a wonder there are so few on-lookers as the Novis always attracted a crowd. Perhaps it is early in the day!
Gerald Walker Photo

On Pole Day, May 15, Bobby drove 22 laps in the Ferguson and the decision was made to try to qualify it later that day. The team had not been assigned an official line position in the draw and this forced Unser to wait until all of the cars in the qualifying line had made their first attempt or taken a wave off before he would be allowed to make a qualifying run. Late in the afternoon, the crowd saw the bulky #9 Ferguson Novi leave the pit area to make its first attempt. As usual, when a Novi came out on the track, the public once again cheered wildly. Unser made an impressive run averaging 157.467 m.p.h. over the four laps with the fastest lap a 157.950 m.p.h. clocking. This made the Ferguson the 8th fastest car of the day and the quickest of the front engine cars to make the field! And that with a car which had completed only 22 laps before the official attempt. Bobby was the last qualifier on Saturday due to the waiting period. One is left to wonder what speed Bobby might have obtained in the lighter #6 car if it had not been heavily damaged, for after its earlier runs it was considered the faster ride. In what seemed like standard operating procedure, the Novi plans had once again gone awry. Who would have anticipated that the Ferguson would be in the show while the highly touted expectations for #6 went unfulfilled.

On hand during the proceedings was Sherwood Egbert, Studebaker's former president, who had orchestrated the company's purchase of STP. As noted earlier, the Granatelli entries now lacked the Studebaker's company name, though STP remained a subsidiary.

While all of this was going on in the Novi camp, the first day of qualifying was a thrilling one. Defending Indy 500 winner and National Champion, A.J. Foyt, established a new qualifying record (161.233 m.p.h.) as well as a new one lap record (161.958 m.p.h.). He was at the wheel of the #1 Sheraton-Thompson Special, a year old Lotus-Ford rear engine car. Foyt's ride was set up by George Bignotti, his chief mechanic who was earning a reputation as a mechanical wizard. This marked the fourth straight year that a new qualifying mark had been established. Foyt's qualifying average bettered Jimmy Clark's record time by almost 2.5 m.p.h. Sitting on the front row next to pole sitter Foyt would be Jimmy Clark in the #82 rear engine Lotus Powered by Ford Special, while Dan Gurney in the Yamaha Special would round out the row in a third Lotus-Ford. In all a total of 21 drivers qualified on opening day. The fastest rookie in the field was Mario Andretti with a very impressive 158.849 m.p.h. run.

The day's only frightening incident happened when Jim Hurtubise virtually demolished the Tombstone Life Special as his ride plowed into the fourth turn wall when the throttle stuck. The car went to the outer wall hitting on the right side shearing off the rear wheel. The car then bounced along the wall for about 200 yards, did a half spin and stopped in the middle of the track. While the car was totalled, Jim emerged without serious

(1965) Bobby Unser receiving accolades as he returns to the pits following a successful qualifying run in the Ferguson after the Granatelli 4WD had been wiped out in a crash the previous day. I.M.S.

injury. Although, the car was badly mangled no fire erupted as the car was using the new Firestone resilient fuel cells. The crash again proved the worthiness of the new safety rules implemented by USAC.

The #59 STP car made an appearance that day with Art Malone at the wheel. During his practice run he left a trail of oil as the roadster was leaking oil. When the mechanics looked over the car they discovered the leakage was due to an O-ring that had permitted water to seep into the oil. Despite being a front engine car, the third Novi entry was rather popular with two drivers. Not only did Malone show an interest, but so did Jim Hurtubise. With his severely damaged Tombstone ride given no chance of being repaired to qualify, Herk was busily looking for a replacement ride.

Jim, a very popular driver, was fast becoming a folk hero due to his uninhibited spirit and carefree approach along with the every present smile and his devil may care style of driving. Hurtubise followers had increased since the previous year's 500 as he was now applauded for the sheer grit that he displayed. One week after the 1964 running of the 500, he had been involved in a tremendous accident in the Milwaukee 100 mile race. While running third just past the half way point, Herk was following the two front runners when the lead car experienced a mechanical problem. The car immediately behind the leader was able to veer away, yet Hurtubise's car ran over one of the second car's tires and bounced off the wall with the car catching on fire. The North Tonawanda, New York resident was burned over 40 percent of his body. The badly burned Hurtubise was flown to the government burn center located at the Brooke Army Medical Center in San Antonio, Texas. While still recovering, an undaunted Jim talked about his ultimate return to racing. It was quite obvious that there was no shortage of determination in his desire to return to the sport he loved. The plucky fellow would spend months on the road to recovery. After his discharge from the burn center, he had to make periodic trips to San Antonio for follow-up treatments. The layers of skin that were damaged due to the burns and that treated by plastic surgery greatly reduced his body's ability to regulate body temperature which could pose a real problem for a driver as cockpit temperature soared. With respect to his being a nervy driver, long-time friend Parnelli Jones said that Herk was "probably the bravest driver I've ever known" as he spoke of the fearless nature displayed by Jim.

As the 1965 season opened, Jim had contracted to drive for a trio of Indianapolis businessmen handling their DVS Special. The initials were derived from the first letter of the men's last name: George Deeb, Robert Voigt and Richard Sommers. Hurtubise had the DVS Tombstone Life Special ready for action in the 1965 season opener at Phoenix, a 100 miler in late March. Amazingly, Herk scored a tremendous comeback (in his first ride in a rear engine car) as he finished a solid 4th finishing behind winner Don Branson, Jim McElreath and Ronnie Duman. Jim's ultra-strong determination to return to the sport he so loved was most certainly demonstrated by the exemplary action he displayed at Phoenix. It was most definitely an extraordinary comeback!

Incidentally, the Phoenix race held on March 28, had muddied the waters with respect to the prowess of the highly touted Lotus-Fords. Three of the four Lotus entries (those driven by Foyt, Rodger Ward, and Roger McCluskey) were forced to the sidelines with an oiling problem as the race was won by Branson at the wheel of an "obsolescent" Offy roadster. While the Lotus cars were less than outstanding that day, rookie driver Mario Andretti had created quite an impression in only his second big car race. Andretti posted the third fastest time in the 24 car field and finished 6th in his Dean Van Line roadster. (His initial appearance in an Indy car had occurred at Trenton in September, 1964.)

Shortly after his Indy wall-banger in the DVS car, Herk made his way to the Granatelli garage to inquire about the availability of #59. Andy listened to Jim's solicitation for a ride and then permitted Hurtubise to take the car out for a test. Jim was again pleased to be at the wheel of his 1963 Indy ride and he was determined to secure the ride for the race if at all possible. Having driven a Novi in earlier Speedway competition, Herk now said, "Its power will throw you back in the seat."

Following the run, he returned to the DVS team owners hoping to persuade them to work

(1965) Hurtubise in the #59 Novi. The pick-up ride is still painted blue with a yellow nosecone. The Kurtis-Kraft 500G roadster appears to be sleek and agile.   I.M.S.

out some sort of arrangement with the Granatelli stable to transfer the Tombstone Life Insurance sponsorship money to the Granatellis in return for a ride in the Novi. After three days of "high-level negotiations," an agreement was reached. The conditions provided for Hurtubise to drive the STP #59 roadster and in exchange DVS would turn over the Tombstone sponsorship money to Granatelli while a commitment was made to carry a companion STP logo. DVS and Granatelli agreed to split the race winnings 50 - 50 with DVS paying the cost for the STP mechanics. DVS partner Dick Sommers has written that the Tombstone money deal amounted to $20,000 and that $15,000 was expended to obtain the #59 ride. Sommers reported that DVS spent $15,000 to save $5,000. Now, if only the prize money would be substantial enough to reward their efforts. Oh, what racing fever can do!

As Art Malone had also been in contention for the #59 ride, the DVS-Tombstone-STP deal closed the door on Art's efforts. It was certainly a coincidence that Art and Jim had been teammates on the Novi team of 1963 and both had racing experience in the same car. Herk had piloted the car in 1963 while Malone was in the cockpit the following year. Now with the DVS-STP deal consummated, Malone's chances were gone and he was left without a ride. When asked about this, Art informed us that he could fully accept this situation. He realized that Hurtubise was an extremely popular driver, a sentimental favorite and one who was desperately seeking a return to the sport. Art declared that the turn of events in no way altered his relationship with Jim as they remained the best of friends.

Art did not see any additional service with the Novi team. Recently reflecting on his Novi experience, Art recalled that after his 1963 run with "Tired Iron" Clint Brawner had offered him a ride in a Dean Van Lines Special for the upcoming Milwaukee race. Art had previously made a commitment to appear at a drag strip show at the behest of a good friend. As a result, he felt an obligation to turn down the Brawner offer. Yet, in hindsight, Art regrets the decision, saying that Clint was the "sort of fellow I could work with" on the champ car trail. Considering the matter further, Art now feels if he had taken the Dean ride that could have expanded his oval track opportunities. Art ultimately returned to drag strip activity and in time secured ownership of the DeSoto Memorial Drag Strip in Bradenton, Florida. He still retains ownership, although the facility is currently leased out. In March of 1997, Art was inducted into the Drag Racing Hall of Fame at Ocala, Florida. With his enshrinement, Art joined a host of drag strip stars from the past including Art Arfons, Don Garlits, Ak Miller, Danny Ongais and Mickey Thompson.

Hurtubise started out practice by running some 150 m.p.h. laps. When he came in he suggested some suspension changes and returning to the track, he reached speeds up to 154 m.p.h. Continuing, Herk showed that he was ready for a return to Indy competition when he made a circuit in the renamed car at a speed of 156.8 m.p.h. during the week of practice. Naturally, Jim had a

(1965) Hurtubise prepares to move out. The #59 has been repainted as Herk moved over from his wrecked DVS Tombstone Life of Arizona Special. The sponorship carried over to the Novi, thus it sported Tombstone and STP advertising.   I.M.S.

leg up on other possible drivers as he was already familiar with the Novi and he had definitely indicated that his Milwaukee accident, a year earlier had not diminished his skills. To some fans, he remained one of the masters of the roadsters.

On Saturday, May 22, the third day of time trials, Jim became the fastest of 11 qualifiers in the #59 Tombstone-STP Special. The Novi put together an impressive 156.863 m.p.h. average with the fastest lap being a 157.288 m.p.h. The last practice lap Jim made prior to the run was reported to have been a 158.061 m.p.h. Jim's qualifying time was more than a full mile per hour over the second fastest qualifier of the day, and more importantly he was the tenth fastest qualifier overall. In addition, he was the fastest second weekend qualifier. The engine used was that from the badly mangled #6 4WD. As the day's fastest qualifier Jim earned the $1,200 awarded to each day's fastest qualifier. When the qualifications had closed, Jim was positioned in the 23th starting spot. The Novis were the 8th and 10th fastest qualifiers in the field. Unser's mercury fast performance had lost some glitter when Hurtubise made his stunning and slightly slower (.604 m.p.h.) run in the rear drive car than Bobby's in the 4WD. Yet, it must be recalled that Unser drove a car that had come almost straight "out of the box." That is, without any extended track testing. As it were, Hurtubise averages were new records for the roadster type car.

After Hurtubise's run an exuberant Andy Granatelli said, "He's a brave driver...with courage beyond that of anyone...He's a super human being." Granatelli also declared, "There was no mistake in putting him (Hurtubise) in the car." With his ever present optimism regarding the prowess of the Novis, Granatelli suggested that if Herk had been in the car earlier he might have reached a 160 m.p.h. average. For his part Herk said, "We'll have it running for the race. Then, those other guys better watch out." One account labeled Hurtubise as the "Novi tamer." Having placed the car in the front row in 1963, Hurtubise certainly was familiar with the car's capabilities. In his book Hurtubise, Bob Gates reports that after qualifying Jim said, "Man that tiger was really roaring. It was doing some sputtering and I never did get the rpms I should have. But when it took hold-vrooooom-It really roared. It's a helleva race car, and I'm glad to be back in it." Following the run, Andy informed reporters that he had worn his STP suit several times the previous year and on each occasion some problem befell the operation. He then concluded that he was indeed superstitious for he did not wear the STP outfit plastered with the STP logo this time around.

(1965) Andy offering some last minute advice to Art Malone before Art takes to the track. With the size of the crowd, it could well be a qualifying day. I.M.S.

The two Novis driven by Unser and Hurtubise had provided stellar performances as they were the two fastest front engine cars of the six in the starting lineup. The fastest of the remaining front engine cars (driven by Gordon Johncock) qualified at a speed 1.851 m.p.h. slower than Herk. It was obvious that the brute power of the Novi had enabled the cars to make the field. Over short distances the Novi still had more than enough power to be reckoned with by the other teams. Endurance was the burning question. It is interesting to note that despite all signs of the classic Indy roadster being overwhelmed by the rear engine cars, there were people who still believed that the front engine car was the way to go at Indy - at least for the short term. Building a new front engine car for the Novi demonstrated that the Granatellis were among the group, even if it was a 4WD. Yet, ace roadster car builder A.J. Watson, who had already started building rear engine cars, seemed to be willing to demonstrate that if a roadster had more power it could match the rear engine cars of which a majority were Ford powered. Therefore, he fitted one of his roadsters with a Ford V-8 placing driver Don Branson in the car for practice. However, time restrictions prevented Watson from dialing in the car as his primary driver Rodger Ward was experiencing continual rear engine problems. In fact, two-time Indy winner Ward missed the race as did the Ford engine roadster. Branson was to ultimately make the race in a Leader Card entry sponsored by Wynn's Friction Proofing Oil. This Watson built rear engine car sported a Ford V-8 and was to finish 8th. Was this additional supporting evidence of the superiority of the rear engine Fords?

One note of interest regarding the history of the front drive Novis: they had demonstrated their massive power time and time again over the years since their inaugural run in 1941; the year (1965) aptly demonstrated that they had finally lost their reputation as the fastest front drive cars to have ever competed at Indianapolis. Mickey Thompson entered a FWD car, the Challenger Wheel Drive Special, a Chevy powered car. After the fatal accident of Dave MacDonald in one of his cars a year earlier, many blamed Mickey for building unsafe, unstable and dangerous cars. Though not one to succumb to pressure, Mickey, nonetheless "threw away" the rear engine concept of which he had been one of the American pioneers. He returned to front engine cars. Such appears to represent a big step back in time as 27 of the cars in the field featured rear engine powerplants. The Thompson Chevy aluminum V-8 featured a DOHC conversion originally designed by former Indy car owner Gordon Schroeder who had turned his mechanical talents to the construction of racing components. Bob Mathouser of Los Angeles struggled to get the car over 150 m.p.h. He ultimately reached 153.5 m.p.h. Thompson reported that the car had been experiencing tire slippage in the corners. "We've got plenty of power but we haven't been able to get out of the corners the way we would like because the tires want to spin in one spot."

The FWD Thompson car never completed an official qualifying attempt, but unofficially it surpassed the mark set by the old front drive Novis, bettering the one lap record of 139.034 m.p.h. set by Novi chauffeur Chet Miller way back in 1952. Then in 1965 Bob reached 153.374 m.p.h. before the car threw a rod. The Indianapolis Star carried a story on Mathouser's run under the headline, "Bob Mathouser Breaks Front Wheel Drive Record." In recounting Mathouser's speed, Mickey stated that the time "shows how much progress has been made in chassis and engine development over the last 14 years." On Friday, the Thompson crew was setting up the engine for a Saturday qualifying run with the M/T Challenger Wheel Special when a crack was detected in the main web. The discovery prevented any thought of a qualification attempt on Saturday. The following day, the last day to qualify, Thompson's car never made the show as the engine blew as Mathouser was about to take the green flag. As a consequence, Chet Miller's official 4 lap record time remained.

On Monday the 24, a newspaper headline read: "Fastest 500 Field Filled." The account included the field's average of 156.058 m.p.h. During Sunday's hectic action four cars were bumped while drivers Johnny Boyd, Masten Gregory, Al Unser and Bill Cheesbourg made the field.

Thompson Special in the last row.

With respect to the racing tires, 21 of the starters (15 rear engine cars, the two Novis and the four Offy roadsters) were equipped with Firestone tires. The wide 9 inch "Indys" would have to perform well to surpass the previous year when 12 of the cars did not change a Firestone during the entire contest. An even dozen of the qualifiers had chosen Goodyears including A.J. Foyt on the pole with the record speed in a Lotus-Ford. Changes were certainly plentiful as the race marked Goodyear's return to the 500 for the first time in 43 years. The so-called tire war was in full swing. The field contained 27 rear engine cars (17 Fords and 10 Offenhausers), four Offy roadsters and the two front engine Novis.

(1965) Car owner Mickey Thompson rolling his M/T Challenger Wheel Special on pit lane. Driver Bob Mathouser walks alongside smoking in the pits. While the front wheel drive failed to make the race, Mathouser unofficially clipped off laps that surpassed the existing record for a FWD set by Chet Miller in a Novi in 1952.   I.M.S.

Eleven rookies joined the field which was one short of the record at that time. The rookies consisted of Mario Andretti, Billy Foster, Jerry Grant, Masten Gregory, Arnie Knepper, Gordon Johncock, Bobby Johns, Joe Leonard, Mickey Rupp, George Snider and Al Unser. In time, members of this rookie class would post a total of seven 500 wins. The future winners consisted of Al Unser (Bobby's younger brother) who would have four wins: Gordon Johncock (two victories) and Mario Andretti (one victory). Al Unser made the field on the last day after the Maserati engine in his Frank Arciero entry blew the previous day. Working with A.J. Foyt, he then placed a Sheraton-

A surprise was noted on Carburetion Day when the #59 Novi was pushed from Gasoline Alley to the track. The car had changed in appearance as the blue and yellow paint job in which Herk had qualified the car had been replaced with a fluorescent red with black and gold leaf trim. The paint job was the result of the STP/Tombstone Life hookup.

Of greater importance that day, Unser's car, without warning, came to an abrupt halt on the back straight -"like a dying shark." One account reported that the engine had "moaned and died in Bobby's hands." When the engine was torn down that night it was discovered that a small metal piece had found its way into the engine from the track surface. The engine could be repaired in time for the event, although the team would not know if everything was in working order as the cars were not permitted to return to the track before the race. Following the mechanical problem, Bobby was asked about the alledged Novi jinx. He replied, "Maybe I believe the Novi Jinx, maybe I don't. I was beginning to wonder."

Once again on race day both the Novis appeared on the track with the leftside tires whitewalled for identification purposes. Photos of the 1965 starting grid show the "Big Red #9" with an electric blanket over the oil tank to warm the oil before starting the engine. The air entry into the front radiator was also covered with a blanket. The #59 also had an electric blanket at the radiator entry. Such a move was uncommon at the time. In preparation, Herk, due to his scarred hands, had a mechanic tie a bandana over his nose and mouth as he would be wearing his open face helmet.

With the display of the green flag, the field was quickly on the move. Many felt that Jimmy Clark was the man to beat and only A.J. Foyt, who drove an older Lotus, was in a position to beat the "Flying Scot." Yet, for the Novi team, misfortune once again struck early. While Hurtubise's car was off to a good start, not balking as it built up revs coming down the front straightaway, a problem quickly developed. With the transmission in second gear, Jim had applied power in shifting into high and the transfer box was not up to the sudden power surge. Hurtubise was to say, "The car was performing perfectly. I got on the gas and I dropped it into high gear and coming out of turn one I could feel a rumble in the transmission gears. I knew something had happened, it must have been when I shifted or when I got on the gas. When I got on the back straightaway it got worse and worse and I knew I had to pull out" of the race. An STP spokesman allowed that Jim had probably "stabbed the gas too quickly with his over anxious right foot." Either way, two favorites were out of the race - a Novi and Jim Hurtubise.

Just as had occurred the last two years, a Novi was almost instantly eliminated from the race. The wider rear tires did not spin on this occasion, thus aiding in the stripping of the gears. It was all Herk could do to pilot the limping #59 back to pit lane under power. Hurtubise, thus, became the first retiree of the day and for the second time in three years the Granatellis had one of their cars certified as finishing last! Such causes one to wonder about the alleged ever-present Novi jinx. Jim was not the only driver who retired with gearbox problems that year as seven other drivers fell victim to broken transmissions or rear end gear failure. It seems reasonable to accept the explanation that some gearing was not able to handle the additional power available in the engines and the "sticky tires" of that year. Bear in mind that the new tires did not permit much wheel spin compared to the narrow tires of the past. The new generation tires had such tremendous gripping power it appears that when drivers mashed the throttle too quickly the gearbox was subject to greater stress, thus increasing a possible malfunction at the transmission.

(1965) A classic photo showing the start of the race by the sterling race photographer Armin Krueger. Bobby Unser in the Novi Gas Treatment Special is in 5th place after having started the chase from the 8th spot. The lead car is Jimmy Clark who has nudged out pole sitter A.J. Foyt. They are closely pursued by Parnelli Jones and Dan Gurney. Note that all four cars in front of Unser are rear engine products.
Armin Krueger Photo

Bobby Unser certainly had more luck than Hurtubise as he moved the #9 Ferguson up to 7th place the first 22 laps after starting 8th. It appears that he was racing a bit more with his head than strictly with a lead foot. He lost a few positions for a brief time, then gained some of the ground back after several of the drivers in front of him

(1965) Catch me if you can! Bobby Unser leading A.J. and Parnelli. The pair are both driving Lotus race cars. Note Bobby's bandanna. His day was over at lap 69 with an oil line problem. Parnelli finished 2nd to winner Jimmy Clark in a flip flop of the 1963 race results. I.M.S.

retired. At 55 laps he was in 5th place. At that point he made his first pit stop with only fuel being added as no tire changes were necessary. The pit action consumed 56 seconds and Bobby rejoined the field in 14th place. Then on lap 69, while running in 5th place, it was all over. An oil line to the supercharger broke, forcing the Novi to retire from the race.

Bobby Unser was to report, "All of a sudden I looked at the oil pressure gauge and it was down to nothing. The engine just started to vibrate tremendously bad and of course I kicked it out of gear and the engine died immediately. I came into the pits, still thinking that with some change that Andy Granatelli and the boys could fix it in the pits. And they took the hood off, started checking the spark plugs and a few things like that. Sure enough, Andy reached down and picked up an oil fitting and it had broken right in two." The car was then pushed to Gasoline Alley with a dejected Bobby still in the cockpit. Little did anyone realize at the time the historical significance of this retirement. Bobby was classified 19th in the standings.

The race was won by Jimmy Clark, the "pride of Duns, Scotland." Clark was the first foreign winner since English born George Robson captured first place in 1946. Clark's win was also the first at Indy by a rear engine car; plus he was the first winner since 1946 who used anything other than an Offenhauser engine. Clark was totally in command as he lead 190 of the 200 laps. The car was using Firestone rubber. Many felt there was some justice in the fact that Clark had won in view of what had faced him in the 1963 race. If it had not been for fate and the chief steward, Clark might well have won two years earlier. Second place went to Parnelli Jones in the #98 Agajanian-Hurst Special while 3rd place was earned by rookie Mario Andretti in a Dean Van Lines Special with Al Miller finishing 4th in the Alderman Ford. The first four spots went to rear engine cars. The highest placement achieved by a front engine car was the 5th obtained by Gordon Johncock in the Weinberger Homes Special. The next four places went to cars with rear engines. Rookie Mickey Rupp was 6th while fellow neophyte Bobby Johns was 7th. Johns was in a team car to that of winner Clark. Florida driver Johns, a NASCAR veteran, was in the #83 Lotus Powered by Ford Special. Rookie Al Unser finished 9th beating out brother Bobby by ten positions.

As for the Novi fans, it was a bitter pill to swallow. A V-8 had finally won the Indianapolis 500, but it was not a Novi. The highly devoted Novi fan must have wondered just how many times a V-8 Novi should have won the race with ease. Now some questioned if there was any realistic chance that a Novi would ever win. Only two

(1965) Bobby out in front of Len Sutton who is in a rear engine Byrant Heating and Cooling Special. The tires on the Novi were once again painted white. I.M.S.

of the first 17 finishers were in cars with front engine placement: Johncock and then Eddie Johnson in a Chapman Special (10th place). Both cars used Offy power with an A.J. Watson chassis.

For all practical purpose, the rear engine revolution was now an established fact. The rear engine car was now the accepted way to go. This left the future of the entire Novi stable in doubt. That is unless they should join the "Society of Rear Engine Racers" or concentrate upon further improvements on the front engine drive or the 4WD concept. If they had an alternate plan in their hip pocket it was time to use it, otherwise the future appeared rather bleak. On the surface, it certainly appeared that the present Novi stable of cars was most likely out of contention.

remarkable event in the long history of the Novi, for it represented the first time in 24 years that a Novi was entered in any race on a closed circuit track in the United States other than the Indianapolis 500.

The two 1962 Kurtis chassis were entered under the name of STP Special and they carried the numbers 6 and 59. The #59 was the same car that Herk drove in the July Atlanta test sessions. The other roadster, entered as #6, represented something of a surprise as this was the number used on the Granatelli built 4WD that was badly wrecked in practice at Indy that May with Bobby Unser at the wheel. It was the first public appearance of this particular car that year. It was painted yellow with a black offset stripe, reminiscent of its 1963

(1965) The winner of the 1965 race, Scotsman Jimmy Clark. The Lotus Powered By Ford Special would carry STP sponsorship the following year.
I.M.S.

After the 500, the #59 STP car was gone over in preparation for some tire testing. Jim Hurtubise then drove the car at the Atlanta International Raceway one and a half mile banked asphalt oval in July and proved that the car was still fast - at least over the short haul. Herk clocked a new record for closed one and a half mile tracks on July 9, with an average speed of 164.5 m.p.h. during a tire test. In doing so he broke Lloyd Ruby's week old record of 163.400 m.p.h. set with a rear engine Ford powered car. The testing preceded a 250 mile USAC race set for August 1 at the five year old Georgia track. With the encouraging performance by a Novi during tire testing at Atlanta, the Granatellis decided to enter their two roadsters in the upcoming 250 miler. It was a

Indy outing. The #59 had retained its fluorescent red as used at Indianapolis during the race.

The Granatelli camp believed that the Atlanta race might prove to be beneficial on the learning curve as they had experienced handling problems with the cars in the past. It was felt that the roadster might prove to be better suited for high speeds on a banked track such as Atlanta. Prior to the race Andy said, "This could be our race...and anything the Lotus and the Lola can do, we can do better."

Recalling the race Andy said, "Atlanta was a high bank and we had a chance to compete there because we could use more throttle." In further reflection on the decision years later, Andy said, "Atlanta was so bumpy that it was a waste bringing the cars there. So bumpy and with all that extra power. We ran pretty fast but..."

Jim Hurtubise was assigned to drive the #59 while the #6 was provided for five-time Indy veteran Bud Tingelstad. Bud's best Indy finish had been a 6th the year before in a Federal Engineering Special. The Granatellis had asserted that Greg Weld would be the driver of the #6 car and such was listed in the program. Although an up and coming driver, Weld was considered by USAC to lack sufficient experience with the championship cars, thus he was not permitted to accept the Atlanta ride. However, the champ car newcomer had been permitted to take the Indy rookie test in May. He passed that driving test at the wheel of Wally Weir's Halibrand Shrike #19 Mobil Gas Special. However, on one occasion Chief Stewart Harlan Fengler was less than impressed by Weld's driving and after a spin-out, "sat him down for the rest of the day." The Mobil car assignment was eventually given to Chuck Rodee who put it in the 500.

(1965) The pace lap at Atlanta in August. The Novi is considerably larger than all other cars - even the roadsters. Foyt on the pole with Billy Foster alongside. Herk is on the outside of the third row while eventual winner Johnny Rutherford is to his left in #2, the Moog St. Louis Special. I.M.S.

Some might be surprised in learning that Bobby Unser, a Novi driver for the last three years at Indy, was not involved in the Atlanta preparations with the Granatellis. This was due to the fact that Bobby's contract with the Granatellis was an "Indy only" obligation, for he wished to drive the entire championship circuit. At the time, Unser was driving car owner Gordon Van Liew's Vita Fresh Orange Juice Special. Bobby's time in the Vita Fresh car was 162.954 m.p.h. Both Novis qualified for the race. Pole sitter A.J. Foyt reached an average of 166.512 m.p.h. By comparison, Foyt's Indy record set the previous May had been a 161.233 m.p.h. The time was declared a new world record for a one and one-half mile closed track breaking Herk's time in a Novi set just weeks earlier. Still, Jim qualified with an impressive 161.483 m.p.h. average for the 6th starting position in the 30 car field. Tingelstad qualified for the tenth spot averaging 158.963 m.p.h. Bud was unhappy with his speed, for in practice he had reached 162.1 m.p.h. That time was recorded early in the morning while the actual qualifying attempt was made as the day's activities were about to end. Andy has said that the cars were not detuned for Atlanta, but that full throttle play was not used on the mile and one-half track.

Before the race started, Hurtubise jokingly told Bobby Unser that he (Jim) would be happy if he could last for more than 30 laps. Herk, still recovering from the horrendous injuries incurred in the Milwaukee incident, did not have overwhelming faith in his physical capacity to go the distance on the banked oval in a powerful Novi. Not only would he be driving a front engine car with the heat moving through the cockpit, but the atmospheric temperature was going to be a major factor as well. The weather bureau had predicted an Atlanta temperature on race day as somewhere between the mid-80s to the low-90s.

At the display of the green flag, Jim fell back into the field somewhat reminiscent of his falling back in the field after leading the first lap of the 1963 Indy 500. This time however, he dropped back much further. But Jim had learned a lesson at Indy two months earlier. Instead of flooring the car to regain positions as quickly as possible, he unwound the Novi gradually. This approach was aimed at preventing another gearbox failure or clutch problem. The "play safe" strategy certainly paid off, for to the surprise of many, Jim held down the second spot in the race for sometime. But the ride in a Novi on the track was a tiring one and Herk became physically weak during the latter stage of the race and was unable to maintain his speed. During the last 7 laps, he had to slow the pace in order to make it to the finish "as exhaustion caught up with him."

(1965) Atlanta action and what a variety of cars. Bud Tingelstad is in the #6 Novi with Johnny Rutherford in a rear engine Ford at his right. Sammy Sessions is in front in Pete Salemi's Central Excavating Special - a dirt track car.   I.M.S.

As it turned out, he managed a highly commendable 4th place finish.

Bud Tingelstad did not make it to the finish, although his car did. The heat within the cockpit was too much for Bud and he eventually pitted for a relief driver. It was reported that his feet had developed blisters. Vince Granatelli believes that the combination of the high banked track and the powerful Novi played a role in Bud's departure from the cockpit 60 laps from the finish. To several observers, Bud's eyes seemed to completely fill his goggle lenses as he pitted. The Indy veteran had certainly never driven anything comparable to the Novi. Unser's Vita Fresh Orange Juice Special, a rear engine Offy, quit at 55 laps and he was available to take over the driving. Unser then brought the Novi home to a 14th place showing. That both Novis finished and seemed to do surprisingly well may be due in part to the fact that there were only 12 rear engine cars entered in the race. The Atlanta 250 witnessed a variety of cars; rear engine creations; Offy roadsters and several dirt cars, all competing on the asphalt. The Novis were a welcome addition to this wide array of styles. It was a remarkable feat for the Novis to see the checkered flag, something seldom experienced during the cars long career. Perhaps, the Novi V-8 preferred to compete under super hot conditions. Remember, Duke Nalon had not experienced mechanical troubles when he ran in the hottest Indianapolis 500 mile race ever held - 1953.

The race and its winner's purse of $17,250 went to Johnny Rutherford, a 27 year old driver from Fort Worth, Texas. He was at the wheel of the Moog Saint Louis Special, the rear engine Ford Rodger Ward had failed to qualify at Indy that May. The triumph marked his first champ car victory and it was also the first Indy type race held at the Georgia track. Fellow Texan A.J. Foyt was forced to the sidelines while leading when the right rear suspension on his Sheraton-Thompson Special broke in turn two on lap 108 of the 167 lap chase. The broken suspension caused the car

(1965) Bobby Unser getting seated in the #6 Novi after Bud Tingelstad came into the pits seeking a relief driver. Tingelstad looks on from the left. Unser was available due to his Vita Fresh Orange Juice Special suffering a mechanical malady earlier.   I.M.S.

to spin crazily into a steel rail before skittering into the infield area. Foyt definitely had been in charge as he had lapped all but Billy Foster, Johnny Rutherford and Hurtubise by lap 40. Mario Andretti finished second in a Dean Van Lines rear engine Offy, while Billy Foster finished third in a rear engine Ford in front of Herk. The victorious Rutherford made reference to the strong centrifugal forces exerted on the bank oval as he said the forces moved him "so far over I was seeing the world sideways and ended up with a crick in my neck." Little wonder then that Herk had to show perseverance as he returned to racing, competing on a banked oval after nearly a year's layoff. While USAC envisioned great hopes for the infusion of champ car racing in the South, only 27,000 fans were on hand for the inaugural outing.

While Andy was later to criticize the bumpy track, as he left the facility to catch a plane following the contest, he asserted that he had learned one thing from the event: "We ought to enter more races."

was met with more than passing interest by the Granatellis though it failed to make the race. When the brothers reached a point where they felt a dramatic change was necessary for their future racing endeavors, growing consideration was given to the use of a gas turbine entry. The thought of using a turbine was not new. As early as 1955, a turbine powered car had taken to the Speedway oval for some experimental work. A KK3000, owned by the Firestone Tire and Rubber Company, was used in some running sessions (see Automotive Quarterly, Vol. 30, No. 4, pg. 75 or The Kurtis-Kraft Story by Ed Hitze, pg. 44 and 48-49.)

The turbine had a great deal to offer at Indy and there was a lack of any restriction on the power output of such a power plant. Any size turbine was allowable. Therefore, in early 1965, the Granatellis had given the green light to such a project. The eventual turbine engine was to become a four wheel drive vehicle, making use of the knowledge gained with the Novi 4WD cars. The car was to have its engine mounted in a

(1965) Jim Hurtubise in the #59 Novi on the Atlanta track. The race was to represent the last competitive action ever undertaken by a Novi. I.M.S.

The Granatelli brothers had suffered another disappointing month of May at Indy that year. It had been obvious that if they wanted the Novi to remain a viable commodity at Indy some dramatic changes had to be undertaken. To get rid of the front engine cars was perhaps the first move to be initiated. We have made several references to the Granatellis having started preparations for a highly futuristic type car earlier that year. In 1962, car owner John Zink of Tulsa, Oklahoma, had appeared at the Brickyard with his Trackburner turbine powered entry and the car

position far to the left with the cockpit on the right side of the chassis. To insure a greater chance of success, the chassis was to be built to fit a Novi V-8 if the turbine engine presented insurmountable problems and would perhaps not be competitive. An alternative plan would therefore be within reach. A Novi was intended to be the alternative as a turbine car was now the desired goal. When the turbine decision was made it did not signal an abrupt end to all Novi activities as the experimental turbine work would not be short ranged or a quick fix.

INTERMEZZOS

Pit Masters

Some sources attribute part of Jimmy Clark's 1965 success to the appearance of the Wood brothers on his Indy pit crew. Glen and Leonard Wood were the car owners of one of the more formidable NASCAR teams. Such was due in part to their reputation as being the "fastest pit crew in the world." Clark's two pit stops consumed a total time of only 44.5 seconds. No tires or adjustments were made, although 58 gallons of fuel was added in approximately 15 sec. at each stop.

The Lotus team sought faster pit stops and the Wood brothers reputation of making pit stop work into something close to an art form was brought to their attention. The fact that they used Fords in NASCAR competition and the Lotus team likewise made use of the Ford powerplant lends credence to the fact that they were "summoned by Ford." It has been said that the appearance of the brothers serving an Indy car with their masterful pit stops "left the competition slack jawed." Remarkedly, the brothers had never serviced an Indy car, much less a rear engine racer.

Johns Goes North

As noted earlier, joining the Lotus team was NASCAR driver Bobby Johns of Miami, Florida. Reportedly, the Ford Motor Company "had pressed for a star driver" in the team's second car but Colin Chapman had resisted.

Andrew Ferguson, Chapman's right hand man during the 1960s, stated that Colin preferred a "lesser known but reliable driver" so that Clark could shift over to the "backup" ride if his mount faltered for any reason. It was felt that such a move would not enrage Ford, the American media and we assume the race fans as well. Johns, who drove a Ford on the NASCAR circuit, lived up to expectations and then some as his car was the third fastest qualifier on the second Saturday though he was relegated to the 22nd starting spot.

In a revealing account, it has been reported that when the race began Johns felt that his throttle power had dropped noticeably and when coming off the corners the car was flat. Stopping later, the pit crew informed him that the car was "okay, just drive it." It turned out that his #83 Lotus had a higher gear installed so that he could not come close to reeling in Clark. However, the "Florida Flash" drove on to a praiseworthy 7th place finish.

Johns reports that he obtained "super mileage but lacked horsepower" as the fuel nozzles were set for a fine spray. Quite understandably, Bobby has pointed out that under revised rules he was the first NASCAR driver permitted to "cross over" to USAC and not lose his NASCAR license.

Herk in the South

While Jim Hurtubise had displayed some trepidation as to whether he could endure the rigors of running a Novi at Atlanta in the 250 miler in 1965, he most certainly must have found the track to his liking. Herk returned to Atlanta in late March, 1966, to win NASCAR's Atlanta 500 in a 1966 Plymouth owned by veteran USAC car owner/driver Norm Nelson. With the car bearing the familiar #56, Jim brought home first place honors after starting 5th. His closest pursuers were Freddie Lorenzen and Dick Hutcherson, both a lap down. Indy veteran Paul Goldsmith, who also competed with the Southern based stock car organization, finished 4th three laps down. During the event, Hurtubise had experienced a vibration problem so he decided to stomp on the gas and "get the show over with." Car owner Nelson said Herk "doesn't know what it is to slow up. Wide open is the only pace he knows."

Earlier that year, Jim had finished 6th in two NASCAR events. The first came at Riverside, California in January. The other 6th place finish was achieved in the Daytona 500 the following month. The open wheel veteran certainly demonstrated that he was equally at home in stock cars.

Prior to attending a Daytona 500 race several years ago, one of your authors entered the Halifax County Historical Society Museum in Daytona to view the NASCAR memorabilia on display. The very first driver photo noted, due to its prominent display, was that of Jim Hurtubise. One might have expected such an honor to go to one of the early NASCAR stars such as Buck Baker, Lee Petty, Fireball Roberts, Joe Weatherly or Daytona's own Marshall Teague. But such was not the case.

Qualifying Photos of Novi Drivers, 1963 - 1965

Jim Hurtubise - 1963
Kurtis - Kraft 500 K - built in 1962 - Finished 22nd

Art Malone - 1963
Kurtis - Kraft 500 F - built in 1956 - Finished 31st

Bobby Unser - 1963
Kurtis - Kraft 500 K - built in 1962 - Finished 33rd

Art Malone - 1964
Kurtis - Kraft 500 K - built in 1962 - Finished 11th

Jim McElreath - 1964
Kurtis - Kraft 500 K - built in 1962 - Finished 21st

Bobby Unser - 1964
Ferguson P104 - 4WD - built in 1964 - Finished 32nd

Bobby Unser - 1965
Ferguson P104 - 4WD - built in 1964 - Finished 19th

Jim Hurtubise - 1965
Kurtis - Kraft 500 K - built in 1962 - Finished 33rd

Chapter 16

Preparations For Another 500 - 1966

Champ car owners who planned to enter one or more cars in the Indy 500 harbored the usual burning desire to have everything in place by the arrival of spring. The Granatelli brothers certainly were no exception, as they and their crew had been busy in preparing a Novi over the winter months of 1965-1966.

Yet, things did not go well at the Paxton-STP camp, for during several tests with the Novi-Ferguson 4WD it was discovered that the car still did not handle properly. The Granatellis decided that Vince should go to England to consult with Colin Chapman, the famed chief designer and owner of the Lotus team. Chapman's reputation was that of one of the finest chassis designers in the world. It was reported that Chapman's relationship with Ford had "begun to fade" and his agreement with the Ford Motor Company was to expire at the end of 1965. Therefore, his services as a consultant were available. Vince met with Chapman and received some suggestions for the Granatelli project.

Following Vince's return from England, Andy became involved in discussions that ultimately lead to STP sponsoring the official Lotus factory team for the 1966 race. Sponsorship of the Lotus effort would be in addition to entering a Novi.

The 1966 Indy Lotus was another technical wonder. Chapman had opted for a 252 c.i. (4.2 liter) version of the British Racing Motors H16 engine. The H16 engine was essentially two flat 8 cylinder engines with one block mounted above the other. They were to use a single crankcase with the crankshafts coupled to a single flywheel. BRM had such an H16 engine under development as new Formula One rules allowed 183 c.i. (3 liter) unblown engines to replace the unblown 91 c.i. (1 1/2 liter) formula in use from 1961 through 1965. The #16 was a massive engine, using a number of components that had previously seen service in the 91 c.i. BRM V-8 engines. At what point Chapman determined to make the move to the H16 is unknown.

The Lotus-STP contract was signed in March, 1966, at the STP headquarters, then located in the Chicago suburb of Des Plaines, Illinois. Granatelli, Chapman and Clark were all on hand. The STP-Lotus connection was to remain intact through 1969. Studebaker publication relations representative, Bill Dredge, said that while the Chapman-Granatelli cars would run as a team with the same sponsor and coloring, the two camps would operate separately. The STP-Lotus deal ultimately called for the use of a Ford engine as Andy considered the H16 to be a "mechanical sandwich." Andrew Ferguson described the business arrangement this way: "Team Lotus joined forces with the enthusiastic Andy Granatelli, head of STP Studebaker Corporation and famed for his mechanical expertise."

The Granatellis were then concentrating heavily on a turbine powered car (with a side-by-side chassis) as the cockpit was to be placed alongside the turbine. Continuing attention was also given to a Novi powered car in case of trouble. The turbine chassis frame was finished in March and was about ready to be assembled into a complete car. Then disaster struck! The frame was dispatched to another firm for the heat treatment process. One of that firm's employees made a dreadful mistake during the procedure which resulted in the lightweight frame being damaged to a point beyond repair. Of course, this meant the end of any 1966 competition with the turbine program. It was the second major set back for the STP Indy efforts in 1966 when one considers the continuing handling problems experienced with the Ferguson.

During that same month, another important engineering factor occurred. The Granatellis were developing a revised Novi engine allegedly capable of rpms beyond the magical 10,000 red line limit. Remember that the original design of the block called for the use of three main bearings as designed in 1940 when some 7,500 rpms would be the top end. Over the years, the Novi had come a long, long way when one considers the demands placed on the fabled engine; yet, a three main crank had remained.

Prior to the chassis disaster with the turbine, the Granatelli brothers had not completely shuttered their Novi project. The Granatelli built 4WD Novi was sent to the one mile Phoenix International Raceway for testing that March. A Phoenix newspaper made it known on March 11, that the car might even be entered in the upcoming Jimmy Bryan USAC 150 mile national championship race. The race was scheduled for March 20, and the Novi was to be driven by Greg Weld.

With the hiring of Weld, the Granatellis appeared to be maintaining a youth movement which started with the hiring of Bobby Unser and Art Malone in 1963. Rookie Weld was only 22 years old. His age aside, Weld had some outstanding racing credentials to offer. The young Kansas City, Missouri driver had begun racing while still in his teens, driving super modified cars in the area around his hometown. In 1963, Weld captured first place in the third running of the now famous Knoxville Nationals that evolved into the most prestigious sprint car race in America. In 1964, Greg moved on to the tough IMCA sprint car circuit - the same sanctioning body that had helped other drivers to hone their skills before they moved on to the then premier USAC sprint car ranks. This group would include drivers such as A.J. Foyt, Parnelli Jones, Jim Hurtubise, Jim McElreath and Johnny Rutherford.

Running with IMCA in 1964, Weld finished 10th in the point standings, and his skills were impressive to the point that he was named Rookie of the Year. With such an outstanding showing by the young Missourian, the following year he graduated to the USAC sprinters. The first year was most certainly a Cinderella story as he lost the driving title to Johnny Rutherford by a minuscule two and one-half points. Talk about tough competition: Following in the point standings were Bobby Unser (3rd); Jud Larson (4th); and Roger McCluskey (5th). The speed displays and talents of Weld did not go unnoticed as the Granatellis signed Greg to drive their sole Novi entry in the 1966 Indianapolis 500. One must concur with the notion that such would be a tough assignment, for not only was there that enormous Novi power, but the acclimation to 4WD as well.

On Saturday, March 12, eight days prior to the third annual Jimmy Byran Memorial Race, the Novi undertaking at Phoenix suddenly soured when Weld crashed the car rather heavily. Granatelli described it thusly: "Greg Weld slashed it into the wall and wiped it out." In spite of this mishap, the Arizona Republic reported in its March 17 issue that one of the Novis was entered for that Sunday's race, although it was not certain that the car would be ready. The following day, the paper published an entry list that did include a Novi. On race day, another entry list was published and it again listed the Novi, although it did not provide any car number! In an accompanying article the reporter referred to the car as being a doubtful starter.

Unfortunately, the car did not engage in the qualifications held prior to the race. Of 31 cars entered, only 23 qualified for a field which permitted a 24 car grid. Thus, the Novi might well have had a chance to make the field had an attempt been made to qualify. The car was not listed in the official program, however a teasing one-half page photo of the Novi engine appeared in the program.

In They Call Me Mr. 500, Andy Granatelli stated that the car had been wiped out in the test session. This most probably was the March 12 incident. If heavily damaged it was a rather firm excuse for not making the field. But then, how did the Arizona Republic come up with the news about a Novi being entered? To compound the dilemma,

(1966) Andy was down to a single driver for 1966, sprint car driving ace Greg Weld. The second year rookie was pegged to pilot the most powerful piston engine at the track that year. Only the name of chief mechanic Vince Granatelli appears on the cowling along with Weld's name. Several crew members have expressed disappointment that their names failed to ever appear on any Granatelli Novi.   I.M.S.

the March 16th issue of the Phoenix Gazette carried a statement that the track's general manager, Harry Redkey, had announced that the Granatellis had filed an official entry blank for the upcoming event. The story also reported that this would mark the first time that "the power-laden Novi creations will be driving competitively outside the two and one-half mile Indianapolis track." The veracity of the article has to be questioned, even if one considers only the assertion of a first running of a Novi outside of Indianapolis. As Novi followers were well aware, such cars had run at Monza, Italy in 1957, and at Atlanta in August of 1965. To make things even more difficult to understand, it is far from certain which car had been used in the sessions. A great deal of uncertainty prevails regarding the whole Phoenix episode. Perhaps the STP press kit released at Indianapolis that May might shed some light on the matter as it mentioned that plans called for Weld to compete in the Phoenix race before the Indy 500.

According to USAC records, no official entry was made for the car to compete at Phoenix. USAC has stated that the wall smacking incident must have occurred during a private test session. All of this certainly leads to intense confusion. As for Andy, the Phoenix episode is strongly etched in his mind. Whenever he talked about the run he would run out of words to describe the shrilling effect of the mighty Novi's roar bouncing off the nearby Estrella Mountains. Vince Granatelli has mentioned that he only drove a Novi once and it was at Phoenix. Even with a helmet on, he recalls the extraordinary echo that reverberated off the mountains and across the desert.

With the Indy 500 just around the corner, the Granatellis were now in deep trouble as their turbine plans had to be delayed and the Novi was now judged to be outdated. Surely a dilemma existed. Without an improved Novi on hand, the Granatelli built 4WD Novi chassis was prepared for duty one more time. It was only to be a stop gap measure.

Some relief for any future Novi project might have been the fact that USAC had postponed an anticipated engine formula change. The alteration would be a move to smaller engines that permitted only 183 c.i. (3 liter) unblown engines and 122 c.i. (2 liter) blown engines. The decision was made after the 1964 race. The existing maximum capacities were now to be retained for an extended period of time. The reason for this change of heart is reported to have been due to pressure applied by team owners who were unhappy with the idea of having to buy new engines so quickly after abandoning the Offys for the new crown jewel - the Ford V-8 engines. But could the Novis benefit from this postponement to win that all-elusive victory?

The Novi arrived at Indy on Wednesday, May 4, parked in a truck behind the garage area. It seemed apparent that the Novi squad wished to keep the car out of sight as long as possible. With its arrival, one newspaper reported that the Novi V-8 was going under the alias of the STP Oil Treatment Special. Once the popular car became synonymous with the Novi label, any effort to change its identification would be futile.

(1966) The Novi featured a long-nose cone. With the side vents, it resembles a snake head! Andy is in conversation with Greg Weld. Crew members are in STP pajamas once again. The publicity generated by their apparel in 1965, undoubtedly played a role in the retention of the garb for another year.
Bruce Craig Photos

The next morning the car was unveiled and Weld took to the track shortly after the car had passed the mandatory tech inspection. The car, entered as the #15 STP Oil Treatment Special, was painted fluorescent red (or as some called it "STP rocket red") with black and white trim, while the oil tank was chrome. The car was essentially the Granatelli built 4WD. Weld, having completed the rookie test the previous year, was now ask to undertake only a refresher session. By May 9, Weld had completed the last phase of the testing, running in the 145 m.p.h. bracket.

NASCAR veteran Cale Yarborough took the rookie test and was to put the Jim Robbins' Special in the race while another rookie, Gary Bettenhausen, son of the late Tony Bettenhausen, was refused permission to take the test. USAC advised the young stock car driver to obtain some open wheel experience before returning to the Speedway.

The BRM H16 powered Lotus did not make an appearance as the BRM factory was working overtime to obtain a reliable H16 for Formula One competition. Reports suggest that there was only a single prototype of the 4.2 liter engine built and this engine was said to be even more unreliable than the earlier smaller capacity F 1 engine. [Authors' note: a BRM spokesman was quoted as saying that the 4.2 liter version blew up faster and into more pieces than had the F 1 version. The H16 engine was used by both BRM and Lotus F 1 teams, but it proved to be very unreliable. During practice for the American Grand Prix in October, 1966, all of the Lotus engines let go. The BRM factory team then loaned one of their high milage spare engines to Lotus to enable Jimmy Clark to start the race. Ironically, this was the only time that a BRM H16 won a race!] So much for any thought of an Indy BRM H16. The STP team had every intention of entering six cars: four Lotuses, one Novi and one unspecified entry. Only two of the Lotuses appeared; an updated version of the type 38 chassis in which Jimmy Clark had won the previous year's 500 and a new Lotus body for sophomore Indy driver Al Unser. Incidentally, two other 38 chassis were sold to American interests. These cars were to be driven by Mario Andretti and A.J. Foyt.

All of this left Colin Chapman with no option other than to make do with the Ford powered 38s. This time the cars were not officially backed by Ford. But since Colin had reverted to the Ford powerplant, the company was willing to offer encouragement and more importantly, practical support. All of this in spite of Chapman's desire to move to BRM power. The European share of the STP racing team came up with only half of the entered equipment with the American team supplying the remainder. While STP sponsored Chapman's pair of cars, there was no difficulty in distinguishing between the Chapman crew and the Granatelli crew. The Lotus members wore bright red coveralls and not the polka dot STP apparel. The Chapman team's red uniforms were contrary to the traditional green worn by British racing teams in Formula One. Some referred to the cars as now being painted "STP Racing Green."

The sole Novi entry had few changes. The driveline had been slightly modified and a hypoid gear unit replaced the spur gears used in the past. The expectation was to achieve a greater tolerance in a Paxton modified differential at the top end of the horsepower output. In order to study the weight distribution for the upcoming turbine project, the radiator of the Novi was removed from the front and installed vertically at the rear deck next to the car's headrest. The radiator was enclosed in a box shaped housing while the right flank of the box (also forming the headrest) was extended in height to create a tail fin similar to those seen on the Kurtis 500F Novis of the past. This radiator location was conceived as a method of simulating some of the weight distribution anticipated with the forthcoming turbine car. Such made the car look big and heavy. Figures have been released reporting that the car had a 97 inch (246.4 cm) wheelbase and an overall length of 170 inches (431.8 cm). The overall height was 30 inches (76.2 cm) and the width 70 inches (117.8 cm) with a ground clearance of 2 inches (5.8 cm) with the car offset 2 inches to the left. The fuel tanks were reported to be able to carry 74 gallons (287.1 liters). The main tank was in the rear of the car and an auxilary tank was located on the left side. Both were of the flex-bag type with polyurethane baffling made by Firestone. Firestone also supplied the tires that were mounted on Halibrand cast magnesium alloy wheels with 16 x 9½ inch rims. The water tank had a capacity of 5 gallons (19.4 liters) while the oil tank carried 7 gallons (27.2 liters). The tank remained on the left side beyond the bodywork. The car used a wishbone layout suspension with inboard springs and Monroe adjustable shocks.

The overall appearance lacked the streamlining present in Novis entered in the past by the Granatellis. Even Andy Granatelli considered it a

(1966) The Novi carried only a right side mirror. What if a car approached on the driver's left side? The radiator, mounted at the rear, appears to create a blind spot for Weld. This shot shows the car carrying a shorter nosecone.

I.M.S.

less than appealing racer for he said, "I built a monstrosity, I built a car that everyone will laugh at." This was due to the alterations from its original configuration. One account asserted that the car "looks different from anything seen in years at the Speedway."

To this day, Andy recalls the laughter emitted by onlookers at their first sighting of the car with the radiator placement. (Yet, the laughter was absent the following year when the turbine, driven by Parnelli Jones, ran away from the field.) The car was entered in the hope of making the race with the Granatellis desiring to learn more about a fully independent suspension 4WD chassis. As stated, this was part of the ground work for a turbine "attack" which had now been moved back a year.

Development of the V-8 engine had continued over the winter and the newest version of the powerplant reached an all-time high power output with a stunning 837 horsepower at top revving speed of 9,000 rpms with the possibility of a bit more torque yet available. To obtain this new power output the engine used ram injection and an increased blower speed of five times the engine speed - 45,000 rpms. Apart from the power increase, the ram tube injection system was said to offer a better response coming off of the turns. Two induction tubes were located on top of the V-8 engine in the valley. Each of the tubes had outlets to the individual intake ports. There has also been talk of the engine being tuned to run in a lower torque range to allow higher power output at lower rpms. For practice, a maximum of 9,800 rpms was mentioned with a claimed power output of 700 horsepower while for race conditions a similar power output at 9,000 rpms had been cited. <u>Indianapolis Star</u> reporter George Moore wrote that "with any luck at all, the new four wheel drive Novi will be the most competitive one ever built."

The engine was reported to weight 470 pounds and the entire car was listed at 1,600 pounds. Believe it or not, despite the fact that the Novi V-8 pumped out more horsepower than it had ever done before, it now lost the reputation of being the most powerful engine at the Speedway! The Granatellis had seen their planned turbine project forced to be shelved for the short run while car owner Norm Demler entered a T58 General Electric turbine car that made it onto the track. A rush to introduce a turbine was now intensified by the Granatellis what with Demler's entry. The Demler owned roadster, equipped with a gas turbine, came up with no less than 1,250 horsepower. The

(1966) Prior to Weld's car moving into the pit area, the tire pressure is being checked by Firestone personnel. Note the offset in the chassis. I.M.S.

car, identified as the Jack Adams Aircraft Special, was assigned to driver Bill Cheesbourg. Helping with the Indianapolis turbine project were representives from both General Electric and Bell Aircraft. However, the car failed to qualify for the event. The Novi V-8, with its 837 horsepower, remained the strongest piston driven engine entered. Beyond the Novi and the Demler, the turbocharged Offenhausers were able to produce the most power. The Ford domination (almost exclusively used in rear engine cars) obviously helped end the era of the unblown Offy. The power disadvantage of the "straight" or standard Offy was too great to be competitive when used in a rear engine chassis. This had led to the development of a new blown version of the Offy to keep the old four banger alive. The private development of a destroked and turbocharged Offy proved its racing potential. The Drake Engineering Company (Louie Meyer had sold out his interest to partner Dale Drake) produced an optimal 168 c.i. (2.8

liter) version of the Offy. These engines could be run with either a Roots blower or a turbocharger conversion. The Roots version could reach 540 horsepower while the turbocharged Offy was capable of 625 horsepower.

A great deal of the credit for the virtues of the turbo powered version must be given to the long-time racing mechanic/innovator Herb Porter. The inexperience of many drivers and mechanics with blown engines and the feared unreliability of the turbo engine resulted in limited use of the turbocharged Offys by competitors. Maybe such skeptics should have gone to Porter whose vast knowledge included considerable work in experimentation with the blower and then the turbo. Or, one could have gone to the Granatelli team for the possible use of a Paxton designed blower.

In addition to the unique Demler turbine, California car owner Al Stein had another 4WD creation on hand. The car was powered by twin Porsche Model 911 six cylinder engines. The driving assignment went to former Novi pilot Bill Cheesbourg. The versatile Cheesbourg was to spend time in the cockpit of not only the 4WD Porsche but the Demler car as well. However, like the Demler car the 4WD Porsche failed to fulfill expectations and also failed to qualify.

A second built 4WD, the Ferguson had been entered by the STP team and it carried the familiar #59. This entry may have been for the new turbine powered car (or if necessary Novi powered) chassis that was heavily damaged earlier that year. It is of little consequence, as the (phantom?) car failed to reach the Speedway.

(1966) Greg loose in a corner. Note the smoke at the right tires. Driver Johnny Boyd has moved low to avoid contact. The difference in the frontal area between the Novi and a rear engine car is considerable.   I.M.S.

The centrifugal supercharger, similar to that used on the Novi, was not the one hooked up to any of the blown Offys. This was largely a result of a lack of torque performance by some supercharged Offys. Because of this unpredictable behavior by centrifugal blown Offys, mechanics went over to the more controllable Roots blower. They wanted the greatest possible power, although it took some time and effort to familiarize themselves to its characteristics in order to harness all available power. The power output of these blown engines were in the neighborhood of that of the Ford Quadcam. However, it was still a far cry from the massive power of the blown Novi V-8.

In early track shakedown runs, Mario Andretti had his Dean Van Lines Brabham Ford up to 160 m.p.h. Other drivers picking up speed early included A.J. Foyt with a practice lap at close to 158 m.p.h. in his new Lotus. Jimmy Clark was close behind followed by rookie Carl Williams.

The Novi no longer was able to gain the attention previously accorded its presence. Things were not going that well with the elaborate car. An engine replacement became necessary when an oil fitting broke after only three laps on May 10. In the previous two days, Weld had not driven the car at all. Another very obvious change in the car

(1966) The beginning of the end...Weld looses it in the third turn.   I.M.S.

(1966) The spin continues as the car heads for the wall. With the tires smoking, the rear of the Novi is engulfed in a haze of smoke.   I.M.S.

(1966) The car smacks the wall in the north short chute. This mishap was to become the swan song in the Novi saga.   I.M.S.

was the adoption of a more streamlined nosecone which made the car 11 inches (27.94 cm) longer. The virtue of such an alteration is questionable and one could wishfully wonder if it might well have been of value in a photo finish! However, the cone proved ineffective and was removed.

On May 11 with the engine replaced, Weld hit a top speed of 159+ m.p.h. which was considered just within the competitive range. Yet, the following day his top speed reached only 154 m.p.h. Meanwhile, a number of rear engine crews had their cars turning laps in excess of 160 m.p.h. with ease and few of the front engine cars seemed to pose any real threat for the rear engine opposition.

On May 13 the last day prior to the first day of qualifications, the traditional draw for the qualification lineup was held. Andy Granatelli drew the coveted #1 -the right to send his car out first in a qualification attempt. In previous years, the early dispatch of a Novi would have created enormous excitement, yet the trackside atmosphere appeared subdued. However, Weld was not able to take advantage of the draw. During the traditional early morning practice, prior to qualifications, all hope of making the starting field that day was lost. Weld had to make a dive into the infield to avoid a collision with a car in front of him. The car was driven by fellow Kansas Citian, rookie Carl Williams who hit the wall in his #77 Dayton Steel Wheel Special. The damage to the 4WD Novi was substantial to the point that it prevented a qualification attempt that day. Thus, the first out honors fell to 1959 and 1962 Indianapolis winner Rodger Ward who posted a time of 159.468 m.p.h.

Sophomore driver Mario Andretti won the pole position, capturing it with a new track record of 165.899 m.p.h. In all, seven cars broke A.J. Foyt's year old qualifying record of 161.233 m.p.h. Among those cracking the previous qualifying mark was Jimmy Clark in his STP Gas Treatment Special, a factory Lotus, with a 164.144 m.p.h. clocking. Such a time positioned him in the front row next to Andretti. Filling out the front row would be another sophomore driver, Californian George Snider in a Sheraton-Thompson Special at 162.521 m.p.h. in a team car to that of A.J. Foyt. A total of 18 cars qualified on Saturday and five more on Sunday.

Tragically, the first day's qualifying session was marred by the fatal crash of 38 year old driver Chuck Rodee. His car slammed into the first turn wall during his second warm up lap prior to taking the green flag and he was instantly killed. The death marked the first driver fatality during a qualification run since the deaths of 'Stubby' Stubblefield and his riding mechanic, Leo Whittaker, in 1935.

For the Novi crew, it was a matter of repairing the #15 STP Oil Treatment car for another attempt and they succeeded in having the car ready for the second day of qualifications. Weld went out with the car, but after a single practice lap he had to park the car on the grass as the engine was smoking badly. The oil line that supplied lubrication to the supercharger had worked loose. The malady prevented any attempt to qualify that day. Was all of this the reemergence of the Novi jinx, hex or whatever one might wish to call it?

For a few days, the Novi STP crew maintained a low profile as they remained inside their garage working on the entry. As it turned out, the engine was experiencing a fuel pickup problem. Late in the week, Vince Granatelli confirmed the fact saying, "We've been in trouble (with the fueling situation) ever since we got here." On May 17, some practice time was obtained with the Novi. On the following day, Weld was out in the Novi once again making some 40 laps reaching the 157 m.p.h. range using the smaller nosecone. On Friday, May 20, the last day before the second weekend of qualifications, Greg managed to move the Novi up to a speed of 159.5 m.p.h. with an average of 158.9 m.p.h. over four fast laps. The burning question evolved around whether such would be fast enough to make the field if he could duplicate the performance during an official qualifying attempt. The fact the car was running that well can be attributed to the massive effort put forth by the crew. They had worked night and day to have the car in proper running order.

According to George Moore, the car's malady was the failure of the supercharged V-8 picking up fuel. Moore reported that the crew changed the manifold on the car going back to the setup used prior to the switch to the ram jet system that had been adopted when it first reached the Speedway. Moore stated, "that the fuel/air ratio is even more critical because the engine is being fed by the supercharger. When fuel and air are rammed into an engine under pressure, the air temperature tends to rise even more than on a non-supercharged powerplant." Moore reported that when this occurs it "amounts to a red hot bellyache. If the crew can go back to the old setup which it has run in the past and keep the cantankerous V-8 churning for four laps of a qualification run they may work their way out of the woods. Otherwise, like the man said, they got problems."

On the third day of qualifications (May 21), Greg Weld made an official qualifying attempt, but it was waved off when he was unable to do better than 158.256 m.p.h. reached on his first two laps. Inexplicably the car had run faster during a warm up lap as he had been clocked at 158.758 m.p.h. Obviously, the speed movement was in the wrong direction! The car was pushed back into the qualifying line to have another shot later in the day, but when the 6 P.M. track closing arrived there were still seven cars in the qualifying line in front of the #15 STP Special. During the day, ten other cars qualified to fill the field.

It all came down to the last day of qualifying. Once again it was heavy duty pressure time for a Novi, a familiar old tale. That the car was able to even make an attempt that day was due in large measure to the dedicated and unrelenting efforts of the crew. Early that afternoon as Weld left the pit lane he created a bit of panic as the car was leaking fuel through a loose fuel line. Fortunately, trouble was averted and the crew quickly repaired the leak. Weld was once again pushed off for a final attempt. Coming off the third turn on the first warm up lap, the car began a slide that covered 550 feet before slamming into the outside wall with the right front wheel. The front and rear suspension on the right side collapsed. A quick assessment revealed that the damage was too extensive to be repaired in time for Weld to go out again. The STP crew was devastated and it was a sad sight to see the car brought back to Gasoline Alley on the hook of a wrecker. Weld came out of the accident without any injuries and was released to drive again, if he could obtain another ride.

Granatelli wondered why the car wound up on the wall on the last day instead of the very first. The STP crew would not have had to work like slaves an entire month only to see their hopes dashed in the waning hours remaining of the last qualification period.

Two hours later, Weld was on the track again as he was able to procure a late ride in a car owned by the 1960 Indy winner, Jim Rathmann, with reported co-owners astronauts Gordon Cooper and Gus Grissom. The ride was originally assigned to NASCAR veteran Lee Roy Yarbrough. Weld spun the #76 Pure Firebird Special and hit the fourth turn wall in another attempt to make the starting field. Once again, Weld was able to walk away from the wreck. The car was a rear engine racer so perhaps Weld simply did not have sufficient time to fully acclimate himself. Weld's driving experience at the Speedway through the month, until that last afternoon, had been restricted to the front engine 4WD Novi. Thus ended another fruitless year for the fabled Novi. The lone Novi entry had failed to gain headlines from any splendid performances. Instead, any ink devoted to the Novi seemed to be saved for the string of aborted efforts. In discussing the 1966 events with Andy, he remembered Weld as being "a hard driver. But he was a dirt car driver. He was never a sophisticated asphalt driver."

(1966) After all the years at Indianapolis, the Novis last departure from the track was under power supplied by a wrecker. The crippled car represented the last in a line of once feared Novis. Note the flat spot on the right front tire. As the accident occurred on the last day of qualifying insufficient time remained for repairs.
I.M.S.

It should also be noted that Greg did make the Speedway race in 1970 finishing 32nd as a piston let go after 12 laps. Further Greg captured the USAC Sprint Crown in 1967. The following year, he was third in the sprint car standings behind champion Larry Dickson and runner-up Gary Bettenhausen.

With the field filled going into the last day of qualifying, only two cars were bumped as Ronnie Duman (158.646 m.p.h.) and rookie Larry Dickson (159.144 m.p.h.) made their way into the starting field. Incidentally, Al Unser had been experiencing difficulties putting his STP Oil Treatment Special into the field as a result of a number of nagging mechanical problems. However, when he did qualify on the third day at 162.272 m.p.h., the speed with his Lotus was the sixth fastest posted for the starting field. As a footnote, we might add that former Novi driver Jim Hurtubise drove a rear engine Gerhardt Offy in the race. In fact, Fred Gerhardt, a Fresno, California, car owner/builder had six of his chassis make the race; the most chassis from any one manufacturer. As to the tire war, it was close to a draw as 17 cars were shod with Firestones while 16 were mounted with Goodyears.

As for the Demler turbine car, author Roger Huntington reported in his <u>Design And Development of the Indy Car</u> volume that the car was eventually declared unsafe by USAC officials. Owner Norm Demler claimed he "was banned because the car was showing too much speed potential - up to 260 mph on the straights - and track officials felt there would be a hassle with other car owners if the car qualified. I don't know. The car never showed much lap speed potential and cornering was erratic." If the car was capable of such extraordinary speeds an improper chassis setup and/or inadequate brakes would be understandable if the racer had to slow down from 260 to 140 m.p.h. or so. Several car owners asserted that with the car's potential speed, the brakes would be insufficient when cornering. Outstanding Indy chief mechanic Danny Oakes (a former leading West Coast midget driver) has said that Demler should have jumped on the turbine project earlier, thus allowing time to iron out its wrinkles.

For the STP group, they could find great consolation from the fact that the two STP sponsored Lotus-Fords driven by Jimmy Clark and Al Unser made the starting grid. For the record, Bobby Unser who had driven a Novi for the three previous years, had moved over to the Vita Fresh Orange Juice Special on a full time basis. While he started 28th with a 159.109 m.p.h. clocking, he was to finish 8th. The 1966 starting field consisted of 32 rear engine cars and a lone roadster. Bobby Grim, driver of this Watson-Offy, posted a four lap qualifying average of 158.367 m.p.h. which was the slowest speed to make the field. His ability to qualify the "Old Hack" was to be credited not only to Bobby's skills and determination, but to the fact that the car was a turbocharged Offy maintained by Herb Porter. You may recall

(1966) While no Novi was in the starting lineup for the first time in four years, the Granatellis had STP sponsorship with the Colin Chapman team. Jimmy Clark (seen here) finished second in his STP Gas Treatment Special while teammate Al Unser, Sr. was 12th in another STP sponsored rear engine Ford. Both chassis were Lotus products.   I.M.S.

that it was Porter who had earlier carried out work with a turbocharger bolted to an Offenhauser.

Pace car driver Benson Ford must have been happy with the fact that 24 of the cars were powered by V-8 Fords while only nine Offys made the race. Three of these Offys made use of turbo power. In all, 13 cars posted qualifying speeds of 160 m.p.h. or more while seven were in the low 158 m.p.h. range. Remember Weld had posted practice laps in the 158 to low 159 m.p.h. range. Oh, well!

thirty minutes, the race was restarted. The race's early leader was pole sitter Mario Andretti in the Dean Van Lines car who remained up front until a valve problem was experienced. Jimmy Clark then assumed the lead having to thwart the challenge of Lloyd Ruby. The Scot then spun, but recovered to continue, though he lost ground. Lloyd Ruby became the new leader, holding on for 68 laps until he experienced a cam tower problem while he held almost a full lap lead. Some hasty work was performed and he was back out on the track before a black flag was displayed

(1966) The race winner, Englishman Graham Hill. He was the first rookie winner since George Souders in 1927. Graham's son, Damon, would win the Formula One title in 1996. The elder Graham had captured the title in 1962 and 1968. I.M.S.

The race started horribly as a massive accident occurred as the field attempted to work through the first turn on the first lap! In the bedlam that followed, the field was decimated as one third of the cars were eliminated. With the straightaway leading into the first turn looking like a salvage yard, the red flag was displayed. Unbelievably, the race stoppage marked the second time in just three years that the world famous race had been halted. Prior to this stoppage, no previous 500 had been red flagged for anything other than rain. The 1964 red flag was waved when the fiery inferno in turn four occurred as the second lap was underway. Fortunately, no injuries were incurred in the 1966 calamity, although major challengers such as A.J. Foyt, Dan Gurney and Don Branson were instantly eliminated from the contest. Another of the unfortunate drivers who never made it through the first turn was Bobby Grim.

After a delay of slightly more than an hour and

for oil leakage due to a broken cam stud in his Yamaha Bardahl Gurney Eagle. With the luckless Texan out, the race appeared to be in the hands of Jackie Stewart in a Bowes Seal Fast Special owned by John Mecom, Jr. until the oil pressure went away with only ten laps remaining. At the time, Stewart held a half lap lead. Englishman Graham Hill, driving an American Red Ball Special, a rear engine Lola-Ford owned by John Mecom, moved into first place to receive the checkered flag. Hill's prior racing experience had been outstanding as he won the Formula One Championship in 1962 and finished second in the standings the next three years. Graham had been at Indy in 1963, but did not qualify for the show. He was now back to take the driving assignment originally given to Walt Hansgen, who had been killed at Le Mans a month earlier. Hill, a resident of London, England, became the second foreign winner in two years and the first rookie winner of the 500 since

George Souders in 1927. The National Speed Sport News aptly headlined the event with "England's Graham Hill Wins Crash-Marred 500." Thirty years later Graham's son Damon would win the Formula One title. Graham had captured the F 1 title in 1962 and 1968.

Jimmy Clark placed second in his STP Gas Treatment Special after a rather eventful ride. He spun twice during the race which certainly played a role in his final placement. The Granatellis protested the results as they felt the scoring for Clark had been in error as they thought the tabulation system had missed one lap. However, the protest was denied. As it turned out the team's scorekeeper had been in error. In spite of the miserable year for the Novi, the Granatellis had witnessed some success. This resulted from the second place finish of Jimmy Clark's STP sponsored car, in spite of the two spins. Further, Al Unser finished twelfth in his STP sponsored car after spinning while running third. Finishing third was former Novi chauffeur Jim McElreath. The top three finishers all used Firestones.

Interestingly, Rookie-of-the-Year honors went to Jackie Stewart rather than to race winner Hill. Stewart appeared to have the race in his hand with his Bowes Seal Fast Special until it dropped out on lap 190 while holding that comfortable lead. He was awarded 6th place.

The Novi had failed once again in 1966 and such is rather understandable. It had been a late effort with a car that had an unconventional chassis layout with the exception of the 4WD setup. Still, the team judged their time at the track to be valuable in one respect as they were able to devote time to work on the new suspension setup. They came away with additional knowledge regarding their future 4WD Indy car project, so the dejection in not making the race may have been tempered a bit. Then one might consider the run to have been something of a commercial success for Andy Granatelli, as winner Hill and the next seven finishers used the STP oil product.

Changes within the STP team were on their way. The Novi V-8 was incorporated into these plans, but were they actually to be realized? A good deal of the Novi popularity seemed to have evaporated. Was the luster and attraction of the Novi as a realistic competitor now all but gone? Some remaining diehard Novi fans felt that it seemed reasonable to assume that their darling was rapidly approaching retirement status. Was the Novi now to become a racing relic?

However, there was another remarkable event with respect to the Novi. After the 1966 set back at Indy which saw the sole Novi eliminated on the last day of qualifications, one would wonder what was left for the fabulous old Novi engine. As it turned out the Granatellis were not finished with their Novi powered car for 1966. Just as a year before, the decision was made to run the Atlanta USAC championship race. This time the contest would be the Atlanta 300 scheduled for June 26. If the renewed Atlanta assault was a surprise to some, a greater surprise was the fact that the team did not arrive with the newer 4WD car, but entered the faithful old #59 roadster. One can assume that the Granatelli decision to enter the race was belated. The "Probable Entries" contained in the souvenir program listed 43 cars, yet no Novi was cited. Greg Weld was once again assigned the driving duties and in early practice he posted a fast lap of 158.40 m.p.h. In short order, he moved it up to 165 m.p.h. Then the alleged Novi jinx presumedly made another appearance - a starting gear broke half way through the final qualifying session to end any hope of competing in the event! As it turned out, the slowest car in the field qualified at 153.539 m.p.h. Thus, if it had not been for this mechanical malfunction, Weld and the Novi surely would have made the starting grid of 30 cars with ease. Had he maintained a speed in the neighborhood of his practice times he would have started from about 8th position.

Former Novi pilot Jim Hurtubise received top billing in a local advertisement for the forthcoming race. The ad noted that he had won NASCAR's Atlanta 500 race at the Atlanta International Raceway on March 27. Meanwhile, the Novi was loaded on its truck for the long return trip to Indianapolis. The USAC race (with the track having 24 degree banking in the turns) was won by pole sitter Mario Andretti (169.014 m.p.h.) in a Dean Van Lines Special. Hurtubise did not fare too well as he finished 26th in a Gerhardt Offy.

Why the Novi was entered is not clear. Possibly it was the thought of the stellar performances of the two Novis entered the previous year. Whatever the case, a Novi had now missed qualifying for two races in a single year. This certainly represented a sad twist in the Novi saga. It appeared that the Novi project had now run up a dead end street. Only a major alteration in chassis development could breathe new life into the career of the Novi. There was enough going on in the Granatelli STP-Lotus operation to give cause as to whether such would actually occur. While the Granatellis still owned the Novis, the racing emphasis for the brothers was definitely changing.

Chapter 17

Is Retirement Temporary?

If it had not been perfectly clear to the Granatelli brothers in 1965, by 1966 they had to have fully realized that any front engine car was now outdated. The rear engine revolution was complete except for a few diehard traditionalists who still believed that the roadster was the only way to go at Indy. The group included a resolute and iconoclastic Jim Hurtubise.

Adopting the Lotus team for sponsorship proved that the Granatelli STP operation had certainly changed its position. Admittedly, events had created a major change within the Granatelli team even while the Novi operation was still active. Although, a Novi was running in 1966, it appears that in all likelihood it was only due to the fact that the new weapon, a turbine powered car, was irreparably destroyed during its construction.

After May 1966, the Granatellis concentrated heavily on their turbine program for the following 500. Thus, the legendary Novi V-8 was temporarily delegated to backup status as the turbine was being sorted out. We will follow the time of the "temporary" retirement of the Novi to see how it was terminated while its successors carried on under the banner of the STP racing team.

The temporary assignment was slightly tenuous as Andy apparently was holding something of "an ace up his sleeve." While the turbine project went forward Andy's ace became common knowledge when a George Moore article appeared in the Indianapolis Star on September 1, 1966. Moore reported that Jim Hurtubise was going to construct a front engine Novi. The clincher to the article stated that the undertaking was to be carried out in conjunction with Andy Granatelli and the car would retain a front engine location. The package called for a roadster style car and it was to be "modernized" with a different steering geometry, four wheel independent suspension, shocks placed within coils and solid axles. The key was to be weight, as Herk was aiming for 1,400 pounds, only 50 over the minimum weight requirement. According to Moore, Andy acknowledged that he was not in agreement with Herk on all phases of the construction, yet he was prepared to go along with the basic concept. The bottom line is that the project did not come to past. In his biography on Herk, Bob Gates did not mention such a joint venture. However, the Gates account does mention that Jim was building a new car. The chassis was to be referred to as a Mallard. Jim envisioned that it would weight in at 1,350 pounds while using an Offy. The car did not make the field for the 500 race in 1967 which meant that Jim missed his first race since his rookie year in 1960.

Perhaps the turbine project left Herk "out in the cold" as the Granatellis at some point had decided that their turbine was ready for its unveiling, or possibly Herk and Andy had a falling out somewhere along the way. Granatelli failed to mention the project in his autobiography though he did mention several other possible projects that were to be Novi powered. Before closing off this account, we checked with racing mechanic Don Shepherd, who along with fabricator Bill Henderson assisted Hurtubise in constructing the Mallard. Don does not recall any Hurtubise-Granatelli agreement regarding the roadster so it may well have been a deal that quickly soured. In Don's words, "If there was a deal it sure fell through."

A turbocharged Watson-Offy roadster had bettered the speeds of the 4WD Novi front engine car in 1966 when Bobby Grim qualified for that year's race with the lone front engine car in the field. The front engine 4WD concept seemed to offer no future for the Novi program. If the famed supercharged V-8 was ever to see service again it would have to be installed at the rear of the chassis. Some consideration had been given for such a car earlier. You may recall that in 1961, Andy Granatelli had advanced such a plan for the Novi.

The revolutionary car was to be built by either John Cooper or Jack Brabham. Yet, no tangible steps were undertaken. In 1963, Granatelli once again gave some thought to such a car. The plan went unfilled as they decided to concentrate on the adoption of the 4WD for the Novi cars. After the non-qualification of the lone Novi for the 1966 race, a rear engine Novi once again came under consideration. The information that follows was provided from sketchy sources and is given based on what we have unearthed. The plans called for Fred Gerhardt to build a chassis strong enough to support a rear mounted Novi V-8. Gerhardt had earned a sound reputation since he had become involved in the construction of Indy car chassis. Gerhardt had built the chassis for the cars that finished 4th and 5th in the 1966 race. The 4th place car was driven by Gordon Johncock in one of the rear mounted Ford V-8s, while 5th was awarded to Mel Kenyon in a Gerhardt owned rear engine Offy. In addition, he also had four other entries in that particular contest. The previous year a Gerhardt built car had finished 6th and Fred saw three more of his chassis in the field.

In spite of such achievements, it would appear that Gerhardt would face a strong challenge in building a chassis capable of carrying the large Novi engine in the rear. It would be something completely different as the Novi was far heavier than the Offy or the Ford. Yet, one must concede that the Ford Quadcam was also a big engine, so perhaps the problems faced were not insurmountable. The Gerhardt chassis had never used any engines stronger than the officially claimed 625 horsepower of the turbocharged Offenhauser engine. It appeared quite obvious that a super strong chassis setup would be needed to handle the weight and power of the demands imposed by the Novi.

The prospects for a rear engine Novi could be considered promising. With the main part of the weight distribution close to the wheels and with the larger tires, more grip or traction for such a car could be stunning. That is if the gearbox could handle the load. With the gearbox mishap of Jim Hurtubise and the rear drive Kurtis roadster in 1965 in mind, this possibly represented a sizable obstacle. A stronger gearbox was not impossible. Perhaps, a rear engine combined with 4WD would provide an excellent opportunity to improve traction and tire wear. Such chassis already existed. Shortly after World War II, Porsche had built its Type 360 for the Cisitalia company. In addition, BRM of England had built a 4WD mid-engine F 1 car in the mid 1960s for test duties, not to mention Harry Miller's 4WD Miller-Gulf cars! In other words, a rear engine 4WD was a realistic option.

Considering what the other rear engine rivals possessed, it seems likely that the car would have been heavier, with or without 4WD. The old bug-a-boo of tire wear could conceivably remain a major problem. There is also some doubts about the fuel consumption figures of the Novis compared with those of the recently introduced blown Offys. Another concern deals with the size of the engine. Was it possible to create a slim looking rear engine car with a behemoth Novi V-8 in the back? Further, consider placement of the fuel injection and air intake to the supercharger. Only time would tell.

Despite all of the good intentions and preliminary work that may have been carried out with this rear engine Novi project, it fell victim to a change in plans by the Granatelli team. When the turbine work was resumed, it became clear that the brothers would have to devote virtually all their time and attention to the new creation. No matter what their loyalty may have been for the legendary V-8 screamer, the Granatellis made the decision to focus their primary attention on the turbine. Once that decision was made the Novi V-8 was put aside.

The official entry list for the 1967 running of the 500 included the #59 assigned to the STP team. Surprisingly, this entry was listed as carrying an eight cylinder engine of 168 c.i., thus making it a supercharged entry with the exact bore and stroke as used by the Novi V-8. One is left to conclude that the entry could have been for the #59 rear engine Gerhardt-Novi. In The Illustrated History of the Indianapolis 500, author Jack Fox listed the 1967 STP #59 entry as a non-qualified car with a turbo engine. The reason cited by Fox for non-qualifying is correct as no Gerhardt-Novi chassis or any car bearing the #59 reached Indianapolis.

Details about possible engine reworking are difficult to find. A limited number of publications provided an indication as to the type of development carried out for a 1967 Novi. These facts may surprise individuals who are unfamiliar with the concept.

In a preview for the upcoming 1967 Indy race, the May 25 issue of AUTOCAR carried an article entitled, "They're Not Complaining This Year," by Roger Huntington. He wrote,

> "I mentioned Granatelli's Novi engine earlier. This year he replaced the high boost supercharger with a medium boost Roots type with the idea of getting better mid-range torque for acceleration off the

turns. Horsepower is reduced from 850 to 650 at 8,000 rpms but Andy claims better overall lap speeds in the early test."

Confirmation as to spec changes can not be confirmed, though we must assume that Huntington had gathered the information from some source. No details were cited with respect to lap speed testing. However, Huntington, who passed away in August, 1989, had garnered a solid reputation as a leading technical automobile racing writer.

Another reference, although very brief, was contained in the May 1, 1967, edition of <u>Automotive Industries</u>. It cites a rear engine Novi using a Roots supercharger. If in fact such was to be the case it certainly is a surprise, for the blowers had been centrifugal for a long-time. Why sacrifice 200 or so horsepower?

Remember that the supercharged Offys of the 1950s did have great power, but a poor torque range. Then in the mid 1960s, the Roots blown Offys demonstrated a better performance, even if somewhat underpowered compared to what a centrifugal blower might well have achieved. When it came to blowers, the Roots overall performance was rated above the centrifugal style unit. One can only surmise how the Novi V-8 would have reacted with a different blower.

It is well-known that in 1966, the turbocharged Offys pumped out even more horsepower than the Roots blown versions. Thus, we are left to wonder if a change was coming: Why did the Granatellis not consider the turbo unless they preferred to use the time honored Roots? Such a blower was considered mild when compared to the turbocharger and the centrifugal supercharger. Or did the Granatelli work with the Paxton muddy the waters?

Apart from the confusion regarding possible blower modification, Huntington had stated that Granatelli claimed better overall lap speeds in early tests. We can only wonder where and in what kind of car these tests had been carried out. Had a Gerhardt been built and used or had one of the front engine cars been used instead? If such is true, one is left to wonder who drove the car during such testing.

When we talked with Andy regarding this alleged testing, he firmly stated that no rear engine Gerhardt nor the Roots blower engine had ever been assembled. So how all the news about the car and engines made it into the press leaves one in the dark. Looking back at it, Andy had more than good reason to stop the project at some point. One must bear in mind that the Granatelli operation had a car in the works offering considerably more potential. At some point it became obvious that the turbine was the way to go for the Granatelli brothers, so any Novi efforts were set aside for the year.

If the advent of the rear engine cars had not been enough to provide the Granatellis and others with an obstacle, the new rule regarding the maximum capacity of supercharged engines at only 161 c.i. (2650 cc) certainly appeared to make them obsolete as the rule was to take affect in 1969. One might consider the loss of a mere 9 c.i. as insignificant. Some of the critics of such a reduction certainly realized that the power lose resulting from the reduced capacity could be regained by moving up the boost. If the sanctioning body really wanted to cut down on the power of blown engines they could have instituted a far smaller c.i. engine. The switch from 170 to 161 c.i. supercharged engines was totally unnecessary to bring the power down. The Granatellis contended that such a rule change was more or less a political gesture to either Offenhauser or Ford. If true, it eventually worked, particularly for the Offenhauser which was made even more over square than it had been since the blown 168 c.i. version that was introduced in 1966. This reduced piston speed enabled the higher revving Offy to eventually break the magic 1,000 horsepower barrier.

A good deal of the magic and aura of the Novi engine was based on the use of the centrifugal supercharger. For veteran Novi fans, the Novi would have lost a good deal of its originality due to the installation of a turbo. For some, the magic of the Novi had already dissipated with the new ownership though the press had continued to refer to the Granatelli cars as simply Novis. Somehow, many long-time fans who heard the Novi name most often thought in terms of the front drive cars, or at least Welch's use of the first rear drives in 1956, 1957 and 1958. The history of the early Novis seems to be best remembered rather than the later models - including the 4WD. Thus, the Novi legend is largely rooted in the late 1940s and the early 1950s. The fact that one of the supercharged FWDs is almost always on display at the IMS museum helps play a significant role in keeping the early Novi in the public eye and mind.

Chapter 18

What Might Have Been

Over the years, there has been discussion among some Indy racing aficionados as to whether a Lotus-Novi project was ever considered in the 1960s. In an attempt to get to the bottom of this, we contacted the public relations department of Team Lotus as the team's owner, Colin Chapman, had died in late 1982. Consequently, we were directed to his former aide Andrew Ferguson.

Ferguson said he was unaware of any discussions between Granatelli and Chapman over the possibility of equipping a Lotus chassis with a Novi V-8. However, he did state that for Team Lotus there was never any real need for such an arrangement since at the time, Lotus was starting up with its Indy activities. As a consequence, the business relationship between Lotus and the Ford Motor Company was strong and healthy during 1963-1965.

Yet, it is known that from 1966 on relations between Ford and Lotus regarding the Ford engines were not on the same footing as had been the case when the Lotuses were virtually overt Ford factory entries. Also, bear in mind that in 1966, Colin Chapman was prepared to make the switch to the H16 BRM engine. Granatelli also denied any Lotus plans as he realized the Novi engine would be too heavy for the rear engine chassis. With respect to Ferguson, sad to say he has now passed away. His demise came in late 1994, at the age of 65 as he was working on a volume set to honor the 30th anniversary of the Lotus victory at Indianapolis. So much for an alleged Lotus-Novi program.

Continuing on with potential Novi prospects, Granatelli revealed one "last secret weapon" that he had in mind. Plans to build such a car had been made earlier. This was a contingency plan if the turbine was not ready to be fully competitive. Plans were thus laid out for a new Novi. It would be a side-by-side chassis unit somewhat similar to the car Smokey Yunick had introduced for the 1964 competition. Yet, such plans were sidelined as a result of the success being achieved with the turbine powered car. If a side-by-side chassis using a Novi engine had in fact occurred, no doubt the car would have had a fantastic leftside weight bias. Even the far lighter turbine side-by-side cars were above the minimum weight so it seems quite logical that a Novi powered version would be far heavier. In such a case, road handling, chassis behavior and tire wear challenges would have been renewed.

A Novi side-by-side conceivably might well have had more power than a turbine powered version. One never knows how it might have been able to perform if constructed. Since some thought had been given to a Roots blown Novi, the question arises as to whether a side-by-side would have been driven centrifugally or with a Roots.

Another consideration dealing with a possible Novi project has also drawn little attention. With the enormous Novi car weight, the Granatellis tried to do something about this by using more magnesium on the existing engines whenever possible. The project went so far as to actually building at least one magnesium crankcase. The pinnacle of such a "weight watchers program" was the introduction of an all-magnesium engine.

Likely, such a project would have been another potential heart breaker for the Granatellis. This is due to the fact that in later years the Cosworth engine firm in England tried to develop a magnesium version for their all-conquering Cosworth V-8 Formula One engine. The project failed as the durability of the lightweight engine simply lacked the stamina to withstand the demands imposed. Reportedly, the bearings were highly susceptible to damage, particularly when the engines were cold. The alloy used had a rather unstable nature when exposed to a wide heat range. This inconvenience was not worth the savings of some additional weight loss, so Cosworth scrapped the project. It seems reasonable to assume that if Cosworth experienced such a fate, the Granatellis would have been destined to meet the same dilemma. Still, such a consideration by the Granatellis underscores their efforts with the beloved Novi.

Another problem a magnesium constructed Novi would have been confronted with dealt with fuel. Magnesium alloys are corrosion sensitive when matched with methanol fuel. In the late 1930s when Art Sparks and Paul Weirick ran their "Little

Six" engine, which contained magnesium parts, they used the less aggressive ethanol fuel. Ethanol is an intoxicating agent in liquors, thereby taxed by the Federal Government. Sparks managed to solve the problem in the 1930s by securing a license. If the Granatellis had used a magnesium Novi engine, it would have been interesting to see how they would have resolved the fuel problem. If the use of ethanol had been the solution would it have been allowable under the existing USAC rules?

While we have already touched on the rumor of a Roots blown Novi, we can move on to another type of compressor, that being the reintroduction of the turbocharger. The Cummins Diesel had been the real turbo pioneer back in 1952, although there was no follow up at Indy in the years thereafter. Then in 1966, the turbocharger literally breathed new life into the Offy. We asked Andy if he ever considered the use of a turbo on the Novi. He replied in the affirmative and with a bit of pride in his voice asserted that with such a setup the dyno had registered 980 horsepower. Keeping in mind that the turbo Offys were producing 625 horsepower at top range, the 980 horsepower figure certainly was impressive. Regrettably, we have never seen such an engine at the track. It appears to have been another project that never actually got off the ground.

With the new size requirements, the loss of sweep volume for some blown engines did not appear to be a major problem, but it turned out to be far more than that for the Novi. The big block had been designed for a greater sweep capacity, reducing the stroke by installing a new shorter stroke crankshaft. This meant that new cylinder blocks would have to be cast to compensate for reduced compression. If the bore was narrow, a problem would occur, as there would be smaller blocks to consider. In such a situation, the Granatellis might well have had a tiger by the tail. It would cost them a bundle to obtain the new parts to keep the Novi within the rules. With the reduced engine size announcement, the decision was made by the Granatellis to pull the plug on the Novi. A possible "wonder weapon" was being sidelined by a new rule imposed by USAC. Naturally, Andy claims that the amount of engine capacity the supercharged engines relinquished would be far too small an amount for the intended goal. As rules were rules, it was the final death blow for the glorious and legendary Novi engine.

Why USAC selected to reduce blown engine size is open for discussion. They might have perceived the notion that this small amount of lost sweep power would be of little consequence. Or could there be another reason for the new lower maximum capacity rule? We have been informed that two other reasons were behind the alteration.

First, Vince Granatelli (Andy's son) has stated that the new formula was implemented as a political favor to Ford. According, to Vince, the Ford had a 161 c.i. engine available, thus it might be possible that the rule was made to please Ford. The 168 c.i. specs used in 1968 offered little success for the turbo Ford Quadcam V-8. While very powerful, the fuel consumption efficiency was a major concern. Yet, it must be pointed out that 1968 was the first year for the turbo Ford and they had to learn how to "crawl before walking." The men who had worked on the development of the turbo Offy in the past had experienced their share of problems as well.

There is a bit of irony if this circumstance is in fact true since Lew Welch had maintained such a close relationship with the Ford Motor Company and Henry Ford in his first years as an Indy car owner. Was the Ford Company responsible in part for the beginning and then the end of the Novi?

The second version for instituting the 161 c.i. rule was voiced by Andy. While Vince blamed Ford for the 161 c.i. rule, his father faulted the Drake Engineering Company, the producers of the Offenhauser.

According to Andy, the Drake organization had a sizable inventory of cylinder blocks on hand for the turbo Offys. However, they reportedly were constantly leaking water when bored out to 171 c.i. But the blocks could tolerate a slightly lower capacity. To salvage their hardware and save writing off thousands of dollars worth of castings they were alleged to have done their best to obtain a lower capacity for blown racing engines. Whether true or not, the 161 c.i. rule was carried out in 1969 and with it the elimination of the Novi from the active list of contending Indy engines. Theoretically now both Ford and Offy faced fewer problems with both engines available in the 159 c.i. conversion.

The demise of the Novi, the engine that Andy once claimed he would rather win with one time at the Speedway than three times with a turbine, was yet another blow for him. In his mind, Andy felt the drop to a 161 c.i. supercharged version of the Novi would render it totally ineffective.

In researching Andy's efforts to remain competitive, he informed us that he had seen a twin turbocharged Ferrari V-12 at the Italian factory when he was there to discuss a possible Ferrari - Granatelli link-up. Franco Gozzi, a spokesman for Ferrari, recalls taking part in a meeting with Enzo Ferrari, the Granatelli brothers and Mario Andretti. At the session, possible plans for a blown 2.8 liter Ferrari engine to be developed from their 3 liter F 1 powerplant were discussed. Gozzi reports that the "project was considered, but it was never carried out."

Chapter 19

SOME REFLECTIONS

The Novi powered cars were entered in the Indianapolis 500 over a period extending beyond two decades. At its introduction in 1941, the car was referred to as a Winfield. When racing resumed in 1946, the cars were referred to by the media and the public as Novis. For some inexplicable reason, many fans saw little difference between the cars, although over the years the cars certainly differed in chassis layout. Somehow it is not entirely correct to talk about the career of the Novi, as the plural is more apt. Be that as it may, this is a detail overlooked by many.

None of the Novis ever won a race, although they often were among the favorites to enter Victory Lane. On many occasions they were considered the cars to beat. They provided more Indy history than the vast majority of Indy cars following World War II. No doubt, the post-war Indy history would have been far different if the Novis had not been present in their annual quest for fame and fortune! Fame it received, but that elusive victory was another matter. There is no doubt that the Novis were one of the main drawing cards at the Speedway, year in and year out. Although the Speedway could survive without them, their presence certainly added to the track's illustrious history. They certainly offered considerable grist for fans, racing historians and Indy history books.

An excellent example as to the Novis role was contained in a statement made by a celebrated driver who never drove a Novi, but who has played a significant part in the Speedway's history: Mario Andretti. In a discussion with Mario about the Novi, he offered the following observations, "The Novi was historical. The thing was a very exciting package, but it was never successfully executed. I think there are a lot of dreams there that were a part of the project but it lacked good basic engineering. Otherwise it should have been more successful. And they were not."

Its power was too strong and ahead of its time for a track of that nature and tire technology was not sufficient to cope with the weight and enormous speeds. Additionally, the chassis placed too heavy a demand on its drivers. In short, the Novi was not the right "package" for Indy, to borrow a term from Andretti.

Another problem relates to the fact that they were raced only once a year. During the earlier phase of the Welch era, very little testing was provided for the cars. When driven on the Salt Flats, such an activity was not nearly as helpful as testing on an actual oval racing facility. When the Granatellis assumed ownership, testing had increased as race cars were being tested at Indy on a more regular basis. The Granatellis, therefore, had the benefit of being able to test at the Speedway as Firestone tire tests had become a rather common practice during the 1950s.

Another consideration is that during the Welch years of ownership, the team searched for more power instead of using the power already at hand. The team overlooked the opportunity to maintain the available power while trying to conserve fuel and reducing car weight.

Yet, in spite of all this, the Welch era provided the positive fan fixation that created the Novi legend. The Granatellis had a more scientific approach as to the conversion of the Novi power. Andy's personal view regarding the Novis was quite different from the way Lew Welch thought about them. One consequence was that in the Granatelli years some of the Novi magic was lost. For while the Granatellis had built two of the most interesting Novis, what with their four wheel drive, it just did not seem the same. Andy also had a number of interesting plans for the engines, yet the Novi lacked the same allure as in the past. Although, the Granatellis improved on the power output, the end results were not as positive as that accomplished during Welch's ownership. Admittedly, the Granatellis ran the cars when front engine technology was becoming outdated. As for Welch, he ran the FWDs in years when they were considered all but dinosaurs due to the accepted racing technology employed at the time.

One is left to wonder how different things might have been if the Novi had remained active and changed in chassis form along with further development on the engine. Interestingly, in an article published in the 1967 Clymer Indianapolis 500 Yearbook, Offy's chief engineer Leo Goossen stated that he believed the Novi could be more than a threat for the Offy and Ford powered cars. Bear in mind that Goossen's Offy had been on the scene before the Ford Quadcam arrived in 1964. One can only wonder what kind of development suggestions Leo might have come up with if he had been involved with the Novi throughout its career.

Then of course, there is the matter of the alleged jinx. If one is superstitious, he/she may believe that all failures were due to some form of hex. On occasion, it was nothing more than pure bad luck. However, on several occasions it was the result of bad judgment or off the target concepts.

It is easy to criticize the Novi, but we have the virtue of hindsight. Welch, the Winfields, Goossen and Marcenac were a strong group of men who could spawn new ideas. If they had been able to remain together the story might well have had an entirely different ending.

Perhaps, if Welch had given more consideration to endurance than flat out speed, results might have been different. During the Welch era, the Novi team placed greater stress on power and ways to obtain it. As with a number of other teams, limited emphasis was given to aerodynamics. It is reasonable to assume that if increased attention had been rendered to chassis behavior, cornering, tire wear and car weight, the results might well have been improved. Some outside observers noted the lack of a chassis specialist within the team. Such an individual might well have improved on the entire package while retaining a front wheel drive system. Perhaps these observers had in mind someone akin to Lou Moore, builder and owner of the FWD Blue Crown cars that won the race in 1947, 1948 and 1949. There are people who believe that the FWD Novi may well have won a race if Lou Moore had worked on them. That is, if Moore wanted to use Novi power in the first place! One can speculate that if Welch had switched to a rear drive years earlier, the outcome might well have been different and a Novi victory would have been more likely.

Based on the judgments of Parnelli Jones and A.J. Foyt after their test drives in the Novi, the Granatellis came up short in obtaining a decent handling roadster chassis. Yet, they did appear to work on the element of handling and an effective power transfer to a much greater degree than had the Welch team.

Any effort to provide an accurate and succinct conclusion regarding the influence of the Novis and their engines with respect to the history of motor racing is not an easy task. Examining what they contributed to racing technology, it must be noted that they were the most powerful cars during their Indy tenure. Yet, what discernable use was made from such an exerted and extended effort? Just as the general technology to employ massive amounts of horsepower was becoming available, the Novis were retired from racing.

The virtue of the Novi was its raw power and the tremendous speeds on the straightaways. Such caused them to be feared, respected and somewhat revered; particularly during the Welch years. They often appeared to present a psychological advantage over a number of the other drivers.

As for modern day technology, the Novi has little to offer. The Novi front drive is considered to be the fastest such Indy car ever built (if one excludes Bob Mathouser's aborted qualification run with Mickey Thompson's 1965 Chevrolet). They were also among the first cars to be built with a lower center of gravity. Yet, with lower gravity and the additional power, the cars could only be driven on the paved oval at Indy as they were totally unsuitable on the dirt tracks, any short track, or for that matter even those with limited corner banking.

The Novi rear drives never contributed any remarkable or important features into racing technology. Their fame and reputation rested largely upon several achievements. Ralph Hepburn's sizzling new track record in 1946 that broke the existing qualifying mark by over 3 m.p.h; Duke Nalon's superlative pole sitter runs in 1949 and 1951 and Chet Miller's record run in 1952. Further, one year they had the fastest car at Indy with Paul Russo's 146.6 m.p.h. practice lap in 1956; the Monza closed track record of 176.826 m.p.h. set by Tony Bettenhausen in 1957 and Jim Hurtubise placing one in the front row for the 1963 running of the 500.

A contribution of sorts, from a technological point of view, was the tail fin used on the 500Fs. They were pioneers in this phase of car construction if one discounts the few times tails were used - primarily in the 1930s. Prior to the 1994 Indianapolis race, it was noted that mini "fins" made up the top part of the engine cover on some of the entries. Interestingly, these modified fins were referred to in print as a "Novi mini fin" component. The Mercedes-Benz powered Penkse cars entered in the 1994 running of the 500, including that of the eventual winner Al Unser, Jr., used the so-called Novi mini fin. According to Karl Ludvigsen, Mercedes aerodynamists used this shape of engine cover due to the powerplant's tall plenum-chamber.

Of more importance was the four wheel drive. Although, obsolete for Indy with their engine location in the front of the chassis, they proved to be a forerunner of a rather successful employment for a unique single seater 4WD race car at Indy. Although, a 4WD never won at Indy, a few that were built met with a measure of success, as the Granatellis aptly demonstrated with their turbines. The 1968 Lotus possibly proved to a degree, the merits of 4WD and aerodynamics just as with the 1967 "Silent Sam." Sam was about on par with the power of the piston driven engines, while the Lotuses were woefully underpowered when compared to the piston cars. It has been estimated that the Lotuses had somewhere between 450 to 480 horsepower available on race day in 1968, while the turbo cars, that might attempt to run at full boost, were in the 600 horsepower range.

Further, another angle deserving mention in a critique of the Novi deals with the use of the supercharger. While there were sporadic efforts using supercharged engines, the Novi was the only supercharged engine presented for competition at every Indy race from 1946 through 1966.

Further, although the engine had its disadvantages, such as its weight and only two valves per cylinder (and perhaps other items that were not optimal), several car owners looked with envy at the Novi wishing they were available. The power output of the Novi was unmatched during its career with the exception of the Demler turbine of 1966. The Novi, the only blown engine, was the link between the era of the supercharged Formula One racers and the earlier glorious period of American race cars. The Novi was eventually followed by the turbocharged cars that were to dominate at Indy. The Novi had become the only continual blown engine as they had all but disappeared from Europe in 1952. Therefore, the Novi was the only race car in the world that continually employed forced induction.

From its beginning, the Novi was one of the engines with the highest absolute power output ever placed in a race car that campaigned on closed circuits. At one point, only a few of the Mercedes and Auto Union "Silberpfeile" ranked higher in power output. In time, the Novi surpassed the claimed 646 horsepower of the 1937 Mercedes Grand Prix car.

The Novi had the highest power capacity ratio of all American built racing engines until the turbo Offy took over. We do not consider the 1,250 horsepower of the 1966 Demler as being a purebred race car as it was not piston driven. Yet, the Novi never became the engine with the higher power ratio of any race car. This honor was held by the catastrophic BRM V-16. This BRM engine, with twice as many cylinders and double stage centrifugal superchargers, had only half the capacity of the V-8 despite giving away 91 c.i. (1.5 liter) to the Novi. The BRM V-16 produced a claimed 585 horsepower in 1953. At that time, the Novi was reported to have an output of approximately 550 horsepower. In conclusion, the blown engine made a return into the racing world with the Novi being the lone notable link to the glorious pre-war heyday of supercharged racing engines.

Since the Novi engine never won a 500 in spite of its power advantage, it must be said that obviously its contribution to the history of motor racing engineering cannot be called extraordinary. Nor were there any imitators, although a few car owners tried unsuccessfully to purchase Novi engines. A "Novi copy," commissioned by car owner Howard Keck, slated to use a newly designed supercharged V-8 engine, failed to materialize.

Yet, one interesting feature of the Novi is overlooked by many people. The Novi V-8 configuration came closer than other V-shaped powerplants in relationship to the everyday passenger car. The American passenger car (V-6 or V-8) had a bigger sweep and often a single camshaft with push rods, though we concede there were differences. Without question the Novi was the only consistent Indy car entered with a V-8 under the hood. Yes, the Novi had dual overhead cams and was blown to gain power. Such was certainly at odds with the designs presented by passenger car manufacturers. On the other hand, many champ cars used a four cylinder engine, a configuration that was not the norm with American passenger cars. A contributing factor in the demise of the Novi was the belated, but successful testing of the turbocharger.

In the turbine car, the driver was positioned alongside a Pratt and Whitney engine. Following the testing program, the car was entered in the 1967 race. Parnelli qualified sixth fastest to start from the outside of the second row. At the start of the race, he took off like a rooster with its tail feathers on fire, leaving the field behind as "Silent Sam" or the "Whoosmobile" seemingly cruised the two and one-half mile Indy oval in an effortless manner. Although, the race was halted

(1967) The Granatellis had now parked the Novis as they switched to a turbine powered car. Parnelli Jones came within several laps of winning in the STP Oil Treatment Special. A gearbox malfunction forced his exit from the race with only 4 laps remaining.   I.M.S.

after 18 laps due to rain, when it resumed the following day, Jones picked up right where he left off. That is until lap 196 when his superb ride in the STP Turbine was abruptly halted due to a broken transmission bearing. At that point, A.J. Foyt moved into first to achieve his third 500 triumph.

The Granatellis then began to lock horns with USAC with regard to the annulus area (air intake) for turbine engines. Yet, driver Joe Leonard qualified an STP Oil Treatment Special for the 1968 race, and in so doing established a new track record of 171.599 m.p.h. Once again with a victory close at hand, Leonard was sidelined on lap 191 with a fuel shaft problem. Continuing the feud with USAC (that eventually lead to a court case), the Granatellis nonetheless moved on. The following year, STP had Mario Andretti at the wheel of their STP Oil Treatment Special, a Clint Brawner built Hawk chassis powered by a turbo Ford. The Granatellis finally achieved a 500 victory, something they had struggled for, on and off, for over 23 years (1946-1969). With the victorious Hawk, the dream of a Novi victory was absolutely dead. That is, if in fact it had not been dashed several years earlier with the introduction and achievements of the turbo cars.

While the illusive 500 victory was not achieved, creating many broken dreams, there was an exception in future years. Driver Bobby Unser, who piloted a Novi his first three years at the Speedway, won the Indy 500 on three occasions after leaving STP. The fabled Novi was, therefore, a springboard in his Indy career.

In spite of all the failures, the people who saw the Novis in action would not easily forget them. There may have been other cars that enjoyed short term popularity, but then the memories fade. For example, how many charismatic stories and details are general knowledge regarding the winning car of say 1959; or 1969 or 1979? All the grandiose considerations rendered in behalf of the Novi fell far short of reaching the desired goal, yet who is to fault the efforts and dedication made in behalf of the beloved Novi? But times being what they are, it is very difficult to imagine that any car marque or car owner will equal or surpass the popularity, magic and mystique that belongs to the Novi legend. The road to Indy's Victory Lane turned out to be the "Boulevard of Broken Dreams" for those who put their faith in the Novis.

Chapter 20

THE GRANATELLI NOVI YEARS IN PERSPECTIVE

At this point, permit us to make some observations relative to the Granatelli portion of the Novi era. The Granatellis opted to drop the Novi name when they submitted official entry forms for the cars. The only concession they made with respect to identifying the Novi heritage was a small decal on the side of the cars asserting that they were "Novi Powered" along with the silhouette of a swift moving race car. Just why this was done was not clear. Possibly, they feared the so-called Novi jinx would diminish or evaporate by dropping the Novi names on the entry forms. When Andy was questioned about the Novi name being left off the form to eliminate the jinx, he stated that superstition and fear had nothing to do with it. Thus, it is more reasonable to assume that the brothers had nothing to do with the business functions of the original Novi owner and wanted a change. In spite of the lack of the Novi name on the entry forms and only the minute name on the sides of the cars, such did not deter the press from continuing to refer to the cars as Novis throughout the Granatelli years of operation. It is interesting to note that even the Granatellis referred to the cars as their Novis and not by another label such as Paxton or STP Specials. Even publicity material constantly referred to the Novis or the Novi engine.

To some fans, the omission was a turn-off for the legendary engine. Yet, on the other hand one must realize that if the Granatellis had failed to pick up on the Novi purchase in 1961 the Novi history might well have ended right then and there. The heart of the legend was still the V-8 engine and that was to be found in the cars then owned by the Granatellis. Some veteran fans might find argument with this, contending that much of the magic of the Novi under Lew Welch was gone. However, one could reasonably assert that the resurrection by the Granatellis must have win some degree of acceptance and appreciation, even among detractors.

For some people, the Granatelli era with the Novi is not held in the same regard as much of the luster seemed to have diminished. No doubt some of this feeling is due to the personal feelings people had with respect to the Granatellis and Andy in particular. Andy became well-known at Indy in the 1960s with the Novis and the turbines, but this did not translate into popularity with large numbers of people. The cars were popular with many, but this did not transfer over to the new owner. In Parnelli, author Bill Libby offered this observation in the 1961 section of his work:

> "Dark, fat and flamboyant, the brilliant Granatelli had risen to a position of power in the automotive world, but he walks so heavy he made most people in racing move away from him. When Liguori hung the latest Novi on the wall in 1961, some fans wept for the car, but many in racing laughed at its owner."

Another account, Indy Racing Legends by Tony Sakkis states, "From the very beginning Granatelli was controversial. Even when he finally won the race in 1969 with Mario Andretti, Granatelli had successfully pissed enough people off so that he had almost no friends at the two-and-a-half mile oval...with the possible exception of himself and possibly his brothers, nobody called him Mr. 500."

It is rather common knowledge that numerous negative remarks have been made with respect to Andy. This work is not intended in any way to be a personal attack on the Granatellis or Andy. The Granatellis were more than willing to take time to talk with us with respect to the years they spent at Indy.

But if Andy Granatelli was not that well-liked, the Novis were. Lew Welch had found himself in a somewhat similar position. During the Welch years there was certainly no outpouring of popularity toward the Michigan businessman, but few would deny him a victory with the Novi. Further, without a doubt, a victory under the Granatelli Novi banner would have been almost (or even) as popular. The fact that the Granatellis placed a Novi in the front row for the 1963 race provided some warm and glowing thoughts with respect to the Novi operation, be it Granatelli owned or not. Further, no earlier front row of cars had ever topped 150 m.p.h. in qualifying. To enhance the glory of this rewarding assault, one can recall the ever popular Jim Hurtubise actually leading the race's first lap driving a Novi. The euphoric spell was fleeting, yet it was to be cherished by any number of Novi followers. Decades later, the first lap drama often comes into discussion when the Novi and/or Herk are mentioned.

It would be a natural reaction to compare the two Novi owners. In some respects they bore similarities, while at the same time they were quite opposites. As an example, Lew Welch was the introvert who did not seek recognition for himself, but only for the Novi masterpiece of which he was so attached. On the other hand, Andy Granatelli's presence was always duly noted at the Speedway. Andy would spend virtually the entire month of May in Indy while Welch's routine normally called for appearances only on weekends as qualifications were underway and the race was close at hand. Otherwise, if circumstances did not call for his attendance he would be found at his Novi, Michigan plant, or the West Coast at the Ford reconditioning plant, or at some business function as he was the epitome of the workaholic.

Without question, both men were keenly involved in champ car racing; they both had the racing bug and they were willing to support the "habit" with their own money. Yet, herein lies a difference as well. Although Welch was receptive to sponsors, he did not pursue them as aggressively as the Granatellis. Such was understandable in the first Novi years at the Speedway, yet as time marched on, Andy was in a position to secure additional funding without any real hassle. Welch, meanwhile, had an obstacle what with the repeated failures of the Novis. Andy had the Grancor Wynn Special (Jim Rathmann driving) finish second in 1952 and the Grancor Elgin Piston Pin Special (Freddie Agabashian driving) finished fourth the following year. Such splendid finishes in the early 1950s certainly enhanced the Granatellis racing resume.

While Welch certainly used his Indy creations to promote his company products, his funding lacked the support rendered by Studebaker, though admittedly the Studebaker expenditures were aimed at helping to save the firm from extinction. But then Lew Welch had been in a personal financial pickle, what with the Texas oil wells disaster that was compounded by the faltering Novi automotive stores. It goes without saying that Granatelli used the Novis to a greater advantage to publicize Studebaker, STP and Andy Granatelli.

Both men had come up the hard way and developed stubborn streaks. Welch insisted many times that activities be carried out in accordance with his wishes. Backing down or compromising were quite foreign to the industrialist. Andy also stood his ground, to put it mildly, even when it came to conflict with his brothers over one matter or another.

This study certainly is not intended as anything approaching a psychological comparison. Such would serve little purpose for this volume even if the authors were qualified to perform such an approach. If this type of study was undertaken Welch would suffer, as unfortunately, we lack an autobiography of the man's life while many are familiar with Andy Granatelli's book. Thus, any behavioralist would come up short in this approach. The best we can do is to undertake a study of their Indy records with the Novis. Yet, even here a flaw exists. Welch had FWD cars in the early years before switching to the rear drive. On the other hand, the Granatellis were not confronted with the ever challenging demands of the FWD Novi. Granatelli's Novi rear drives failed to make the 500 the first two years (1961-1962) and then he introduced the 4WD, a concept that Welch never employed. Without access to financial records, one is left to merely surmise as to the amount of money supplied by the owners and that provided by outside funding. The fact that Granatelli was able to field three cars in the 1963, 1964 and 1965 races is a good indicator of the availability to attract "outside" money, although outside is a bit strong as he was responsible to Studebaker and in later years to its successors in the matter of accountability when racing dollars were balanced against the corporate returns.

Comparing their records, we have Welch with 16 years of Novi participation at the Speedway and Monza while the Granatelli stretch lasted only six years. If we consider merely numbers, Welch had 17 Novis in the various races out of 27 entered, while the Granatellis had eight entries make the race of the 14 entered. Welch cars placed 3rd once, 4th twice and 10th twice. Of the three 500s with Granatelli Novis the best finish was an 11th, although two did score 4th and 14th place finishes at Atlanta in 1965. Their Indianapolis records are as follows:

	Welch Era		Granatelli Era
Entries	Placement	Entries	Placement
1941		1961	
One	4th	One	DNQ
1946		1962	
One	14th	Three	DNQ
1947		1963	
Two	4th & 21st	Three	22nd, 31st & 33rd
1948		1964	
Two	3rd & DNQ	Three	11th, 21st & 32nd
1949		1965	
Two	25th & 29th	Three	19th, 32nd & DNQ
1950		1966	
Two	DNQ	One	DNQ
1951			
Two	10th & 25th		
1952			
Two	25th & 30th		
1953			
Two	11th & DNQ		
1954			
One	Bumped		
1955			
One	DNQ		
1956			
Two	33rd & DNQ		
1957			
Two	4th & 15th		
1958			
Two	10th & 18th		
1959			
Two	DNQ		
1960			
Two	DNQ		

CHASSIS

Welch	Granatelli
12 front drive	0 front drive
5 rear drive	6 rear drive
0 4WD	2 4WD

When we look at the results we see that in three years of racing the Novis, the Granatelli team had only two finishes above 20th. The 19th achieved by Bobby Unser and the 11th earned by Art Malone. Thus, Malone's finish was the best ever achieved by the Granatellis with the Novis. While it is difficult, if not truly unrealistic, to compare the Welch years to the Granatelli years, one might still conclude that the Novis achieved a more distinguished record under Lew Welch's ownership. In the Granatellis behalf it must be pointed out that the results were influenced in part by being in the wrong place at the wrong time. As an example, Unser's 32nd place finish in 1964 was caused by the fire in turn two and the somewhat questionable call on Hurtubise in 1963 with respect to the "oil leak." Then in 1965, the highly touted Granatelli built 4WD was eliminated the day before qualifications due to its involvement in the accident when Ebb Rose spun in front of Bobby Unser. Without a shadow of doubt, the car was capable of making the field. Finally, there is the influence of the long pause between the crash and the restart in 1964, with respect to the refiring of the Malone and McElreath cars. On only three occasions did a Granatelli car suffer from a mechanical failure; Malone in 1963 and Unser and Hurtubise in 1965.

Then there were three years of non-qualifying as well. If some thought the Granatellis had dropped the Novi name from the official entry forms to avoid the so-called Novi jinx it certainly did not work that way for the result was just the opposite. To say that the Granatellis did not do enough to keep the Novis running would be misleading at the very least. For as with the Welch team, experimental work was continuous, although the Granatellis had the highly beneficial advantage of track time. Before we leave the comparison game, we might point out that Welch's Novis broke the track record several times, set on the pole twice and also were eliminated by crashes while leading - not once but twice.

The Granatellis had some good ideas on how to improve the V-8 engines and raise the power output from 500 horsepower to over 800 horsepower. Further, adopting four wheel drive was an example of their experimental work. If we have to criticize the Granatellis for any developmental mistakes, it would be the fact that they made the wrong choice in remaining with front engine cars. But then other car owners were also reluctant to take to the so-called "funny cars" i.e. those with rear engine placement. In spite of much consideration in building such a rear engine car, the Granatellis never seemed to move beyond the planning stage.

The development of race car chassis took a real turn from the beginning of the 1960s and the Granatelli option did not appear to be the correct choice. Most ironic was the fact that Andy had envisioned several plans but they were never realized.

The evolution process the Granatellis chose (whether right or wrong) was executed far more carefully than that under Welch. Maybe criticism of the Granatelli Novi operation is deserved if one envisioned the promised success with the car. This rests with Andy's continuing exhortations - great promises yet very limited success. As for the Welch era, the ballyhoo was largely from the press and not from the the team's ownership.

While the Novis often experienced misfortune under Lew Welch, the Granatellis suffered bad

The above photo appeared in the 1965 STP press kit. In this often used shot, Andy Granatelli is seen working at the dyno. It is believed the Novi engine being tested was one of the front drive crankcase engines with a new head. No protective barrier, Andy?

Authors Collection

luck in a similar way. It has already been mentioned that in the years the cars made the race, they appeared to be habitually hampered by one form or another of bad luck.

It is not entirely equitable to compare the Welch - Granatelli era in a reasonable and just manner. The results table above may allow the reader to draw his or her own conclusions.

In spite of what the critics may have said, we have to conclude that at the very least the Granatellis may well have saved the Novis from an otherwise earlier and ignominious disappearance from the Speedway. Keep in mind that during Welch's last two years at the track, the twin entries were completely uncompetitive. The Granatellis enabled the Novi to make a return to the racing world even if such was not highly successful. While they were the last descendants of the front engine Novi cars, they defended the Novi reputation with some honor in 1963, 1964 and 1965. (Hurtubise placed a front engine Novi in the front row. In 1964, Unser had the second fastest front engine car in the field.) For those who had always claimed that the Novi was the wrong concept from the very beginning, they would probably conclude that the Granatellis postponed the inevitable - the final execution of an engine that was never well suited for the Speedway in the first place. But even these critics seemingly would have to admit that the Granatellis along with Lewis Welch greatly enhanced the unique history of the world renowned Indianapolis 500.

INTERMEZZO

A Brief Granatelli Critique

A flamboyant Andy Granatelli, a showman of the first order, was not a favorite among some of the other crews, nor by a number of other car owners. His modus operandi was judged to be excessive showboating and his ego overly zealous. Yet, the Novi was a crowd favorite. It must be remembered Andy, Joe and Vince were the individuals who were responsible for bringing back the Novi for its last attempts to reach the most exhaulted place in American auto racing - an Indianapolis 500 win.

Andy may well have been auto racing's answer to P.T. Barnum, the famed circus impresario and his style of showmanship. P.T. was said to have told the press, "Say anything you want about me as long as you spell my name right." A transition to Andy Granatelli seems logical. Taking this supposition and applying a bit of poetic license, one might well imagine Andy as saying `say what you will about me, but spell my name right and be sure to mention STP.'

Whatever the reader's judgment may be, bear in mind that Andy played a key role in greatly expanding STP's role in the sport. In time, the company became one of the very top supporters and sponsors in racing - and the Granatellis played a pivotal role in that important involvement. Further, one should not overlook the Granatellis bringing Valvoline into auto racing, and away from its sole West Coast support of drag racing.

Every Granatelli detactor we talked with - to a man, extolled his masterful touch as a promoter. They were all quick to point out that while he was busy promoting Andy Granatelli, he was also selling auto racing. He may well have suffered a severe case of decal mania, yet racing was publicized, thus granting it greater visibility.

The public relation folks at STP may have worked overtime, yet the proof of the pudding was in the eating - company profits - if we may use a slightly distorted homily.

During Andy's tenure at STP sales soared from $9,000,000 annually to $100,000,000. As this astronomical growth occurred, one newspaper account stated that "the man became as well-known as the product he promoted." Granatellis falling out with STP may well have been due in some measure to that factor.

Yet, racing proved to be a beneficiary as STP and Valovine, two major automotive operations, were brought into the sport on a major scale and they have played instrumental roles in the continuing growth of auto racing.

The Novis presented the Granatellis with a source to expand STP, yet bear in mind that the brothers had operated the Paxton supercharger operation for several years before the STP opportunity emerged. Their arrival at the Speedway with a sole Novi, left as a part of the distressed Lew Welch inventory, provided a new chapter in the Novi saga. The entry of STP, via the Studebaker Corporation, did not occur until 1963, although the Paxton firm had been acquired by Studebaker earlier (see Chapter 24).

Chapter 21

ANDY GRANATELLI'S RECOLLECTIONS OF THE NOVI PROJECT

Without a doubt it would have been most interesting and helpful had we been able to talk to Lew Welch and gone back over the years in which he owned and entered the Novi race cars. Fate did not permit this to happen, though we were able to converse with brothers Andy and Vince Granatelli. This input has been used in the text. Apart from talking about various aspects of his involvement, Andy also brought into our conversations other points of view. Through such statements one becomes well aware of Andy's strong feeling and infatuation with the Novi project.

One of the factors that makes Andy very proud was that the team was able to increase the Novi horsepower so that in time they managed to have the engine producing up to 837 horsepower. He also mentioned that in 1963, they had been able to obtain 741 horsepower competing against 400 horsepower Offys. This was due in good measure to the adoption of the Bendix fuel injection system. In reflecting on his feelings, Andy has said, "All of this was a total waste of time because the Offys only had 400 horsepower, the good ones, so we had almost double the horsepower but we didn't know anything about how to make a car handle with that kind of engine in it."

Granatelli also reiterated a point made by a number of drivers - the Novi had a reputation for not finishing races. Art Cross had a brilliant but brief tenure at the Speedway (2nd, 5th and an 11th in only four starts). When Art retired, he said that Andy tried to lure him back to the Brickyard. Art asserts that a major stumbling block was the inherent undependable nature of the Novi. As pointed out earlier, in discussions with other drivers, they echoed similar sentiments.

Andy enjoyed discussing his first year at the Speedway, not solely because it was his first year as a car entrant, but in being on hand to witness the Novi and its extraordinary power as displayed by Ralph Hepburn. Andy recalls:

"In 1946, I could see Ralph Hepburn coming out of turn four and all you could see with the Novi is the cloud of smoke, blue smoke. The tires were spinning both front drive wheels. The whole car was like coming out of a movie in other words like a ghost...He (Hepburn) was very old to drive any car, let alone the Novi but he did a great job. He qualified at 133 m.p.h. [Author's note: a new track record-133.944 m.p.h. breaking the existing record by over 3 m.p.h. which had been set by Jimmy Snyder in 1937.] He was always very modest. He (Hepburn) said a young guy could qualify this car with 140 m.p.h. You know, those were trucks. Don't ever get the idea that those front drive Kurtis cars were driveable. They were not driveable. Those cars had a locked front end on them...You didn't have a chance...if you spun locking the front end. It was not steerable and it took all your might to turn the car and those cars were heavy. They were something like 3,000 pounds and that's why they had all that tire wear."

When the front drives came up in discussion, the fatalities in these cars (Hepburn and Chet Miller) are often mentioned. Andy, who practiced as a rookie in 1948 driving a front drive, informed us he had a feeling that he knew what killed Hepburn and Miller.

"They tried to get the car back on the track and with the Novi Special, once you stood on the gas, which ever way the nose was pointed, that was the way the car was going to go and they both drove straight up into the wall and got killed when the steering wheel hit them in the chest and I remember that and whenever I lost a front wheel drive car here, I took it down on the grass gladly and stayed there. I didn't try to get back on the track."

Andy then mentioned the fact that if a car had moved down onto the grass and the skinny tires became dirty with sand, pebbles, etc., the grip that the tires offered in returning safely onto the track was so minimal that it became even more hazardous.

While discussing the 1948 race, we mentioned the various accounts with regard to the reason Duke Nalon had to make that late pit stop that may have cost him the race. Since Andy had known the engine so well we were interested in hearing his theory as to what happened. His response was a near classic. According to Andy, "every team owner and sponsor has some reason to tell different versions about a car's retirement or failure. Some sponsors don't even tell the true facts. Occasionally, an owner doesn't even tell the actual reason(s)." Before we could proceed, Andy immediately said, "If a car is sponsored by STP, I wouldn't want anybody to know if an engine blew up." Such a statement by Granatelli reminds several veterans of the time when Andy reported that one of his cars had been sidelined due to "a sudden loss of power." A driver standing nearby, overhearing this, muttered, "Yeah, due to a hole in the side of the engine."

Regarding the mechanical weaknesses and mistakes regarding the Novis, Andy was willing to offer some observations. In his judgement, the following had been an error.

"The Novis should have had intercoolers on them. I know it had an intercooler on in the early years. But the intercoolers were so heavy that one man had difficulties in lifting one up but I didn't realize then as much as I realize now that an intercooler was absolutely mandatory."

Continuing, Andy said;

"Let me tell you what the basic problem on the Novi was. I know now it was the oil sump system; the oil sump and pumps were not big enough for that engine. When I think back now after all the experiments, had I been able to put a bigger sump pump on it then I could have put a vacuum in the crankcase. This would have eliminated a lot of problems. A lot of temperature problems occurred."

Again the matter of weight came into play and a bigger oil pump would have in one respect defeated their purpose. A great deal of what Andy learned about the engines came at the dyno. He claims to have spent thousands of hours behind the dyno. "I won a race every year on the dynometer, no question about that." Then he mentioned the magical subject: the sound and noise of the Novi. Andy spoke in magnificent terms when mentioning the Novi sound. He said, "If you want to hear a sound that would be at Phoenix when we ran the Novi and the sound would echo (off the nearby mountains). You'd run it and hear that noise come back. It was a sound you wouldn't believe." When we mentioned to Andy that during Jean Marcenac's testing of the Novi on the dyno people blocks away complained about the noise, Andy reacted with his voice rising in volume, "Several blocks around? When I ran them at Santa Monica, are you kidding? Five miles away they complained." According to Andy, "the Novi was the only car you could hear around the entire race track. The Novi could be heard above every other car all around the track, all the time." Then he recalled, "But we lost that sound somewhere along the way. We missed that sound. The last time I heard that sound was in the early '60s, but with changing the head design and changing the port design, putting the injection on it, cam timing changes and the various exhaust manifolds as we got different style cars, we lost that sound. Not that it wasn't an impressive sound, but not that real Novi sound." As to its loudness, Andy informed us that the Novis had been measured as high as 130.8 decibels. The human ear reaches the pain level limit at 120 decibels. Granatelli stated, "I use to run the engines on the dynometer with ear plugs and muffs on like they used with jets and when the engine hit a certain sound on the dyno the ear muffs would pop off your ears from the vibration. The ceiling plaster would start falling. The exhaust pipes were attached to hoses that went out into the alley and if anybody would walk by it would knock them over. You can't believe what I'm talking about. It was something else."

Regarding the volume of exhaust gas produced by the Novi, we lack sufficient information to offer solid data. However, we feel we can provide some information as to the noise level as to the amount of air moving into the engine. We began by considering the air intake of the Novi, the Offy and the Ford Quadcam V-8. Our calculations call for all engines running at their average rpms for a full lap at the Speedway. The consideration also involved the notion that they could not run at full throttle through the turns. Because of the four stroke principle, the rpm value must be divided by two to calculate the volume of air taken in. For the Novi, we took what we think must have been an average boost level provided by the supercharger for the full lap.

	Novi	Offy	Ford Quadcam
Capacity (liter):	2.8	4.2	4.2
Average RPM:	6,000	4,000	5,600
Boost level:	2.5	1	1
Volume air taken in:	21,000	8,400	11,760

Keeping in mind that these figures are estimated and based on conservative figures, it can be seen that the Novi took in a far greater amount of air than the two unblown engines. Knowing that the Novi had the highest fuel consumption of the three engines it becomes clear that the Novi indeed produced a tremendous amount of exhaust gasses. As Andy indicated, it is difficult to fully comprehend the noise element. Those who heard a Novi running will most certainly support the notion that the noise level of the Novi was all but indescriblable.

It is recalled that at one point the Granatellis had a sound barrier erected behind the Santa Monica shop in an effort to defuse the noise away from a pub a block over that had its backside facing the common alley. Vince chuckled as he recalled that such a measure was of little consequence as the patrons still quickly departed from the bar when a Novi engine was fired up.

When the matter of engine reduction rules came up, Andy asserted that the expense would be too large an amount of money to make the change. He went on to another subject which made a lot of sense, especially when one recalls when he was considered the 'enfant terrible' among the Indy car owners. Andy asked, "What would stop them from changing the rules again next week." In a firm manner Andy asserted, "When we stopped with the Novis it was not because they were old fashioned at all." And indeed, if it comes to the level of power performance they were certainly not yet outdated. The opposition had yet to reach the power outputs the Novi was capable of producing.

While some contend that the Novis were rapidly becoming dinosaurs due to the failure to place the all powerful engine at the rear, Andy had great faith in the car. Yet, the very promising turbine beckoned.

Chapter 22

The Early Granatelli Years

To be completely factual, the Granatelli "years" began with the arrival of Vincent Granatelli, Sr. as an immigrant to the United States at the age of 18. The young Italian came from a village near Palermo and he was a part of the large wave of Europeans looking for a better life in the promised land. In 1918, Vincent and Carmine Cardinal were married. The couple were to become the parents of three sons, Joseph (born May, 1919), Anthony (born March, 1923) and Vincent, Jr. (born January, 1927).

As the boys grew up in Chicago during the depression years of the 1930s, they were not strangers to the hard way of life. For a time the family had to live with relatives and draw relief aid. For the elder Vincent there was a scarcity of funds for the family; a rather common denominator with millions of Americans due to the economic upheaval of the time. As resilient and creative youngsters, the brothers quickly learned of ways to acquire funds, even if they came a few pennies at a time. As an example, the brothers trooped from their home in north Chicago down to the site of Chicago's 1933 World's Fair, located adjacent to Soldier Field a distance of more than nine miles. Joseph (known as Joe) and brother Anthony (called Tony in earlier years and later Andy) noted the numerous soda bottles in and about the fair grounds and realizing that each would bring a two cent refund, they began gathering up the glass containers. Then as they began the long trek back home, they would stop at stores along the way turning in a portion of the bottles to collect "their" refunds. A great family lose occurred in 1935 when Carmine Granatelli passed away. Vincent, Sr. lived until 1977.

Along the way the youngsters developed a love for automobiles. By the time the boys were in their mid to late teens, they were beyond the basic fundamentals of the operation of the automobile. In time this led to Joe and Andy obtaining employment in garages. With his additional income, Joe was able to purchase a 1938 Ford that he hopped up. The car was to sport an overdrive and a blower. Andy would later have his first car, a 1934 Ford with a 1939 Mercury engine. Through thrift and diligent work they were able to procure sufficient funds to secure a lease on a corner gas station on the city's north side. A hefty $500 loan from a neighborhood merchant went a long way in helping to secure the lease from the Texaco Oil Company.

Then in 1944 came the big break. The brothers opened a speed shop on North Broadway - then an automobile row in Chicago. A name was not difficult to come by as the Granatellis formed a corporation entitled Grancor. Having learned through the grapevine of the very active hot rodding activities in southern California that predated World War II and realizing that the Chicagoland area contained a significant number of hardcore hot rodders, they were ready to meet the needs of fellow speedsters. Opening their garage, identified as the Grancor Automotive Specialists, they advertised the business as centering around their work at souping up Ford V-8s. When rebuilt with modified racing equipment, the Ford was considered to be the hot setup. The firm advertised that it performed "motor building and repair, muffler work of all kinds and served as a distributor of racing equipment of all kinds." The muffler angle may appear a bit whimsical or meager with respect to a car's performance. However, some of the hot rodders were content merely to have the custom made mufflers that emitted a deep throated sound as their cars roared down the street in an authoritative macho manner. Yet, beyond the "music" from the dual exhaust system there was the benefit of the pipes relieving back pressure with the increase in engine speeds. For some hot rodders, the addition of spinner hubcaps on the front wheels and wheel skirts on the rear was all they really desired, while others wanted to add top-notch speed equipment. For the intense hot rodder the Grancor inventory included Winfield products, "Winner of the Field" and "Second to None," Mallory coils and condensers, Jahns custom made racing pistons, Harmon and Collins cams, Norden steering and the ever popular Smithy's California style mufflers, among other items.

As the business grew the Granatellis had parts built by speed manufacturers with the Grancor name stamped on the products. Their work became known to not only hot rodders but racing personalities throughout the Midwest. Their reputation was such that the February, 1950 issue of Mechanix Illustrated, a national publication, contained a story by noted automotive authority Tom McCahill entitled, "How to Hop Up Your Car." In preparation for his article, Tom contacted Grancor "whose Ford engines hold the record for flat tops." From a standing start it had taken a Ford 15.9 seconds to reach 60 m.p.h. With a new Grancor setup, McCahill's 1949 Ford passenger car's time dropped to 15 seconds flat. Prior to the addition of the duals, the car's top speed had been 92.3 m.p.h. Then the Granatellis added aluminum heads as they removed the Ford cast iron pieces. This was followed by the installation of a dual intake manifold and an oversized Merc carb. With this work completed, the 1949 Ford was then clocked at speeds up to 112 m.p.h. Such publicity certainly was a great assistance to the Grancor reputation and business operation. The brothers had also become quite active in various forms of racing which garnered much additional publicity.

The Granatellis had entered a car in the 1946 Indianapolis 500 (which will be covered in the next chapter). Approximately a week prior to the race, Indy driver Duke Nalon was permitted to take to the track in an experimental run in a Paul Weirick owned sprint car powered by a Sparks/Weirick engine to test the effect of a pair of JATO (Jet Assist Take Off) rockets then used for aircraft carrier planes to aid in quicker takeoffs from the ship's deck or to assist heavily loaded military aircraft that were required to use short runways. Driving at about 80 m.p.h. Nalon set off a two second rocket that increased the car's speed to approximately 100 m.p.h. The detonation created a huge trail of white smoke. A later test with a four second rocket raised the top speed to about 110 m.p.h.

Perhaps picking up on the eye-opening exhibit of smoke and noise generated by the JATO setup, Andy was to spend time that summer touring with Frank Winkley's promoted International Motor Contest Association (IMCA) racing shows on the circuit's promotions at county fair tracks throughout the Midwest or at Al Sweeney's track productions. The navy surplus JATOs were purchased as military surplus at $10 each and Andy would do a lap or two in the "Grancor Rocket Firebug" car to the great delight of the assembled crowd. Andy was later to refer to the activity as "playing the beer and cotton candy circuit." His participation that summer in the IMCA shows provided some important lessons in showmanship and business acumen that would prove to be important for the Granatellis. Frank Winkley and Al Sweeney were masters at racing promotion and some of it most certainly rubbed off on Andy.

The racer that carried the rockets had a bit of Indy history itself as it had been entered in the 1934 running of the 500 classic event by a Chicago Ford dealer, Don Hulbert. The car failed to make the race though it was the second alternate. The bulbous shaped car sported a tail as did several other cars; perhaps a forerunner to the enormous wing on the Granatelli's #75 car. Although the body had been altered, the Hulbert car contained a Ford V-8.

With the close of World War II, racing resumed in the Chicagoland area as was the case across the nation. Many track owners scurried about to quickly resume racing. The tracks included the renowned quarter mile paved track at Soldier Field. Similar to the Los Angeles Coliseum, Soldier Field was built primarily for football games and other outdoor show activities. However, the perimeter around the field offered sufficient space for auto racing. The Chicago Auto Racing Association provided the sponsorship for A.A.A. sanctioned midget racing and the weekly shows attracted many outstanding racing veterans such as Sam Hanks, Ronnie Householder, Teddy Duncan, Mel Hansen, Duane Carter, Johnnie Parsons, Duke Nalon, Frank Burany, Tony Bettenhausen, Pete Romcevich, George Tichenor and Gus Klingbeil.

Meanwhile, the Granatelli brothers, having recognized that the metropolitan Chicago area had hundreds of young males with souped up prewar cars, began to think in terms of some sort of hot rod racing program. They were well aware of the origins of the California Roadster Association and its large following in addition to all of the hot rod runs occurring north of Los Angeles at Muroc Lake, El Mirage, Rosamond and elsewhere. Also involved in the California activities was the Southern California Timing Association. As a consequence of this beehive of activity out west the Granatellis, in conjunction with several others, formed the Hurricane Racing Association in July, 1947. The events held at Soldier Field that summer attracted substantial crowds to say the very least. As an example, an estimated 35,000 spectators were on hand for the first hot rod show. Driver Pat Flaherty, coming in from California for his first Hurricane hot rod show, recalls how

(1948) Ray Erickson poses behind the wheel of his #9. After one race, a fan coming out of the stands referred to the car "as a dog." Picking up on that, the next week Ray appeared with a new car identification - K-9.   Authors Collection

(1948) Another tangle. Not much protection for the drivers. The packed stands attest to the popularity of the Granatelli hot rod shows.   Bob Sheldon Photo

astonished he was at seeing 35,000 to 40,000 fans in attendance for the evening's activities. The entries consisted largely of stripped down cars of late 1920s and 1930s vintage. The vehicles ran without fenders, bumpers, glass, etc. Many of the cars contained customized cams, late model steering, multi carbs and other items intended to create additional speed. In this essentially pre-television era such entertainment was an excellent draw. With Joe Granatelli as president and Andy serving as vice-president the Hurricane circuit soon spread to other facilities located at Rockford and Springfield, Illinois, Milwaukee and Kokomo, Indiana among other sites.

Such racing was also being carried on in neighboring Indiana and as a consequence a number of the top drivers from that area, members of the Mutual Racing Association which pre-dated World War II, would tow their rods to Hurricane shows for the purses were considered substantial enough

(1949) Dick Rathmann in a hot rod built by A.J. Watson and Dick. The rods did not capture much beauty, yet some of them had hot equipment and could move. This chassis was a 1924 model with a 3 inch open rear end and a tube axle. The engine, with Weiand racing heads, was fueled by a Stromberg carb setup as an alky burner. The engine had a 3.8 bore and stroke. Dick recalls "it having real pick-up."   Authors Collection

HOT ROD RACES

The Hot Rod pictured above holds all Midwest Hot Rod records. Powered by a "Grancor Firebug" engine and driven by Joe Granatelli, this car set a world's record of 127.76 M.P.H. in Aug. 1944.

SOLDIER FIELD
CHICAGO

Wednesday Night   •   August 27, 1947

OFFICIAL PROGRAM... 25c

(1947) The photo caption states that Joe set a world's record with this rod in August, 1944, reaching a speed of 127.76 m.p.h. No further details were provided. Note the huge dual airhorns as well as a "riding mechanic." The program cover was from the first hot rod race sponsored by the Granatellis at Soldier Field in Chicago.   Authors Collection

to make it worth their while. In fact, the inaugural Soldier Field hot rod feature show was captured by Jim Morrison of Muncie, Indiana. By the latter part of 1947, word of the substantial Hurricane payoffs were sufficient to lure some of the top California roadster/hot rod drivers to Chicago where they stayed busy on the circuit. This group included drivers such as Dick and Jim Rathmann,

(1952) Stock car star Jim Rathmann piloting one of the cars owned by Joe Beccue. While Jim drove this pink colored Cadillac, brother Dick drove Joe's pink Ford. The owner had been a vacumn cleaner salesman turned car dealer with a passion for racing. The "secret weapon" on the Beccue cars was a longer, stronger right front spindle to keep the tire from folding under.   Authors Collection

Don Freeland, Pat Flaherty, Chet Bingham and Chuck Leighton. Some of the top drivers from Chicago included Willie Sternquist (who went on to win the first year's hot rod championship), Allen Swenson, Ray Erickson, Nick Karelas and Gilbert "Skippy" Michaels. Mutual drivers coming over from Indiana included Ralph "Smokey" Stover, Jim Morrison, Sam Skinner (all from Muncie), Dick Fraizer from New Castle as well as Red Renner of Woodburn, Indiana. From Wisconsin came several hot shoes including Norm Nelson who would later become a star USAC stock car driver and owner. The Granatelli brothers also participated in several of the early runs.

"Booger artist" Al Swenson in his devil-may-care ride.   Authors Collection

The hot rod activities provided enough thrills and spills to keep the crowds coming as the Hurricane group returned to Soldier Field in 1948. Hurricane billed the shows as featuring "sensational hot rod races." The program included 4 ten lap races, a 6 lap handicap affair, a 15 lap semifinal and a 25 lap feature. For this activity the general admission was $1.00 per adult tax included and 50 cents per child.

The spills and chills aside, after several years the battered and beaten hot rods appeared to have lost some of their luster. While Soldier Field was capable of handling crowds up to 100,000 spectators the crowds began to drop off drastically as interest in the hot rods diminished. Stock cars were to then step in to fill the void. This venture proved successful as attendance picked up with crowds in excess of 30,000 not being uncommon.

Showing further signs of his budding promotional

(1950) A two car tango - Les Olson in #55, a 1937 Chevy, and Willie Sternquist in a 1939 Ford. Do not let the empty seats mislead you. Most fans sat in the first and second turns or along the straights. The horseshoe shaped Soldier Field stadium had been built to house over 100,000 spectators.   Authors Collection

(1954) Promoter Andy Granatelli, along with starter Art Kelly and the trophy girl presenting the feature winner's trophy to stock car driver Larry Odo.   Bob Sheldon Photo

talents, Andy made use of "booger" artist tactics to add spice and excitement to the early stock car shows. Granatelli employed several drivers, known as booger drivers, who would attempt to perform such moves as knocking the leader off the track; intentionally creating a wreck by spinning out and taking several cars along with him. The role of such drivers are described by Andy in his autobiography. Those he engaged included fellows like Rudy Tici, "Marblehead" Thome and Al Swenson. In short order, Al became quite profficient at such moves and accordingly he was financially rewarded by Granatelli. A part of the show included numerous trackside runs by the ambulance to the scene of the latest "crash." A ketchup bottle was carried surreptitiously by the rescue attendants to add a bit of "blood at the accident" scene. Al Swenson well remembers Andy's trips through the pit area urging the drivers to provide some thrills and chills as he proclaimed "let's get some action, let's get some action!" Once news of the "exciting, breath taking and thrilling shows" made the rounds in Chicagoland, the crowds rapidly increased. With the hype, the specialized talents of the booger artists were no longer necessary.

Some of the participants were drivers who had been competing in the hot rods. Among the hot rod drivers who moved into the stock cars were the Rathmanns, Nick Karelas, Pat Flaherty, etc. as well as some of the top-notch area stock car drivers such as Tom Pistone and Gene Marmor. The 1952 stock car finale was advertised as "one of the biggest nights of racing ever held." No one could accuse the Granatellis of being shy with respect to their grandiose advertising.

Back at the Grancor shop business prospered. One of the biggest successes came with the introduction of the Fordillacs. Such were 1949 or 1950 Ford chassis in which the big 100 horsepower V-8 Fords were replaced with crammed in Cadillac engines that were capable of 160 horsepower. Andy was later to estimate that over 100 of the popular creations were assembled. Working on the assembly was Jim Rathmann when not otherwise engaged in racing. Jim reports that a conversion could be completed in a day's time.

Yet, another venture emanating from the Granatelli shop was drag racing. California had served not only as a hotbed of souped up hot rod

(1952) The action has switched to stock cars as the hot rod fad passed. The new racing venue attracted huge crowds to Soldier Field.
Bob Sheldon Photo

activities on the desert floor, but many nightly drag runs down the all but deserted highways during the wee hours of the morning. When it was quite apparent that a following existed for some sort of organized activity to say nothing of a legalized form of drag racing, the Orange County California Drag Strip was created. Being within the realm of extremely active participants and promoters, the Granatellis were quite aware of the direction of the mushrooming growth in California drag racing. Race driver Jim Rathmann was also aware of the potential of drag strip racing. Rathmann was on his way to becoming an astute automotive entrepreneur. (During this time he would shortly have a speed shop in Miami before establishing a General Motors dealership in Melbourne, Florida).

The Granatellis began to investigate the possibilities of such a promotion in the Midwest. Andy made a quick trip to the coast to check out the Orange County operation. Returning to Chicago, he informed his brothers that the potential rewards were quite positive. With that they made a decision and began scouring the Chicagoland area for a suitable drag strip. As luck would have it, along with Jim Rathmann, they found such a site, an abandoned Navy airstrip located at Half Day, Illinois, a short distance northwest of Chicago. Drag races were to be conducted on Sundays over the one and one-eighth mile paved timing strip that was 150 feet wide. The drag races were broken down into different classifications that included motorcycles, sports cars (manufactured models only), stock cars (that must "be stock appearing except for exhaust and ignition system") and finally souped up cars in various categories. When the dragstrip first opened in the early 1950s, the crowd was so enormous that the handling of the multitudes was beyond the realm of possibility. Crowd control went out the window, yet after their early experiences conditions improved. Organized dragstrip racing had been introduced into the Midwest and the Granatelli organization was instrumental in its appearance.

It was obvious that the Granatelli operation had mushroomed beyond anybody's expectations with the possible exception of the Granatellis. Their endeavors included the work associated with the speed shop, serving as a speed distributor, promotion of hot rod and then stock car activities and finally the dragstrip operations. In time, the Chicago Auto Racing Association, under the direction of Art Folz, was to unite with Hurricane once the hot rodders moved onto the scene and ultimately with the stock cars. On top of all of this was the Granatelli participation in some champ car contests and in the Indianapolis 500 Sweepstakes - the race that offered the biggest single purse in automobile racing. With their addiction to hot engines and speed it was only natural that their attention would turn to the world famous race.

DRAG RACES

EVERY SUNDAY 10:00 A.M. TO 5:00 P.M.

HALF DAY SPEEDWAY

LOCATED 2 MILES NORTHWEST OF HALF DAY, ILLINOIS, ON U.S. HIGHWAY 45

(BETWEEN STATE HIGHWAYS 21 & 83)

1⅛ MILE PAVED TIMING STRIP, 150 FEET WIDE

Write or Call for Free Decal and Further Information

BUSINESS OFFICE
5150 N. WESTERN AVE.
CHICAGO 25, ILL.
LOngbeach 1-9195

An April, 1952, postal card from the Granatellis announcing their immersion into drag racing at the Half Day, Illinois paved strip northwest of Chicago.   *Authors Collection*

Chapter 23

THE KATZENJAMMER KIDS ARRIVE AT INDY

With their all consuming interest in automobiles, and more importantly auto racing, it was no surprise that the Granatelli brothers would harbor thoughts of participating in the Indianapolis 500 Mile Race. With the conclusion of World War II in the latter half of 1945 it was announced that under new ownership, spearheaded by Terre Haute, Indiana businessman Anton "Tony" Hulman, the classic event would be resumed. While the track was in sad shape after four years of virtually total neglect, the first post-war Memorial Day race would nonetheless be held in May, 1946.

One might imagine that in time the Granatellis would ultimately work their way up the rungs of the ladder of racing success to eventually attempt to compete at Indy. After all, some drivers struggled for years to participate in the annual contest without success. As for car owners, they found participation a true challenge, what with only thirty-three cars in the starting field and with probably twice that many entrants. The Granatellis were certainly no different in one respect from many other speed merchants. They were to become afflicted with the all but incurable "Indy Fever." Andy has spoken in terms of how the Speedway had a "special brand of hypnotism, and it sets up an impossible dream...it draws me as it does the rest of them (car owners)."

The Granatellis were in a state of perpetual motion, for they were involved in many facets of automotive work and to them it appears nothing was impossible if one sets his mind to reach a goal. The sky was the limit! Thus, when entry forms for the first pre-war 500 race were received by the IMS, one was from the Grancor Corporation of Chicago - the Granatelli brothers working their way up the ladder. Nonsense. They would instantly shoot for the moon.

The irony of the Granatelli entry rests with the fact that they had acquired one of the ten Miller-Fords built in 1935 when the Ford Motor Company intended to dominate the field. Only a quartet actually qualified for the race and the same mechanical snafu eliminated these cars from the race. A beleaguered and very unhappy Henry Ford then ordered the cars to be warehoused and padlocked until he decided the fate of the cars. As noted in Volume I, one of the cars was made available to Lew Welch, who was to commission the design and construction of the first Novi engine. The Novi engine (or Winfield as it was originally referred to) made its initial entry in the 1941 running of the 500 with Ralph Hepburn at the wheel of the six year old Miller-Ford chassis. The FWD chassis most certainly was not designed to house a powerplant capable of enormous horsepower that went way beyond what the front wheel drive Miller-Fords were meant to handle. They had been constructed to carry the relatively lightweight Ford V-8 when constructed back in early 1935; not a brute of an engine such as the colossal blown V-8 Novi. Other Miller-Ford chassis were ultimately made available and the Granatellis were fortunate to be able to secure one of the Miller-Fords for the 1946 race without having to be out of pocket money for construction, alteration, etc.

Listed as driver was Chicago native Danny Kladis, a noted driver with a feisty nature, a laid back style and a hearty laugh. The peppery Kladis did not appear concerned by the dangers of the sport. Danny's approach was noted in his attitude - "If the car has four wheels and a steering wheel I don't give a damn about anything else." The 28 year old had started racing in 1934 at the Evanston Speedway in Illinois with the sprinters. The following year, Danny began driving midgets as this new venue blossomed in Chicagoland. Kladis competed against some star studded-fields that included the likes of Tony Willman, Jimmy Snyder, Harry McQuinn and Emil Andres.

Kladis certainly had his work cut out for himself. He faced several tough challenges for not only was he a rookie at the demanding Indy track, he was slated to drive a front wheel drive car. Kladis had absolutely no experience with front wheel drive and to add to his challenge the car's chassis was eleven years old. Danny recalls that driver Chet Miller, a veteran of 12 Indy 500 runs, had told him to drive a little harder into the turns and if the car tries to get away steer to the left. With just several days of qualifying remaining, Kladis was doing around 100 m.p.h. and members of the advisory board of veteran drivers "were not exactly excited with (his) driving at the turns." Yet, he was allowed to continue to practice. At one point Danny lost control of the Grancor Special going into the first turn and the car jumped the creek that runs under the track. Danny recalls that a dragline was needed to help extricate the antique car. Of course, the blue and silver colored car was not the only aged racer at the track, for with the war recently completed, only a few new cars had been constructed for the event. Perhaps such helped Kladis. The #59 Grancor Corporation Special managed a speed average of 118.890 m.p.h. during its run to make the field. Of the cars in the starting field, only seven had qualifying times below 120 m.p.h. In fact, only one car with a slower time than the Grancor entry made the contest. Driver Al Putnam was in with a 116.283 m.p.h.

Two cars were bumped from the contest. One was the Army Recruiting Special, a Studebaker powered car with rookie pilot Buddy Rusch at the wheel. Its time had been 116.268 m.p.h. The Rusch car was owned by race driver Bud Bardowski. Bud was cited in one newspaper account as "The People's Choice." Such sentiment transpired from the fact that Bardowski had purchased the car with his Army discharge money. A survivor of the infamous Bataan Death March, Bardowski had spent forty months in a Japanese prisoner of war camp. With Bud not fully ready to drive, the chore was handed over to Rusch. The second bumped car was the Singer Special, driven by Charlie VanAcker who recorded a speed of 115.666 m.p.h. Charlie was driving Al Singer's Voelker engine car.

The biggest news during the entire qualifying process was Ralph Hepburn's red hot qualifying speed of 133.944 m.p.h. for the 500 derby. In the words of W. Blaine Patton, sports editor for the <u>Indianapolis Star</u>, "A chilled, shivering but patient crowd estimated at 22,500, sat under threatening weather conditions until late yesterday afternoon at the Indianapolis Motor Speedway and they were rewarded with the greatest driving feat in the 30-year history of the famous 2 1/2 mile course." The record smashing run was made in the Novi Governor Special, a newly constructed front drive Kurtis-Kraft that housed the eight cylinder engine. Hep's run included 2 laps at better than 134 m.p.h. His fourth lap was the fastest at 134.449 m.p.h.

With some of the racing teams frantically working to iron out the bugs from their pre-war engines, qualifying was extended through Tuesday, May 28. The qualifying runs were permitted up to

(1946) The "Katzenjammer Kids" are ready for their first 500 race at Indianapolis. The brothers sit on the pit wall with several helpers as driver Danny Kladis poses with the 11 year old, two seater Miller-Ford. Their Grancor V-8 Special finished 21st as the fuel switch was inadvertently turned off during a pit stop.   I.M.S.

sundown (8:08 p.m.). As sundown approached three cars were on the track being timed in their qualification runs. The trio consisted of Tony Bettenhausen, George Connor and Billy DeVore. Bettenhausen had qualified another car earlier, but it had to be withdrawn as a defective crank could not be readily replaced.

Naturally, the Granatellis had opted for a Ford what with their work in the Granatelli shop dealing almost exclusively with the flathead Ford V-8. While Danny's speed was nothing to brag about, the mark set was a record for a flathead engine. Noting the Granatellis' frenzied garage exploits and what some perceived as antics, they were referred to as "The Katzenjammer Kids" and the tag was to stick. The term was derived from a noted comic strip created and drawn by Rudolph Dirks (1877-1968). The comic strip featured the "mischievous antics of Hans and Fritz" who it seemed spent every waking hour involved in one crisis or another. It was obvious that the young crew from Chicago were novices at champ car action to say nothing of Indianapolis. To this day, some old-timers still use the Katzenjammer term in talking about the Granatelli operation. The Chicago-based crew took it all in stride and actually displayed some fondness for the tag. Years later, Vince Granatelli was to laughingly refer to some of their Speedway methods as akin to "an Italian fire drill."

In recalling that year at the Speedway Kladis said, "I was known as the Wonder Boy because every time the car went out members of other crews wondered if the car would be able to make it around." He recalls that the car experienced numerous problems and the "Kids" had to change engines several times. Seldom was he able to put in more than four or five laps before some mechanical problem emerged. Beyond that the car's cockpit was huge, what with it having been built in the era of the two man cars. In addition, Danny barely topped five feet in height. In order to better position himself, Kladis taped several Indianapolis phone books together and sat on them in order to peer over the cowling. The time established by Kladis had the Grancor Special begin the long race from last spot. One consolation - you cannot start further back in the field! In the race, the Grancor car held its own against the other contenders until its second pit stop. After the car was refueled, Danny shot out of the pits only to have the engine die as he came off the second corner. Dashing to the scene, several of the Granatellis saw that the #59 car was already on the hook for the trip back to Gasoline Alley. The towing across the infield was an automatic disqualification.

Andy has made reference to the "mysterious fact that the fuel switch on the dash panel was discovered to be in the off position, suggesting that as soon as the fuel in the carbs was consumed the engine died." Danny Kladis relates the situation thusly: "As I came in for fuel I turned the selector valve to on from the three gallon reserve tank. When I came off the second turn the engine died and I brought it to a halt on the apron." Danny was to later relate that while the fuel handle appeared to be in the correct position the valve was in the shut off position as the serrated plate on the dash behind the valve had worked loose and slipped out of place to give an erroneous reading. Danny said that as the three carburetors went dry the car's power disappeared. He then noted that many versions of what went wrong had been mentioned over the years. He asserted that a A.A.A. official told him that the car could not be towed around the track and "as I was green at the Speedway, I didn't know all the damn rules." Having been towed across the infield the car was disqualified. It has been said that perhaps this was the first time in Speedway history that a car in perfect running condition was eliminated from the race.

As a consequence, the car was awarded 21st place, winning prize money of $875. With all of the "antiques" in the field, the attrition rate was high, for only nine cars were on the track when George Robson received the checkered flag. As it were, one of the seven cars that had qualified under 120 m.p.h. finished 5th. The Noc-Out Hose Clamp Special, started by Joie Chitwood, earned that spot though Joie sought relief. After the Spike Jones Special, driven by Sam Hanks, was eliminated Sam was available for service and he took over Chitwood's place for the last 200 miles or so to make the respectable showing. The Ralph Hepburn Novi which had been so dominate in qualifying went out after 121 laps to be classified 14th.

It was quite obvious that the Granatellis were far from distressed by the entire Indy exposure for they returned the following year with two entries. By this time, the brothers had acquired another of the 1935 Miller-Fords. Kladis was back to pilot one of the Miller-Fords now numbered 57. The Granatellis had acquired some sponsorship from a Ford dealership, Camco Motors, located several blocks south of their speed shop on Broadway. Driver Pete Romcevich, another midget veteran, was assigned the Camco Motor Special #59 Miller-Ford with the Ford powered setup and the front wheel drive being retained. While Danny was unable to obtain sufficient speed for a qualifying run, Pete managed to make the grid, although his time was approximately a mile an hour slower than what Kladis had achieved a year earlier. The 255 c.i. Ford started 17th and finished 12th with what was listed merely as a "mechanical failure." Andy has asserted that the fault rested with the magneto drive, for the spiral grooves had been cut backwards. The condition caused the engine oil to drip off the timing gears rather than to return to the crankcase.

In assessing their fortunes, or one might say misfortunes, the Granatellis appeared to believe that the Miller-Fords had gone beyond their years as the two Millers were then offered for sale. An advertisement in a racing publication cited the availability of "Two Indianapolis Cars for $10,000." The ad stated that "both of these cars have proven themselves on the Speedway. One was the Grancor V-8 that holds the flathead record of 119 m.p.h. and the Camco V-8 that placed 11th (sic) in 1947... These cars are ready to run and there are extra parts galore. Will consider trade for championship car or midget cars." In actuality, the official record indicated a speed of 118.890 m.p.h. and the Camco finished 12th in 1947.

Following the Grancor efforts at Indy in 1946-1947 detailing their endeavors for the following two years is at best a trying experience. To unravel the "Grancor puzzle" is a challenge as there were a number of cars bearing the Grancor name. Several entries carrying the Grancor name were owned by other parties. The individuals agreed to carry the Grancor name in exchange for tires and fuel. To further cloud the situation, several of the formal entries failed to designate a driver or the cars ended up using different powerplants than what were submitted on the entry forms. Driver assignments often shifted abruptly in those years; particularly in May when the Speedway was a beehive of activity. Piecing the available information together, the following scenario represents the key ingredients as it was reconstructed.

In 1948, four Granatelli entries were received. Driver assignments for two of the cars went to Anthony Granatelli and Pete Romcevich while two entries failed to list drivers. Listed entrants for the car to be driven by Andy were Joe and Andy (the #39 car), the #59 car of Romcevich had Grancor Auto Specialists listed as the entrant. The #69 was entered by Grancor Werner and the powerplant was an eight cylinder 181 c.i. Maserati supercharged engine. Finally there was the #85 Grancor-Werner Special, with a new Offy.

Failing to dispose of the Miller-Fords, Andy had made the decision to drive one of the cars. The car entry asserted that the power would be supplied by a Mercury engine. Romcevich departed from the team in early May only to trash Norm Olson's car on May 15. The frame was bent so badly the car could not be repaired in time for the upcoming speed chase. The tough Romcevich, Serbian by heritage, failed to make the 500, thus the 1947 race in the Granatelli ride marked his only appearance in the prestigious contest. The resident of Gary, Indiana, lost his life in a 150 mile midget race in June, 1952 at Detroit.

In preparing for the race, Andy had some tough sledding as he was a victim of a mild slide in the southwest turn while practicing on May 15. The press reported that the crowd "had another shock when Anthony Granatelli of Chicago spun." Andy had passed the rookie test earlier (May 8); yet, he experienced some problems during the following days that prevented him from making a qualification run until Saturday, May 29, the last day of the time trials. After three laps at better than 123 m.p.h., Andy had the car whip about as he worked through the first turn. The right front tire had let go and the car smashed into the outside retaining wall. The Grancor car then rolled over before coming to a halt. Andy was helped out of the car by track personnel. While the car was severely damaged, Granatelli was able to walk to the nearby ambulance for transfer to Methodist Hospital. His injuries included a fractured wrist, cuts and bruises. His crew believed that Andy's presence of mind in diving into the basement - dropping below the cowling - may well have saved his life. The Indianapolis Star, in reporting the accident, stated that Andy had spun three times during earlier practice "but was making a determined effort to get the car into the starting field when the crash occurred." According to some accounts, Joe and Vince made a hasty departure from the hospital after determining that Andy's injuries were not life-threatening. They rushed back to the Speedway in an effort to get Manuel Ayulo into the starting field in another Grancor car. Yet, time had run out as qualifications closed! As for Andy, the crash ended his abbreviated Indy driving career.

Having a bad case of "Indianapolis fever," the Granatelli's had attempted to place several other cars in the starting field. The #85 was to be driven by Cliff Bergere who had left the Novi team after a spat with car owner Lew Welch. This Granatelli car did not make the race and one knowledgeable source stated the car "still seemed to have had bugs that needed to be worked out." The other car was the aforementioned Manny Ayulo ride. In Andy's autobiography, he refers to the car as "our little dirt machine." Jack Fox's 500 History identifies it as the Conrad (Connie) Weidel Special. It was listed as having Mercury power. No further information was available on the #69 car, therefore the assumption must be that it saw no track action or very limited time on the track at best. The brothers had attempted to place four cars in the 1948 classic, yet they came away empty handed.

The following year (1949), the Grancor operation certainly went all out as the brothers were involved, to one degree or another, with a total of six cars at the Speedway. They were so serious about their 500 endeavors that a sign was posted at the north Chicago speed shop reading, "Positively no work until after

173

(1948) The Indy driving fever caught Andy until this crash "turned him around." The wall smacker ended his driving efforts. It was about the end of the line for the now ancient Miller-Fords. I.M.S.

the 500." At the time Joe stated, "We'll win the 500 maybe not this year, but some year."

Looking at the cars carrying the Grancor name, one notes that the Granatellis were gaining experience with engines other than those of the Ford Motor Company as Offy power was used with several of these entries. Drivers Hal Cole and Byron Horne were to handle the two cars owned by the Grancor team. An accident early in the month with Horne at the wheel severely damaged the team's remaining front wheel drive Miller-Ford. As it turned out, Horne never did make a 500. Physical injury imposed by the windscreen may well have played a big role in this decision. Their other car was a Kurtis-Kraft 2000 carrying a four cylinder Offy and it was to be driven by Cole. Hal qualified at a speed of 127.168 m.p.h. to start from the fourth row.

The remaining four cars, all receiving Grancor sponsorship (that apparently translates to their providing Firestone tires and fuel), were to be driven by Pat Flaherty, Dick Fraizer, Jim Rathmann and Travis "Spider" Webb. The Granatellis were certainly familiar with the racing talents of Flaherty, Fraizer and Rathmann as all had participated in Hurricane hot rod action. Meanwhile, Spider had one year of experience at Indy. As for the success of the sponsored cars, the Grancor Specials did not prove to be truly significant. The #37 car driven by Spider was a 270 Offy housed in a Bromme chassis. The entry form listed Louis and Bruce Bromme as the official entrants. Like Cole, Webb made the race, yet his time in the event was non-existent as the car's transmission was inoperative on race morning, thus when the field pulled away he was scored dead last with zero laps completed.

Hoosier driver Fraizer, handling an Offy owned by brothers Frank and John Heuer, failed to make the race as he simply could not squeeze sufficient speed from the #59 Grancor Special.

Flaherty, the 1948 Hurricane Hot Rod Association's title holder, also failed to make the show as his qualifying time of 120.846 m.p.h. was too slow. The car had been constructed in large measure by A.J. Watson then in his second year as a Speedway mechanic. The Flaherty car was actually owned by Watson, although it bore Grancor identification. Watson used a Barney Navarro constructed engine that carried Navarro heads and manifold.

The remaining Grancor Special was a chassis purchased from the brothers by Jim Rathmann. The future 500 winner tried to make the show with a 264 Offy powerplant. This car also failed to qualify, although Jim did make the show. He climbed into the Pioneer

Auto Rebuilders Special, owned by John Lorenz, and registered a clocking of 126.516 m.p.h. Rathmann completed 175 laps before being flagged to an 11th place finish. Incidentally, Rathmann was to return to the Speedway for the next 13 years and he made every race.

With the number of cars entered under the Grancor banner, the activities involved in the preparation for the event itself must have been a terrific downer for the Chicago gang. Six cars carried the Grancor banner, yet only one started the race while another was left at the starting line.

Hal Cole, a veteran of two previous 500s, did not fair as well as his previous run in 1948. In that event, he went the full distance to finish 6th in the City of Tacoma Special. This time around he finished 19th going out at 117 laps with a bad rod bearing.

While the Granatellis were experiencing their problems at the Brickyard, they were witness to the continuing achievements of the Novis. Driving a Novi, Duke Nalon not only set fast time but started from the pole and was pulling away from the entire field when the rear axle snapped sending his car into the wall setting off a fiery blaze.

The Granatellis had been quite taken with the power demonstrations of the Novis during the early post-war years, and in Andy's case, it seemed to be one of total enthrallment. While the Novis had demonstrated their enormous power and speed they failed to win the race. Nalon had finished a respectable third in the 1948 race in a Novi as a late pit stop possibly denied a victory to the Lew Welch team. The predominant cars during the period were the FWD Blue Crown Specials owned by former 500 driver Lou Moore. Mauri Rose drove a Moore car to victory in 1947 and 1948 while teammate Bill Holland won in a companion car in 1949.

For the 1950 running of the Indianapolis classic, the Grancor squad had determined to zero in on a single entry and to fully concentrate on improving their showing. Former Californian, Pat Flaherty, then residing in Chicago, was selected to drive the #59 Grancor Auto Specialist/SABOURIN Special. Dr. Raymond N. Sabourin, D.C., a noted chiropractor provided sponsorship. As noted, the Granatellis were well aware of Flaherty's racing talents, for while he was a rookie at Indy they were versed on his abilities having seen him in action in many of their hot rod and stock car shows.

By 1950, the Granatellis had relinquished any hope of trying to be competitive with a Ford or Mercury setup as their new Kurtis-Kraft 3000 contained a 270 Offy. Such a move is reminiscent of Lew Welch. Welch gave up on Ford power in the late 1930s when he had an Offy placed in his 1935 Miller-Ford. The Granatellis attractive Kurtis-Kraft started from the 11th position and finished 10th when the race was red flagged at 345 miles due to rain. While there was certainly room for an improved showing, the performance by rookie Flaherty was certainly respectable. In retrospect, the Granatellis had four entries make the previous four races and the results were not sterling: a 12th in 1947 with Romcevich, 19th in 1949 with Hal Cole, 21st with Kladis in 1946 and last place in 1949 with Webb. Consequently, Flaherty's 11th place finish was certainly a step in the right direction.

The following year, the Katzenjammer Kids were back at the Speedway with the familiar #59 on their Grancor Auto Specialists car. It was the same car that Flaherty had finished 10th with a year earlier. This time the driving assignment went to Freddie Agabashian whose career with midgets and sprinters preceded World War II. Further, he was a veteran of the last four 500s. Freddie posted a qualifying speed that had the car start from the fourth row. In the race, the clutch let go on lap 109 providing the team with a 17th place finish. A step backward, but the Indy fever would not relinquish its hold on the Granatellis.

In 1952, the Granatellis were back to a two car operation; the Kurtis-Kraft 3000 and a Bruce Bromme built chassis. The driver assignments went to Jim Rathmann and Spider Webb. While Spider enjoyed more success than in 1949 when his Grancor ride failed to leave the starting line, he was now in the chase; at least for 162 laps. At that point an oil leak placed him on the sidelines for a 22nd place finish. Jim Rathmann qualified at 136.343 m.p.h. which placed him on the pole of the fourth row in the Grancor Wynn's Special. Only six drivers qualified faster for the race. As it began, Rathmann immediately moved up to join the frontrunners. He was in contention for the lead throughout the race as he was never lower than 3rd at the 50 mile increments except for the 150 mile mark when he was ranked 4th. The speed contest came down to a chase involving Bill Vukovich, Troy Ruttman and Rathmann. While in command at lap 191, Vukovich had his car's steering break enabling Troy to take the victory flag and in doing so, establishing a new race speed record - 128.922 m.p.h. Rathmann who had been running nose to tail with Ruttman earlier, had been forced to fall back slightly with over 100 miles to go due to a brake lock nut that had worked loose. The second place showing represented a giant step forward for the Granatelli operation and the effort was most praiseworthy.

The following year (1953), Freddie Agabashian returned to the Grancor operation as he qualified and drove the Grancor-Elgin Piston Pin Special. Freddie was at the wheel of a brand new Kurtis-Kraft 500B.

(1953) California driver Freddie Agabashian aboard the Granatelli car. Freddie finished 4th in the Grancor-Elgin Piston Pin Special. The car was a new Kurtis-Kraft 500B.
I.M.S.

Agabashian's time of 137.546 m.p.h. had him start the race from the middle of the front row. It was truly a feather in the Granatellis' cap. Only three drivers posted faster speeds during the time trials. They were pole sitter Vukovich at 138.392 m.p.h., Bill Holland the 1949 winner at 137.868 m.p.h. and Johnnie Parsons, the 1950 winner at 137.667 m.p.h.

The car went the distance though Freddie had to stop for relief as the track temperature soared to 130 degrees. As Agabashian departed the cockpit, Paul Russo stepped into the car to come home in 4th place behind winner Bill Vukovich, Art Cross and Sam Hanks (who needed relief help). With the searing heat that day many other drivers had also sought relief. For the 1953 race, Jim Rathmann had switched over to the Travelon Trailer Special owned by Ernie Ruiz of Modesto, California. Again, he went the distance but fell back to a 7th place finish.

While 1952 and 1953 had been good to the Grancor organization, what with a second place and then a 4th place showing, 1954 was to be brutal. Jim Rathmann was back again with the team for the 38th annual running of the 500. In the draw for qualifying positions, the Grancor team drew #1. As Rathmann completed his warm up laps and started on his run much to his amazement the yellow caution light came on. He thought that perhaps the perennial rabbit might have made its appearance on the track or some fan had possibly thrown something on the track surface. He pulled into the pits and a "conference" was held at the start/finish line between the Granatellis and A.A.A. officials. The officials asserted that Jim had not raised his hand on the third practice lap to signal the start of his timed run as required by the regulations. Therefore, he had been called in by the track officials that included Chief Stewart Harry McQuinn and fellow A.A.A. official Howard S. Wilcox (son of the 500 winner in 1919, Howdy Wilcox). While the officials stood firm, Rathmann and the team, feeling the delay would be slight, kept the engine running. As a consequence by the time the decision was made to "overlook" the alleged rule infraction, three of the cylinders had washed down due to the nitro injector setup on the car. The result was a tremendous loss of power and any attempt to qualify was eradicated. Further, an engine teardown would be necessary. Each car was provided three attempts, time permitting. (In later years, the crew was permitted to display the green flag if they felt their car was ready to qualify as the practice laps ended.) As it were, the first car out to qualify had created the first rhubarb of the month.

Years later in recalling the episode, Rathmann stated that he could not believe that with four officials at the start-finish line with binoculars,

(1952) The Granatelli fortunes at Indianapolis reached a new high when Jim Rathmann finished 2nd in their Grancor-Wynn's Friction Proof Special. Wynn's was an oil additive on the market at the time while U.S. production of STP was still two years away. Further, the Granatelli involvement with the product did not begin until 1963.   I.M.S.

they had all failed to see his raised arm. Jim also reminds his listener that a driver could not raise his arm too high due to the wind velocity as the car was at full speed. He contends that trying to convince the officials was like talking to "a box of rocks."

On the opening day of qualifications, the big story was Jack McGrath as he established a new track record in the Jack Hinkle car. He became the only driver in the field to break the 140 m.p.h. mark. Jack's speed was an amazing 141.033 m.p.h. No other driver was able to get close to his time much less break the 140 m.p.h. barrier. Driver Jimmy Daywalt started next to McGrath with a time of 139.789 m.p.h. in a Sumar Special owned by Chapman Root. Excluding McGrath, the speed differential from Daywalt's time to the slowest car was only 2.116 m.p.h. Hotshot speedster Walt Faulkner, who as a rookie a mere four years earlier, had set a new track record and then topped it the following year in a J.C. Agajanian car, was among those bumped. Paul Russo's 137.678 m.p.h. prevented Walt's participation as he was clocked at 137.065 m.p.h.

The Granatelli Kurtis-Kraft car, which had undergone some revamping since 1953, now had a rebuilt engine in place, had Rathmann qualify at a shaky 137.132 m.p.h. on the second weekend of qualifications, Saturday, May 23. With such a time, it was set to start from the last row. The field was filled that day as competition to make the starting lineup was extremely tough. The competiveness was such that on the same day that Rathmann qualified, Duke Nalon, driving a powerful Novi, was bumped from the starting field by Andy Linden. Duke's time of 136.395 m.p.h. was insufficient. No other bumps occurred that day. Yet, with the keen competition on the last day of the time trials, additional cars were removed from the starting field by faster cars. Among the group was Rathmann in the Grancor car as stellar east coast driver Len Duncan completed his run at 139.217 m.p.h. Rathmann was thus bumped from the starting field and as a result the Granatellis were eliminated from 500 competition that year.

Yet, good fortune was to come Jim's way as he was able to climb into one of car owner Ed Walsh's three Bardahl Specials and with only a few acclimation laps, he qualified at 138.222 m.p.h. Walsh's drivers were to be Sam Hanks, Art Cross and Rathmann. The 1949 winner, Bill Holland, had originally been assigned the third car, but when he could not surpass 135.788 m.p.h. he was called in by Walsh and chief mechanic Harry Stephens.

(1954) Jim Rathmann offers a hand waving salute following his qualification run in the Granatelli car the second weekend. The engine had "washed down" during the "conference" held during the first weekend of the time trials. The grin on Jim's face would disappear as the car was bumped. Jim was then able to move into one of Ed Walsh's three Bardahl entries to make the race. The Granatelli operation at Indy that year was over. They did not return until 1961, and that was with a Novi. I.M.S.

They then replaced him with Rathmann. Holland was to charge that the team was "spread too thin" to be completely effective. Be that as it may, Bardahl had three cars in the 500. In addition to Rathmann, two other bumpees managed to climb into strange mounts the last day to make the contest. The battle to make the starting grid was fierce as a total of eleven cars had qualifying times too slow to make the race.

The Granatellis' car's first day practice laps did not represent the only confusion with respect to flagging. After driver Bob Scott had been bumped in an Ernie Ruiz car (137.504 m.p.h.), he moved into a Ray Brady car. Yet, he "failed to get back in the lineup owing to his error in reading the starter's flag just before the track closed." After three laps that would have put him in the field, Scott misread his pit sign and the flag of starter Bill Vandewater. Bob reduced his speed, returning to the pits believing he had completed the required four laps. When the Californian realized his grievous error tears rolled down his cheeks, and for some hours thereafter he was in a state of great despondency. Scott was to lose his life in a A.A.A. champ car 200 mile race at the Darlington Speedway in July of that year.

With the enormity at not making the 500 mile race after being involved for nine consecutive years at the Speedway, the Granatelli camp was utterly deflated and a monumental decision was ultimately made. In Andy's words, "We were bumped...we were out at Indy. I closed the garage doors on it and the Indianapolis 500 mile sweepstakes."

Andy was completely devastated as he got himself so totally immersed in the fate of the Grancor racing endeavor that it seemed to be an extension of his very being. The disenchantment in not making the race with a car that both he and Rathmann considered to be a top contender cut deeply.

The Grancor team had gained valuable experience, but a "roll of the dice" had now caught up with them. Remember, in 1952 they had earned a second place finish and that had urged them onto the crowning achievement, accomplishing an Indy 500 triumph. Yet in 1954, they found themselves on the sidelines. Andy Granatelli's, They Call Me Mister 500, has a chapter describing the nerve shattering 1954 experience entitled "I've Had It With Indy."

The famed track had a majestic history with many happy tales and countless tales of disappointment. The Granatellis had seen both sides of the coin with a second place finish in 1952 and then the failure to even make the race in 1954. Be that as it may, a farewell to the hallowed racing oval was made by the Katzenjammer Kids.

Chapter 24

FROM PAXTON TO STUDEBAKER

Not only did the Granatellis make the decision to abandon their Indy 500 endeavors, they eventually disposed of their other business holdings in Chicago. These included the Grancor shop, the tie-in with the Chicago Auto Racing Association and the Half Day drag strip. The entire speed shop enterprise was sold or transferred to others. The situation appeared to be a case of burnout. With the disposal of their holdings completed, in 1957 the Granatellis moved west to California - lock, stock and barrel.

Unable to stay away from the automotive speed industry, in short order, Andy made contact with Robert Paxton McCulloch, the president and founder of the McCulloch Company. According to Don Woodward (with McCulloch since 1954), the company had its start in 1946 on Century Blvd. several blocks from what is now the Los Angeles International Airport. The operation was contained in several quonset huts. At this writing Woodward, a company executive, described McCulloch as "quite an innovator" who in some respects was ahead of the times." Woodward asserts, "Engines were McCulloch's life." The company manufactured various products such as chain saws (electric, gas and battery driven), garage door openers, superchargers, outboard motors, over 100,000 two cycle drone engines for the military, high pressure pump nozzles, lawn debris blowers, lawn trimmers and several other related items. At one point (1953), the company had made a noble effort to manufacture passenger cars. The Paxton automobile never moved beyond a single prototype model that was completed before the project was halted.

The Granatellis had heard that one of McCulloch's industrial divisions was available for sale - that unit producing the Paxton supercharger. The division had fallen short of meeting McCulloch's expectations, although several sources have stated that they "sold tons of them." Whatever the reason, a deal was arranged whereby the Granatellis obtained the supercharger subsidiary. The deal was finalized in early June of 1958.

At the time of the Paxton purchase, an executive vice-president at McCulloch was Sherwood Egbert (1920-1969). As a result of the sales negotiations, Egbert and Andy Granatelli became friends. At a later date this relationship would have a direct bearing on the Novi undertaking.

As a footnote, it might be added that McCulloch eventually moved on into oil exploration and real estate investments and in 1971 he sold the manufacturing end of the business to Black and Decker. The McCulloch Company, now privately owned, is headquartered in Tucson, Arizona. It has six other locations where its various products are manufactured. The "cash cow" for McCulloch and the current ownership remains the same - the chain saw.

With the purchase of the supercharger division, the Granatellis took immediate steps to improve on the Paxton blower while garnering publicity for their newly acquired product. At the time McCulloch manufactured the superchargers, their research and development unit had been busily engaged in dealing with several problems relating to the blowers. These consisted of the belt drive gumming up and an even bigger problem was that the drive shafts often twisted when they surpassed 40,000 rpm. Along the way, the McCulloch supercharger had been improved. The five one and one-half inch steel ball bearing housing and the impeller was placed completely within the unit. Incidentally, one phase of the blower business consisted of producing impellers for the military. Under McCulloch, the Paxton was a centrifugal blower that had a one on one ratio, thus lacking any significant power until a sufficient rpm reading was achieved.

The McCulloch firm had sold their completed blowers to several car manufacturers as well as to other accounts. Car manufacturers who had purchased the Paxton in the past included Kaiser (for

179

their Manhattan model) and Studebaker. According to Andy, McCulloch had sold 15,000 of the blower units to the Studebaker Corporation for installation on the company's newest car, the V-8 Golden Hawk with its 289 c.i. powerplant. Such a sale by McCulloch to the Studebaker firm, ultimately proved to be an important milestone for the Granatellis, particularly with respect to racing.

To help promote sales of their new product, in early 1962, the Granatellis had a supercharged stock-bodied car at California's Riverside Raceway to attract publicity. The car used was a 1962 Plymouth Fury sedan. On January 27-28, Andy piloted the Paxton supercharged Plymouth at Riverside to several records. He reached a top speed of 117.41 m.p.h. to exceed the existing record for stock-bodied passenger cars by nearly 5 m.p.h.

Then in March of 1962, the Studebaker board of directors tendered an offer to purchase Paxton. The Granatellis agreed to a deal for a reported sum of $275,000 of which $125,000 consisted of common stock. The Studebaker-Packard Corporation purchase of Paxton Products Incorporated of Santa Monica, California was reported by the Wall Street Journal on March 19, 1962. The account was carried under the headline, "Studebaker Acquires Supercharger Maker, Plans to Stress Power." The media was informed that the Paxton product would continue to be produced in Santa Monica, California, and that Anthony Granatelli would retain the title of President of Paxton. At the time, Studebaker conceded it was moving into more speed and power promotions for its cars. Sherwood

Egbert, who had left McCullock to become president of Studebaker in January, 1961, declared, "If the customer wishes to buy more horsepower than he can use, he will be able to buy it from Studebaker." The announcement of the purchase stated that the Paxton supercharger would be an option item on a new racy prestige car the auto maker was preparing. The new Avanti was the work of renowned designer Raymond Loewy and

(1961) Andy with a supercharged Plymouth that he drove to a speed of 117.41 m.p.h. as the Granatellis' firm, Paxton Products, wished to display the prowess of its supercharger.
Authors Collection

his associates. On several earlier occasions, Loewy had carried out design work for various Studebaker models. The Avanti project had its origin back in 1961 when Egbert approached Loewy regarding the design of a radically different stylistic car that would be sure to catch the public's eye. Egbert had moved quickly after taking charge of the company for Loewy was commissioned to proceed with the projected new car on March 9, 1961. Thus, less than two months after Egbert became president at Studebaker, the company announced the commissioning awarded to Loewy. Some observers viewed the project as a final attempt to save the ailing automaker.

During that same March board meeting, the decision was made to drop the Packard name from the company title. Packard had merged with Studebaker in 1954 with actual production of the car being halted in June, 1958. Removal of the marque was judged a positive step. The Packard, once considered a leading luxury car, was equipped with a Paxton supercharger on its 1957 V-8 model. That same year McCulloch manufactured Paxton blowers for Studebaker's Golden Hawk. The item was later dropped as Studebaker produced its Silver Hawk without the benefit of a blower. The testing of McCulloch blowers also included their placement on Fords at FOMOCO's Williams, Arizona testing grounds where speeds up to 149 m.p.h. were reached. Yet, no evidence was uncovered to show that Ford ever purchased the product in large numbers.

Later that year (August, 1962) under the direction of Andy Granatelli, a fleet of Studebakers arrived at Bonneville in an attempt to shatter a variety of various class and unlimited speed land records from one kilometer to ten miles. The timing was handled by USAC using FIA recognized standards. Among the numerous records established was a 168.15 m.p.h. for a one mile flying start. Andy drove this segment of the undertaking. For the ten mile run the average was 163.90 m.p.h. The company remained busy promoting its Lark and Hawk while attempting to generate vast publicity for the sporty new Avanti.

The entire 1963 line of Studebakers was previewed for the press at the Indianapolis Motor Speedway on September 6, 1962. Egbert was present and he proudly posed on the track's front straightaway with a prototype Avanti containing a 289 c.i. V-8 engine. The car was described by one viewer as "a wedge-shaped sports car unmatched in quality and performance." The supercharged Avanti handled exceeding well and even at speeds in excess of 130 m.p.h. the car moved straight as a arrow. Andy said, "It performed and handled like a true precision-built expensive sports car without the discomforts of a cramped sports car." Andy also stated, "This car will definitely appeal to the connoisseur of fine automobiles." All of the Studebaker models on display (Avanti, Hawk, Lark and the Cruiser) were available with or without a supercharger at the buyer's option. But, the stress on power was most certainly evident.

Returning to Bonneville later that year, the Studebaker folks broke 72 records using a six cylinder Commodore, a Daytona convertible, a Hawk and the Avanti. The Avanti model (in the Class C closed car supercharged category) flashed past the timers at a speed of 170.78 m.p.h. In an experimental Avanti, driven by Joe Granatelli, an amazing speed of 196.62 m.p.h. was reached. The certification was to speed only and not for inclusion in the record books, although company ad-

(1963) Once tied in with the Studebaker Company, the Granatellis had a caravan of Studebakers transported to the Utah Salt Flats for a series of runs. The cars making speed runs included Studebaker's Hawk, Lark and the Commander. The ever-present STP decal can be seen below the #90.
Authors Collection

vertising understandably did make mention of the speed. That particular V-8 used Bendix fuel injection, twin Paxton superchargers, cams ground for high speed performance and a magneto. At the time, it was stated that the package was "initially developed for the V-8 Novi Indianapolis engine." As one would expect, Studebaker procured much advertising space extolling the fact that they had broken dozens of records in "torture tests" at Bonneville as they had demonstrated "Studebakers' endurance, engineering and speed." The automotive corporation's advertising asserted that the Studebakers were "different by design." Following that round of Bonneville testing, company president Egbert predicted at least a 40 percent sales gain for the company in 1964! The fact that the company was "hotly pursuing a performance image" was not lost on avid followers of American automotive activities.

The publicity acquired on the October, 1962, run was enhanced by the fact that the two drivers were women, Paula Murphy of Granada Hills, California and Barbara Nieland of Whitter, California. The trip encompassed 49 hours and 39 minutes and averaged 58.66 m.p.h. Sears tires were also a part of the publicity campaign. Studebaker pointed out that all speed laws were obeyed as the Avanti broke the existing 35 year old mark by over 28 hours. One might note that no mention was made of improved roads since the 1927 run.

That same month, Paula Murphy posted a two-way average run of 161.29 m.p.h. in a test course run with a Studebaker as the company continued its promotional efforts. Having a woman driver undertake the run certainly would help generate additional publicity for the Indiana car builder.

To some, the purchase of Paxton by the

(1963) The fastest of the Studebakers was the Avanti that Joe Granatelli drove to an eye brow raising speed of 196.62 m.p.h. using a hopped up engine. The modified 304.5 c.i. engine carried dual blowers, fuel injection, etc.   Authors Collection

As for the marketability of the Loewy designed Avanti, it failed to serve the purpose as the company's "savior." The new model had been rushed along and corners were cut to get the car into showrooms as quickly as possible. The car had its official unveiling on April 26, 1962, at a Studebaker dealers and stockholders meeting. While some thought the Avanti to be sleek, it drew a considerable amount of criticism. Some critics referred to it as an anteater due to its highly slanted nose and the disproportionate shape of its radiator grill. As for its sloping back, some folks said it reminded them of a duck's back.

Not resting on the speed laurels, the company sought additional publicity by means of a coast-to-coast run; from Los Angeles to New York City.

Studebaker firm made little sense as the car company had been experiencing a slumping market with the various Studebaker models. The purchase of Paxton did not stand alone as the Indiana company had also acquired the Gravely Tractor Firm (a maker of small utility tractors); the Onan Company that produced gasoline and diesel generating machines, a floor finishing firm and a company making low-temperature display cases. Was it simply a case of not putting all of one's eggs in the same basket? If the car operation failed would they then fall back on the other companies? In looking back at Studebaker's records of the 1950s, it was noted that the firm had been experiencing problems during the decade. Some observers felt that it would be beneficial for Studebaker to diversify by buying other profitable industries. The year prior to the Paxton acquisition, Studebaker had purchased the Chemical Compounds Corporation of St. Joseph, Missouri. This key component in the Novi undertaking will be covered in the next chapter.

The various Studebaker divisions were taking in over $100,000,000 per year while the car manufacturer itself was losing money. In 1953, Studebaker had established a record in its car manufacturing when it reached a total of 344,164 units. With its "bullet nose grill," Studebaker was 8th in sales. In fact, its sales surpassed those of such cars as Chrysler, Nash, DeSoto, Hudson, etc. Yet, its annual production was not only unpredictable, but would be dropping. Studebaker had 2,600 dealerships in 1959, but this figure dropped to 2,200 dealers by early 1961. The challenge in the automotive world was somewhat startling as the Studebaker Starliner which began production in 1952 was considered a sleek coupe offering impressive lines and was most definitely an attraction in dealer showrooms. Now it appeared the task of rejuvenating sales would fall within the realm of the Avanti. While some manufacturers were experiencing great sales, others were dying. Before the decade was over, Crosley, Hudson and Nash were gone and Packard had been acquired by Studebaker.

As for Studebakers' Avanti, it appeared the model lacked substantial public support. The availability of a supercharged Avanti obviously held little interest for potential buyers of sports car. The delays in production may well have helped create greater public appeal for the Corvette and the Thunderbird. Evidence of such is noted in the fact that slightly less than 4,000 units of the 1963 Avanti were sold and only 806 were sold in 1964. The Corvette and Thunderbirds had been on the market for several years. Corvette was introduced in 1953 and the Thunderbird in 1955.

As the Avanti sales push continued, the South Bend residents experienced what they referred to as "Black Monday", December 9, 1963. On that date it was announced that the Studebaker South Bend plant would be permanently closed as of December 20. It certainly provided a bleak Christmas for the northern Indiana community and especially the town's Studebaker employees. The company had recently laid off 1,500 individuals. Some 5,000 additional workers were notified on the 9th of their termination. The halt of all U.S. production ended the American corporation activities after 111 years. The closure of the South Bend plant left Indiana without an automobile manufacturing plant, though numerous auto parts manufacturing plants remained. Over the years, 208 makes of cars had come out of Indiana. These included the Duesenberg, the Stutz, the Marmon, the Cord, the Auburn, the Simplex, Durant and the Maxwell, all of which were now just a memory. All future Studebaker production needs would be met by a smaller plant located in Hamilton, Ontario, Canada.

According to one protagonist, "The troubles of Studebaker go back to 1961 when Egbert took over as president. He was brought in to scotch rumors of the sagging car sales." In 1959, the company had manufactured approximately 136,000 units, whereas by 1961, sales were down to approximately 70,000 units. Remember that Egbert had certainly been overly optimistic, for in late 1963 he had predicted at least a forthcoming 40 percent jump in sales for 1964. In fact, no such milestone was reached as production fell from almost 84,000 to a total that did not exceed 47,000 in 1964. In all fairness, it must be pointed out that the company had been in financial hot water for some years before Egbert's arrival.

One Indiana publication, in asserting that Studebaker's problems went back further than the Egbert presidency, declared that "the firm had been in financial trouble for years, even when US auto sales hit a record 7,000,000 in 1962." The account also stated that "since the mid-1950s the Studebaker car was not the seller it had to be to keep up with General Motors Corporation, Ford Motor Company and Chysler Corporation." When Studebaker offered $100 rebates on its late 1960 models, that was a strong hint of sluggish sales.

"The last gasp was the Lark, the first American compact, which sold well at first, but nose-dived when the larger companies matched the car." Sales continued to slide and in 1966 the Canadian plant was padlocked. The Studebaker era came to an end after 114 years with a rather ignominious closure. It died off in spite of various attempts by Studebaker to save the automotive firm.

As for the Granatellis, although they were affiliated with the Studebaker Company, Andy had moved to the presidency of a subsidary, the Chemical Compounds Corporations (STP). This firm was to remain viable while continuing to support auto racing. As for the venerable Hoosier auto manufactoring firm, it became a part of the colorful and historic lore of auto builders that had disappeared over the years.

Chapter 25

Early Studebaker Racing

During the Novis last years, there was an extremely close connection between the Studebaker Corporation and the Granatelli forces. As was briefly noted earlier, Studebaker provided substantial support; first with the Bonneville speed runs made by various Studebaker passenger car models and then in the Novi undertaking at Indy. In fact, the Studebaker firm had a rich racing history that pre-dated support for the Novi project by generations. With such a close relationship between Studebaker and Indy car racing and most particularily with the Novi program, we feel it worthwhile to briefly touch on Studebaker's extended and rich heritage as it pertains to racing.

The firm was established in February, 1852, by brothers Henry and Clement Studebaker as they opened a small blacksmith shop in South Bend, Indiana. On the side, they ran a limited wagon building operation. During the first year of business, they produced a grand total of three wagons. However, in time the manufacturing became highly successful as they were a major supplier of wagons sold in this country. At the time of the Civil War, the brothers were supplying wagons for the United States Army. In time, the operation grew into the largest wagon manufacturing operation in the world. The company motto was an appealing "Always give more than you promised." Even before the turn of the century, the company was competitive beyond the market place as it entered wagons in weight hauling contests.

The death of co-founder Clement in November of 1901 did not deter the company's efforts to complete the first of 20 electric cars. The first buyer was a resident of Macon, Missouri. The second sale was made to the famed inventor Thomas Edison, who had assisted in the development of the electric vehicle.

In 1904, the company began producing gas-powered cars. Partner John M. Studebaker, who had joined forces with Clement and Henry (his brothers), was quite reluctant to make the move over from the electric vehicle. John, nicknamed "Wheelbarrow Johnny," believed the gasoline cars to be "clumsy, dangerous and noisy. They stink to high heavens and are apt to break down at the worse possible moment. In short, a public nuisance." Yet, as is well-known, production did continue and the firm was one of the pioneers in automobile manufacturing. In time, the Indiana firm also began to assemble and sell Studebaker trucks.

In 1925, Salt Lake City, Utah resident David Abbott Jenkins driving a Studebaker created a great deal of publicity for the firm in a challenge race. The hype was due in large measure to the fact that he was competing against a special excursion train from Salt Lake City to Wendover, Utah, a distance of 125 miles. Ab Jenkins came away the winner, although the $250 prize money that he received was insufficient to completely pay for the car repairs necessitated by the run over rough "roads." Fortunately, the car was supplied by a Salt Lake City Studebaker dealer.

The following year, Ab (with relief driving from Ray L. Peck) drove a Studebaker touring car from New York to San Francisco in 86 hours and 20 minutes. For a train to make the trip at that time would have consumed 100 hours. In a later run, Jenkins reduced the cross-country trip time to 77 hours.

In 1928, Studebaker introduced its President's engine that in time "set dozens of stock car records" and was judged by writer Richard Langworth in <u>Studebaker 1946-1966, The Classic Post-War Years</u> to be "one of the finest automobiles to ever put rubber to the road."

Early Studebaker racing "participation" included some board track activity which was very much in vogue in the 1920s, as the company had one of its President roadster's models take to the Atlantic City board track in July, 1928. In so doing, the car broke the existing 24 hour endurance mark for stock cars as the car traveled 2,040.8 miles at an average speed of 85.2 m.p.h. The record was achieved in spite of the rough track surface. The record winning speed at Indy at the time was the 101.2 m.p.h. achieved in 1925 by Pete DePaolo. The Atlanta City team consisted of Ab Jenkins along with a crew of five veteran Indianapolis drivers. The other drivers were L.L. Corum (co-winner of the 1924 Indianapolis 500), Cliff

Bergere, Ralph Hepburn, Zeke Meyer and Billy Winn. The group urged Jenkins to join in the 500 race competition. Yet, his attention as a driver would be largely focused elsewhere. Studebakers also participated in various record hill climb runs around the country with Jenkins doing the driving - establishing record runs time and time again.

With the Atlantic City endurance run completed, the following year a President Eight was selected to pace the starting field for the Indianapolis 500. The President housed a straight eight L-head 337 c.i. engine using a five main bearing setup. The pace car driver was a top Studebaker engineer, George Hunt.

The marque was to remain on the Indianapolis scene for some years, through its participation with a number of race cars. With the implementation of the so-called "junk formula" at the Indianapolis Motor Speedway in 1930, several passenger car manufacturers were to take advantage of the rule changes. Previously, engine displacement had been limited to 91 c.i. The change was intended to attract the builders of passenger cars with their larger stock block engines to the Speedway. The "bait" worked as a number of stock engines were entered over the course of the next few years. The group included not only Studebakers, but Buicks, Hudsons, Hupmobiles, etc. The increased cubic displacement was announced by the A.A.A. *before* the stock market crash of October, 1929. With the nation soon to be caught up in the grip of the Depression, the A.A.A. rule change certainly proved to be a beneficial alternative for those seeking less expensive cars than those that had been running at the Speedway.

It has been reported that by 1930, Studebaker had established 143 records for standard passenger cars with respect to speed and endurance. The claims were sanction by the American Automobile Club. Further, the South Bend company took

(1931) The Hunt Special, a somewhat covert Studebaker factory undertaking with LSR ace Ab Jenkins as car owner. While leading, the car spun as a result of oil from a previous accident. Tony Gulotta is at the wheel while a hatless Jenkins stands next to the riding mechanic.　　　I.M.S.

credit for countless record runs in unsanctioned hill climbs across the country.

Two Studebakers were entered in the 1930 Indianapolis 500, while the potent, supercharged and expensive 91 Millers were banned. Driver Russ "Snowy" Snowberger of Detroit built a chassis (identified as a Russell) in which he housed a President 331 c.i. powerplant. The car, which cost a reported $1,500, went on to finish an admirable 8th. It is worth noting that "Snowy" "dazzled the Indianapolis entries by using Pennzoil." This marked the introduction of the first oil-base petroleum at the track. The result was that other teams began to switch over from the mineral-base oil compounds, such as castor oil, that had previously been the standard. The other Studebaker powered car had a unique background as it was entered by a group of Studebaker Company employees. The Romite Special was driven by J.C. MacDonald (with driver relief) to an 18th place finish in the 38 car field. The car withdrew after 112 laps due to a split fuel tank.

The following year (1931), two Studebakers were again entered in the 500. Snowberger was back with his 1930 Studebaker and captured the pole with a time of 112.742 m.p.h. Only the previous year's winner, Billy Arnold and the 1928 Indy winner Louie Meyer were able to post faster qualifying times. The other "South Bender" car was entered by the emerging endurance king and LSR driving ace Ab Jenkins, now assisted by George Hunt, Studebaker's testing director. The entry was considered an "unofficial" Studebaker entry. It has been reported that Jenkins had factory support in the form of "spare parts" plus the assistance of several Studebaker engineers. Ab's son, Marv, has stated that his dad had ceased his promotional work for the Studebaker firm and that they were in debt to him. To settle the financial obligation, the company offered to provide Jenkins

(1931) Russell Snowberger's 1930 Studebaker powered entry. He was back at the Speedway with the same car in 1931 and he achieved a splendid 5th place showing. Russ' qualifying speed of 112.742 m.p.h. earned him the pole in 1931.   I.M.S.

help in an Indy attempt in lieu of a cash settlement as the firm was strapped for working capital. Veteran driver Tony Gulotta was at the wheel of the Hunt Special with a Studebaker President engine housed in a Herman Rigling built chassis.

The 1931 race gave every indication of being a repeat of the previous year's event when Billy Arnold, lead the pack virtually all the way to win. However, Arnold's right rear axle broke in the northwest turn on lap 162. The incident then sent Luther Johnson crashing into Arnold. Gulotta, who had been running second for quite sometime, inherited the lead. Gulotta's Studebaker then apparently ran over oil spilled from the Arnold-Johnson mishap causing him to crash five laps later. This placed Gulotta 18th in the finishing order. The race winner was Louis Schneider in a 181 c.i. Miller. As for Snowberger, he finished 5th, the highest finish by a stock block production engine. Snowy's car used four downdraft Winfield carburetors which is noteworthy as the Winfield brothers were to play key roles in the creation of the Novi engine.

The dazzling Gulotta/Snowberger speed displays did not go unnoticed at the South Bend headquarters. Consequently, Studebaker felt racing might well offer a golden opportunity for increased sales. The following year was to be the big year for Studebaker at the Speedway as it took a full plunge - entering five Studebakers in the 1932 race. Four beautiful Riglings were constructed and the Jenkins-Hunt car was retained. It has been reported by several sources that the cars "were approximately 85% stock," for not only did the engines come from Studebaker, but the gear boxes, axles, steering and brakes were also factory products. The cars were equipped with dual updraft Bendix Stromberg carbs. With the factory cars using the same grill work and body lines, they were painted different colors for quicker identification. In addition to the factory entries, three other Studebakers were also entered in the competition. When the race was completed, the *factory sponsored* Studebakers had finished 3rd, 6th, 13th, 15th and 16th. The impressive 3rd place finish was accomplished by Cliff Bergere who was later to drive for Lew Welch's Novi team. Finishing in front of Bergere were winner Fred Frame and Howdy Wilcox, Jr. The three non-factory entries finished 20th, 28th and 34th in a 40 car field. The trio all went out with a mechanical failure of one sort or another while two factory entries were eliminated. One was caused by a lost wheel while the other fell victim to an accident.

The following year (1933), nine Studebakers were in the starting field. Unbelievably, the cars finished 6th, 7th, 8th, 9th, 10th, 11th and 12th. All seven of these cars went the full 200 laps! Five of the seven cars were from the factory. The highest finishing factory car was the 7th place finish achieved by

(1932) A happy, dirty faced Cliff Bergere poses in Gasoline Alley following his 3rd place finish in one of the Studebaker factory entries. The company had six cars in that year's race. Bergere would later play a role in the Novi effort, driving for the first Novi owner, Lew Welch, in 1947.
I.M.S.

Tony Gulotta. The company backed off the following year (1934) as only four Studebakers were scattered throughout the starting field with Snowberger having the best finish, 8th in his Russell Special. Over a five year stint (1930-1934), Snowy had finished 22nd, 5th and then 8th twice in a Studebaker. In 1932, Snowberger drove a Hupmobile.

The 1934 official program contained a Studebaker advertisement that pointed out the Indy successes achieved by the firm. It also noted that the company was too busy building the highly sought after Studebakers to take on the added task of competing at the Speedway. At one point in the mid 1930s, Studebaker promoted their creations thusly: "From the Speedway comes their Stamina, From the Skyway comes their Style." What might be noted at this point is that the Depression had really hit the company's pocket book. Therefore, its back-off from direct racing participation after 1933 was not a complete surprise.

Meanwhile, Ab Jenkins had become heavily involved with the Pierce Arrow Company, which had been taken over by Studebaker.

It was assumed that the following Indy 500 (1935) was to be Ford's big year as they were to enter ten cars. Yet, only four were completed in time to qualify for the 500 and the results were disasterious as all went out with the same mechanical flaw. Meanwhile, three Studebakers were entered; all non-factory. Harris Insinger scored the highest finish of the Studes with a 14th place finish. In 1936, the sole Studebaker in the field finished 9th. In 1937, there was once again a lone entry - it placed 10th. This was the same year that Lew Welch, the initial owner of the Novis, had a car in the race for the first time. In 1938 and 1939, a single Studebaker once again made the race with sprint car star Ira Hall at the wheel. His finishes were quite low -24th and 30th.

During the summer of 1939, two Studebaker Champion cars circled the Speedway for 15,000 miles. The fuel consumption averaged out to over 19 miles per gallon at a speed of just over 60 m.p.h. Fuel economy was the name of the game for the Hoosier state's only surviving auto manufacturer.

No further Studebakers made the starting field in the two remaining races prior to the closing of the track in 1941. However, the 1940 pace car had been a Studebaker 2-door Champion sedan.

It is worth remembering that Studebaker had also provided a pace car in 1929. The car, a President roadster, contained a straight eight 337 c.i. engine. One wonders if perhaps the car's presence played any role in the Snowberger and Romite's entries of 1930.

In an excellent sidebar story "Studebaker Puts the '39 Champion to the Test" in Collectible Automobile (June, 1996), writer Richard Quinn covers Studebaker involvement in racing. Quinn stated that,

"No American automaker was more obsessed with speed and endurance than Studebaker during the late Twenties and early Thirties. The famous Ab Jenkins twice drove Studebakers coast-to-coast, setting records not even railroad locomotives could match. Studebakers ran continuously for over 30,000 miles on the board track at Atlantic City, New Jersey, and also set records in California at Culver City and Muroc Dry Lake. By 1930, Studebaker could - and did - claim the title to every official record for fully equipped stock cars, including 143 marks for speed and endurance sanctioned by the American Automobile Club - not to mention hundreds of records in unsanctioned hill climbs... But the Depression was close to bottoming out by then and Studebaker was being forced into receivership, so the company halted its racing activities in 1933."

The centennial year for the Studebaker Corporation (1952) did not go unnoticed. The celebration began in February - virtually 100 years to the day that Clement and Henry opened their small blacksmith shop. On February 15, the centennial year kickoff began with the completion of the company's 7,130,874th vehicle - a 1952 Commodore Starliner hard top coupe. Some intrepid car buffs suggested that it was unfortunate that a 1953 V-8 was not yet available, for it was an extremely beautiful car. For some, the pillarless 1953 coupe received a grade of A+, although it reportedly had slight structural flaws. Yet, in appearance, the car was a match for the most exotic and expensive sport cars coming out of Europe at the time.

Quite naturally, the centennial activities extended to the Indianapolis Motor Speedway. On race day, a caravan of historic Studebaker vehicles circled the race track as "A Century of Transportation" was recognized. Vehicles taking part in the ceremony included a Studebaker covered wagon: the Studebaker Commodore Ab Jenkins drove in setting a coast-to-coast record in 1927 and the #22 Studebaker racer that Cliff Bergere drove to 3rd place in the 1932 running of the 500. Ab and Cliff were on hand to participate in the celebration. Ab drove a 1952 blue Studebaker Commander V-8 convertible that served as the Official Pace Car. A coup would have been achieved if a Studebaker powered racer had made the 500. Such was not out of the realm of possibility; particularily since one of car owner J.C. Agajanian's two entries contained a DOHC V-8 Studebaker.

The Agajanian Specials were assigned to Troy Ruttman (#98) and rookie Allen Heath (#97). While

(1962) Present for the Speedway's celebration of Studebaker's centennial year were several of the cars that had competed in earlier years. Included was the #34 that Tony Gullota finished in 7th place in 1933.   I.M.S.

Troy's Offy powered mount beat the Granatelli car, driven by Jim Rathmann, to the checkered flag. Heath's Studebaker powered car failed to make the show. Whether the car actually put in any track time is unknown. The 1952 Clymer Indianapolis Yearbook carried an article on racing engines authored by the aforementioned, knowledgeable auto racing tech writer, Roger Huntington. He cited the array of engines on hand: the Cummins Diesel Special that Freddie Agabashian placed on the pole; the V-12 Ferrari that made the race with Formula One ace Alberto Ascari; a blown 4 cylinder Offy prepared by "Horsepower" Herb Porter and driven by Andy Linden and the fabled Novis piloted by Duke Nalon and Chet Miller. Yet, no mention of a Studebaker engine. When asked about the situation, A.J. Watson recalled the #97 car, believing that it failed to reach a satisfactory speed and then an Offy was installed, yet to no avail.

An aborted attempt with a Studebaker engine was also made in 1956 and financed by car owner Lindsey Hopkins. The eight cylinder 270 c.i. engine set up by mechanic Willy Utzman failed to reach expectations and thus did not arrive at the track. The Agajanian/Hopkins endeavors are the last known attempts to put a Studebaker in the 500 starting field.

In 1962, Studebaker supplied its last pace car for the Indianapolis 500, a Lark V-8 convertible. The honor had originally been accorded to the Avanti, but it was not in a state of readiness, therefore it served as the "honorary" pace car.

Andy Granatelli continued as Paxton's president until the summer of 1963 when Studebaker President Egbert asked Andy to become president of one of the company's divisions. The unit was identified as the Chemical Compounds Division and its primary product was an engine oil additive identified by its founders as Scientifically Treated Petroleum, or to fit the America

(1962) Also on hand for the 1962 celebration was Studebaker's latest show piece, the highly touted Avanti. It carried the title of "honorary pace car." Constructed by the South Bend firm to stop sagging sales it proved to be less than a smashing success. The company was indeed falling on hard times and was not even in a position to have the designated Avanti bring the field down to the starting line.   *I.M.S.*

fondness for acronyms - STP. The STP firm had been founded in St. Joseph, Missouri in 1954. The STP firm had functioned for several years as an independent company prior to its sale to Studebaker in 1961. The following chapter will explore the origins of the company that was to have such a lasting effect not only with the Novis, but eventually with world-wide motorsports.

With Granatelli aboard, Studebaker announced that its Chemical Corporation Division was being transferred from St. Joseph to its South Bend, Indiana plant. The official press release stated, "Anthony Granatelli of Santa Monica, President of the Paxton division would now head up the STP operation." The top position at Paxton, which remained in Santa Monica, was then passed to Joe Granatelli.

Egbert's business methods were on a fast track and one associate said, "He operates on a one gear ratio -full speed ahead." Egbert initiated some drastic changes in his efforts to sustain Studebaker. Included in the continuing diversification program was the acquistion of Paxton and then STP.

In spite of all efforts, the Studebaker firm continued to experience financial problems, although its 12 other divisions were being successfully operated. The car division had been a money loser since 1959.

The company's success at Indy with its factory production race cars in the 1930s most certainly was not being duplicated in the 1950s and 1960s with respect to its passenger car production. The glory days were long gone, and the early vehicle manufacturer was down to a very limited output from its Canadian factory before the demise of the company in 1966.

(1947) Ab Jenkins (left) stands with his son Marv behind a canopied Novi at the garages where land speed record cars were housed in Wendover, Utah. With them is John Cobb who at the moment appears to be more interested in looking at his LSR car, the Railton Mobil Special.   *Marvin Jenkins Collection*

INTERMEZZO

The Bonneville Salt Flats - Studebaker and Novis......

Packard and Studebaker

The time worn phrase has it that what goes around comes around. In the case of the Studebaker Company, that was quite true regarding car endurance and racing. Studebaker and its subsidary, the Pierce Arrow Motor Company (acquired in August, 1928) had their cars out west on the dry lakes of Southern California and the Bonneville Salt Flats of Utah - circa 1930-1932. Studebaker had acquired Pierce Arrow as that company was experiencing financial woes in the luxury car class "war" primarily against Cadillac and Packard. The Salt Flats effort by Studebaker (and Pierce Arrow) was undertaken to establish new speed records that would hopefully improve the company's car sales.

Ab Jenkins, Utah's "Son of Speed," raced Studebaker cars and Pierce Arrows. In 1932, Jenkins drove a V-12 Pierce Arrow for 24 consecutive hours at an average speed of 112.935 m.p.h. during the course of a 2,710 mile record run at Bonneville. This effort and others by Ab occurred prior to his runs later in the decade with his famed Mormon Meteors. In the process, it was said that "Ab established more world records than any other man in the history of auto racing."

Then in 1947, Ab was on hand at Bonneville when his son, Marv, drove a Novi equipped with a cockpit canopy to several speed records. His average for the two-way run was 179.434 m.p.h. In all, Marv established four new international records and an equal number of national records. Marv was later to serve as Lew Welch's personal pilot, aide and confident. He also served as a Novi crew member for eleven year (1946-1957). [Note Chapter 6 of Volume I for details on Marv's Novi run in Utah.] Marv's mechanical expertise is so astute that several years ago he stripped the Mormon Meteor III to its frame. Then in a painstaking manner, he fully restored the streamlined car. The renovation process, which certainly required extraordinary patience, perserverance and diligency, consumed several years.

When Studebaker returned to the Flats in the early 1960s the purpose was once again to establish a number of record timed runs to help increase car sales.

What goes around comes around.

The attempt by the Studebaker Company to rescue the once highly esteemed Pierce Arrow Company was commendable. The "Good Samaritan" undertaking came to an abrupt halt in 1933 as a consortium of bankers took over the Pierce Arrow operation. With a price reduction in 1931, the cars still had failed to produce the desired results and bankruptcy followed. Under a reorganization plan production continued. Then in December, 1937, the Pierce Arrow undertaking went under and in early 1938 company trustees began liquidation proceedings as they had determined that the company could not survive. One giant step back for Studebaker in the midst of the Depression.

Then came Studebaker's attempted rescue of the Packard Car Company in the 1950s. Again as noted, the Packard program stumbled and fell flat as production was halted in the late 1950s. When it came Studebaker's "turn," the remaining car companies failed to show any interest in a resuscitation - if such was even possible. The history of the American auto industry had fully demonstrated the near futility of attempting to save a firm once it was on a downward spiral. Trying to save such a victim appeared to be akin to throwing a lead weighted "life preserver" to one in the midst of drowning.

Chapter 26

THE BIRTH AND EARLY YEARS OF STP

The latter years of the Novi saga was to witness the Studebaker Company becoming a major player in a product that had first seen the light of day seven years earlier in Missouri. This commercial item was to eventually become a familiar commodity in automotive stores and gas stations across the land.

The town of St. Joseph, Missouri, located on the Missouri River approximately 50 miles north of Kansas City, Missouri, is considered a historic community for several reasons. For one, the town served as a major outfitting post for folks journeying west who wished to participate in the Gold Rush of 1849. Others going West used the community for a jumping off-spot as well. It also served as the eastern terminus of the famed and swift Pony Express service, although the famed fleet lasted only 18 months (1860-1861). Then in 1882, the town was the site of the fatal shooting of the notorious western outlaw Jesse James.

Yet, there is another reason for some to consider the town an historic locality. Some auto enthusiasts and/or race fans can cite an additional important factor as St. Joe was the site for the formation of the Chemical Compounds Company. The small firm introduced what was to become, in a few years, a nationally known product - the automotive additive STP (Scientifically Treated Petroleum). STP played an inexorably strong role in the continuing Granatelli-Novi story as well as other well-known racing venues years thereafter. The contributing role of STP in auto racing has been immeasurable and it all started in an alley garage in St. Joe.

Without the support of the firm, one might well question the degree of commitment that could have been rendered in behalf of the Novi by the Granatellis. Yet, with STP in their corner, the Granatellis had the green light for an extended and strong commitment to auto racing. With its strong role in mind, not only with the Novi saga, but its continuing major involvement in racing, permit us to delve into an account of the company's formative years.

STP's origins in St. Joe began when the acquisition of a German developed petroleum product was available and such came to the attention of a highly motivated businessman C. Dwight Liggett and friend Jack Hill. Over the years, C. Dwight Liggett had been involved in a number of enterprises in St. Joe. In the early 1950s, he was operating several businesses: Wade's Indian Grill Restaurant (for which he had a manager), as well as operating the American Wallpaper and Paint Company and the Liggett Chemical Company from his home located in St. Joe. The chemical company had been selling a sludge remover for septic tanks

Dealing with chemicals was nothing new for Dwight Liggett, for among his on-going business ventures was the Liggett Chemical Company. Liggett provided for the mixture and sale of Nu-Chem fluid, an embalming substance.   Authors Collection

as well as preparing embalming compounds since 1936. Purchasing chemicals for embalming purposes, Liggett prepared the mixtures, thus dealing with chemicals was not new to him.

As a hustling entrepreneur, Liggett's primary work involved employment by the Mills Novelty Company of Chicago Illinois. In this work, Liggett traveled throughout the region visiting organizations, clubs and military posts where the membership had indicated more than a passing interest in obtaining slot machines. There were never any cold calls; only to groups that expressed a desire for the acquisition of the gaming devices. Meanwhile, Hill, the elder of the pair, had been involved in several businesses, but was then semi-retired and seeking a new work outlet for a few years before he was ready to call it quits.

As the pair investigated the German product (that included a trip by Liggett to an industrial fair in Hanover, Germany), they determined that it offered a great potential when added to motor oil due to its friction reducing feature as well as its ability to reduce heat temperatures on moving engine parts. The pair was able to determine that the finished product remained 100 percent petroleum and would blend with all petroleum based oils. The product, following a molecular structural change via "a catalytic action, a synthetic was created. The substance became thick, yet light in weight" while increasing viscosity. The product was also said to lower oil consumption, improve oil pressure, increase compression, lessen engine wear and fight carbon varnish.

The product's formula had been developed by scientists working at Germany's largest chemical complex, the I.G. Farben Company during World War II. The compound was derived as the Germans attempted to enhance the ability to extend and strengthen oil based products. This was due in part to Germany's limited supply of oil as it carried out its highly mechanized blitzkrieg (lightning) warfare. The German war machine was without a sufficient supply of oil as much reliance had to be placed on the rich Romanian oil fields around Ploesti. But the location had been a primary bombing site for Allied bombers due to Germany's crucial need for the vital component.

I.G. Farben, with headquarters in Frankfurt, was a sprawling industrial cartel involved with the manufacture of pharmaceuticals, chemicals, dyes and other products. The organization's scientists and engineers were considered a very prominent force in world technology and commerce. Among the products developed by I.G. Farben were the following: novocain, sulfa drugs, nitrates, various fibers, rocket fuel and synthetic oil (from coal). After World War II, the Allied forces brought about the dissolution of the massive empire by breaking it up into separate units. This was a result of the type and depth of support rendered unto the Nazi government. Liggett and Hill, recognizing the potential of the I.G. Farben produced oil product, entered the picture. The pair made no effort to conceal the source of this product. Early STP ads included one with a caricature of a gentleman wearing lederhosen under the heading "Achtung." The ad then stated that the product was "developed by outstanding Germany petroleum scientists." STP was, thusly, a German developed item that was 100 percent petroleum and it would blend with all other petroleum based oils.

In 1954, the Missourians acquired the exclusive rights to produce the additive for a reported sum of $1,500. The transaction provided them with the exclusive right to produce and sell the solution. With a total investment of $3,000 each, they started the undertaking. It is noteworthy that the pair was completely without any automotive experience and their financial base was quite limited. However, this did not prevent them from pursuing their goal to produce an oil additive of great promise. This type of product was not entirely new, for as they began their small operation other American firms such as Bardahl, Wynn's Friction Proofing, Miracle Power, etc., had been engaged in such a market for some years. When Liggett was recently asked why he felt STP held greater virtue than other oil additives, he asserted that when other additives were heated by a bunsen burner only a brown spot would remain. Yet, when the STP product was put to the same treatment it did not break down. As for STP, only a clear pane remained as the additive evaporated under the direct heat. This was the result of STP being a pure ingredient without any carbon residues. Liggett asserts that the final product was so pure one could place the product on his tongue and even ingest it if so desired without bodily harm as it was toxic free. Liggett has said that there was no way that Bardahl, Wynn's or other additive products could aptly combat the superb demonstration achieved with STP. In his mind, an STP demonstration was an insurmountable advantage used by the Missouri firm.

In typical American style, the infant business had it's origins in October, 1954, in a four-door garage behind Liggett's home at the corner of South 9th and Messanie. They proceeded to produce the additive and then to test it in their own cars. Delighted with the results they passed out samples to friends and associates for further reactions. The feedback was quite positive, thus, they began to make arrangements to manufacture the additive, selecting as a firm name Chemical Compounds. In acquiring their basic oil product from Amoco Oil Company of Tulsa, Oklahoma, they informed Harold Lorenz, the com-

The birthplace for STP - an alley garage in St. Joseph, MO. At the time the structure contained four bay doors. Authors Collection

pany representative, of their plan. In describing their process to Lorenz, he noted that their finished product would result in creating a scientifically treated petroleum. As they sat in the garage talking, Lorenz doodled on a slip of paper.

In preparing the early batches for sale, the pair, with the invaluable aid of helper Lee Pate, simply bored eight holes into a long board and positioned funnels through the holes above cone top cans. Thus, once the cans were filled they were heated and cooled.

As they went about their early efforts, some people with whom they came in contact though the entire undertaking was foolhardy and the pair were crazy. Yet, they were not to be deterred. In their rush to get things moving and to generate a cash flow, the pair had not given any immediate thought to the name for their forthcoming product. Shortly thereafter, Liggett was seated one evening at a local drug store, the Red Cross Pharmacy, owned by brothers Lewis and Victor Rudolph. A number of local businessmen regularly gathered there to take coffee and discuss whatever issues the group declared worthy of their time. Lewis Rudolph, doodling on a piece of paper as he listened to the discussion of the new product, began to fashion out a simplistic logo - STP within an oval. Ironically, the symbol was similar to what Lorenz had earlier sketched on a pad as the group had talked at Liggett's garage. With that, the name was to stick. Thus, the locally printed labels were manually pasted on the cans. The first case was sold to a local automotive outlet, Polsky's Auto Parts Store. Yet, the pair's expectations went well beyond merely local or regional sales.

The plans called for the eventual marketing on a wide-scale level. In order to do so, visits to automotive shows, county fairs, industrial meetings as well as visitations to jobbers and gas stations would be required. Liggett has said that the product was easily demonstrated and therefore it would sell quite well. A primary demonstration consisted of placing a bit of standard motor oil on the tip of a screwdriver and then attempting to hold it between the thumb and the forefinger. The effort was challenging. Yet, when the tip was treated with STP it became impossible for an individual to continue holding the screwdriver. Some jokingly referred to the product as motor molasses, as emptying a can could consume something approaching ten minutes. Considering a demonstration vital to the sale of the product, the company made use of two ounce glass containers. To demonstrate the non-toxicity of the product the salesman could resort to the placement of a bit of the oil on his tongue.

At his summer home at Grand Lake, Colorado, Liggett became acquainted with brothers Robert and Herbert Bruhn, the owners of several automotive stores in Denver, Colorado. In recalling the early efforts to promote the STP product, Robert Bruhn said that the challenge was nothing short of monumental. One factor dealt with the well established automotive additives already on the market. At one point, Robert remembers how despondent Liggett became due to the lack of orders. Bruhn assisted Liggett in an effort to induce sales at Denver auto outlets. Bruhn states that as sales failed to materialize Liggett resorted to giving out samples, hoping that would help. Then, "pay dirt" was struck as an order came in from a Chrysler dealership located near one of the Bruhn's stores. It turned out to be the ice breaker for sales in that area.

STP's struggle also involved criticism from the major oil companies. In fact, the year STP began operations, <u>CAR LIFE Magazine</u> (March 1954 issue), carried an account entitled, "Are Oil Addities Dangerous?" Both sides were covered as two writers presented their case to the readership. The negative position was taken by the advertising director for Mobiloil while the affirmative side was addressed by the chief engineer for Miracle Power an oil additive. The final resolution of the possible merits of the additives rested with its users. Ironically, the inside front cover of that particular periodical carried a full page ad for Bardahl and it contained an endorsement from the reigning A.A.A. national driving champ, Sam Hanks who said, "Bardahl makes any car run better."

In Liggett's words, "Hill was no road man, thus, the rigors of travel fell on my shoulders." By all appearances, Liggett had the innate qualities of a top drawer salesman. He went so far as to say, "Sleep is a waste of time." Bruhn remembers Liggett leaving St.

Joe at 4 A.M. and driving to Denver (approximately 700 miles away) arriving by noon. And if push came to shove, Liggett would "go on down to Santa Fe, New Mexico the same day" for more promotional work.

As good fortune would have it, in a short time another St. Joseph resident, Robert DeHart, joined in the venture. DeHart had returned to St. Joe after service in the air force to go into the vending, jukebox and pinball machine business. One account asserts that since DeHart lacked an office, Liggett and Hill offered him a spare desk to count out the coins taken from the machines and a bit of space to work with his machines. In the process, DeHart became interested in the STP process. Not only was DeHart ready to join in the venture, he was already interested in "anything automotive." Thus,

(1960) In the early years, the product was heavily promoted at auto shows, county fairs, trade exhibits, etc. Shown are: (left to right) a security officer, Herbert Bruhn, a Denver STP distributor, C. Dwight Liggett, co-founder of the firm and a salesman. *Authors Collection*

was formed the triple partnership as DeHart sold his business and joined the pair. It has been reported that Hill's investment amounted to $6,000. In the early years, the trio were their own canners, salesmen and distributor. Many a day's work went well into the evening with no days off be it Sunday or holidays. With DeHart's involvement, the business was incorporated with a total of five stock holders: Robert and Lillian DeHart, James and Geneva Hill and Liggett.

Robert Bruhn suggested to Liggett that the fledgling company take on distributors who would be solely responsible for handling the product in their territories. The idea proved acceptable and the Bruhns became the first STP distributor as they sold the product in their automotive stores as well as handling distribution

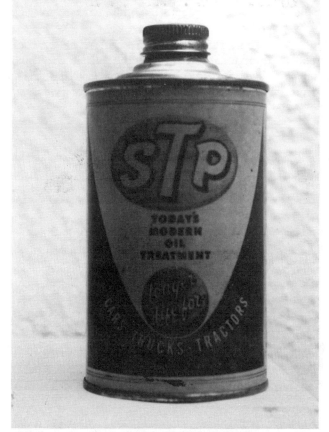
The first container used by STP was a cone top can with a screw cap and a paper label. Robert Bruhn Collection

In the evolution of STP, the third can produced carried a litho label bearing the Magic notation that was soon discarded. Robert Bruhn Collection

for the state of Colorado. Other early distributors were located in nearby states such as Kansas, Oklahoma, and Wyoming.

Liggett has reported that at its peak, Chemical Compounds had 28 or 29 distributorships and this made account posting rather easy when one considers that less than 30 invoices had to be dispatched each month. Liggett says he insisted that the company establish a policy of going that extra mile for their distributors as these individuals had gone out on a limb for an unknown product. Liggett stated, "If they stuck with us we supported them in every way possible." Along this line, Liggett mentioned that a St. Louis, Missouri automotive firm contacted him in St. Joe regarding the possible purchase of a quantity of STP. While emphasizing the virtues of the product, Liggett informed the caller that a possible purchase would have to be made through the state distributor or one of his jobbers and not directly from the St. Joe plant. Distributors were carefully selected and as a result, only one necessitated being released. All the distributors had to agree to sell at a fixed minimum price ($1.35 per pint) which in time caused the Federal Government to consider litigation charges of price fixing. From the company's standpoint, STP did not want any distributor trying to undercut another with lower prices. The St. Joe business, standing squarely behind their loyal distributors, did not relish the thought of any cut-throat pricing activity.

As business continued to improve, STP was placing substantial orders for the base product in 55 gallon drums and cans were secured from American Can Company in lots of 20,000 with lithograph printed labels. The lithograph label was the third one designed and the first to carry the term "magic" in phantom like letters above the now familiar STP logo. The term magic was later dropped, for in Liggett's words it appeared to denote some sort of "hocus pocus snake oil" advertising.

With the increased demand, the notion of pouring the molasses like substance into funnels was long gone as Chemical Compounds had invested in a motor driven canning machine. Further, the production now had the cans sealed with a lid as the use of screw top cone cans was halted. As the STP distributors interested more and more jobbers, service stations and auto parts stores into carrying the product, word of mouth advertising served them well. People were intrigued when they heard that oil consumption decreased; engines would run smoother and quieter and hydraulic valve lifter noises disappeared. The company then began to make the now familiar STP logo decals available for their sales outlets. Promotional plastic STP shirt pocket protectors with the logo were used by service station attendants, mechanics, salesmen, etc. It was another form of advertising that proved to be quite valuable.

Unsolicited endorsements for the product began arriving at the St. Joe garage/office. For example, a printing press operation in Phoenix was suffering with machinery that "badly" overheated during long runs. The firm reported that after STP was added the heat subsided. The Missouri firm acknowledged that the product was not only suitable for automobiles, but trucks, tractors and other machinery and that they were testing it for possible use in aviation engines. A Lubbock, Texas trucking firm sounded ecstatic as they determined that their trucks' mileage increased by one mile per gallon of fuel "which will pay handsome dividends...as our fleet makes over 2,000,000 miles per year." One letter reaching St. Joe stated that the addition of STP to transmissions stopped leaks at the seals on Diamond T and Reo trucks. The virtues of the product were further enhanced when scientific testing by a university had its researchers declare that the product "had a marked effect toward increasing viscosity with oil, particularly at high temperatures." STP reported that companies using the products included bakeries and cotton mills in the Carolinas, etc. One letter arriving from a woman in Oregon encouraged the company to consider canning small containers of the product in order for mothers to be able to use it in coping with baby diaper rash. Though the company disclaimed its effectiveness for medicinal purposes, it strongly endorsed its use for machinery.

In time, the 9th Street garage in St. Joseph was unable to provide sufficient space for the thriving business. As a result, the partners had this building constructed. It was close to the city's rail yards, thus, providing for easier shipments of STP products.   *Authors Collection*

However, this did not mean filling the engine with five or six quarts of STP. On one occasion, the St. Joe office was contacted by an automotive rebuilder. The Tulsa, Oklahoma mechanic complained that he could not quickly turn-over a newly overhauled engine after filling the crank case with STP. He asked, "What should I do?" The reply: "Take out the drain plug and allow the rebuilt engine two days to drain. Then place ONE container of STP in along with the regular motor oil!"

Staying busy, the firm was then to introduce two other products, although they were to play second banana to the oil additive. One new product, Auto Blitz, was intended for use in automobile fuel systems. The can directed its users to add six ounces to each tank full of fuel (15-20 gallons). The super concentrated fuel treatment was designed to keep the fuel system clean as well as to help maintain clean firing chambers, valves, pistons and spark plugs. Auto Blitz was offered in six ounce, one gallon and five gallon containers or in 55 gallon drums. The other product, Diesel Blitz, was intended to keep injectors clean on trucks as it was advertised to prevent carbon and wax build-up while providing greater fuel economy. Customers were informed to apply one quart for treatment of each 100 gallons of fuel. It was made available in one quart containers, one gallon, five gallon or in 55 gallon drums. As for STP, it could be purchased by dealers in case lots of twelve cans-actually a bakers dozen as an extra can was included as a bonus incentive.

As sales continued to grow, a Kansas City advertising agency was called in to assist. By 1959, STP had expanded to the point that the firm had to have larger quarters. They had a 50 x 100 foot building constructed on South 6th Street and as business boomed there was a need to rent additional storage. With STP being shipped out aboard truck and railroad cars, business was certainly mushrooming. Witness to this is the fact that in its initial year (1954), the company showed gross receipts of $2,000; in 1955 the receipts had advanced to $6,000; and by 1956 they had jumped to $90,000.

DeHart pointed out that a big selling point dealt with the fact that "our product was 100% petroleum and would blend with all petroleum based oils." With the aid of the Kansas City advertising agency, ads began to appear in the <u>Saturday Evening Post</u> and other periodicals. They also sponsored the Mr. Ed's Talking Horse comedy show on television; Art Linkletter handled some of the commercials while well-known sportscaster Bill Stern did the radio commercials for a year.

The firm not only used radio and television to promote the product, but it also noted that several distributors and sales outlets were using auto racing to further promote the product. On occasion, a distributor, jobber or independent gas station owner would sponsor a local racer. In time, the St. Joe company would also begin using auto racing for advertising purposes.

As the company grew, it's Kansas City advertising agency enlisted the services of several national celebrities. They included radio and television personalities, Art Linkletter and actor Alan Young with his side-kick "Mr. Ed," the talking horse. Do you imagine the product afforded Mr. Ed more horsepower?
Robert Bruhn Collection

An advertisement extolling the virtues of STP. In later years, some money generated by sales helped to underwrite the Novi operation as well as other forms of automotive competition.
Robert Bruhn Collection

Earl Kouba, known as "The Ol' Hay Burner," in an Offy powered midget sporting early STP sponsorship. The Colorado farmer/part-time racer is holding off the pack that includes Carl Williams (in 3rd place). Williams eventually made it to the .500 classis where he competed in six races. The above action occurred at the Englewood Speedway in Englewood, Colorado in 1958. STP was on its way.   Leroy Byers Photograph

It has been impossible to this point to determine precisely what jobber or independent gas station was the first to sponsor - i.e. provide partial financial support for race cars at the many tracks scattered across the Midwest in exchange for publicizing STP. We do know that the STP decal began to appear on midgets, sprinters and stock cars and in no time it was a well recognized logo.

STP's home office then became involved in a national campaign that involved an attempt to break the land speed record at the Bonneville Salt Flats. Driver/car builder Athol Graham made a run in his homemade streamliner, "The City of Salt Lake," in December of 1959. Jointly sponsored by STP and Firestone, Graham was clocked at 344.761 m.p.h. which was just a shade under the record held by an American driver. At the time the world record holder was Englishman John Cobb who had average 394.1 m.p.h. on the Utah Salt Flats in 1947.

When STP celebrated its 40th Anniversary in 1994, it was reported that the first use of STP in an Indy car occurred in 1958 in the John Zink Specials driven by Jimmy Reece of Oklahoma City, Oklahoma and Ed Elisian of Fresno, California. Zink, of Tulsa, Oklahoma had been the winning Indy 500 car owner in 1955 and 1956. Mr. Zink is unable to recall the circumstances, yet he well remembers Mr. Charles Soule, STP's Oklahoma distributor. Soule is credited by some with introducing the product to auto racing. A close inspection of the qualifying shot of Elisian's ride shows several decals, including those of Perfect Circle, Champion Spark Plugs and Bowes Seal Fast. Reece's ride also carried a Monroe shock absorber sticker, yet neither car bore an STP decal.

Early on STP encouraged the promotion of the additive by its distributors through the sponsorship of race cars. The scene is the Colorado State Fairgrounds at Pueblo in 1958. STP leads the way with driver Warren Hamilton in a stretched midget that housed an Offy.   Leroy Byers Photograph

Graham having been reared in nearby Salt Lake City was quite taken with the notion of Bonneville and the numerous speed records that various individuals had set there. His City of Salt Lake was a creation powered by a 3,000 horsepower aircraft engine with the cockpit canopy being grafted to the body from a P-51 Mustang fighter plane. On the nose of the car was an oversized oval STP decal that had become so familiar in the United States and was on its way to becoming one of the most identifiable logos in the world.

"STP helped me break the friction barrier again on the Bonneville Salt Flats. Just ran 344.761 MPH" -- Athol Graham

The STP Company joined in the action as it helped sponsor, along with Firestone, the 1959 LSR attempt by Salt Lake City driver Athol Graham.
C. Dwight Liggett

Graham was the owner of a general auto repair shop in Salt Lake City where STP was available. He publicly proclaimed that Salt Flat speeds caused tremendous engine strain and terrific heat, yet "I can say without qualification that STP made the difference in reducing the possibility of a lubrication or mechanical breakdown." He also stated, "I am sold on STP as the greatest friction-reducing agent ever developed."

Graham was to attempt a second go at breaking the LSR in August of 1960. In lending his name to the company he closed an endorsement letter with "I'll be seeing you on the sports pages."

During Graham's 1960, attempt he was two-thirds of the distance between the starting pit and the measured mile traveling in excess of 300 m.p.h. in the bright red car when the rear wheels lost traction. According to several accounts, this caused the car to move into a side way skid and flip, landing on its right side before it tumbled 4,000 feet across the saline bed before finally coming to a halt in an upside down position. Removed from the wreckage, Graham was flown to a Salt Lake City hospital where he passed away within minutes.

Some observers felt that the car had too much power and acceleration for the 4,200 pound creation. Further, the winds were clocked at up to 15 m.p.h. blowing at a 45 degree angle across the flats. This most likely contributed to Graham's failure to retain control of the racer. In spite of the tragedy, STP through its outlets, was to continue to support auto racing.

As the major oil companies became aware of the success of the new product, they began making reference to it as nothing more than "snake oil" or "mouse milk." As the sales of the STP oil additive soared, the rapid acceleration in sales may well have caught the major oil companies off guard.

The negative reactions were met head on by various users of the product. For example, the well-known aircraft engine firm, the Lycoming Company of Williamsport, Pennsylvania, recommended that STP be added to aircraft reciprocating (piston) engines, (Production Test Spec. No. 600, December 15, 1961). The firm later issued a service instruction bulletin (No. 1059, July 6, 1962) that strongly recommended that all Lycoming

Company engines be pre-lubricated at assembly to prevent scoring before the engine oil completed its first cycle. Parts for pre-lube included cam lobes, valve guides and supercharger bearings (where applicable). In closing, the bulletin noted that the company "has had success" with several pre-lubricants. The four products listed included STP. In fact, it was first on the list.

In March, 1961, the St. Joe Gazette informed its readership that the Studebaker-Packard Corporation of South Bend, Indiana had acquired the STP organization. The Studebaker offer to buy the firm came at a time the Missouri company was grossing $10,000,000 per annum. The Wall Street Journal reported that STP had pre-tax earnings of $1,250,000. At the time STP was approached for a buyout, the distributorships were located throughout the United States, Mexico and Canada. The tendered offer, reported at $10,000,000, met with the approval of Liggett, Hill, DeHart and the wives. The sale stipulated that the partners were to retain a 30 percent interest following the Studebaker acquisition.

With the sale completed, the STP operation was to remained in St. Joe. Liggett continued to serve as president of the Studebaker subsidiary with direct assistance from Bob DeHart. Over the course of the next several years, disenchantment arose among the founders regarding the overall management of the subsidiary from the South Bend corporate offices. Liggett reached the point where he felt it necessary to dispatch an accountant to South Bend on several occasions to determine what expenditures were being derived from the STP end of the Studebaker operations. In the early months of 1963, the South Bend office began discussions regarding a move of all STP activities to South Bend.

At the time, Sherwood Egbert, President of Studebaker-Packard, apparently was having differences of opinion with Liggett regarding several matters. Missives began to fly between South Bend and St. Joe. The St. Joe office had engaged the legal expertise of an Ames, Iowa law firm to represent it as difficulties continued. Liggett and his associates were of the opinion that there was an "implied understanding" that the operation would remain in St. Joe, although such was not stipulated in the sales contract. When it became clear to Liggett that such a move was unavoidable he sent a bulletin to the distributors announcing that he would "terminate my service as of July 31, 1963." He also informed the distributors that he would "continue to have a substantial interest in the future of the Division for many years." In early July, Egbert dispatched a registered letter

Robert P. DeHart - one of the trio of owners of Chemical Compounds - i.e. STP. His participation in the undertaking enhanced it's rapid growth. The photograph was taken at the Studebaker plant as the sale was finalized. Courtesy of Mary Ann DeHart

(of six pages) to Liggett that included a directive that he (Liggett) was no longer to engage in any future decisions within the Chemical Compounds Decision. Egbert also stated that while there was no intention to move the division at the time of the acquisition "no one could have committed the Corporation against the possibility of a move in the future. After all, circumstances do change."

On August 1, the Chemical Compounds Division officially moved to South Bend. Robert DeHart was retained by Studebaker to serve as Acting General Manager during the continuing transitional period before Studebaker made adminstrative changes. DeHart's services were then severed as per plans hammered out during the discussions regarding the move. Egbert held to the position that the move to the corporate offices would prove to be beneficial as it would combine all of the corporation's automotive divisions: Studebaker and the licensed Mercedes-Benz distributorship as well as the Defense Products Division at one central location.

As Liggett severed his managerial ties with the Indiana based firm, his letter of resignation (which seems obligatory in the business community) stated, "It is my feeling that the greatest growth for Chemical Compounds still lies in the future. Good luck and good selling."

The trio of Liggett, DeHart and Hill are to be commended for their perseverance in remaining

C. Dwight Liggett is pictured several years ago as he and his wife Edith celebrated the New Year in Hong Kong.
Courtesy of C. Dwight Liggett

with the new products during the tough formative years. Their hard work and dedication went a long way in making the STP product a familiar sales item by the time they departed from the operation. They had been resourceful and completely dedicated to do whatever was involved in promoting and selling their company's product.

With the departure of Liggett, the Studebaker organization announced that the president of its Paxton division, Andy Granatelli, would move into the role of chief executive of Chemical Compounds. With Granatelli's racing background, he was readily able to acquire sponsorship for a continuation of the Novi racing endeavor from the South Bend's corporate offices. American ingenuity had created a market for STP and it was on solid ground when sold to Studebaker. Support for the product rests with the fact that with the closing of Studebaker, its STP division remained in operation and prospered. In time Liggett sold his remaining stock to Studebaker for a seven figure amount.

Since the sale and departure of STP from St. Joseph, two of the three early owners have passed away. James Hill died in 1966 and Robert DeHart in 1994. C. Dwight Liggett, at age 85, spends a portion of each year in Zurich, Switzerland, while the remainder of the year is spent in the United States as he is a legal resident of Nevada.

INTERMEZZO

Master Salesman

While folks quickly recognize the STP logo and many are familiar with items produced by the corporation, probably only a small hard-core group of public relations reps going back some years, long-time participants in racing and perhaps a handful of diehard fans are aware of the invaluable contributions made in behalf of STP by master salesman, William "Bill" Dredge. Bill worked with the promotion of STP and its product line shortly after the Studebaker take over of the St. Joseph firm.

Dredge had worked as auto editor for the Los Angeles Times and no doubt had made the acquaintance of Sherwood Egbert, then working at the McCulloch Company in Los Angeles. Bear in mind, McCulloch had attempted to build an automobile in the mid-1950s and was engaged in the production of the Paxton automotive superchargers.

Dredge was hired by Studebaker as a public relations director and before his services were ended he held the position of Vice President for Public Relations. Bill's writing career had started before World War II and it was resumed upon his discharge from the U.S. Navy. The tenure as Times auto editor covered the years 1959 to 1962. At that time, he left to join the Studebaker operation at the behest of President Egbert. In so doing, he was to become associated with Andy Granatelli at the STP Division as they worked to further enhance the product name and witnessed a steady increase in sales. The ideas that Bill came up with were often extraordinary to say the very least. The STP logo stickers were plastered all about the team's equipment at Indy right on down to the galvanized water spout can. Give away decals ran into the thousands and they seem to pop up all over the place.

Further, as a former newspaper man, Bill was extremely adroit at handling the needs of members of the press. He could adjust his materials to provide for the particular needs of the many individuals in the press corp with whom he remained in constant contact. While he may not have produced the first press kit used in auto racing, he is credited with creating the first fully useful, well-rounded product for the racing press members. A kit was prepared for the 500 and as conditions dictated, Bill would see to the availability of updated versions. A reporter did not have to open the cover flap to check for a possible update, for if the kit was altered, it carried an oversized rubber stamp marking - "REVISED."

Deke Houlgate, a fellow public relations pro who has been engaged in the same work as Dredge, refers to Bill as a motorsports legend who knew the reporters by name and was able to deal with them on a basis that provided the particular data they would be most interested in obtaining. When press members were invited by Dredge to a session, they knew full well that it would be time well spent. Bill made sure of that. He was able to garner maximum exposure for STP and the forms of advertising were outstanding and different.

Going to work for Dredge, Deke recalls that each morning at 6 A.M. Bill would be on the telephone to dictate a three page story that he wanted disseminated across the country. Handling promotion west of the Rockies, it was then Deke's task to see that the info went out to the wire services within that region. With respect to maximizing STP, Deke asserts that Bill knew exactly which buttons to press to get a job done.

If press members desired black and white photos, color shots, slides, etc., Bill would see that such needs were taken care of. Interviews? No problem as Bill would set the ball into motion. As a great innovator, Bill scored a number of coups. One was seen with the special full-size supplement that he had inserted in every copy of the Indianapolis Star printed on race day, May 30, 1965. The eight page spread carried a vast amount of information for the race fan. In addition to extolling the virtues of STP at Indy, the supplement carried material on the use of the product in LSR efforts, motorcycle drag racing, stock cars, dragsters, etc. The entire supplement was printed in color and it certainly did not go unnoticed. Similar inserts were also used in 1966, 1967 and 1968.

At the end of the supplement, readers were offered the opportunity to purchase an STP decal t-shirt; a poplin wind breaker or mechanic overalls - like the familiar STP "pajamas" worn by the STP crew for several years. In his promotional efforts, Dredge seemed to have limitless possibilities for the time: stick on STP decals were handed out in untold numbers. Other items produced by the company included paper hats, felt hats and key chains to cite only a few.

Beyond the normal track work with interviews, personal business contacts and the like, Dredge found time to play a big role in the production of several STP film documentaries. The cinematic productions were made available to television outlets and military units scattered about the world. Yet, while Bill was instrumental in the production of the movie undertakings, he would be listed in the closing credits merely as a technical coordinator.

When Dredge and Andy put their heads together, new, sure fire ideas were often the result. However, Bill remainded in the background a great deal of the time. The pair had an intuitive instinct for drawing media coverage into every promotion they dealt with.

Following his retirement from racing, Bill retreated to his home in Baja, Mexico where he so enjoyed the area. He kept in touch with friends though he missed the personal contacts and the activities that abounded at any given motor racing event. Several times Bill journeyed north to visit with friends; even making it back to Indy. He passed away in March of 1989.

Chapter 27

The Remaining Novi Hardware

With the halt in the Novi racing program it seemed only suitable that in time some of those famed race cars would see museum duty. Further, it would appear that they would be extremely popular with a significant number of race fans. The question then arises as to what was built and still available from the past. Any vintage race car collector or museum now wishing to possess a Novi would be confronted with a seemingly insurmountable obstacle. There is an extremely limited number of engines and chassis available. Further, would the current owner(s) be willing to part with such desirable racing memorabilia? Possibly the only way to acquire "such" would be via a reproduction.

According to several reports, only one engine was built the first year (1941) and this engine was also used in 1946. Two other engines were added in 1947. From that point on the team had only three engines for two cars for several years. An article in a 1954 issue of Hot Rod Magazine mentioned three existing engines with a sufficient quantity of spare parts to build up two additional engines. When the front drives were retired, their engines continued to see service as they were placed in the 1956 500F rear drive roadsters. New crankcases were built for the rear drives, but other engine parts were salvaged for further use. Up until 1958, there was still talk of only three complete engines with spare parts. In 1960, noted racing writer Bob Russo said that there had been five engines built since 1941. One is left to wonder if this was exclusive of all spare and replacement parts that had been built over the years. This seems to be a feasible consideration. Even Radio Gardner, who was with Lew Welch from day one until the Novi operation was sold, was unsure as to the exact number of engines cast during the Welch era.

Several types of cylinder blocks were produced to meet changes in bore and stroke. The fact that several different cylinder blocks were used over a long period is borne out by the following: One of the authors had the opportunity to inspect a complete, original Novi engine. A careful check of the engine provided the following data: The right-hand block contained the following markings; USAC 1956 and a USAC 1957 with an additional number - 27. You might recall that Tony Bettenhausen's 1957 Novi ride was identified as car #27. The left-hand block had similar stamping, but with A.A.A. 1951 and A.A. 1952 (the third A is not visible). Both blocks contained another marking, #248. Its significance is unknown.

In the years the Granatellis owned the engines, additional blocks were built to increase the inventory. Andy asserts that he had five engines when the Novi project came to an end. Photos appear to confirm this fact. We have also found evidence of the remains of the magnesium engine the Granatellis attempted to develop to reduce engine weight, although it was never actually used in practice. One informant told us that the Granatellis used the retired front drive crankcases for dyno testing, with some moving parts being removed to be used in the rear drives that eventually were placed in the cars. Yet, one crew member denies this account so a cloud remains. Rumors have persisted as to the whereabouts of several of the engines.

In returning to Welch's first car, the rebuilt Miller-Ford chassis used in conjunction with the first Winfield-Novi engine, it can be reported that this car still exists. It is currently in a private collection in Colorado. The car has been totally restored in full Novi trim. While the car lacks its original engine the owner had a single replacement powerplant built, having engine components cast as necessary.

As for the front drives, the 1947 car which gained its greatest fame while Duke Nalon was at the wheel, is housed at the Indianapolis Motor Speedway Museum and Hall of Fame. The museum acquired the car from Lew Welch. The cream colored #54 Novi Grooved Piston Special is very similar in appearence as when Nalon drove the car in 1948. For a considerable time it had been painted a bluish metallic grey with a red trim, using 1955 mag wheels and disc brakes. It now sports red wire wheels that were used at the time of Nalon's driving performances. One account declares that while the car was in transit from an exposition in Germany (still bearing a bluish grey paint job), it was damaged. As it had to be repainted, the decision was made to return the color to the original 1948 finish. An additional detail on the restored car is inaccurate as the actual 1948 car had an air scoop in front of the windscreen to permit an adequate air flow into the three Winfield carburetors. Beginning in 1950, when the engine used a single Holley carburetor with its scoop mounted directly on top of the unit a slight alteration was made in the bodywork. The museum car retains the bodywork as used in its final years of racing.

A spokesman for the museum stated that the Novi is one of the more important cars in its collection, representing an era of advanced technology. For this reason, the front drive is regularly on display. In addition, one may assume the immense popularity of the Novi is a contributing factor for keeping the car on display most of the time.

The other front drive car was removed from sight after Chet Miller's fatal crash. The severely damaged car remained in the Welch shop for a considerable period. It was eventually sold minus the engine and ultimately made its way to an outstanding Michigan car restorer.

Moving on to the rear drives (beginning with the 500Fs), one of the cars is known to exist. It is the car entered by the Granatellis in their early Novi efforts (1961-1962). When it was retired in 1964, it remained with the Granatellis and the STP organization. A 1965 STP promotional piece portrayed the car as carrying the lucky #7. The car was then on display in Harrah's Automotive Museum in Nevada. After William Harrah's passing, his collection was broken up and the Novi eventually made its way to the International Motorsports Hall of Fame in Talladega, Alabama. It retains the bodyshape used in its final years of duty. The paint job is the same as that pictured in the 1965 STP promotional pamphlet.

According to Andy Granatelli, the second rear drive car was included in the deal when he acquired the Lew Welch Novi team. Some Novi purists are not absolutely sure as to what happened to this particular car which had gained additional fame and glory in Monza, Italy. A 1963 Popular Hot Rodding magazine article includes a photo of the Novi shop that appears to show a partial outline of said car in the background.

The two Kurtis-Kraft cars built in 1962 were ultimately separated. The car driven by Hurtubise in 1963 and 1965 and by Art Malone in 1964 is in the Indianapolis Motor Speedway Museum. Occasionally, it is made available for viewing. For example, in May, 1989, it appeared at the Indiana State Museum and in May, 1990, it was on display at the Indianapolis Motor Speedway Motel. The motel lobby maintains a single car display on a rotation system from its collection of cars. The aforementioned car carried the bodyshape and colors used when Jim Hurtubise drove it in 1965. Regrettably, like the museum's front drive Novi, it also contains only a mock up engine. The second 1962 car has disappeared from public viewing though some feel it still exists.

The last two cars are the four wheel drives. The Ferguson chassis remains and is now owned by the Motorsports Hall of Fame of America located at Novi, Michigan. We have been informed that the other four wheel drive Novi built by Vince in 1965 was totally shattered and thus cannibalized. Such a report could not be confirmed.

Thus, it appears that six of the nine cars built have somehow survived. Perhaps two more are still around, yet their location and condition are unknown. Only the original Miller-Ford and the Ferguson 4WD are fully restored and in running condition.

It would be interesting to know how many engines were actually built. A 1987 photograph of existing Novi engines indicated that it was possible to identify five engines and the experimental magnesium engine. Determining the number of Novi engines actually cast would be a challenging and most likely a fruitless endeavor.

The engine that blew in 1961, with Ralph Liguori behind the wheel, was reportedly trashed with only a few parts in salvageable condition. You may recall Liguori saying that perhaps only the camshafts could be used again.

Andy Granatelli provided additional details when he stated that the Novi shop had contained all the parts made for the engines and that when everything was gathered up it would be possible to build ten or twelve engines. The maximum number of ready to run engines that they possessed at any given time was five or six. This was particularly true during the years the team ran three cars.

One undisputable fact remains: There are a limited number of authentic Novi parts in private hands. Organizations and individuals who claim they own significant parts that represent something of the original Novi heritage certainly have items that can be considered rare and in some cases of considerable value.

While the Detroit suburb of Novi is a name that knowledgeable Indy car fans can quickly relate to, the town itself did not appear to make any early efforts to equate the car's world-wide fame with the community in any meaningful way. Yet, in time as things changed and the city grew, the fame of the fabled Novis was locally recognized.

The old Welch owned factory had been closed for years and it was left to local leaders to try to obtain an actual Novi if they wished to commemorate the Novi Legend. As the plans were set in motion, a civic committee was formed to acquire a Novi. They contacted Andy Granatelli with an inquiry as to whether he was interested in selling one of the remaining Novis stored in the Santa Monica shop. Originally, Andy did not appear willing to part with the beloved cars to the city of Novi, or to others making requests for the cars or parts. Considering the matter further, Andy ultimately responded to the inquiry of the civic-minded group from Novi, Michigan with a counter proposal. He offered the 1964 4WD Ferguson chassis as a roller (minus the engine and driveline) for $200,000. The offer included two engines and the remaining three engines would also be a part of the arrangement if the civic leaders agreed to acquire the first two engines. With the entire collection in hand, Granatelli promised to provide other memorabilia to perpetuate the Novi Legend.

The committee was without that amount of money and they proposed to buy the chassis for $35,000, but Granatelli kept the engine option open until the remainder of the money could be raised. Fortunately, the committee was successful in its attempt to acquire sufficient local funding to acquire the additional Novi hardware that had remained in California with the Granatellis since 1966. Thus, in the spring of 1983, the Ferguson chassis was shipped from Santa Monica to Novi with plans for its restoration.

The civic group planned to display the Novi in a setting that was to be built, although the Ferguson was not planned as the only display. The decision was made to recognize all forms of racing including Indy cars, stock cars, sports cars, sprint cars, dragsters, motorcycles, racing boats and airplanes. Thus, the plans called for the construction of a building to house a planned museum in addition to the restoration of the car.

With the Ferguson in Novi, Michigan, the major restoration problem dealt with the fact that the driveline was no longer complete as several parts had been used in the 1967 STP turbine car. As a consequence, one might reasonably conclude that the turbine was in part the "son of the Novi." Restoration would be difficult but certainly not impossible. The civic leaders began a search for an individual capable of restoring the famous car. The restorer selected was R.J. "Buck" Boudeman whose restoration facilities are located in Michigan. In the past, Boudeman had restored other race cars and the work was considered nothing short of beautiful, accurate restorations by racing diehards. Buck is a member of the Society of Racing Historians and a Miller devotee completely familiar with the many aspects of the Miller/Goossen/Offenhauser technology heritage found in Novi engines. Under Boudeman's guidance, a Novi engine was completely overhauled and put together. When necessary, new parts were machined to replace those of questionable dependability. The chassis was repaired and rebuilt with the driveline reconstructed with the aid of the Ferguson Company in England. They provided assistance in offering copies of original drawings and blueprints.

In 1988, the Ferguson was a part of the 500 Festival Parade. Such an event is held in Indianapolis each year the day before the race. As the engine and driveline had not been completed, only the chassis with its bodywork were seen.

In March of 1989, the electrifying day arrived when Boudeman had the car ready for a shakedown run. Shortly before 6 A.M., the engine was fired and it roared into life without any difficulties. Buck drove the car around his neighborhood using aviation fuel and the car carrying medium hot plugs. The use of a methanol blend and warm up plugs switching over to racing plugs was totally impractical as the car was not attempting any sort of speed run. The car made several short trips around the streets of Buck's village. Boudeman said that he did not want to attempt more than several passes since he expected the police to arrive to discover that he was running on the roads creating a loud noise. As they failed to appear, he returned to the shop only to hear the phone ringing. It was the local constabulary inquiring as to what was going on. They were well aware of Boudeman's restoration of cars and they were merely checking "things out." Thus, the noise shattering episode was over before it really started.

Boudeman firmly believes that during his restoration work some unusual discoveries were made. In fact, we have already alluded to it in the 1964 introduction of the Ferguson at Indy. During his restoration of the front suspension, Buck discovered that the steering geometry was off. The spec sheets verified his finding. Buck feels the error resulted from the fact that one of the pieces on the system had been improperly installed. The suspension system included a triangular piece which was incorrectly placed. Merely by turning it over during installation the steering geometry appeared to be vastly improved. But since the car was to be restored in its original condition Buck placed the parts as they had been originally fitted. Boudeman now wonders if the car had been designed with a suspension setup like this or whether somewhere in the developmental procedure something went wrong. If one assumes that the present suspension setup was used in 1964 and 1965 such is possible. If this was so, little wonder that the car was not handling properly in 1964 as Novi pilots Jim McElreath and Bobby Unser reported. On the other hand, it might simply be possible that some of the heavy steering reactions were the result of the complicated driveline system with its gears and differentials. You might recall that Granatelli had contacted Colin Chapman seeking assistance which ultimately lead to the Granatelli-Chapman efforts with the turbine program.

However, there is good reason to believe that Boudeman's conjecture is correct. As a consequence, the Ferguson might well have required less effort on the driver's behalf. Boudeman and his assistants discovered several other apparent flaws during the restoration. According to one theory, the steering arrangement for a car works best when the rotation point of the king pin and that of the steering rod, which activates the axle holder, are in a straight line going through the center of the rear axle. Normally, the steering rod is behind the front axle. However, in the Ferguson the rod was located in front of the axle. If the rotation point of the steering rod remained on this imaginary line between the rear axle center and king pin rotation point, the steering point would come too close to the brakes. To avoid that, the steering rod was made narrower and as a result the turning point between steering rod and axle holder was not on the theoretically ideal line. This may well have contributed to the less than perfect track behavior of the Ferguson.

Another detail of the car that evoked some concern for the restorers was that with the supercharger in the front of the car, the power intake point of the front differential had to be angled slightly downwards. As a result, the input into the differential was not in a straight line with the driveshaft as is preferable, so it had a slight angle. Perhaps this was another cause for less than ideal track behavior by the car.

A further observation dealt with the exhaust system. In contrast to the 500K roadsters which had full length exhaust pipes, the Ferguson ran with short exhaust pipes which emitted their thunderous blast in front of the driver, hereby exposing him to an extraordinary amount of noise! While very loud noise can be a cause for fatigue, one must think about what it would have been for a driver to be exposed to the sound for approximately three and one-half hours.

One detail however, shocked the men who restored "Fergie." They discovered that the seat of the car was connected to a rear cross member of the chassis with a metal bracket. They realized with horror that in case of an accident in which the driver seat had been pushed back, this bracket could pierce the back of the driver! Bobby Unser, who crashed the car in the 1964 inferno, was perhaps even luckier than he realized.

The Boudeman restorers, however, made it perfectly clear that all their judgments were made with the benefit of hindsight. Not all current knowledge was available back in 1964 when the car was laid out. One knows how easy it is to ascertain errors with the advantage of hindsight.

Whatever the situation, when it comes to the Ferguson, Boudeman and the individuals and organizations that assisted in the lengthy restoration can be justifiably proud of their great work.

The Novi-Ferguson remains on display at the Novi Motorsports Museum and Hall of Fame of America which is a part of the Exposition Center located in Novi. The museum occupies 20,000 sq. ft. for display of current and vintage racing cars, boats and motorcycles.

The disposition of all the Novis we could locate is touched on in the introductory section for each car in Appendix C. In closing, it might be added that one of the Novis (the 1962 version?) may have been used as a show car at various Andy Granatelli Tune Up Master shops that operated for some years after his departure from STP.

Chapter 28

The Magical Draw of the Novi

One of the most interesting circumstances regarding the Novi relates to the enormity of its popularity. For one reason or another, the Novis were tremendously popular and true crowd pleasers nearly each and every year they were in action. The people who saw them run most likely will never forget the viewing and the sound of "that" engine. Even now, more than a generation after the last of the Novis turned a wheel at the Speedway, they have not been forgotten. The memories surrounding the "Big Brute" and the adoration for them have remained intact with some fans over the years. Even among some younger racing fans who never saw the Novis compete and have to rely on stories and pictures, the car is well-known. The mere mention of the name Novi generates many thoughts among a sizable number of race fans. The unusual name still works its magic. But what was the reason for the Novis to be such tremendously popular cars? There are probably countless theories for such a question.

The Novis created a tremendous amount of excitement, thrills, disappointment and drama in the long history of the Indianapolis track. They were involved in a number of the best known and most famous episodes of Indy 500 history. Even casual fans who follow the sport are probably familiar with the story of the astonishing record smashing run of Ralph Hepburn in 1946; the near victory by Nalon in 1948 (possibly being denied due to the late pit stop); the horrendous crash experienced by Duke a year later; his returning to capture the pole in 1951; the exploding tire on Russo's car in 1956 while running in front of the field and the fatalities of drivers Hepburn and Chet Miller to mention a few of the more significant episodes.

The involvement of these cars, the team and their drivers alone is sufficient cause to make the Novis unforgettable and difficult to avoid. The Novis played such a prominent role from 1941 through 1966 that they can not be ignored. Further, why was fan support continual when in reality they proved to be an annual disappointment?

Most certainly the Novi was a perennial favorite of many fans each and every year in spite of their continual disappointing showings. Yet, they were to suffer from one or more problems virturally every year they were at the Speedway. Much of the time the public is devoted to the underdog in the game. Yet, some years - particularily during the early years, the Novi was not always considered to be an underdog. However, examining the entire career of the cars, they were much closer to the status of underdogs than the unbeatable cars some believed them to be. Somehow, racing fans idolized the Novi year after year. Part of it might rest with the fact that much of the time they were handled by very popular drivers.

It could also have been that they always made a terrific showing and displays of extraordinary speed - as long as they held together. The sight of one of the powerful Novis overtaking car after car on the straightaways with such ease was most certainly racing excitement at its best. Some of the fan adoration may have been due to their continuing notoriety at the track year after year. Another angle relates to the fact that they were something more than just another "boring" Offy powered car. Maybe it was the spine-tingling overwhelming noise created by the V-8. It produced such an amazing sound - a song of power! The fact that they failed to win year after year must have drawn some crowd support and sympathy for cars that had demonstrated their superiority nearly every time out, only to suffer yet another misfortune. Another possible factor is that they always seemed to be among the most eye appealing cars at the track.

Thus, there are a number of reasons that can be cited for the tremendous popularity and well-loved Novis on behalf of the racing public. Without a doubt, the Novi was the most powerful car at the track during its years. Serving as proof of this fact was Hepburn's record shattering qualifying run in the first 500 outing after World War II. It thereby drew considerable attention and interest. This early impression was not easily forgotten by anyone who witnessed that first pre-war race. This most likely helped lay the foundation for the popularity of the Novi legend - a legend capable of continuing as long as the 500 is held.

As the years go by, many veteran Indy fans and racing oldtimers still can remain busy discussing stories and strong memories regarding the Novi and its role at the Speedway. Andy Granatelli has stated that he received letters into the late 1960s from fans asking him to bring the Novis back into competition.

The strong memories of the Novi were off to an early start in its very first years. Possibly the movies played a small role in this popularity. In 1949, "The Big Wheel" was filmed. The story deals with a young California driver who tries to gain fame at various dirt tracks. The driver, Billy McCoy (played by Mickey Rooney) is the son of a former driver who had lost his life at Indianapolis. The film is far from realistic and a number of scenes are total poppycock. Inserted in the movie are a collection of some of the more spectacular accidents of 500s backed up with studio shots of McCoy in action with his car. Included in the film is actual footage of the major wreck of the previous 500 in which Duke Nalon's Novi crashed and the ensuing inferno. The producers used the wall of fire created by the burning Novi to have McCoy's car catch fire in order to provide for a spectacular finish. In the movie, this was suppose to have occurred on the last lap of the race. Of course, this caused racing fans who knew what actually occurred to wonder how the producers could explain the fact that a racing car could create such a horrible fire while crashing on the last lap. Factually, the accident had occurred on lap 24. One is left to even question why the producers never sought permission of Duke Nalon with regard to using the crash in which he almost lost his life. Nalon was unaware of the use of the accident footage until he was informed of its inclusion within the film. A normally unflappable Nalon was less than pleased with the movie. The use of this piece of film and the fact that the movie is shown with some regularity may be one reason why the crash may be such a well-known incident.

A curious fact about the making of "The Big Wheel" movie is that Nalon's Novi was used as a stand-in for Bill Holland's Blue Crown, the winning car in that year's 500. While the original Blue Crown was not available for studio shots of the car, Nalon's rebuilt Novi was located in Jean Marcenac's Burbank shop close to the Hollywood studios. The car was painted to resemble the Blue Crown. Thus an irony; Nalon's rebuilt mount made it into the movie disguised as its biggest rival at the Speedway!

A large 37 inch x 23 inch red bordered poster was sold some years ago tracing the history of the Novi heritage. The poster had head shots of all drivers known to have driven a Novi at the Speedway, be it in practice; qualifying or in the race itself. Further, a year-by-year chronology relates the fortunes and misfortunes that befell the cars. The poster of the Novi years was simply entitled NOVI. It was the work of Rick Whitt of Indianapolis. Whitt received assistance from Duke Nalon as he traced the Novi history.

Many other examples can be cited of the continuing Novi's lore:

Some years ago Steve Bonesteel of Fresno, California, a stained glass artist, created a beautiful, (2½ ft. x 3½ ft.) stained glass window that portrayed the blood red #29 Novi driven by Paul Russo. In addition to the sale of the glass window, Bonesteel also sold posters of the stained glass work of art. Further, several oil paintings of the Novi have been seen from time to time.

The #29 blood red Novi driven by Paul Russo in 1956 was featured in this beautiful stained glass work of art by artist Steve Bonesteel of California. The black and white reproduction does not do justice to the remarkable work. The intricate glass work was also reproduced as a poster.
Courtesy Steve Bonesteel

The public appeal for the Novi has been translated into artist renderings as early as 1953. For example, an original work of art by Virginia artist John Orfe graced the cover of the June, 1953 issue of Speed Age magazine. The eye appealing colored illustration has the #21 Novi Purelube Special roaring down the front straight with Chet Miller at the wheel.

(1992) At an autograph party held in Indianapolis at the release of Vol. I, fans Paul and Fran Snowden had Duke Nalon sign the oil painting they own. It features Duke in the #54 Novi Grooved Piston Special now housed at the I.M.S. Museum and Hall of Fame. *Authors Collection*

In 1994, Larry and Dale Wright of Evansville, Indiana began producing vintage racing t-shirts bearing "famous, infamous and novel racing machines from decades past." Among their first six selections was the #54 Novi driven by Duke Nalon. The quality is outstanding and accurate what with Dale's broad background in painting and knowledge of racing history. Their firm, Over Time Machines, is a division of their Over Hill and Dale Studios that has been in operation for over 30 years.

Certainly one of the most unique rememberances of the famed Novi comes in the form of Indiana limestone. Eddie Evans, owner of Architectural Stone Sales of Bedford, Indiana, with the invaluable help of his sons John and Bill, carved a limestone copy of the #54 Novi. The actual dimensions were obtained prior to the commencement of work. The car is actually a two-thirds model, for in Eddie's words, "We did not have a long enough stone to do a full scale model." The stone used is of a high quality and was formed an estimated 300 million years ago. In view of such, Evans states that with the age of the stone "the Novi shall last that much longer." When the car was displayed at a meeting of the Winchester Old Timers Club at the famed Winchester, Indiana track, driver Duke Nalon posed with the marvelous creation and declared that it would make a nice headstone for his final resting place.

The cigar-shaped body was planed lengthways, and from that point on, all remaining bodywork was carved by hand. The wheels were turned on a lathe and the spokes and Firestone letters were cut by hand using a pneumatic air hammer and chisels.

The Bedford area is located in the heart of the state's tremendous limestone deposits. Such limestone has been used in major building projects around the country including the Pentagon, the Empire State Building, state capitals, government and university buildings, etc.

While the Evans had previously created scaled down models that included an Indy car, a sprinter, a midget and a 1970 Plymouth Road Runner, they had never carved a model on the scale of the Novi. Eddie is a long-time race fan who owns a collection of original race cars. Mr. Evans, a 40 year veteran in the stone business, is quite understandably a devoted race fan as he attended his first 500 in 1950. Recently, the Evans opened the Antique Auto and Race Car Museum at Bedford that features a wide selection of race cars.

When the Over The Hill and Dale Studios of Evansville, Indiana, decided to reproduce nostalgia t-shirts several years ago, the beloved #54 Novi was among the very first to be printed. Bruce Peters, son of George & Barbara Peters, models the shirt. *Authors Collection*

A three-quarter scaled granite model of the #54 Novi. The fabulous work was created by Eddie Evans of Bedford, Indiana, with the help of his two sons, John and Bill. Posing with the car at a Winchester Old Timers meeting at the famed Winchester, Indiana track, Duke acknowledged that the stone work would make an excellent marker for his final resting place!
Courtesy of Eddie Evans

It would be most difficult to locate any book detailing the history of the 500 without noting some reference to the Novi, be it a detailed account, or at the very least an oblique citation. As an example, author Brock Yates devotes a chapter in his book, <u>Famous Indianapolis Cars and Drivers</u>, to the Novi. The volume was published in 1960, so the Novi saga relates solely to the Welch years of ownership. Mark Dees' monumental book, <u>The Miller Dynasty</u>, also devotes a chapter to the Novi. Another book citation would be Roger Huntington's <u>Design and Development of the Indy Car</u>, which contains several paragraphs of Novi info located in different chapters. C. Lee Norquest, a true blue devotee to the Novi and its active history penned an early booklet entitled <u>The Fabulous Novi Story</u> in 1963. With its popularity, later updated editions were printed. This particular publication, reprinted over the years had its last release in 1965 and is now out of print. Lee's dedication to the Novi is obvious as one keeps in mind that his writing was a "labor of love." It is the only known publication devoted entirely to the Novi during its career.

The famous car has also attracted considerable attention in foreign publications. To cite only two examples: <u>History of the Racing Car, Man and Machine</u> by Giovanni Lurani (published in Italy, then in the United Kingdom and finally the United States), offers a colored shot of the Novi on a double page spread. A more recent English publication, William Court's <u>Grand Prix Requiem</u>, contains a chapter entitled "The Heavy Burden: A Tragedy of Three Novi Men and Their Cars." The chapter is devoted to recounting the Novi careers of Ralph Hepburn, Chet Miller and Rex Mays. Without question, other Novi references could be located if one cares to pursue the matter further.

In addition to the numerous stories contained in foreign publications relative to the Novi, there has also been a somewhat unique approach. A very popular comic book series originated in Europe in 1957 by Frenchman Jean Graton includes some Novi adventures. His fictional hero is driver Michel Vaillant. Since the first book appeared over 51 different comic publications and a few special editions have been printed.

Michel is the son of an imaginary French car producer, Henri Vaillant, who builds the Vaillante cars. The elder Vaillant has a racing department and Michel is the first driver on the factory team. The fictional stories continue as an ageless Michel endlessly faces the stiffest opposition - year after year. In the various volumes the young Vaillant competes in many forms of motor racing, including Formula One, sports cars, touring cars, etc. In two of the comics, Vaillant is seen competing in the NASCAR series with special dispensation from Bill France. The Vaillant team enters the Indy 500 in five of the comic books. The first issue witnesses Michel's initial experience at Indy.

Vaillant's major American opponent for his opening challenge at Indy (supposed to take place in 1957) is a very unsympathetic Steve Warson. Warson drives a Vanwall in Formula One events and a Lister-Jaguar at Le Mans. At Indianapolis he is assigned to a Dean Van Lines Special. Unbelievably, when the race is started Steve is driving

The fame of the Novis certainly has not been limited to the United States. A number of foreign books provide varying amounts of space to the Novis. This included the well received comic books of Frenchman Jean Graton. Admittedly, Graton has taken some liberty with the story lines in the 50 plus comic books thus far printed. The cover illustration pictured presumedly shows the terrifying 1964 Indianapolis 500 crash. In spite of the loss of two drivers, no cars flipped. The Novi coming through the fiery holocaust is the Jim McElreath car. Note the STP decal on the headrest and the skull and crossbones emblem on the helmet!! This particular issue is entitled, "Panic in Indianapolis."
Courtesy of Jean Graton

a Novi Special described by Graton as being a powerful car. This particular car resembles the 1956 500F Novi. Yet, there is no reference to an official Novi team. Michel wins Indy but at the season's close he refuses to claim the championship!

We contacted Jean Graton to verify a few facts regarding the Novis he used in his comic books. He told us that he selected a Novi for Steve Warson for this 1957 adventure as he felt it to be a car with the proper background for a man like Steve. The inspiration for the car came from a book which Graton received from Bill France.

A second Vaillante Indy adventure took place in 1964. Michel Vaillant and Steve Warson as friends, teammates and Vaillante drivers faced stiff opposition from a team called "Texas Drivers Club," a team which had a score to settle with Steve Warson. One of the Texas Drivers had a Lotus-Ford, the other two drivers had Novis, instantly recognizable as the 1963 versions of the 500K, the cars driven by Hurtubise and Unser that year. Again, there is no sign of an official Novi team or Granatelli cars. Michel once again wins Indy. Both the Novis retire early from the race when one of the drivers refused to eliminate the Vaillante drivers during the contest, but instead took out his teammate in the other Novi who was willing to do so! An interesting feature on the cover of this comic book is a Novi taking a corner to the right!

Jean Graton's fantasy went so far that when he needed an American built Formula One car for an adventure in 1958 he created one with the name "Novi Europ." This car has a straight 6 engine with a Novi tailfin. It contested only one race, driven by Steve Warson, but was parked thereafter because the car constantly had to change tires. Asked about why and how the Novi Europ came into existance, Graton had the following explanation: The creation of the Novi Europ was to underline the connection between Steve Warson and the Novi in the preceeding book. When he drove a Novi at Indy.

The very same Novi Europ returns in a 1988 issue released to commemorate 30 years of Michel Vaillant adventures and the 50th album within the series. In an imaginary contest for vintage cars (to give the author another chance to bring back some of the cars of the earlier books), Steve Warson drives the Novi Europ in a race for front engine F 1 cars. Curiously, of all the opponents in these races, the Novi Europ is the car which receives the most attention from Graton. The extended attention given to this non-Vaillante in the 50th book in which vintage cars appeared was explained by Graton with the statement, "It was evident to me that the Novi Europ was one of the cars which deserved to be brought back from the past."

A picture from one of Graton's books shows a #7 with the familiar dorsal fin. The Novi name is carried on both the nose and hood of the car.
Courtesy of Jean Graton

As noted earlier, the #54 Novi appears to be what has been described as "an on going center piece" at the Indianapolis Motor Speedway Museum. Small scale toy models of the car have also appeared down through the years.

A current member of the Indianapolis Motor Speedway press room corp, the ever pleasant Bob Clidinst, makes handcrafted models of various race cars and has built approximately 25 Novis from very detailed 1/24th prints that he has drafted. Bob's patience certainly shows in the beautifully crafted finished product. He has compiled the exact measurements for the two Novis housed at the Speedway.

Another supplier of Novi models is Bill Jorgensen, also of Indianapolis. He supplies resin molded cars ready for assembly, painting and detailing. The model in question is the FWD Novi in 1/24th scale.

The very same FWD Novi has also been available as a 1/43th scale white metal kit, made by Precision Miniatures in Costa Mesa, California. Duke Nalon's 1948 version is known to exist, perhaps more versions have been released over the years.

Garage 97 Models of Indianapolis offered a 1:24 resin kit of the Ferguson-Novi 4WD as driven by Bobby Unser in the 1964 race.

Over the years there have been several factory runs of Novi model race cars. One of these has been produced by a slot car company, MRRC, located on the English Channel island of Jersey. They are on a scale of 1:32. Oddly enough, this car is a rough resemblance of the Ferguson car as it was driven in the spring test sessions in March, 1964, before it was damaged in the garage fire. While the actual car was heavily modified during the reworking, this slot racer Novi certainly resembles one of the least known disguises of the Ferguson.

Regarding oddball Novi items, remember the imaginary Novi Europ from the Michel Vaillant Comic Series? A French company, Jade Miniatures of Aix-le-bain, France has released 1/43th scale resin models of some of the cars which appear in these albums. The Novi Europ is one of these imaginary cars released in kit form. The Warson's 500 inspired car is scheduled for release as well.

In 1994, the STP firm celebrated its 40th year of operation. To commeraie the occasion, the firm introduced a series of six plastic STP Oil Treatment containers that bore labels featuring various cars and drivers associated with the company over the years. One of the six anniversary containers carries a color shot of the Novi driven by

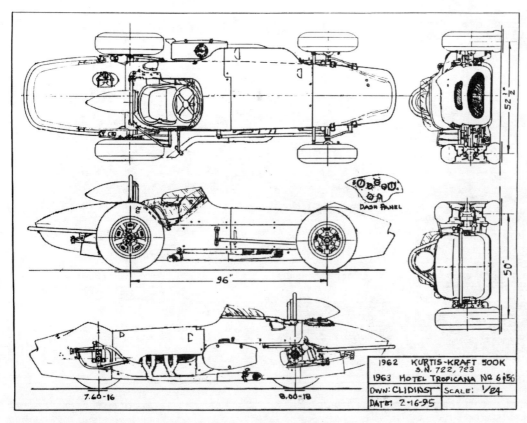

Many models of the various Novis have been custom made over the years as well as several production runs. Bob Clidinst, who works for the I.M.S., has created a number of hand built Novis. He works from measurements he has taken by hand. The above 1/24 scale drawing was for use with the 1962 Kurtis-Kraft 500K, the Hotel Tropicana Special.
Courtesy of Bob Clidinst

Jim Hurtubise in 1963 that started from the front row. The caption below the photo reads in part "STP sponsored the popular Novi car, a 2,000 pound, 775 horsepower super race car. Jim Hurtubise, pictured here was one of STP's top drivers." Other containers featured STP drivers Richard Petty and Gordon Johncock. In no time the STP containers became collectibles as the supply was quickly sold out.

Another recollection of the rich Novi heritage came at Indy prior to the running of the 1994 race. A handful of the cars offered a silhouette line that included a distinctive fin along the top of the engine cover. Such was necessary on the PC 94 Penske cars containing the Mercedes Benz due to its tall plenum chamber. Some track siders, upon seeing the change, made referrence to the engine bonnets as being "mini Novi type tails." While they fell far short of the enormous tail fin on the #75 Novi of the early 1960s, the mere recollection denotes the strong impression left by the Novis.

Another bit of reminiscence of the Novi was present in 1994 as the cover of the official program contains a collage of noteworthy events in the track's long history. Among the five illustrations is the start of the 1963 race portraying Parnelli Jones and Hurtibuse leading a pack of cars down the front straight as the race began.

Currently, popular items at race tracks are various, colorful lapel and/or hat pins featuring a number of famed drivers and cars. The Novi has not been overlooked as several such items have been manufactured. Driver Duke Nalon's name is carried on one of the limited number made available. The Novi featured is the Novi Grooved Piston Ring Special while another pin carries the name of well-known Novi mechanic Radio Gardner. The Novi Motorsports Museum of Novi, Michigan, also released lapel pins with a red Novi, resembling their #9 Ferguson car. Two sizes are known to exist: a big one of about one inch and a smaller version that was available in later years.

On page 35 of Volume One was pictured an example of the 1947 IMS Pit badge that features the record breaking 1946 Novi driven by Ralph Hepburn. Pit badges are a popular item among the Indy 500 memorabilia collectors and the 1947 Novi badge is among the most popular. The 1947 badges were available in both the silver and the bronze variety, the first ever pit badge of which the two versions existed.

Because of the popularity of the 1947 badges, they are among the highest prized badges and therefore less affordable for many. A cheaper alternative was a keychain which featured the pit badge minus the number. The rim of the rear wheel was absent in order for keys to be attached. Alternative or not, the keychain remains a collectible item for diehard Novi fans!

The 1947 pit badge was also used on a 1947 Christmas gift given to the friends and business

In this age of popularity for racing pins, the Novi has not been forgotten. The pin in the upper left features the #54 Novi and the name Duke Nalon while a companion pin in the opposite corner carries the name Radio Gardner. Between them is a keyholder, a replica of the 1947 pit badge. In the middle row are the 1947 bronze and silver badges that feature the record smashing Novi driven by Ralph Hepburn a year earlier. Between the numbered badges are three Novi pins that had been sold at the Motorsports Hall of Fame in Novi, Michigan.   *Authors Collection*

associates of the Hulman family. The gifts were copper colored ash-trays with a raised impression of the Novi located in the center. The impression is identical to that used for the 1947 pit badges, but without a badge number under the car.

Among other Novi items are the highly sought after 6 in. x 9 in. color postcards. The cards printed included Chet Miller (1952), Tony Bettenhausen (1957), Paul Russo (1957), Jim Hurtubise (1963) and Art Malone (1964). Some 5 in. x 7 in. also exist, in color and black and white as well as some standardized sized postal cards. All of these cards were released in the 1950s and 1960s.

In 1995, an Indianapolis business that had been established in 1945 (the same year the Hulman family acquired the historic Speedway), had a private printing of some memorable events that span the five decades. The printing included a series of oversized (9 in. x 13½ in.) "firsts" photos. The set begins with a photo depicting Ralph Helpburn at the wheel of the record smashing Novi in 1946. The caption is entitled "The First of Many Years of **THE AWESOME NOVI**." The other illustrations in the set consist of The First Roadster, (Vuky In 1953); The First Woman Driver (Janet Guthrie); and The Beginning of Modern Rear Engine Revolution (showing Jack Brabham in the 1961 Cooper-Climax).

It is worth noting that eight of the individuals who played integral roles in the history of the Novi have been honored with enshrinement in the prestigious Indianapolis Motor Speedway's Hall of Fame. While Lew Welch is the only conceivable inductee whose racing career was basically centered around the Novi, the remaining honorees also played significant roles with the storied V-8 Novi brute as well as with other racing track activities during their extended and illustrious Indianapolis 500 adventures. The individuals are drivers Cliff Bergere, Ralph Hepburn, Chet Miller, Duke Nalon and Bobby Unser. They are joined by mechanics Jean Marcenac and Ed Winfield. Beyond this, it can be pointed out that in July, 1992, as part of the third annual induction ceremony sponsored by UNOCAL 76 at the International Motorsports Hall of Fame (located at the Talladega Superspeedway), Andy Granatelli was added to the roster of individuals who have played significant roles in the sport of auto racing.

The magical draw of the Novi remains - within the racing fraternity and among the diehard fans. For example in May of 1996, the annual Indianapolis 500 Oldtimers Club banquet honored those living drivers who have sat on the pole, set fast time or established a new track record. For the affair one car was placed on display in the hotel banquet room: the #54 Novi Grooved Piston Special that Duke Nalon placed on the pole in 1949

(1958) This postal card size photo was a popular item with Novi admirers and 500 memorabilia collectors. Paul Russo drove the car to an 18th place finish. Directly behind Russo in the t-shirt is the well-known Novi mechanic Radio Gardner.   *Courtesy of Richard Smith*

following his setting of fast time for the race. Nalon captured the pole again in 1951 driving a Novi.

In retrospect, the removal of the Granatelli wrecked car on the last day of qualifications in 1966 ended the big brute's racing career. The powerful V-8 entered Gasoline Alley not under power or a tractor push, but on the hook of a tow truck. Yet the Novi was not officially shelved until the turbine proved workable, but its last track showing had been made. Further, Bobby Unser's STP Gas Treatment Novi coasting into the pits after 69 laps of the 1965 Indianapolis 500 marked what was to be a Novi's last racing appearence at the Speedway.

Irregardless, the Novi Legend continues.

(1996) The Indianapolis 500 Oldtimers Club and the Indianapolis Motor Speedway saluted those drivers who started the race from the pole, set one and/or four lap qualifying records or established the fastest qualifying run for any given year. On hand were the following drivers: (left to right) Duke Nalon, Gary Bettenhausen, Scott Brayton, Rodger Ward, Johnny Rutherford, Parnelli Jones, Arie Luyendyk and Len Sutton. The car selected to appear with the drivers was the famed #54 Novi Duke placed on the pole in 1949.
I.M.S.

Chapter 29

THE AFTERMATH

The year 1966 was pivotal for both the Novi undertaking and for the Studebaker Corporation as both came close to an end that year. In the fall of the year, the Studebaker plant in Canada was closed, thus bringing to an end 114 years of continuous operation by the once proud Indiana born company. As noted earlier, the year also marked the last appearance of a Novi at the Speedway in a racing capacity.

There was word that fall that Jim Hurtubise was going to create a new Novi in conjunction with the Granatellis, but as noted, the project failed to materialize. The Granatellis chose to move on with their turbine project and entered the 1967 race with such a creation. The Novi was then to move into the pages of racing history.

While Studebaker had folded, its subsidiaries continued to function under new ownership. Some divisions were retained by the Worthington Corporation and under the reorganization plan the company name was changed to Worthington-Studebaker. This permitted the proud use of the familiar Studebaker name. As for Worthington, previously it had been involved in the manufacture of scales of all types.

The Paxton production unit was repurchased by the Granatellis as the Studebaker Company began relinquishing its subsidiaries. They continued to produce the blowers at the Santa Monica plant. Several years ago the Paxton operation was moved out of Santa Monica to Camarillo, California. In the latter part of 1995, the company announced the production of its latest model blower - the Novi 2000. The centrifugal blower was reported to provide 27 pounds of boost level.

In 1968, STP went public and the following year shares were listed on the America Stock Exchange under the symbol, "STP."

After their prolonged, six year struggle with the Novis followed by two heartbreaking years with their turbine powered cars, the Granatelli dream was finally realized. Mario Andretti drove an STP Special to victory in the Indianapolis 500 mile race in 1969. After wrecking the primary car (a 4WD Lotus-Ford Turbo),

Mario had to use his backup car. Unfortunately, for Novi followers victory was achieved with a Clint Brawner built Hawk chassis using Ford V-8 power rather than that of a Novi V-8.

In discussing Andy's reaction to the seemingly unattainable victory, Andretti reports that while the world thought an emotional Granatelli was merely giving him a kiss on the cheek, it was more involved than that. Making reference to Andy's being a "deal maker," Mario said that Andy had informed him that if he could pull off an Indy 500 win or capture the national championship the agreed upon driving fee would be doubled. Mario stated that when he pulled into Victory Lane Andy uttered an `expletive' into his ear (Indy Car Racing, January, 1995).

Four years later (1973), a second triumph was achieved as Gordon Johncock won the 500 in the STP Double Oil Filter Special Offy turbo powered Eagle. The car was owned by Pat Patrick. While the victory was another feather in the cap for STP, it was bittersweet at best. The race was halted on lap 133 after intermittent rains had dragged on the event for three days before being declared official. The race was to claim the life of STP driver David "Swede" Savage as well as an STP crew member who was struck by a support vehicle as he dashed toward the accident scene in turn four.

The year was to be less than one of great achievements for Andy Granatelli as it was announced on October 12, that he would part company with STP as of March 26, 1974. The board of directors controlled 55 percent of the stock and voted to replace Granatelli as board chairman. Yet, he was retained as a consultant for a short time. For his part Granatelli said, "I chose to step down in order to maintain my self-respect. There were policy differences with the board which I refused to accept." One newspaper account stated, "One of the known reasons for his ouster was the lower earnings for the last nine months of the year as compared to last year and declining stock prices." The market price had been reduced approximately 50 percent during that period. STP had closed at eight points on Friday, October 12. During the last year it had been as high as 18 7/8.

Granatelli's departure notwithstanding, STP's sales rebounded and climbed steadily over the years. It has become a standard staple throughout the years as customers can purchase the oil treatment as well as many other STP products at outlets across the land. Sales have extended beyond America's shores reaching into Europe, South America, Australia, etc. Items now sold by STP include not only the standard oil treament product but what appears to be an entire automotive inventory of additives. The list would include Fuel Injector and Carburetor Cleaner, Super Concentrate Gas Treatment, Octane Boost, Intake Valve Cleaner, Power Steering Fluid, Transmission Fluid, a Vinyl Protector (Son of a Gun), oil filters, air filters, AP-75 Multi-Purpose Lubricant, etc.

The company continues to support racing in many forms. This includes Indy type racing, stock cars, midgets, late models, motorcycles, dragsters, etc. You name it and STP most likely plays some sort of sponsorship role. The company's involvement in racing can be matched by only a few other corporations, such as Valvoline, Pennzoil and UNOCAL. (In the early years of support, it was the Pure Oil Company, later replaced by UNOCAL in a takeover.) The STP involvement has extended over four decades and its contingency program has been known to honor over 25 champions in a single racing season.

During its 40 plus years of operation, STP has been associated with countless drivers. Indy car drivers would include Mario Andretti, Michael Andretti, Jim Clark, Wally Dallenbach, Roberto Guerrero, Gordon Johncock, Tom Sneva, Danny Sullivan, Jim Hurtubise, Joe Leonard, Graham Hill, Art Pollard, Al Unser, Sr., Bobby Unser, Art Malone and Jimmy Vasser. NASCAR drivers would include Freddie Lorenzen, Buddy Baker, Bobby Hamilton, John Andretti, Kyle Petty, Richard Petty and Wally Dallenbach, Jr.

STP's support of the Indianapolis 500 continues to the present. For the 1997 race the company provided associate sponsorship to the #2 Glidden/Menards Special driven by sophomore sensation Tony Stewart. The Indiana driver was in contention for a 500 victory until the John Menard car brushed the wall with only a few laps remaining. Yet, Stewart continued and completed the 200 laps for a strong 5th place finish.

The NASCAR driver list is much shorter for as many fans are well aware, Richard Petty carried the STP banner for much of his illustrious and phenomenal racing career. After one year with the Daytona based sanctioning body, sponsoring the car driven by Freddie Lorenzen, STP joined forces with Petty. In 1972, he won the Daytona 500 with STP sponsorship in their first year together.

Richard Petty recalls that the sponsorship came about in some measure as a result of Chrysler's withdrawal from stock car sponsorship. This decision left Petty without a substantial sponsor. Knowing that STP had been quite active at Indy for some years, Petty stopped at STP headquarters (then located in suburban Chicago), as the North Carolinian speedster was on his way to NASCAR's season opener at Riverside, California. He wished to "talk with Granatelli and STP about sponsoring our car and we worked up a sponsorship." That association has lasted longer than any other major automotive team-sponsorship. The tie-in between STP and Petty is such a natural as it has worked out so well for both parties. Richard's charismatic charm and tremendous racing skills translated into vast media coverage - print, photo and via television. Petty Racing Enterprise celebrated its 25th year with STP in 1996. The celebration includes current driver Bobby Hamilton piloting the #43 car painted silver in three races during the season: the Daytona 500, the Brickyard 400 in

(1961) The Novi Special housed at the International Motorsports Hall of Fame Museum in Talladega, Alabama was transported to Birmingham for the Third Annual Induction Ceremony. The dorsal finned car last competed at the Speedway in 1963.
Authors Collection

Indianapolis and the season finale at the Atlanta track. At other NASCAR contests on the schedule, the Nashville, Tennessee, driver drove an STP car carrying the company's traditional colors of red, white and blue.

The cover of Dr. John Craft's volume, <u>Vintage and Historic Stock Cars</u>, carries a colored photo of a quickly recognizable Richard Petty #43 STP car. The STP history and logo hold such a famous spot in auto racing it is little wonder that such a picture selection & placement occurred.

Over the years, STP has been owned and operated by several corporations. They include Beatrice, Esmark and Union Carbide Corporation. Union acquired STP in 1985 and the following year the automotive branch was acquired by First Brands of Danbury, Connecticut. Twelve years later, STP remains a viable part of the corporation's overall business functions. In addition to the various STP products, the corporation has also sold items such as Simoniz, Prestone, Glad Bags, Jonny Cat Litter and trash can liners.

Another Studebaker connection to the Speedway occurred in 1981 when the stock block Studebaker Cliff Bergere drove to an impressive 3rd place in the 1932 race was added to the Indianapolis Motor Speedway's museum. Museum director, Jack Martin, accepted delivery of the attractive vintage car from Ralph Salvino, director of STP's motorsports program.

Recognition of STP's long standing commitment to the sport was underscored by the use of the STP logo on the pit badge used by the Speedway in 1978.

Another form of Novi recognition, even though it represents only a portion of Andy Granatelli's extensive racing career, came in 1992 when he was inducted into the International Motorsports Hall of Fame. Other inductees that year included Alberto Ascari, Louis Chevrolet, Louie Meyer, Wally Parks, Eddie Rickenbacker, Curtis Turner and Rodger Ward.

Driver Gary Bettenhausen has been quoted as saying that the STP connection with racing "has been a long and auspicious marriage and racing has been a primary beneficiary."

In retrospect, one wonders what the situation with STP might have been in regard to auto racing if it had lacked the "shot in the arm" from the much revered Novi racing program. Where would STP be without the Novi and vise versa?

The company has most certainly come along in splendid fashion since its creation in a back alley garage in St. Joseph, Missouri. The STP saga is a fine example of what ingenuity, hard work, dedication and a first class commitment can do in this country. While the early STP operation is now just a memory, the undertaking has every right to display its familiar logo on billboards, banners, or speeding race cars.

(1962) Among the group of racing luminaries inducted into the International Motorsports Hall of Fame that year was Andy Granatelli. He is seen here with co-author George Peters.
Authors Collection

Chapter 30

Commentaries and Memories

With the willingness of countless people stepping forward to reminisce with respect to their Novi memories we felt that the readers of this volume might well enjoy some of the edited accounts.

Robert Steele,
Denton, TX
"As a boy I watched and listened for Jim Hurtubise and Bobby Unser and others in the Novis at the Speedway. Everyday they woke me from my sleep with joy."

Larry Wright,
Evansville, IN
"I was ten years old when I attended my first auto race. It was the first reborn 500 mile race at Indianapolis (1946) and I had never been at an auto race, so I had no prior experience to draw on. My initial excitement in seeing a field of racing cars pass in front of us, as I stood at the infield fence between turns one and two, was quickly heightened by a thunderous roar that preceded a flash of blue passing by. It was as if some force or energy was being unleased upon the Speedway that far exceed any other presence. Soon I recognized the long, low slung blue racer as the "Novi Governor Special" driven by Ralph Hepburn. The Novi thunder would certainly win the heart of a sightless person! In addition I have been grateful all of my 48 years since that day in May 1946 that as a 10 year old lad I heard that thunder and saw the speed of the Novi. I am appreciative that I lived during all the Novi years, even though the years of frustration of their failures were bitter."

George Moore, writer
<u>Indianapolis Star</u>
"When this blown mount had its tail twisted it begins providing horsepower... something like the national debt."

Wilbur Shaw, President of
Indianapolis Motor Speedway
in a 1947 correspondence to a friend.
"We will expect a real showing with those two perfectly wonderful automobiles (Novis)."

<u>National Speed Sport News</u>,
May 11, 1994
"While it never won the 500, the high-pitched, supercharged Novi screamer was so fast, so powerful and so dangerous it drew fans to Indianapolis by the truck load. Speedway records reveal attendance zoomed whenever the 2 ton car was scheduled to qualify."

Anonymous Speedway Resident,
"When they started the Novi it shook the walls and knocked the pictures around on the wall. We left the pictures lopsided for the month as long as the Novis were still in action."

Bessie Lee Paoli,
Indy car owner
"It was always a thrill to see them run. I wanted to be there whenever they ran."

Robert Boyer,
Bloomington, IN
"When a friend took me to the track on the first qualification day of 1951 I was already quite familiar with the Novis and they were my favorites. It was quite a thrill to see Duke Nalon drive one of them to a new track record that day. I also attended the race that year and the following year. I was serving in the military during 1953 and 1954 and didn't get to visit the track those years, but I've been at the track every year from 1955 on."

Steve Longmire,
Naperville, IL

"My uncle got tickets to the race every year and in 1958 called my mother in Peoria, Illinois, to see if I would be interested in going to the race. I was on the next bus to Indy. He told me about the Novi and I thought it sounded really cool. I was not prepared to say the least. That race car was the most awesome looking and sounding car I had ever seen. I'll never forget it."

(1995) Sharing memories at the Speedway are two former Granatelli drivers, Ralph Liguori and Danny Kladis along with fellow Indy veteran Ernie McCoy.   *Authors Collection*

Cowboy O'Rourke,
Race driver

"Without a doubt it was the most spectacular car that ever competed at the Speedway. When Duke buckled up the collar on his beautiful coveralls and strapped on his helmet (as he prepared to take a Novi out) the crowd would scream in delight. Or when a Novi was pushed out from the garages, with Duke walking behind it the fans would go wild."

Bob Estes,
Indy car owner

"The strongest memory I have of the Novi was the year Tony Bettenhausen drove one at Monza, Italy. With the speed he ran, other European teams did not want to have anything to do with the race. Only the Jags were willing to stay."

Inscription on placard placed in front of the #59 STP-Tombstone Life Special that ran in 1965 - IMS

"The scream of the super Novi engine is considered one of the great classic sounds in auto racing history. The engine, far ahead of its time, produced over 700 horsepower when competitive engines of that day were barely topping 400 horsepower."

Bob Veith,
Indy race driver (1956-1968)

"They were something else...(they) could shatter your ear drums...you had to get away from behind them with all that racket. When the Novi drivers stood on the gas they could spin their wheels in the middle of the backstretch."

Gary Valente,
Cleveland, OH

"I was lucky enough to have seen the Novis run during the early 1960s and I still get goosebumps when I remember its scream."

(1996) Pictured in a suite at the Indianapolis Motor Speedway are (left to right) Ralph Salvino, Duke Nalon and Bob Falcon. Ralph served as Director of Racing at STP for many years beginning with the "Granatelli era." His work involved not only champ cars, but stock cars and other venues as well. Duke, without question, was the most famous of the Novi pilots. Bob served as a tech rep for Ted Halibrand's operation at the Speedway for years.
Authors Collection

Tom Savage,
Auto racing writer

"My most vivid memory of my boyhood days at the Speedway was the sound and sight of the powerful Novi. Sitting in grandstand H you had a clear view of the front chute and the fourth turn. The rest of the course was out of vision. When

Duke Nalon had the Novi on the track, you didn't have to see it, you could hear it! He would punch the throttle on the big brute just off the second turn and heading down the incredible long back chute. The noise generated by the powerful supercharged V-8 would build and build as he raced toward the third turn. It sounded like 1,000 sirens wailing as we listened but could not see it. The car would come into view between the third and fourth turns on the short chute. The screaming of that engine would bring tears to your eyes, build goosebumps on your arms and make the hair on the back of your neck come to attention. That was almost 40 years ago but I can still remember the sound of that Novi cranking up on the back chute. The ungodly scream of the Novi that sounded like 10,000 tornado sirens ignited at the same time."

Jep Cadou,
National Speed Sport News
September 25, 1985
"The monster man could harness, but never really tame the ill-fated machines which were all-time fans' favorites at Indianapolis."

Louie Meyer,
Three time Indy winner
"Tremendous crowd pleasers."

Pat Flaherty,
1956 Indianapolis 500 winner
"The Novi was too big, it was too heavy." Pat also stated that Andy offered him all kinds of money to drive a Novi in hopes of being the first to crack the 150 m.p.h. barrier. Flaherty's retort was, "I wouldn't drive it for twice" the offered amount.

Auto Week,
March 3, 1983
"This unforgettable noise and power were to make the Novis the most popular cars on the track for two decades."

Indianapolis Motor
Speedway Race Program
The 1991 official Indianapolis 500 program carried a feature providing a flashback of the track's first 75 years. In a caption used with the 1967 turbine the narration declared that: "If not the most popular ever (that would undoubtedly be the Novi)..."

Troy Ruttman,
1952 Indy winner
"Driving an old car - a pre-war job my first year at the Speedway (1949), a Novi roared by me like I wasn't even there."

Paul Russo,
Novi driver
(written on an autographed 1956 qualifying picture)
"Thanks for the greatest ride in my life to Jean Marcenac."

Bob Harkey,
Indy race driver (1964-1976)
"As I was working to adjust to the Speedway and my rookie test, I came down the front straightaway. Without any warning Jim Hurtubise passed me and the roar of that Novi engine all but had me jumping out of my skin."

Russ Stone,
Cincinnati, OH
"It was a great car driven by many great drivers. I wish I had made a tape of that engine at full song! I have never heard anything like it, or felt it so deep in my chest."

Michael Garabedian,
Novi/STP crew member
"I began working with the Novi crew in 1965 when I was only 20 years old. Dad (Wally) had been with the Granatellis for several years. I well remember that in the 1965 race Herk went out early - after only 1 lap to finish last.
Andy called Wally cousin and others picked up on the name. The Granatellis treated Dad great. Every time I see Andy, which is about once a year, I make sure to thank him for the treatment given my Dad.
The Novi crew had rooms on the top floor of the Speedway Motel. After a hard day at the track the crew would board an old bus Andy had and we would ride to a nearby MCL cafeteria for dinner."

Another source recalls how Andy would always bring up the rear, paying the dinner bill for the entire crew.

After Volume I was published we received correspondence from Bob "Buck" Rogers who resided in Oklahoma. Mr. Rogers informed us that he had served on the Novi team during several of the Granatelli years. As a result he proved to be a valuable first-hand source of information. Additionally, of his own volition Bob penned the following memories; (slightly edited here) detailing some of his experiences and feelings regarding the Novi project. It is our hope that you will find this material as interesting as we have. Unfortunately, Bob passed away in January, 1996 prior to the final draft of this volume. Buck's letter follows:

"The first time I heard about the Novi was in 1941 when I read about it in the National Speed Sport News. My brother use to receive it each week in Canada. I started reading it because he had a lot of buddies who he raced against back in the 1930s and then I got into car racing. I lived in Calgary in the early 1950s and with a group of buddies we would sit around talking racing. The discussion included the Novi. We were always wondering what it consisted of though we knew it was supercharged. So I go back a number of years and I'm still a lover of the Novi, always was.

Of all the cars running at the Speedway in the 1950s the Novi was the magic name. You could talk about 32 other cars making the race and they would always mention if a Novi made it. If you stop and look it was amazing. I know there was a diesel and a Maserati but the name Novi was a magic name with me.

In 1961, I went to work for the Granatellis. They had their work ethics and you did as you were told and you'd get along. When you first start working there they would go through your toolbox and throw away any tool that was chipped or had the chrome peeling off. A lot of guys quit on the spot when they would do that.

I'll admit that they use to kind of let me get away with a lot more than other people. Andy use to borrow my little pocket screwdrivers all the time and never return them. I use to get on him about that all the time. Then one day he walked up to me and gave me one of those big 3 ft. screwdrivers in return. They also gave me a roll-away Snap-On toolbox that went to the mechanics putting cars on the front row as we did in 1963.

Even today none of the V-8s make an exhaust noise like the Novi. It was like a bunch of banshees going down the backstretch. In 1963 we did some tire testing at the Speedway. Parnelli was there in his #98. We had the Novi and Andy ran the Studebaker Avanti as well. I look back now and wish I had had a tape recorder. Parnelli got into the Novi and took a couple of laps. If you look at it, and think about it, there we were, two cars at the Speedway in August on a calm day with no other cars present. To hear that Novi going down the backstretch running about 180 and coming by the grandstands it was kinda eerie. We use to swear that it rattled the rafters in the main grandstand. I just never heard anything like it. The Novis were not lucky cars, but when you take 31 or 32 other cars and they only allow a 33 car field your odds really drop.

Having read about the Novi my dream was to drive one in a race. Well, I got older and I got banged up a bit and I gave up driving. I thought the next best thing would be to work on the Novis at the Speedway and I did that.

In 1961, I learned that Andy had bought the Novis and that he was going to have one at the Speedway. I moved down there (Indianapolis) in April. I worked at a Buick garage and on the weekends I worked part-time for sprint car driver Elmer George. When Indy practice started I spent a lot of days out at the track having decided I was going to work on the Novi. I knew Andy and Joe from the early 1950s because I had bought a couple of heads from them when I was racing up in Canada. I didn't know if they would remember me or not, because that was a long time ago and racing in Canada was not that popular. Anyway, I introduced myself and met some of the crew. Andy told me they were here for practice and if I wanted a job I could have one if I moved to Santa Monica, California.

In August with my wife Lois, we moved to Los Angeles where I worked for another Buick garage and pestered Andy about getting a job. Finally, Joe called and said I could start the next Monday morning. At the time the Granatellis were working on the Paxton blower. They made some changes and really improved it. Then along came the Avanti. I built a lot of those engines. In fact, one of my engines broke a lot of records up on the Bonneville Salt Bed. But that's another story. When we returned from Utah the team started working on two new chassis that Andy had bought from Frank Kurtis. In May we went back with the two new cars and we had Bill Cheesbourg and Chuck Stevenson as our drivers. We had some handling problems and I don't know what else. I do know that in the closing minutes of qualifying on the last day Cheesbourg was in line when the gun went off. There was a rookie in front of us and Andy had run up and was going to pay him off if he would take just one lap and pull in, but he went the full four laps. I think we did screw up on the lateness of the day, but that's just my opinion.

223

While we didn't make the race we stayed to watch it. Andy gave my wife a ticket on the backstretch while the rest of us viewed the race from wherever we could.

Shown are Barbara Peters (whose work on the Novi study warrants her co-authorship if she would only agree) and the late Bob "Buck" Rogers and his wife Lois. Buck, who worked as a Novi crew member, offered considerable help and encouragement that was most appreciated.   *Authors Collection*

These are my own thoughts of working for the Granatelli brothers. There have been many stories and rumors about them and I have my own thoughts and opinions. When I started with them I was told about how they fought, called each other names and that they were called the Katzenjammer Kids. Some people looked down on them as not the best, but it never really bothered me. I never even thought about it.

You know in 1963 if you take a look at the pictures of the qualified Novis with driver and crew you will see that the same crew was on every one of the cars. Back then you worked night and day when you worked for the Granatellis. We use to say that if anybody ever invented the 25 hour day it was going to be Andy. I had no complaints on the work hours or anything like that.

When we were at Indy we use to eat a lot of White Castle hamburgers. Our crew called them "slippery bombers." You use to get 10 hamburgers for a buck. Then Andy brought in a refrigerator and we would have sandwiches. Once in a while the entire crew would go out and eat. I remember the first year and a half working at Paxton Products, the Granatellis' home base in Santa Monica. There was a restaurant, The Pigeon, down the street about 3 blocks. We worked long hours, 7 days a week, and we'd get pretty hungry. Andy use to let us go down and eat at the restaurant. We could have anything we wanted. Then on one occasion one of the fellows decided he would take his entire family in to eat and he must have had 10 or 11 people that Sunday. They all ate steaks and what ever, the guy signed his name to the check just like always. About a week and a half later Andy called a meeting and canceled any future company paid for meals at the restaurant. We lost eating there and I understood why.

For the 1963 race we'd planned on taking back the two year old Kurtis. Then we got ahead of schedule and they decided they would also take back the old #75 which was 8 years old. I really liked that old car with its big fin on the back. Joe put me in charge of rebuilding it. I felt like it was my car. We didn't have a driver yet. We qualified all 3 cars that year, one of them being the old #75 or as we called it "Tired Iron." That was something to be really proud of.

Let me close with several personal thoughts. I had stuttered all my life-the Granatellis must have liked me or I would not have been there. We use to have talks and Vince told me they were going to cure my stuttering. I thought it odd that they would take that sort of interest in me. After about three years I was almost cured. I have the Granatellis and my wife to thank for that.

I quit a couple of times. Once I quit and moved up to Minneapolis. In February, Andy called me and asked what it would take to get me back. I told him and he said he would let me know. Two days later I received a letter and a bunch of credit cards. The Granatellis had informed me to call the movers and to start packing up. We didn't even load up, we just packed up what we needed and the movers loaded the remainder of our belongings. The moving expenses were paid from the Santa Monica office.

Another time we were going to the Speedway and Lois was pregnant. Andy called me in and said why don't you send your wife back home for the delivery and I said I didn't have the money. He said to go ahead and do it and he would be good for the hospital bill, the plane fare and all that. I was really shocked. My wife gave Andy a big hug and a kiss and he told her that was the most expensive kiss he had ever gotten."

Bob "Buck" Rogers
Crew member on Granatelli-Novi team

Smokey Yunick,
Race car builder and owner
Indy cars and NASCAR

"The Novi was the greatest thing here. Too bad they never made it work here. That mechanic that worked on that machine all those years (Jean Marcenac) never got 1/10th the credit he should have. What I saw was that nobody on the team knew anything about handling. Everybody was an engine man. Bud Winfield was as good an engine man as there was as I remember. I was impressed with Marcenac for that day and time. But as impressive as it was it (the Novi) never came close to winning. It hit a place where it almost made Broadway. Mickey Thompson almost had the car first. If Thompson had got the Novi he'd probably have taken off and cleared this tower or something (laughing).

Returning to Marcenac, Yunick said, "He didn't have any paid help, just a bunch of stooges. He didn't go to a hotel. He slept in Gasoline Alley on a cot. I guess around 2-3 o'clock I would go by and he was still working. I'd go in and say are you ever going to bed and he would just be mumbling and talking to himself - 'I've got to finish this up' or 'I've got a little problem here.' He'd put that lock on the inside so that you couldn't get in and he would just go to sleep. He'd only be down 2-3 hours and he would be up again. I'd go over to the hotel or wherever we were staying about 3 in the morning and come back at 7. Marcenac was working when I left and he was still working when I got back. I'd say are you going to eat and he'd reply I'll go over there and get something later, pointing to a nearby food booth.

I know when Russo drove the Novi it would come off four and up there near the end of the pits once in a while you would see a little puff of black smoke and by the time it got to the start-finish line that (expletive) had passed you and both rear tires had lite up. When he busted a tire in the race he came down to where I was standing. I said, 'Do you see that?' If he hadn't busted a wheel he would have lapped this field five times. I was looking right at the car when he hit the wall."

(1966) As part of the 50th annivesary of the Hulman-George family ownership of the Indianapolis Motor Speedway, drivers competing in the 1946 contest were honored. Danny Kladis (center), Granatelli's 1946 driver, was joined in the festivities by former 500 winners Rodger Ward, Johnny Rutherford and Parnelli Jones. With them is co-author George Peters.   Authors Collection

Clarence Cagle,
Superintendent of Grounds, 1946-1977
Indianapolis Motor Speedway

Preceeding one of the early 1950s Indianapolis 500s, Clarence Cagle had a premonition "that someone was in there (inside the track) doing something they shouldn't be. I had seen marks on the blacktop, tire marks where they were accelerating and I couldn't believe what I was seeing. I knew that during the day I wasn't having any of this so this particular night I thought I would go over. As I was walking over in my bathrobe and pajamas Mr. Hulman drives in wanting to know where I'm going. I told him that I had a feeling something irregular was going on in the infield and he said why don't we just go over there together. As soon as we got over into the infield we hear this rev and a car flashes across in front of our headlights because I didn't turn my lights off. Mr. Hulman said 'Do you think that could happen'. I said yes I could because of having seen the tire marks. Thank the Lord we didn't get anybody hurt and it is one we can laugh about today, but at the time it was very serious to me. Since the Granatellis couldn't get out onto the track they were using the infield road (now identified as Hulman Blvd.). The Granatellis knew they were caught and that they had to get the car back to the garage. They wanted to fire it up and return it under power but I wouldn't allow it. They had to push it back."

Cagle considers the Granatellis friends, saying "everytime I see Andy's wife Dolly, I remember how she contacted me one May saying she had an urgent concern. She said to me, `Clarence you are going to cause my husband to have a heart attack'. I looked at her and said, Dolly, I don't want anybody to have a heart attack, but I'm saying to you that I'm going to run things accordingly and if you don't want him to have a heart attack you had better keep him home." Continuing Cagle said, "They were under pressure and they (the Novis) weren't running like he thought they should be running and you know when you live with these people you can walk in to their garages."

Regarding his relationship with the Granatellis, Clarence said, "There was another incident that I remember. It is a good thing that race drivers, when not on the track, act like kids. They seem to get into so much mischief. Andy and his brothers had a deal that rewarded the driver of any car using STP. Each would receive a bicycle. The stated objective being that the drivers could pedal around to get physically fit and still not have to walk. We can get so crowded at Indy in May and they had a shipment of bikes delivered. They had enough bicycles that they were stacked up in front of their garage doors and in the immediate area. I objected to that and they said well what will you do about it. I said just watch me. I had my radio with me and I called for one of my garage trucks. My object was to put them in a compactor but they found room in the garage for them while the truck was coming."

In closing our discussion, Mr. Cagle said, "I use to set my watch by the time they would leave Chicago coming down here because they could outrun every state police car we had in Indiana. Boy, I will tell you they would really come down the road with those Fords using Cadillac engines." There will never be another bunch like the Granatellis and "maybe its good we don't have them, but on the other hand they are still supporting racing and I know a lot of others that aren't."

Jim Wilson,
Indianapolis television sportscaster
Indianapolis, IN
"Andy Granatelli, being interviewed by Tom Carnegie, said that his autobiography, They Call Me Mister 500 was second on the best sellers list to which Carnegie shot back, "Fact or Fiction."

Robin Miller,
Sports writer
Indianapolis Star
"It all started when my dad took me to the Indianapolis Motor Speedway and I watched the Novi lumber down the front straightaway. It was love at first sight - and sound.

Rodger Ward,
1959 and 1962 Indy winner
"In my first year (1951) at Indy I felt comfortable with everything until Duke Nalon went by in that Novi."

Bob Gates,
Author of Hurtubise
"To its owner and thousand of loving fans, the Novi seemed only to bring a mixed bag of joy and tragedy, with the emphasis on tragedy."

Johnny Boyd,
Indy race driver, 1955-1966
Best finish 3rd in 1958
"Bob Christie and I were talking about the Novi just the other day (May, 1996). We mentioned the thrill of listening to those things run. I said to Bob at the time there are two things that are most vivid in my memory as far as the Novis were concerned. First, I would have given ANYTHING to have had a Novi with George Bignotti as my mechanic. We would have probably detuned the engine to the point we would avoid the tremendous amount of horsepower it generated and conserved on rpms. If I didn't win a race with it then I would have been surprised.

George knew how to apply the horsepower to the race track and that's what you need. You can have all the horsepower in the world but if you can't use it - it does you absolutely no good. Unfortunately, I saw the Novi being used as just a horsepower vehicle and not a handling automobile.

The other thing I vividly remember about the Novi occurred in 1956 when I was driving George's newest roadster (the Bowes Seal Fast Special) and I thought I was flying as I caught Bob Sweikert. I was going by him on the front straighaway and I thought I had this race captured because I'm passing everybody. Then I hear this tremendous ROAR and I thought Sweikert had jumped out of gear. I looked over my right shoulder and Paul Russo was going by me in a Novi -I was flat out down toward the end of the front straightaway and I said to myself there was nobody that could get by me in that Bignotti car. Paul went by me giving a little nod and wave. By the time I came out of the second turn he was already halfway down the back straightaway. He didn't give me "the friendly" race driver salute. Old Paul just gave me a little wave. He was a guy that I thought the world of. Those are the two strongest memories I have concerning the Novi. They were a tremendous asset to racing and you know anybody that heard the Novi run at the Indianapolis Motor Speedway wouldn't easily forget them. The crowd knew when the Novi was on the race track and it was a thrill to hear that roar."

Jim McWithey,
Indy driver, 1959-1960
"When the Novi was near you on the track it really gave you a vibration. I'll guarantee that."

Ted Hollingsworth
Speedway, IN

Ted, an astute observer of racing, is well versed on the subject with heavy emphasis on champ car racing. A life-long Hoosier resident, Hollingsworth has been at the I.M.S. for years in one capacity or another. From 1957 through 1963, he served as the Public Relations Director for Bowes Seal Fast Company, an Indianapolis firm that had been heavily inolved in racing as a sponsor since the early 1930s. During Ted's tenure with the firm, he worked with Bowes drivers including Johnny Boyd, A.J. Foyt, Freddie Agabashian, Jud Larson and Bob Veith.

In other capacities, Ted was responsible for bringing Budweiser into Indy racing and he conceived the program that has recognized the fastest rookie each year for over two decades. At present, he is the promoter of the very popular "Thunder in the Dome" midget racing program held at the RCA Dome in Indianapolis every January. With his business acumen, he has had an inside view of Speedway activities. With this insight, Ted's thoughts with regard to the Novi undertaking was shared in an informal conversation. Ted's observations follow:

"Following Chet Miller's fatal accident in a Novi in 1953, the jinx tag was strongly attached to the Novi program. Media members even alluded to the Novi being a death car, although the term did not receive public exposure as such.

I found it difficult to understand the fatal crashes of Ralph Hepburn (1948) and Chet Miller (1953) due to their experience with front drive race cars. Then along comes driver Rex Mays, probably devoid of much if any front drive experience, and he placed a Novi in the front row at Indy (1949), leading the race for some time following the departure of teammate Duke Nalon from the race.

Sitting in the shade of the trees in the first turn was a popular pastime with many drivers and crew members when they were not involved with duties associated with their own cars. I recall more than one driver saying in effect; I have no desire to drive a Novi as I don't believe the damn thing will go 500 miles. Back in those days drivers did not have contracts providing for a base pay of sufficient consequence. If they did not make the show and do reasonably well it would be a light trip to the bank. I feel that some drivers were in the Novi cockpit as they hoped to use it to show that they could handle the rascal. Such would look good on a resume and might well enable them to secure a better, more reliable ride down the road.

With a few exceptions the Novis did not fare all that well. The Novis were like the Buicks entered years later. Like the Buicks, the Novis had very limited success. Other than Al Unser, Sr.'s splendid 3rd place finish driving a Buick in 1992, the GM product enjoyed very little success. What sort of endurance did the Buick possess for all the effort rendered in its behalf over the years?

The 'marriage' between Andy Granatelli and the Novi worked to the advantage of both the individual and STP. In time Granatelli's name and STP became synomous and the arrangement worked well for both parties, at least for a number of years. The Novis may have been in their declining years, yet the timing was right. A year earlier or later may well have produced different results."

With respect to the Granatelli youth moment regarding drivers, Ted offered the following observations:

"The heavy Novis were not conceived for finesse driving and those drivers who could manhandle a car secured the best results, be that as it may. Hurtubise was not a finesse driver, but he frequently got the job done. He would go as fast as he could as long as he could. If the car failed, he would be ready to climb into another ride. He was definitely a flat-out driver. The Novi needed someone who could manhandle or master the car and Herk fit that description.

Another driver in this category was Bobby Marvin. He only knew one way to go, and that was fast. Unfortunately, he did not live long enough to get into 'his' Novi. Death cut short his brief, but very promising career. Marvin was as fearless a driver as I have ever seen. He was on the verge of showing his great sprint car abilities, when he died in a racing crash. Great potential was there, he was young and eager and the last thing on his mind dealt with the possibility of getting hurt. Bobby Unser was made for a car like the Novi. The Unser-Rose crash was a severe blow for Bobby what with the Novi camp possessing the new, lighter 4WD. The potential was terrific."

Ted asserts that,

"At one point Paul Russo was an excellent Novi driver and he could run the wheels off the supercharged V-8 Novi.

Art Malone proved that a straight line drag car racer could adapt to an oval racing configuration."

In referring to the Novi, Ted chuckled as he said, "The driver had to be in charge. My gosh, we're talking about the Novi like it was human."

Hollingsworth acknowledged that race fans are loyal to those products that support racing and that "Andy Granatelli and his associates did a remarkable sales pitch. The company product line not only became well-known, but it sold well. Amazingly well in fact."

Actually, Andy's sales pitch style reminded Ted of a snake oil salesman, while he acknowledged the extraordinary selling power that Andy evoked. "The Novi was an ideal way to introduce STP into racing - and in a big way by the ultimate salesman."

As the conversation was closed with the ever low-key Hollingsworth, he noted a benefit of STP that he had used to his own advantage. Growing weary of squirrels making their way up to his backyard bird feeder, Ted placed some STP on the pole. After the squirrels had made several runs at the pole only to slide down, they would back off and take a good run at the pole. Once again failure and by now befuddlement had overtaken the squirrel. When Ted's wife, Barbara, declared such to be cruel, Ted pointed out that the pole treatment in no way hurt the animals. Barbara's comeback - "It is still cruel." In time, a squirrel guard was placed on the post, but the once pesky squirrels may have already become totally perplexed and in a state of dischantment moved elsewhere.

SOME LASTING PHOTO MEMORIES

"The Feet Have It"

(1951) A most unique photo opportunity we could not overlook, though it only became available after the release of Vol. I. Mechanic Radio Gardner had gone into the cockpit head first during the race after Duke Nalon came into the pits with the #18 Novi Purelube Special. Suspecting a blower problem, the carburetor had been removed in order to check for a broken supercharger shaft. With the blower behind the engine this was the quickest way to check the unit. Duke was out of the race at lap 151 to be awarded 10th place.   Authors Collection

Herk relaxes with his favorite beverage after a brutal race, while his throttle foot is positioned in a container of water as it receives a cooling off.   Authors Collection

"How Times Can Change"

In its first Indy appearance (1941) the Novi is pushed from Gasoline Alley to the pits by a sole mechanic - the ever dutiful Radio Gardner. Driver Ralph Hepburn is seated in the 1935 built Miller-Ford that carried the original Novi powerplant.   Authors Collection

(1964) From a one man job of pushing in 1941 we note that by the 1960s the pit crew membership had dramatically increased as noted in this qualifying shot.   I.M.S.

BIBLIOGRAPHY

BOOKS

Calvin, Jean.
Those Incredible Indy Cars.
New York, New York: Sports
Car Press, 1973.

Clark, Jimmy.
Jimmy Clark at the Wheel.
New York, New York:
Coward & McCann, 1966.

Clymer, Floyd.
Indianapolis 500 Race Official Yearbooks, 1961-1966.
Los Angeles, California:
Floyd Clymer Publications, 1961-1966.

Court, William.
Grand Prix Requiem.
Sommerset, England:
Patrick Stephens Lit.
c/o Haynes Publishing Group, 1994.

Davidson, Donald.
Donald Davidson's Indianapolis 500 Yearbooks, 1974-1975.
Indianapolis, Indiana:
Donald Davidson, 1974-1975.

Dorson, Ron.
Stay Tuned for the Greatest Spectacle in Racing.
Speedway, Indiana:
Carl Hungness Publishing, 1980.

Ferguson, Andrew.
Team Lotus, The Indianapolis Years.
Sparkford, Sommerset, England:
Haynes Publishing, 1996.

Fielden, Greg.
Forty Years of Stock Car Racing,
Vol. II. Surfside Beach, South Carolina:
Galfield Press, 1988.

Flamming, James M.
Chronicle of the American Automobile - Over 100 Years of Auto History.
Lincolnwood, Illinois:
Publications International, Ltd., 1994.

Fox, Charles
The Great Racing Cars and Drivers.
New York, New York:
Grosset and Dunlap, Inc., 1972.

Fox, Jack C.
The Illustrated History of the Indianapolis 500.
Speedway, Indiana:
Carl Hungness Publishing, Fourth Edition, 1994.

Friedman, Dave.
Indianapolis Racing Memories 1961-1969.
Osceola, Wisconsin:
Motorbooks International, 1997.

Frommeyer, Fritz.
"Against All Odds: Studebaker At Indy."
1979 Indianapolis 500 Yearbook.
Speedway, Indiana:
Carl Hungness Publishing, 1979.

Gates, Bob.
Hurtubise.
Marshall, Indiana:
Witness Productions, 1995.

Granatelli, Anthony (Andy).
They Call Me Mister 500.
Washington, D.C:
Henry Regnery Company, 1969.

Hitze, Ed.
The Kurtis - Kraft Story.
Danville, Illinois:
Interstate Publishing, 1974.

Hungness, Carl.
GO, The Bettenhausen Story.
Speedway, Indiana:
Carl Hungness Publishing, 1982.

Huntington, Roger.
Design and Development of the IndyCar.
Tucson, Arizona:
HP Books, 1981.

Jenkins, Ab and Wendell J. Ashton.
The Salt of the Earth, Ab Jenkin's Own Story of Speed.
St. George, Utah:
Dixie College Foundation, 1993.

Kirby, Gordon.
Unser, An American Family Portrait.
Dallas, Texas:
Anlon Press, 1988.

Langworth, Richard M.
Studebaker, 1946-1966, The Classic Postwar Years.
Osceola, Wisconsin:
Motorbooks International, 1993.

Libby, Bill.
Great American Race Drivers.
New York, New York:
Cowles Book Company, Inc., 1970.

Libby, Bill.
PARNELLI, A Story of Auto Racing.
New York, New York:
E.P. Dutton Company, Inc., 1969.

Ludvigsen, Karl.
Mercedes-Benz, Quicksilver Century.
Isle Worth, Middlesex, England:
Transport Bookman Publications, 1995.

Lurmni, Giovanni.
History of the Racing Car: Man and Machine.
New York, New York:
Thomas Y. Crowell Company, 1972.

Neely, William.
Tire Wars, Racing with Goodyear.
Tucson, Arizona:
Aztex Corporation, 1993.

Norquest, C. Lee.
The Fabulous Novi Story,
1963 & Supplements 1964, 1965 and 1966.
Indianapolis, Indiana:
Norquest Enterprises, 1963-1966.

Nye, Doug.
Cooper Cars.
Osprey Publishing, Ltd., 1983.

Nye, Doug.
Theme Lotus 1956-1986.
Motor Racing Publications, 1986.

Pomeroy, Laurance, F.R.S.A., M.S.A.E.
The Grand Prix Car, Vol. II.
London, England:
Motor Racing Publications, Ltd.

Radbruch, Don.
Roaring Roadsters.
Driggs, Idaho:
Tex Smith Publishing, 1994.

Riggs, L. Spencer.
Pace Cars of the Indy 500.
Fort Lauderdale, Florida:
Speed Age, Inc., 1989.

Sakkis, Tony.
Indy Racing Legends.
Osceola, Wisconsin:
Motorbooks International, 1996.

Scalzo, Joe and Bobby Unser.
The Bobby Unser Story.
New York, New York:
Doubleday & Co., Inc., 1979.

Sommers, Dick.
Eddie Called Me Boss.
Indianapolis, Indiana:
Warren Publishing Co., 1979.

Thompson, Mickey and Griffith Borgeson.
Challenger: Mickey Thompson's Own Story of His Life of Speed.
New York, New York:
Signet Books, 1964.

White, Gordon E.
Offenhauser.
Osceola, Wisconsin:
Motorbooks International, 1996.

BIBLIOGRAPHY

NEWSPAPERS

Atlanta Journal	Atlanta, GA
Arizona Republic	Phoenix, AZ
Bedford Times - Mail	Bedford, IN
Chicago Herald American	Chicago, IL
Chicago Tribune	Chicago, IL
Illustrated Speedway News	Brooklyn, NY
Indianapolis News	Indianapolis, IN
Indianapolis Star	Indianapolis, IN
Indianapolis Times	Indianapolis, IN
Los Angeles Herald-Examiner	Los Angeles, CA
National Speed Sport News	Harrisburg, NC
Phoenix Gazette	Phoenix, AZ
St. Louis Post-Dispatch	St. Louis, MO
Santa Barbara News Press	Santa Barbara, CA
Salt Lake City Tribune	Salt Lake City, UT
Santa Monica Evening Outlook	Santa Monica, CA
The Wall Street Journal	New York, NY

BIBLIOGRAPHY

PERIODICALS

The primary periodical sources used were: AUTOCAR, Autosport, Car and Driver, Modern Rod, Motor Trend, Motoring News, OPEN WHEEL and Stock Car Racing.

Biro, Pete.
"Four Wheel Drive: Studebaker STP Special."
Sports Car Graphic (November 1964).

Brown, Arch.
"Classic From South Bend."
Car & Parts (November 1996).

Davidson, Donald.
"The Novi Comes Home to Roost."
Autoweek (May 16, 1983).

Davis, Jr., David E.
"Indianapolis 500."
Car and Driver (August 1964).

Duck, Harvey.
"Racing's Top Sponsor."
Stock Car Racing (March 1996).

Duerksen, Menlo.
"Andy Granatelli."
Car & Parts (August/September/October 1986).

Eggert, Bill.
"Crowd Pleasing Novis Are Back With Old Whine."
Indianapolis 500 Mile Race Year Book (1963).

Ferguson, Andrew.
"Those Lotus Indy Cars."
Historic Racing (October 1994).

Frank, Len.
"1932 Studebaker Indianapolis Special."
Motor Trend (November 1984).

Garnier, Peter.
"Indianapolis 500-Mile Race."
Autocar (June 5, 1964).

Garnier, Peter,
"Peter Garnier's Personal View of the Indy Spectacular."
Autocar (June 19, 1964).

Gibbs, Steve.
"Bakersfield U.S. Drag Championships."
Popular Hot Rodding (June 1963).

Glatch, Thomas.
"Studebaker Saga."
Circle Track (July 1988).

Girdler, Allan.
"The Reign of Frank Kurtis."
Automobile Quarterly, (1972) Vol.11, No.4.

Granatelli, Anthony (Andy).
"Paula Murphy as I See Her."
Auto Racing Magazine (March 1970).

Graton, Jean.
Michel Vaillant Comics.

Grenier, Mildred.
"STP Got In Gear In St. Joseph."
St. Joseph Magazine (October 1977).

Hoyt, Wade.
"The Novi, Indy's Would Be Exploding Star."
Autoweek (March 21, 1983).

Huntington, Roger.
"Full Report Indianapolis 500."
Autocar (June 11, 1965).

Huntington, Roger.
"Indianapolis 500 Racing to Rule..."
Autocar (May 28, 1965).

Huntington, Roger.
"Indy Time Again..."
Autocar (May 22, 1964).

Huntington, Roger.
"They're Not Complaining This Year..."
Autocar (May 25, 1967).

Huntington, Roger.
"Tune Up For Indianapolis."
Autocar (May 25, 1962).

Jordan, Michael.
"The History of 4WD."
Car & Driver (June 1992).

Kerchner, Mike.
"25 Years Racing On The Edge."
National Speed Sport News (February 14, 1996).

Kollins, Michael J.
"The Novi Story: Part 1-7."
Wheels (July 1985).

Lamm, Michael.
"Andy Granatelli: Business As Usual."
Collectible Automobile (April 1996).

McCahill, Tom.
"How To Hop Up Your Car."
Mechanix Illustrated (February 1950).

Martin, Bruce.
"The Greatest Race Of Them All."
Indy Car Racing (January 1995).

Moore, Bob.
"The Wood Brothers at Indy."
American Racing Classics (October 1992,) Vol.1, No.4.

Nehamkin, Lester.
"Hot Ones for Indy."
Popular Hot Rodding, (June 1963).

Newton, Harry.
"The Cooper Scoop."
Car and Track (April 1992).

Nielssen, Eric.
"2750 C.C. - Over 700 B.H.P."
AutoCar (April 17, 1964) Part I, (April 24, 1964) Part II.

Nye, Doug. "
A Power In The Land, The Coventry Climax Story."
Automobile Quarterly, Vol.32, No.2.

Owen, David.
"The Magnificent Failure of the BRM V16".
Automobile Quarterly, (1976), Vol.14, No.4.

Peters, George.
"Brickyard Bomber."
Four Wheeler (June 1986).

Rudeen, Kenneth.
"Close Call For A Jones Boy."
Sports Illustrated (June 10, 1963).

Summar, Donald J.
"The Twyford Four-Wheel-Drive Motor Car."
Automotive History Review (Fall 1981) No.14.

Scalzo, Joe.
"Brothers - Jim and Dick Rathmann."
Circle Track (March 1990) Part I.

Scalzo, Joe.
"Mad Dog."
Circle Track (June 1988).

Scalzo, Joe.
"The Novi."
Circle Track (June 1983).

Springer, Wilson R.
"Fastest Gal On Wheels".
L.A. Herald Examiner (January 5, 1964).

Titus, Jerry.
"Indianapolis 1965, The Year of the Lightweight."
Sports Car Graphic (August 1965).

Weernink, Wim Oude.
"Vierwielaandrijving? Spyker Was De Eerste!"
Autoselect (July 1983).

Waid, Steve.
"Ralph Salvino."
American Racing Classics (1994, Vol. III.).

Quinn, Richard.
"Bold Dollars: The Studebaker Champion Of 1939-1940."
Collectible Automobile (June 1996).
Publications International, LTD.

Whitt Photo Service.
"Novi Poster."
(1984).

The following articles were also consulted. However, authorship was not cited:

"The Sport."
AutoCar (February 26, 1965).

"Indy Novi-Ferguson."
AutoCar (March 27, 1964).

AutoCar (April 24, 1964).

AutoCar (April 28, 1961).

AutoCar (May 28, 1965).

Automotive Industries (May 1967).

"Face to Face: John Cooper."
(Interview with J. Cooper.)
Competition Car (September 1973).

"Indianapolis Make-Ready."
Modern Rod (July 1965).

"Indy Prelude."
Modern Rod (July 1965).

"The Ferguson-Novi: Four Wheel Drive Indianapolis Race Car."
Motoring News (March 26, 1964).

"Fabulous Ferguson First."
Motor Racing (November 1961).

"Hot One for Indy."
Popular Hot Rodding (June 1963).

BIBLIOGRAPHY

RACE PROGRAMS

The Atlanta 250, August 1965

The Atlanta Championship 300, June 26, 1966.

The Indianapolis 500 Mile Race, May 1991.

Jimmy Bryan 150, Phoenix, March 20, 1966.

VIDEOS

Way of a Champion 1964,

A Diary of Courage 1965. Produced by STP with Bill Dredge listed as Technical Adviser.

The Racer's Edge, An Inside View of STP Racing's Greatest Moments - 50 min. 1996

Design for a Winner, The 1963 Indy 500, Indy 500 Video Series, Indianapolis Motor Speedway, 26 min.

APPENDIX A

REGISTRY OF CARS

During the years that the Winfield/Novi V-8 was at Indianapolis, a total of nine cars were built using this engine. The nine cars can be divided into six different types. In the following summary these types and individual cars are cited. This summary and designations are used for correlation for the following APPENDICES and identifications given within this book.

Type 1: Rebuilt 1935 Miller-Ford chassis Reworked for 1941 race to house first Novi Engine.
Chassis number: 1

Type 2: Front drive Kurtis chassis, two cars built, one in 1946 and the second in 1947. Generally known as Front Drive Novis.
Chassis numbers: 2 (1946) and 3 (1947)

Type 3: Rear drive Kurtis-Kraft Roadster chassis, two cars built in 1956. Usually referred to as the Kurtis-Novi 500F.
Chassis numbers: 4 and 5

Type 4: Rear drive Kurtis-Kraft (500K) Roadster chassis, two cars built in 1962.
Chassis numbers: 6 and 7

Type 5: Ferguson built chassis with Ferguson four wheel drive system (4WD), built in 1964. Official registration is Ferguson P104, but generally referred to as the Ferguson-Novi or Novi-Ferguson.
Chassis number: 8

Type 6: Granatelli built chassis with Ferguson four wheel drive system, built in 1965. No special designations given.
Chassis number: 9

Apart from the cars built, there were several other plans for Novi powered cars which did not reach completion for various reasons. To make this overview as complete as possible, these projects are listed in a separate section.

Authors note: The first two chassis listed herein were never raced by the Granatellis. However, they are listed here for purposes of continuity.

APPENDIX B

ENGINE VARIATIONS

The Novi engine, which made its debut in 1941, underwent various modifications over the years. However, the Novi name tag was to remain. Even when the entry forms did not identify them as Novi Specials the public and the press nontheless continued to refer to them as Novis.

In this overview a summary of the major versions of the Novi V-8 will be listed.

Most differences over the years were to be found within the engine.

This list is merely a reference point to provide some insight as to the evolution the V-8 went through over the years. The listed registrations were arbitrarily selected by the authors.

Type 1: The original engine built in 1941 under the 183 c.i. rules.

Type 2: The two engines built in 1947. Their only difference from the original engine dealt with the engines spark plugs. They were slightly inclined in the blocks while the first engine had the plugs mounted in a straight line.

Type 3: The rebuilt engines used in 1948. They were reported to have used several parts from the older engines. They had some minor changes in specifications. The new type registration is given for this reason.

Type 4: The version introduced in 1950 with the new bore and stroke dimensions that made them even more oversquare.

Type 5: The version first used from 1953 when the intercooler was removed.

Type 6: The rebuilt engines used in the rear drive roadsters from 1956 on. The crankcases were redesigned due to the adoptation of a rear drive line.

Type 7: The version used in 1957 with the shorter stroke for the new 171 c.i. maximum capacity rule for blown engines.

Type 8: The version using the dual ignition systems introduced in 1958.

Type 9: The Granatelli reworked engines debuted in 1962 with the new smaller supercharger and several other changes.

Type 10: The reworked engines used from 1963 on with the smaller port cylinder blocks.

Type 11: The 1966 engine using ram injection.

Type 12: The all-magnesium development engine built by the Granatellis.

Type 13: The Roots blown version reportedly developed in 1967.

APPENDIX C

A Summary Of The Cars And Their Careers

A summary of all Novi race results follows. An attempt was made to verify each driver for the various cars. Possibly some names have been overlooked. To the best of our knowledge only one of the first five Novi chassis were a part of the Granatelli portion of the Novi Era.

The abbreviations represent the following:

Year:	Year of action
Car #:	Car number
Driver(s):	Driver(s) who drove the car that year
S/Q:	Starting position/Qualifying time ranking
F/laps:	Race placement/Number of laps completed

CHASSIS 1: 1941 MILLER FORD-WINFIELD V-8

The first car equipped with the Winfield/Novi. The chassis was basically one of the ten 1935 built Miller chassis used in the catastrophic Miller-Ford V-8 stock block project of that year. From 1938 on, one of the cars was owned by Lew Welch and originally raced with an Offy under the hood. Herb Ardinger, Cliff Bergere and Ralph Hepburn finished 6th, 3rd and 29th with it respectively in 1938, 1939 and 1940; Ardinger had relief from Russell Snowberger and Bergere in 1938. During practice, the car was tried out by the legendary Italian driver Tazio Nuvolari. The last two years it carried sponsorship from the Bowes Company of Indianapolis.

In 1941, the first Winfield V-8 was placed within the chassis and entered for that year's 500. Hepburn started 10th with 28th fastest time and finished 4th with the car using a partially blocked throttle. The car was very difficult to drive as a result of too much weight and power for a chassis not suited for an engine with the torque possessed by the Winfield V-8. The chassis still exists. The car, owned by Robert Sutherland of Denver, CO, is not on public display. However, it has appeared at several vintage car shows.

Performance Record

Year	Car#	Name	Driver(s)	S/Q	F/Laps
1938	54	Offenhauser Special	Nuvolari	Practice only	
			Ardinger	14/24	
			Bergere	(Relief)	6/200
			Snowberger	(Relief)	
1939	54	Offenhauser Special	Bergere	10/15	3/199
1940	54	Bowes Seal Fast Special	Bergere	21/9	29/47
1941	54	Bowes Seal Fast Special	Hepburn	10/28	4/200

CHASSIS 2: 1946 KURTIS-NOVI (WINFIELD V-8) FRONT DRIVE

This was the first of the true Novi cars. Designed in late 1945 and early 1946 by Bud Winfield and Leo Goossen. Front drive chassis, built by Frank Kurtis in early 1946. Driven by Ralph Hepburn who set new one and four lap track records on the last day of qualifications. Was easily the fastest car in the race, but retired in latter half of race. In 1947 driven by Cliff Bergere. Bergere again nominated to drive the car in 1948, but left the team after several spins, declaring the car unsafe. Ralph Hepburn took over and was killed while warming up the car to qualify. Could not be repaired in time for that year's race. Rex Mays drove the rebuilt car in 1949, qualified second, but retired after 48 laps. For the next four years it was Chet Miller's car. Miller did not qualify in 1950; was third fastest in 1951 and the fastest with new track records in 1952. Dropped out of the race early on both occasions. In 1953, Miller unofficially broke the 140 m.p.h. barrier, but was killed the day before the first day of qualifications. The car was not repaired, but retired from active duty. The car is now in private ownership and efforts to restore it are underway.

Performance Record

Year	Car#	Name	Driver(s)	S/Q	F/Laps
1946	2	Novi Governor Special	Hepburn	19/1	14/121
1947	18	Novi Governor Mobil Spl.	Bergere	2/4	21/63
1948	12	Novi Grooved Piston Spl.	B. Winfield	Practice only	
			Bergere	Quit after practice	
			Hepburn	Killed in accident	
1949	5	Novi Mobil Special	Mays	2/4	25/48
1950	43	Novi Mobil Special	Miller	DNQ	
1951	32	Novi Purelube Special	Miller	28/3	25/56
1952	21	Novi Pure Oil Special	Miller	27/1	30/41
1953	15	Novi Governor Special	Miller	Killed in accident	

CHASSIS 3: 1947 KURTIS-NOVI (WINFIELD V-8) FRONT DRIVE

The sister car of the older front drive (chassis 2). Built in late 1946 and early 1947. It was identical to the original Kurtis-Novi. Made its first appearance at Indy in 1947. Was originally entered as #22 and was to be driven by Sam Hanks, but as a result of the A.S.P.A.R. strike the ride was eventually qualified by Merril "Doc" Williams. Had been renumbered 54. Both driver and Welch were unhappy, so the car was driven in the race by Herb Ardinger until lap 69 when he was replaced by Cliff Bergere. Car came home 4th. Was entered in 1948 for Chet Miller who left the team to drive another car. Duke Nalon took over the car and finished 3rd after losing a chance of winning the race as a result of a late unscheduled pit stop for fuel.

In 1949, Duke Nalon won the pole position, lead first 23 laps until the famous fiery crash in turn three with a 29th place in the final results. Car extensively rebuilt for 1950 when Nalon again drove the car, but did not qualify for the race. In 1951, Nalon won the pole again after setting track records that were bettered one week later. Chet Miller had driven the car in practice to set it up for Nalon. All sorts of problems prevented the car from doing well in the race. After 151 laps the engine stalled and 10th place was the result.

In 1952, Nalon qualified fourth on Pole Day, but was out of the race after 84 laps with supercharger problems; classified 25th.

In 1953 with Nalon in the car, qualified 26th. Survived terrible trackside temperature until lap 191 when a car in front of him spun causing Nalon to drive into the infield to avoid a crash. Finished 11th.

Was the only Novi entered in 1954. Slowest qualifier on Pole Day as a result of misunderstanding between driver Duke Nalon and team owner to abort the attempt and was eventually bumped from the field. Entered one last time in 1955 with Troy Ruttman and Paul Russo taking turns in the cockpit. Duke Nalon and Marshall Teague also drove car during some testing. Car did not qualify as gearbox broke beyond repair during qualifying attempt. Car was then retired from racing. Restored for exhibition duties and presented to the Indianapolis Motor Speedway Museum by Lew Welch in the late 1950s. Remains on display there. Is not in running condition as it lacks a Novi engine.

Performance Record

Year	Car#	Name	Driver(s)	S/Q	F/Laps
1947	22	Novi Governor Special	Hanks	Assigned driver but left team over misunderstanding	
	54*	Novi Governor Special	Jackson	Practice only	
			B.Winfield	Practice only	
			Williams	4/19	DNS
			Ardinger	Relieved by	
			Bergere		4/200
1948	54	Novi Grooved Piston Special	Miller	Practice only	
			Nalon	11/1	3/200
1949	54	Novi Mobil Special	Nalon	1/1	29/23
1950	38	Novi Mobil Special	Nalon	DNQ	
1951	18	Novi Purelube Special	Miller	Practice only	
			Nalon	1/2	10/151
1952	36	Novi Pure Oil Special	Nalon	4/8	25/84
1953	9	Novi Governor Special	Nalon	26/30	11/191
1954	8	Novi Special	Nalon	DNQ/44	Bumped
1955	18	Novi Automotive Air Conditioner	Ruttman	DNQ	
			P.Russo	Practice only	
			Nalon	Practice only	
			Teague	Practice only	

*Car originally entered as #22, later renumbered 54.

Chassis 4: 1956 Kurtis 500F-Novi

This was the first of two rear wheel drive chassis cars built in the spring of 1956 for car owner Lewis Welch. It was the sixth variant in the line of Kurtis 500 type roadster chassis, and was dubbed 500F. The chassis was specially adapted to accept the heavier and bigger Novi V-8 engine.

Entered for the first time in 1956, it was driven by Paul Russo who broke the 145 m.p.h. barrier with an unofficial track record of over 146 m.p.h. He then qualified on Pole Day with a disappointing 143+ m.p.h. average for eighth spot on his second attempt. Duke Nalon then drove the car during practice for possible relief duty.

Russo made a glorious run to the front during the first ten laps of the race only to crash in turn one when a rear tire blew on his 22nd lap.

Russo was again assigned the car in 1957. He was the fastest qualifier in the field, but he did not have a chance at the pole as he was a third day qualifier. He again lead the race, but eventually finished 4th with a not too healthy engine.

The Kurtis went to Italy for the Monza 500 with Paul Russo again at the wheel. He qualified 7th fastest, but did not start the race due to an engine breakdown.

Russo again was assigned the car in 1958. However, he was involved in the well remembered first lap third turn accident but managed to continue in the race after repairs. He completed 122 laps. After several more pit stops for repairs the car was withdrawn, finishing 18th.

In 1959 and 1960, the car failed to qualify with Paul Russo behind the wheel. Again due to malfunctioning engines.

The car was sold to Andy Granatelli in the spring of 1961 and made an unexpected appearance after heavy rebuilding. No driver was assigned, but some car testing was carried on by Dick Rathmann who unofficially registered the second or third fastest time . Rathmann could not secure a release from his original entry so plans to have Rathmann qualify the car had to be cancelled. Ralph Ligouri was then given a turn at the wheel, but the car crashed with a blown engine. After repairs, Ralph tried again but to no avail. Russ Congdon took over, spun the car but no major damage was incurred. For safety reasons and as a result of a reported lack of experienced drivers the car was withdrawn.

The chassis sat in the garage in 1962 and was never sent out onto the track.

Art Malone was assigned the ride in 1963. He made the field handsomely but was third to retire for the day after 18 laps when the clutch/transmission problem could not be resolved. The eight year old car was then retired from racing action.

The car was stored in the Granatelli shop for a time before being placed on display in Harrah's Automobile Museum in Reno, Nevada. The collection was broken up following Bill Harrah's death. This 1956 Kurtis was then placed in the International Motorsports Hall of Fame Museum located adjacent to the Talladega Superspeedway in Alabama. It retains the 1963 bodywork. The current paint job is very likely one given in 1964 for promotional duties.

Performance Record

Year	Car#	Name	Driver(s)	S/Q	F/Laps
1956	29	Novi Vespa Special	P.Russo	8/1	33/21
1957	54	Novi Automobile Air Conditioner Special	P.Russo	11/1	4/200
1958	15	Novi Automobile Air Conditioner Special	P.Russo	14/17	18/122
1959	38	Novi Diesel Engineering Special	P.Russo	DNQ	
1960	49	Novi Special	P.Russo	DNQ	
1961	75	Paxton Products Supercharged V-8 Special	D.Rathmann R.Liguori P.Russo R.Congdon	Practice only Practice only Practice only Practice only	
1962	75	Hotel Tropicana Special	———	No track appearance	
1963	75	STP Special	A.Malone	23/25	31/18

Monza 500 Performance

Year	Car#	Name	Driver(s)	S/Q	F/Laps
1957	54	Novi Tidewater Oil Getty	P.Russo	7/7	13/DNS

Chassis 5: 1956 Kurtis 500F-Novi

The sister car to chassis 4. Was built at the same time (Spring, 1956) and was identical in specifications during Welch Era. Has been listed behind its sister car as a result of poorer showings.

Was entered for the first time in 1956, intended to be driven by Jimmy Davies. Davies left team after several practice sessions for "personal safety" reasons. Car then test driven by Duke Nalon and Marshall Teague, but eventually assigned to Eddie Russo who was unable to qualify when rain prevented any chance of making the field.

Was assigned to Tony Bettenhausen in 1957, who qualified on the last day. Made an impressive showing, moving to the front before experiencing trouble with the throttle cable which cost so much power lose that the car dropped back through the field to finish 15th.

Bettenhausen was fastest qualifier in Monza 500 that year, establishing a new Monza closed circuit speed record of 176.826 m.p.h. Lead one lap but was first to retire from the starting field.

During 1958 practice, tested by Paul Russo then driven by Juan Manuel Fangio who later declined the ride. Bill Cheesbourg took over and was the only qualifier on the last day of qualifying. Bill came through the first lap tragedy by going through the infield. Was not able to retain top speeds due to slight damage, yet finished 10th going the full distance.

Dempsey Wilson took over in 1959 and 1960, but could not qualify as a result of engine malfunctioning.

This car was reported to be included in the deal when Andy Granatelli purchased the Novi outfit. The car was never to compete again. Vince Granatelli, Andy's son, has said that the car may have been cannibalized for parts. According to Andy Granatelli, the chassis was sold off shortly after he obtained it. No known public appearances by this car since 1960. Present location, if intact, unknown.

Performance Record

Year	Car#	Name	Driver(s)	S/Q	F/Laps
1956	31	Novi Air Conditioner Special	Davies	Practice only	
			Teague	Practice only	
			Nalon	Practice only	
			E.Russo	DNQ	
1957	27	Novi Automobile Air Conditioner	Bettenhausen	22/9	15/195
1958	54	Novi Automobile Air Conditioner	P.Russo	Practice only	
			Sachs	Practice only	
			J.Rathmann	Practice only	
	6		Fangio	Practice only	
			Cheesbourg	33/29	10/200
1959	34	Novi Diesel Engineering Special	Wilson	DNQ	
1960	47	Novi Special	Wilson	DNQ	

Monza 500 Performance

Year	Car#	Name	Driver(s)	S/Q	F/Laps
1957	27	Novi Tidewater Oil Getty	Bettenhausen	1/1	12/45

Chassis 6: 1962 Kurtis 500K-Novi

One of the two chassis built in 1962. As this car had a longer career and achieved better results, it has been assigned the lower chassis number. It was one of the last Kurtis Roadster chassis ever built.

This chassis was delivered in April, 1962. It was entered and driven by Chuck Stevenson, yet all kinds of teething problems prevented a qualifying attempt.

The car was rebuilt and entered in 1963 for Jim Hurtubise. He qualified third fast but was blackflagged in the race after 102 laps for oil spillage. The car made the last leading lap for a Novi when "Herk" lead the field on the first lap.

It was again rebuilt and entered in 1964 for Jim McElreath who left the car when it persistently failed during the first two qualification attempts. With one attempt left, Art Malone took it over and qualified the car for the race. It was not involved in the second lap disaster, but the long pause between the accident and the restart caused the plugs to foul. Malone dropped back but finished 11th and was on lap 194 when the checkered flag was displayed. He had been running with little or no brakes for most of the race.

The car was entered as a backup for 1965. It was driven in practice by Art Malone and Jim Hurtubise who had crashed his own rear engine mount. Hurtubise secured the ride, qualified for 20th position, although he had the 10th fastest time in the field. Yet, he finished dead last when the gearbox broke on the first lap.

The car was taken to Atlanta for tire tests in July. There it set a world record for 1 1/2 mile tracks which was broken during qualifying for the Atlanta 250 mile race. The car was entered in that race. It proved to be the only time that the Novis would race on an American track other than Indy. Hurtubise drove the car to a fourth place finish.

The car was then entered for the June 26, 1966, Atlanta 300 race with Greg Weld driving. He did not qualify due to engine problems. As it turned out this was the last event that a Novi entered, appeared for practice and tried to qualify.

The car was placed in retirement and is occasionally on display in the Indianapolis Motor Speedway Museum. It is painted in the 1965 race colors when Hurtubise was at the wheel. It is not in running condition as it is equipped with a mock-up engine.

Performance Record

Year	Car#	Name	Driver(s)	S/Q	F/Laps
1962	16	Hotel Tropicana Special	Stevenson Hurtubise	DNQ Shakedown laps only on Carburetion Day	
1963	56	Hotel Tropicana Special	Hurtubise	2/3	22/102
1964	3	Studebaker STP Special	McElreath Malone	Practice only 30/25	11/194
1965	59	Chemical Compound Division Studebaker	Malone Hurtubise	Practice only Practice only	
	59	STP Tombstone Life Special	Hurtubise	20/10	33/1*

*Car was renamed and repainted when Hurtubise secured the ride. The qualification came after Herk had experienced an accident in the DVS Tombstone car. The DVS owners and the Granatellis worked out a mutual agreement.

Atlanta Performance

Year	Car#	Name	Driver(s)	S/Q	F/Laps
1965	59	STP Special	Hurtubise	6/6	4/166
1966	59	STP Novi	Weld	DNQ	

Chassis 7: 1962 Kurtis500K-Novi

The sister car to chassis 6. They were virtually identical in specifications.

The car arrived at Indy in 1962 with Bill Cheesbourg as the designated driver. Cheesbourg did not qualify and the car was waiting in the qualifying line on the last day as the track closed.

The car was rebuilt for the 1963 race with rookie Bobby Marvin the designated driver. Marvin was killed in a sprint car accident in April, thus when the car arrived at Indy there was no assigned driver.

Several drivers took the car out for practice: Parnelli Jones, Paul Russo, Eddie Sachs, Cliff Griffith, Bill Cheesbourg and Dempsey Wilson. Evenually, Parnelli's protege, rookie Bobby Unser was assigned the ride. Unser qualified handsomely but crashed on the second lap of the race. The official results list him finishing in last place.

For the 1964 race, the car was rebuilt and Bobby Unser was to drive. However, Bobby then moved into the newer 4WD Ferguson. Jim McElreath, who had been slated to drive the #6 chassis but failed to qualify it, then took this car out to easily qualify. The race was halted due to a second lap inferno. McElreath's car was the last to go through the wreckage but the long pause caused the plugs to foul and the car was retired after 77 laps with ignition failure.

The car was not entered in the 1965 Indy race. However, it was qualified by Bud Tingelstadt for the Atlanta 250 mile race. Tingelstadt started the race but was relieved by Bobby Unser who brought it in for a 14th place finish.

The car was retired from racing and is believed to be privately owned. It has made no known public appearances.

Performance Record

Year	Car#	Name	Driver(s)	S/Q	F/Laps
1962	59	Hotel Tropicana Special	Cheesbourg	DNQ	
			Hurtubise	Demo laps	
1963	6	Hotel Tropicana Special	Hurtubise	Practice only	
			Jones	Practice only	
			Sachs	Practice only	
			Cheesbourg	Practice only	
			Griffith	Practice only	
			P.Russo	Practice only	
			Wilson	Practice only	
			B.Unser	16/12	31/1
1964	28	Studebaker STP Special	B.Unser	Practice only	
			McElreath	26/16	21/77

Atlanta Performance

Year	Car#	Name	Driver(s)	S/Q	F/Laps
1965	6	STP Special	Tingelstad	10/10	Relieved
			B.Unser	Relief	14/160
1966	59	STP Novi	G.Weld	DNQ	

Chassis 8: Ferguson P104-Novi

The only chassis built for the Novi engine outside the United States. It was constructed by the Ferguson Company in England early in 1964. The frame was built out of square tubes. The idea for a car powered by a Novi was credited to Stirling Moss who drove a 4WD Climax powered F 1 Ferguson car (P99) in the early 1960s. In 1963 a P99 was brought to Indy for testing purposes. The results were satisfactory, therefore a Novi powered version, dubbed P104, was ordered.

The car was delivered in March, 1964, and tested at Indy during the month but was slightly damaged by a fire in the garage. It was rebuilt in the Granatellis' Santa Monica work shop and was entered in the race. In early practice sessions it was driven by Duane Carter and Jim McElreath, but the car was assigned to Bobby Unser for the race.

Experiments were carried out on the day prior to Pole Day using sodium filled valves. This endeavor turned out to be a disaster and the car was not ready for qualifications that weekend.

On the second weekend of qualifications, Unser qualified for the 22nd spot although he had the 5th fastest time overall. Unser was impressive on the first lap and the second until the Sachs/McDonald disaster. The car was too severly damaged to continue the race, thus finishing 32nd.

A year later the main backup car for Unser was brought out for duties on Pole Day as Bobby had crashed a newer built 4WD chassis the day before. After a few practice laps, Bobby qualified for 8th spot with the 8th fastest time in the field. This meant that it was the fastest front engine car in the field. Unser drove in the top ten until an oil line split after 69 laps and the car had to be retired. These were the last laps made by a Novi on Race Day at Indianapolis.

It was ultimately retired from active duty. The car was returned to Granatellis's workshop and the driveline was used in the STP turbine car of 1967. The suspension lay-out of the car was copied for the turbine car as well. The remaining parts were later sold to the Novi Motorsport Museum in 1983 and was restored to running condition. This work was completed in March, 1989. The car has the 1965 body-shape, but the rear bumper is now missing. The car now carries promotional decals of companies which supplied parts to accomplish the restoration.

Performance Record

Year	Car#	Name	Driver(s)	S/Q	F/Laps
1964	9	Studebaker STP Special	McElreath	Practice only	
			Carter	Practice only	
			B.Unser	22/5	32/1
1965	9	STP Gasoline Treatment Special	B.Unser	8/8	19/69

Chassis 9: Granatelli (Paxton)-Novi

The last of the Novi powered cars that made it to the Indy track. The chassis was designed by Vince Granatelli and was lighter and a more compact 4WD car then the Ferguson built car.

It was delivered in 1965 and was driven in practice by Bobby Unser. On the day prior to opening qualifications, Bobby could not avoid Ebb Rose's spinning car and the car was damaged too severly to be repaired in time to make any qualification attempt.

When the turbine project had to be postponed for one year, the car was entered in the 1966 race. In the rebuilding process the car underwent some massive changes-the radiator was installed in the rear deck to evaluate a possible improvement in weight distribution.

It was driven by rookie Greg Weld who had some hairy moments in it. The first qualifying attempt averaged 158.5 m.p.h. and as a result was waved off. On the last day of qualifications, Weld crashed the car and the last Novi V-8 powered car left the track on 'the hook'. This ended the active career of the Novis at Indianapolis.

There is some indication to believe that this particular car was also the one that appeared at a test session at Phoenix, Arizona, in March, 1966, and was badly damaged in an accident. Some observers believe that it had been entered for the March 20, Phoenix 150 Miler. In his autobiography They Call Me Mr. 500, Andy simply refers to using "our key car". Presumedly this meant the Granatelli built 4WD rather than the Fergie "truck".

According to Andy Granatelli's son, Vince, this chassis was cannabalized. It has indeed disappeared from public viewing.

Performance Record

Year	Car#	Name	Driver(s)	S/Q	F/Laps
1965	6	STP Oil Treatment Special	B.Unser	Practice only (Wrecked in accident)	
1966	15	STP Oil Treatment Special	Weld	Wrecked in accident while warming up for second qualification attempt	

Chassis 10: Paxton-Pratt and Whitney/Novi

This side-by-side chassis was built in 1966. It was a four wheel drive that was to be powered by a turbine engine, but if that engine was not ready it was to be powered by a Novi V-8. The chassis was damaged during a heat treatment process (performed at another facility), thus it was never completed. However, it must be said that the chance that it would use Novi power must have been remote since the turbine engine was ready.

Chassis 11: Gerhardt-Novi

This was another project which was never finalized. It was to be a rear engine Gerhardt chassis with a Novi engine to be built and raced in 1967. Apart from becoming the first Novi powered car with the engine behind the driver, it was reported to make use of a Roots blower rather than a centrifugal supercharger. There has been no further evidence of such a redesigned engine nor any pictures located of a completed car. An official entry form was filed for the car, but the project was cancelled in favor of the "Silent Sam" #40 turbine. The car never arrived at Indy, but due to the official entry form the chassis is listed.

Performance Record

1967	59	STP Gasoline Treatment Special	— —	Did not arrive

APPENDIX D

NOVI RESULTS THROUGH THE YEARS

The following table chronicles the Novis record year by year. The chassis numbers used (#) are those cited in Appendix A. Other abbreviations are as follows: Q. Av. The qualification speed average for the four qualifying laps. S/Q The starting position in the race and the qualification speed ranking. F/laps indicates the finishing position and the number of laps completed.

Year	Driver(s)	#	Q.Av.	S/Q	F/Laps	Remarks
1941	Hepburn	1	120.656	10/28	4/200	Race average 113.573 mph
1946	Hepburn	2	133.944	19/1	14/121	New 1 & 4 lap track records
1947	Bergere	2	124.957	2/4	21/63	Stalled engine-piston failure
	Williams	3	120.773	/19		Driver withdrew after qualifying Novi Governor Special
	Ardinger			4/		Started, relieved after 69 laps by Bergere
	Bergere				4/200	Race average 113.404 mph
1948	Bergere	2	-	-	-	Withdrew during practice
	Hepburn		-	-	-	Died in practice accident
	Miller	3	-	-	-	Withdrew during practice
	Nalon		131.603	11/1	3/200	Race average 118.034 mph
1949	Mays	2	129.552	2/4	25/48	Stalled engine
	Nalon	3	132.939	1/1	29/23	Crashed in Turn 3 while leading
1950	Miller	2	-	-	-	Failed to qualify
	Nalon	3	-	-	-	Failed to qualify
1951	Miller	2	135.798	28/3	25/56	Ignition failure
	Nalon	3	136.498	1/2	10/151	New 1 & 4 lap track records
1952	Miller	2	139.043	27/1	30/41	New 1 & 4 lap track records
	Nalon	3	136.395	4/8	25/84	Supercharger drive shaft failure
1953	Miller	2	-	-	-	Died in practice accident
	Nalon	3	135.461	26/30	11/191	Spun out to avoid another car
1954	Nalon	3	136.395	NQ/44	-	Too slow, bumped
1955	Ruttman	3	-	-	-	Failed to qualify

Year	Driver(s)	#	Q.Av.	S/Q	F/Laps	Remarks
1956	P. Russo	4	143.546	8/10	33/21	Crashed while leading
	Davies	5	-	-	-	Failed to qualify
	E. Russo	5	-	-	-	Failed to qualify
1957	P. Russo	4	144.817	10/1	4/200	Race average 133.818 mph
	Bettenhausen	5	142.439	22/9	15/195	Flagged
1958	P. Russo	4	142.959	14/17	18/122	Leaking radiator
	Cheesbourg	5	142.546	33/29	10/200	Race average 129.149 mph
1959	P. Russo	4	-	-	-	Failed to qualify
	D. Wilson	5	-	-	-	Failed to qualify
1960	P. Russo	4	-	-	-	Failed to qualify
	D. Wilson	5	-	-	-	Failed to qualify
1961	D. Rathmann	4	-	-	-	Practice only
	Liguori	4	-	-	-	Practice only
	P. Russo	4	-	-	-	Practice only
	R. Congdon	4	-	-	-	Practice only
1962	—	4	-	-	-	No driver assigned
	Stevenson	6	-	-	-	Failed to qualify
	Cheesbourg	7	-	-	-	Failed to qualify
	Hurtubise	7	-	-	-	Practice laps Carburetion Day
1963	Malone	4	148.343	23/25	31/18	Clutch failure
	Hurtubise	6	150.257	2/3	22/101	Blackflagged, oil spillage
	Hurtubise	7	-	-	-	Practice only
	Jones		-	-	-	Practice only
	Sachs		-	-	-	Practice only
	Cheesbourg		-	-	-	Practice only
	Griffith		-	-	-	Practice only
	P. Russo		-	-	-	Practice only
	D. Wilson		-	-	-	Practice only
	B. Unser		149.421	16/12	33/1	Crashed
1964	McElreath	6	-	-	-	Practice only
	Malone	1	52.222	30/25	11/194	Flagged
	B. Unser	7	-	-	-	Practice only
	McElreath		152.381	26/16	21/77	Engine failure
	McElreath	8	-	-	-	Practice only
	D. Carter		-	-	-	Practice only
	B. Unser		156.865	22/5	32/1	Involved in 2nd lap disaster
1965	Malone	6	-	-	-	Practice only
	Hurtubise	6	156.863	20/10	33/1	Broken gearbox
	B. Unser	8	157.567	8/8	16/69	Broken oil line
	B. Unser	9	-	-	-	Wrecked in practice
1966	Weld	9	-	-	-	Wrecked during qualifying

PERFORMANCES OF NOVIS ON OTHER CIRCUITS

MONZA 500 (ITALY)

Year	Driver(s)	#	Q.Av.	S/Q	F/Laps	Remarks
1957	Russo	4	166.801	7/7	13/0	Did not start, mechanical trouble
	Betttenhausen	5	176.826	1/1	12/45	Record for the Italian closed circuit high bank track - 176.826 mph

ATLANTA 250 (1965) AND 300 (1966)

Year	Driver(s)	#	Q.Av.	S/Q	F/Laps	Remarks
1965	Hurtubise	6	161.483	6/6	4/166	
	Tingelstad	7	158.963	10/10	-	Relieved by Unser
	B. Unser	-	-	14/160		
1966	Weld	6	-	-	-	Did not qualify

Note: Qualification averages cited for Monza 500 and Atlanta 250 are for one lap. This came about as these races used a single lap qualification speed.

APPENDIX E

UNFULFILLED NOVI PLANS

Although hard evidence is elusive, these were the only known Novi V-8s that were planned but never built.

I. Early Fifties Novi 4WD: The idea for employing 4WD for a Novi car was made by Bud Winfield. Such a plan ended with Bud's death. Tire wear and wheel spin were a problem despite everything he had tried. The plans were cancelled and it was left to Andy Granatelli to try to tame the massive 4WD Novi horsepower some 14 years later.

II. Early Sixties Cooper-Novi: Impressed by the performances of Jack Brabham in the tiny rear engine Cooper-Climax in 1961, Andy Granatelli talked about the possibilities of a rear engine Novi powered car built by John Cooper. Cooper turned the suggestion down as he felt that even the Offenhauser was too heavy for his chassis. Therefore, the heavier Novi was out of the question.

III. Early Sixties Brabham-Novi: Andy Granatelli wrote in his autobiography that he ordered a rear engine chassis to be built by Jack Brabham for 1962. Brabham agreed, but later changed his mind, dropping all Indy plans. Thus, he did not finish the chassis design. Remarkably, this story was denied by Sir Jack Brabham who informed us that although a proposal had been made by Granateli, this was not in 1961 but later (late 1962 or early 1963) and the deal was never accepted by him. When asked about it, Andy Granatelli also denied any work on this project being carried out. Therefore, Granatelli was to acquire two new Kurtis roadsters.

IV. 1966 Paxton-Novi: The alternative version of the planned STP side-by-side turbine car that was to run in 1966. In the event the turbine would not work the chassis was destined to be powered by a Novi V-8. The chassis was constructed but destroyed during the heat treatment process. It is listed in the overview of built chassis as Chassis 10. The chances that it would have been Novi powered was very remote. The replacement chassis was turbine powered and became the famous 1967 #40 'Silent Sam' STP Special.

V. Gerhardt-Novi: Plans to build a rear engine Novi powered car was made by Andy Granatelli in the '60s. It was never realized as he opted for 4WD cars. After the demise of the roadster, such plans were reconsidered and a strengthened Gerhardt chassis was planned to accept a Novi V-8. The Gerhardt had to be strengthened for the heavier and greater power output of the Novi compared with that of the Ford Quadcams and Offenhausers. As the turbine car project seemed to be more promising, the Gerhardt plan was shelved.

*I*NDEX

A

A.A.A., 27, 49, 93, 172, 176, 185, 188, 194, 204.
Adams Aircraft Special, 139.
Adams, Jack, 139.
Agabashian, Freddie, 32, 157, 175-176, 189, 227.
Agajanian-Bowes Special, 108.
Agajanian-Hurst Special, 125.
Agajanian, J.C., 14, 28, 40-41, 50, 59, 65-67, 70, 177-178, 188-189.
Agajanian Special, 27, 188.
Airheart braking system, 41, 85.
Aix-le-bain, France, 213.
Akron, OH, 96.
Albuquerque, NM, 53, 115.
Auburn, 183.
Alderman, Ford, 125.
Alfa Romeo, 84.
Allentown, PA, 14.
American Can Company, 196.
American Grand Prix, 138.
American Red Ball Special, 96, 145.
American Rubber & Plastics Special, 53.
American Stock Exchange, 217.
American Wallpaper & Paint Company, 192.
Amoco Oil Company, 193.
Anderson, IN, 91.
Anderson Speedway, 91.
Andres, Emil, 170.
Andretti, John, 218.
Andretti, Mario, 118-119, 123-124, 129, 138, 141, 145-146, 151-152, 155-156, 217-218.
Angelopolous, Angelo, 34.
Antique Auto & Race Car Museum, 210.
Apache Airline Special, 100.
Apex Metals, 24.
ARCA, 71.
Architectural Stone Sales, 210.
Arciero, Frank, 123.
Arfons, Art, 120.
Arizona Republic, 136.
Arlington, TX, 73.
Armi, Frank, 9.

Armstrong AT10 shocks, 87.
Army Recruiting Special, 171.
Arnold, Billy, 186-187.
Ascari, Alberto, 18, 189, 219.
Ashland Oil Company, 44.
Aston-Martin Cooper, 57.
Atlanta 250, 128.
Atlanta 300, 146.
Atlanta 500, 130.
Atlanta (GA) International Raceway, 126-129, 137, 146, 157, 219.
Atlantic City, NJ, 184-185, 188.
Auto Blitz, 197.
Autocar, 109, 148.
Autocrat Seatbelt Special, 57, 91.
Autolite plugs, 93.
Autolite Special, 5-6, 10-11, 13-17, 38.
Automotive Industries, 149.
Automotive Quarterly, 129.
Autosport , 72.
Autotron Museum, 81.
Auto Union, 154.
Auto Week, 222.
Avanti, 39, 76, 181-183, 190, 223.
Ayulo, Manuel, 174.

B

Bailey, Chuck, 55.
Bailey, George, 83.
Baja, Mexico, 203.
Baker, Buddy, 130, 218.
Bakersfield, CA, 46.
Banks, Henry, 7.
Bardahl, 178, 193-194.
Bardahl Special, 24-25, 27, 177.
Bardowski, Bud, 171.
Barnum, P.T., 160.
Barringer, George, 80, 83.
Bataan Death March, 171.
Bear Alignment, 35, 56.
Beatrice, 219.
Beccue, Joe, 167.

259

Beckley, Jack, 11, 13, 15.
Bedford, IN, 210.
Belanger, Murrell, 92.
Belanger Special, 12, 92.
Bell Aircraft Company, 139.
Bendix Aircraft engine, 41.
Bendix Company, 41.
Bendix fuel injection, 24, 48, 85, 161, 182.
Bendix Stromberg carb, 166, 187.
Bergere, Cliff, 39, 47, 84, 174, 184, 187-188, 215, 219.
Bettenhausen, Gary, 137, 144, 216, 219.
Bettenhausen, Tony, 5-6, 10-15, 17, 19, 38, 97, 137, 153, 165, 172, 204, 215-216, 221.
Bettenhausen, Val, 15.
Bignotti, George, 7, 78, 118, 226.
Bignotti T53, 82.
"Big Wheel," 209.
Bingham, Chet, 167.
Birmingham, AL, 219.
Birmingham Hill Climb, 82.
Black and Decker, 179.
Blue Crown Special, 38, 153, 175, 209.
Bobby Unser Story, 62-63, 103.
Bonesteel, Steve, 209.
Bonneville Salt Flats, 16, 76, 181-182, 184, 191, 199.
Bosch, 6.
Bosch mag, 5-6, 29.
Boudeman, R.J., 206.
Bowes Seal Fast Special, 14, 18, 38, 65, 145-146, 199, 226-227.
Boyd, Johnny, 34, 65, 107, 123, 140, 226-227.
Brabham, Jack, 13-14, 16-22, 30-32, 39, 57, 69, 72, 90, 113, 140, 215.
Bradenton, FL, 120.
Brady, Diamond Jim, 94.
Brady, Ray, 178.
Branson, Don, 14, 48, 51-52, 58-59, 119, 122.
Brawner, Clint, 14, 19, 120, 155, 217.
Brayton, Scott, 216.
Brickyard, 28, 53, 82, 97, 129, 161, 175, 218.
Brisko, Frank, 82-84.
British Leyand Firm, 78.
British Racing Motors H16, 135, 138, 150.
BRM, 138, 148, 154.
Bromme, Bruce, 174-175.
Bromme chassis, 174.
Bromme, Louis, 174.
Brooke Army Hospital, 119.
Bruhn, Hebert, 194-195.
Bruhn, Robert, 194-195.
Bryan, Jimmy, 27, 136.
Bryan Memorial Race, 136.
Bryant Heating & Cooling Special, 19, 30, 125.

Bugatti, 82.
Buick, 30, 32-34, 38-39, 42-43, 108-109, 185, 223, 227.
Burany, Frank, 165.
Burbank, CA, 209.

C

Cadillac, 92, 167-168, 191.
Cadou, Jep, 222.
Cagle, Clarence, 57, 80, 225-226.
Cahill, Mel, 52.
California Racing Association (CRA), 53-54, 165.
Calgary, Canada, 223.
Camarillo, CA, 217.
Camco Motor Special, 172-173.
Car & Driver, 110.
Carburetion Day, 34-36, 45, 123.
Car Life Magazine, 194.
Carnegie, Tom, 50, 55, 226.
Carter, Duane, 47, 57, 69, 92-93, 165.
Central Excavating Special, 128.
Chalik, John, 54.
Challenger: MT, 30.
Challenger Wheel Drive Special, 122.
Champion Spark Plug Company, 93, 188, 199.
Championship Trail, 27, 52.
Chapman, Colin, 42-43, 58, 65, 71, 92, 108, 130, 138, 144, 150, 207.
Chapman Special, 12, 26, 57, 126.
Charlotte Motor Speedway, 71.
Charlotte, NC, 46.
Cheesbourg, Bill, 13, 18, 27-30, 32-36, 40, 100, 105, 109, 123, 139, 223.
Chemical Compound Corp., 182-183, 192, 196, 201-202.
Chemical Compounds Division, 44, 189-190.
Chemical Compounds Special, 116.
Chevrolet, 17, 32, 42, 44, 47, 53, 69, 109, 122, 153, 167, 193.
Chevrolet Corvair, 17.
Chevrolet Lumina, 219.
Chevy Aluminum V-8, 122.
Chicago Auto Racing Association, 165, 169, 179.
Chicago, IL, 6, 12, 17-18, 135, 164-170, 172-173, 175, 179, 193, 226.
Chicago World's Fair, 164.
Chitwood, Joie, 172.
Christie, Bob, 9, 57, 226.
Chrysler, 182, 194, 218.
Chrysler Corp., 43, 45, 183.
Chrysler 300 Convertible, 58.
Citroen, 21.
City of Glendale Special, 3.
City of Salt Lake, 198-199.

City of Tacoma Special, 175.
Clark, Jimmy, 43, 47, 50-51, 57-58, 63-65, 67-71, 75, 92-94, 96-97, 101, 107, 109, 113, 118, 124-126, 130, 138, 140-141, 144-146, 218.
Clancy Special, 77.
Clancy six-wheeler, 81.
Clidinst, Bob, 212- 214.
Climax, 75.
Climax engine, 17.
Clymer, Floyd, 86, 115, 153.
Cobb, John, 190, 199.
Cobras, 76.
Cole, Hal, 174-175.
Coleman Four Wheel Special, 82.
Collins, Bob, 51.
Collins cams, 165.
Collins, Sid, 37.
Colorado State Fairgrounds, 199.
Columbus, OH, 44.
Commodore Starliner, 183, 188.
Commodore V-8, 181.
<u>Competition Car</u>, 21.
Congdon, Russ, 11, 15-16, 19.
Connor, George, 172.
Cooper car, 43.
Cooper Car Company, 18.
Cooper Chassis, 17, 21.
Cooper-Climax, 14, 17-18, 20-22, 113, 21 5.
Cooper design, 42.
Cooper, Gordon, 143.
Cooper, John, 18, 20-22, 30-31, 42, 143, 148.
Cooper/Novi, 21.
Cord, 183.
Corum, L.L., 184.
Corvette, 17,183.
Costa Mesa, CA, 68, 213.
Cosworth V-8, 150.
Court, William, 211.
Coventry Climax engine, 21, 72.
Coventry, England, 72.
Crosley, 183.
Cross, Art, 161, 177-176.
Crosthwaite, John, 31, 39.
Cruiser, 181.
Culver City, CA, 23, 188.
Cummins Diesel, 151, 189.
Cunningham, Briggs, 73.

D

D'Leia, Lou, 23-24.
Daigh, Chuck, 31, 33.
Dallas, TX, 91.

Dallenbach, Wally, 218.
Darlington, SC, 93.
Darlington Speedway, 178.
Davis, Don, 18, 27.
Day-Glo, 104.
Daytona 500, 16, 49, 97, 130, 218.
Daytona International Speedway, 45-46, 141, 181.
Daytona Beach, FL, 97, 130, 218.
Dayton Steel Wheel Special, 142.
Daywalt, Jimmy, 177.
Dean, Al, 14.
Dean Van Lines, 13, 27, 31, 119-120, 125, 129, 140, 145, 211.
Deeb, Jr, George, 93, 119.
Dees, Mark, 211.
Defense Products Division, 202.
DeHart, Lillian, 195.
DeHart, Robert, 195, 197, 201-202.
Demler, Norm, 144.
Demler Special, 14, 31, 34, 139-140.
Demler turbine, 154.
Denver Chicago Trucking Company Special, 39.
Denver, CO, 194.
DePaolo, Pete, 83, 115, 184.
<u>Design & Development of the Indy Car</u>, 144, 211.
"Design For a Winner," 64.
DeSoto, 183.
DeSoto Memorial Drag Strip, 120.
Des Plaines, IL, 135.
Detroit, MI, 43, 75, 173, 186, 206.
de Villiers, 32.
DeVore, Billy, 172.
Diamond T Truck, 196.
Dickson, Larry, 144.
Diesel Blitz, 197.
Dinsmore, Duke, 9.
Dirks, Rudolph, 172.
DOHC, 90, 122, 188.
Drag Strip Racing Hall of Fame, 120.
Drake, Dale, 139.
Drake Engineering Company, 139, 151.
Dredge, William (Bill), 135, 202-203.
Drewry's Special, 33.
Duesenberg, 183.
Duesenberg, Fritz, 10, 58.
Duke University, 71.
Duman, Ronnie, 96, 104-106, 119, 144.
Duncan, Len, 178.
Duncan, Teddy, 165.
Dunlop, 77, 79.
Dunlop-Bendix CV, 88-89.
Dunlop mag alloy rim, 88.
Dunlop tires, 18, 86-88, 96, 98, 100, 107-108.

Duns, Scotland, 125.
Du Quoin, IL, 28, 111.
Durant, 183.
Dutch Grand Prix, 42.
DVS, 93, 109, 120.
DVS Special, 119-120.
DVS Tombstone Life Special, 121.
DVS Tombstone STP Special, 120.

E

Eagle, 217.
Earhart, Amelia, 76.
Eddie Called Me Boss, 67.
Edison, Thomas, 184.
Egbert, Sherwood, 75, 118, 179-183, 189-190, 201.
Elisian, Ed, 199.
El Mirage, 165.
Empire State Building, 210.
Englewood (CO) Speedway, 199.
English Channel, 213.
English Goodwood Circuit, 72.
Epperly, Quin, 13, 16, 28.
Erickson, Ray, 166-167.
Esmark, 219.
Esso, 18.
Estes, Bob, 221.
Estrella Mountains, 137.
Evans, Bill, 211.
Evans, Eddie, 210-211.
Evans, John, 210-211.
Evanston, Illinois Speedway, 170.
Evansville, IN, 210.

F

Fabulous Novi Story, 74, 79, 90.
Fageol, Lou, 83-84.
Fageol, Twin Coach Special, 84.
Fairlane V-8, 43, 47, 90, 101.
Fairman, Jack, 31, 33, 43, 74-75.
Falcon, Bob, 221.
Falconer, Ryan, 107.
Falk, Ron, 6.
Famous Indy Cars & Drivers, 211.
Farben, I.G., 193.
Faulkner, Walt, 177.
Federal Engineering Special, 108, 127.
Fengler, Harlan, 10, 12, 36, 53, 58, 65-69, 115-116, 127.
Ferguson, 75, 78, 85, 87-89, 91-98, 100, 110, 114-119, 125, 135, 205, 207, 213.
Ferguson, Andrew, 130, 135, 150.
Ferguson chassis, 206.

Ferguson Eng. Ltd., 72-75, 77, 79, 92, 206.
Ferguson, Harry, 72.
Ferguson-Novi, 73, 80, 105, 118, 213.
Ferguson P99, 72-74, 84, 88.
Ferguson P104, 73, 77, 89, 111-112, 133-134.
Ferrari, 18, 151.
Ferrari, Enzo, 151.
F.I.A. (Federation of Internationale de L'Automobile), 16, 181.
Fiberglas Special, 49.
Fike Plumbing Special, 53.
Firestone, 18, 48-49, 71-72, 74, 77, 87, 95, 98, 100, 117, 123, 125, 129, 144, 146, 152, 174, 210.
Firestone Tire & Rubber Company, 117.
Firestone Tire Company, 48, 74, 88, 95-96, 100, 112-113, 119, 129, 138-139, 199.
First Brands, 219.
Flaherty, Pat, 7, 13, 69, 166-168, 174-175, 222.
"Florida Flash," 130.
Flying Scot, 65, 124.
Folz, Art, 169.
FOMOCO, 181.
Forbes, Bill, 91, 106.
Forbes Racing Team, 13, 28.
Forbes Special, 106.
Ford, 43, 69, 71, 100-102, 107-110, 113, 122-123, 126, 128-129, 130, 135, 138-139, 144-145, 148, 150-151, 153, 157, 165, 167-168, 175, 181.
Ford, Benson, 101.
Ford, Henry, 43, 151, 170.
Fordillacs, 168.
Ford Motor Company, 28, 43, 71, 75-76, 80, 90, 92, 130, 150-151, 170, 174, 183.
Ford V-8, 106, 109, 122, 137, 148, 164, 168, 172, 217.
Formula One, 13, 17-18, 21-22, 31, 42-43, 72, 74, 77, 84, 88, 135, 138, 145-146, 148, 150, 154, 189, 211-212.
Formula One Championship, 145.
Fort Worth, TX, 128.
Foster, Billy, 123, 127, 129.
Foyt, A.J., 14, 18-19, 22, 38, 49, 50-51, 56-57, 64-65, 68, 74, 78-80, 91, 94, 96, 108-109, 111, 113, 116, 118-119, 123-125, 127-129, 136, 138, 140-141, 146, 153, 155, 227.
Fox, Jack, 148, 173.
Fraizer, Dick, 167, 174.
Frame, Fred, 187.
France, Bill, 45-46, 211-212.
Frankfurt, Germany, 193.
Freeland, Don, 167.
Fresno, CA, 144, 199, 209.
Fuson, Wayne, 34.

G

Garabedian, Michael, 117, 222.
Garabedian, Wally, 34, 222.
Gardner, Derrick, 77.
Gardner, Jim, 71.
Gardner, Radio, 71, 204, 214-215, 229-230.
Garlits, Don, 120.
Gary, IN, 173.
Gasoline Alley, 2, 10, 12, 26, 34-35, 37, 46, 54, 57, 64, 80, 89, 111, 115, 123, 125, 143, 172, 216, 225, 230.
Gates, Bill, 121, 147, 226.
Gates, Bob, 36, 104.
General Electric T58, 139.
General Electric, 139.
General Motors Corp., 43, 169, 183, 227.
George, Elmer, 223.
George, Mari Hulman, 19, 100, 225.
Gerhardt, Fred, 15, 24, 146, 148.
Gerhardt Novi, 148.
Gerhardt Offy, 144, 149.
Glendale, CA, 24.
Glidden-Menard Special, 218.
Goldsmith, Paul, 30, 51, 53, 130.
Goodwood Circuit, 72.
Goodyear, 37, 72, 74, 76.
Goodyear, Scott, 38.
Goodyear Tire Co., 48, 69, 74, 76-77, 79, 95, 113.
Goodyear tires, 48, 55, 69, 72, 74, 78, 87, 90, 98, 123, 144.
Goossen, Leo, 153, 206.
Gozzi, Franco, 151.
Graham, Athol, 199-200.
Granada Hills, CA, 182.
Granatelli, Andy, 1-16, 19-36, 38-42, 44-52, 54-58, 62, 64, 66-67, 69-80, 84-85, 88-96, 98, 100, 106, 109-119, 121-122, 124, 126-127, 129, 135-141, 143-144, 146-170, 172-181, 183-184, 189-190, 192, 202-206, 209, 216-218, 221, 223- 227.
Granatelli, Carmine Cardinal, 164.
Granatelli, Dolly, 226.
Granatelli, Joe, 1-8, 12-13, 16, 19-27, 29-31, 34-36, 38-39, 44-52, 55-56, 65, 69-75, 79-80, 85, 88, 90, 96, 100, 110-117, 119, 122, 126-127, 129, 135-140, 143-144, 146-156, 162-170, 172-182, 189-190, 192, 204-205, 216, 223-226.
Granatelli, Vince, 1-5, 7-8, 12-13, 16, 19-21, 23, 25-27, 29-31, 34-36, 38-39, 41-42, 44-52, 56, 63, 69-72, 75-80, 85, 88-96, 99-100, 110-113, 118-119, 122, 126-129, 135-141, 143-144, 146-170, 172-184, 192, 204-205, 216-218, 223-226.
Granatelli, Vince, Jr., 54, 59, 151.
Granatelli, Vincent, Sr., 164.
Grancor, 164-165, 168, 173-179.
Grancor Auto Specialist, 164, 173.
Grancor Auto Specialist/SABOURIN Special, 175.
Grancor Corp., 170-171.
Grancor Corp. Special, 170-171.
Grancor Elgin Piston Special, 157, 175-176.
Grancor Rocket Firebug, 165.
Grancor Special, 172, 174.
Grancor Wynn Friction Proof Special, 175, 177.
Grancor Werner Special, 157, 173.
Grancor V-8, 171, 173.
Grand Lake, CO, 194.
Grand National, 3.
Grand Prix, 14, 22, 43, 72, 84, 154.
Grand Prix of Holland, 31.
Grant, Jerry, 123.
Graton, Jean, 211-212.
Gravely Tractor Firm, 182.
Gregory Masten, 47, 57, 123.
Griffith, Cliff, 53.
Grim, Bobby, 16, 144-145, 147.
Grissom, Gus, 143.
Guerrero, Roberto, 218.
Gulf Oil Company, 83.
Gulotta, Tony, 185, 188-189.
Gurney, Dan, 30-31, 39, 42-43, 47, 58, 68-69, 75, 96, 108-109, 118, 124, 145.
Guthrie, Janet, 215.

H

Haase, Elmer, 48.
Half Day, IL, 169, 179.
Halibrand binders, 85.
Halibrand magnesium wheel, 87, 138.
Halibrand plant, 96.
Halibrand Shrike chassis, 96, 127.
Halibrand, Ted, 48, 96, 106, 221.
Halifax Co. Historical Soc. Museum, 130.
Hall, Ira, 188.
Hall, Norm, 100, 105-106.
Hamilton, Bobby, 218.
Hamilton, Duncan, 73.
Hamilton, Ontario, Canada, 183.
Hamilton, Warren, 199.
Hanks, Sam, 28, 39, 58-59, 84, 165, 172, 176-177, 194.
Hanover, Germany, 193.
Hansgen, Walt, 145.
Hansen, Mel, 165.
Harkey, Bob, 47, 96, 105, 222.
Harrah, William, 205.
Harrah's Automotive Museum, 205.

Hartley, Gene, 1-7, 33.
Hartz, Harry, 10.
Harvey Aluminum Special, 30-31, 47, 57.
Hatfield Speedway (PA), 73.
Hawk, 155, 180-182.
Hawk V-8 Golden, 181-182.
Heath, Allen, 188-189.
Hedman Hedders, 41.
Heidelberg, PA, 52.
Hemi V-8, 44.
Henderson, Bill, 147.
Henning, Joe, 86.
Hepburn, Ralph, 36, 47, 84, 153, 161, 170-172, 185, 208-209, 211, 214-215, 220, 227, 230.
Heuer, Frank, 174.
Heuer, John, 174.
Higman, Bob, 100.
Hilborn injector, 90.
Hill, Damon, 146.
Hill, Geneva, 195.
Hill, Graham, 47, 72, 145-146, 218.
Hill, James, 192, 195, 201-202.
Hinkle, Jack, 177, 192.
History of the Race Car, Man & Machine, 211.
Hitze, Ed, 1, 24-25, 129.
Holiday Inn, 46, 67.
Holland, 31, 81.
Holland, Bill, 38, 175-178, 209.
Holley carburetor, 33, 204.
Hollingsworth, Barbara, 228.
Hollingsworth, Ted, 227-228.
Holman-Moody Ford, 71.
Hoosier 100, 69, 91.
Hoover Express Special, 14.
Hopkins, Lindsey, 5, 11, 15-16, 38, 107, 189.
Horne, Byron, 173.
Hot Rod Magazine, 204.
Hotel Tropicana Special, 26, 28-29, 34, 44, 49, 51, 64, 70, 73, 75.
Houlgate, Deke, 203.
Householder, Ronnie, 165.
Houston, TX, 117.
Hudson, 183, 185.
Huffaker, Joe, 98.
Huffaker-Offy, 78.
Hughes, Johnny, 82.
Hulbert, Don, 165.
Hulman, Anton "Tony," Jr., 13, 19, 39, 59, 100, 170, 215, 225.
Hungness, Carl, 68.
Hunt, George, 185-186.
Hunt Special, 185, 187.
Huntington, Roger, 144, 148-149, 187, 189, 211.

Hupmobiles, 185, 188.
Hurricane Hot Rod Assoc., 2, 166, 169, 174.
Hurst Company, 100.
Hurtubise, 36, 104, 226.
Hurtubise, Jim, 4, 14-15, 18, 31, 34, 36-37, 40, 45-53, 56, 58-70, 72, 75-76, 92-93, 123-127, 129-131, 134, 136, 144, 146-148, 153, 157-158, 205, 212, 214-215, 217-218, 220, 222, 227-229.
Hurtubise, Pete, 52.
Hutcherson, Dick, 130.
Hydragas suspension, 78.

I

Iacocca, Lee A., 76.
Illustasted History of the Indy 500, 148.
Illustrated Speedway News, 30.
Indiana State Fairgrounds, 91, 111.
Indiana State Museum, 205.
Indianapolis 500, 7, 12-12, 17-20, 26, 27, 30, 36, 39-40, 43-44, 46-48, 50, 53, 55, 57, 65, 69-70, 74-75, 77, 81, 83-84, 90, 92, 95-96, 110-111, 113, 115, 117, 119, 123, 125-126, 128, 135-137, 141, 145-146, 152-153, 155, 157-158, 160, 165, 170-171, 175-176, 178, 184-186, 188, 202, 216-218.
Indianapolis 500 Oldtimers Club, 215-216.
Indianapois, IN, 1, 3, 21-22, 66, 82, 172.
Indianapolis Kiwanis Club, 22.
Indianapolis Star, 9, 13, 36, 50-51, 70, 122, 139, 147, 171, 173, 203, 220.
Indianapolis Times, 1, 9, 68, 79.
Indianapolis Sweepstakes, 82, 169.
Indianapolis Motor Speedway, 1, 6, 10, 14, 17, 24-28, 30, 34, 44-46, 71-73, 113, 149-150, 170-171, 181, 185, 188, 204-205, 210, 213-214, 215, 220-222, 225-227.
Indianapolis Motor Speedway Hall of Fame and Museum, 219.
Indy Car Racing, 44, 217. 29.
Indy Racing Legends, 156.
Internation Motor Contest Assoc. (IMCA), 53, 91, 136, 165.
Insinger, Harris, 188.
Iskenderian cam, 45.
Iskenderian, Ed, 45.

J

Jacobi, Bruce, 47.
Jade Miniatures, 213.
Jaguar, 74, 221.
Jahns Pistons, 165.
James, Jesse, 192.

JATO, 165.
Jenkins, David Abbott, 184-185, 188, 190-191.
Jenkins, Marvin, 184, 186, 190.
Jim Robbin's Special, 14.
<u>Jimmy Clark at the Wheel,</u> 71.
Johncock, Gordon, 122-123, 125-126, 148, 214, 217-218.
Johns, Bobby, 123, 125, 130.
Johnson, Eddie, 13, 31, 97, 102, 106, 109, 126.
Johnson, Luther, 187.
Johnson, Junior, 49, 53.
Jones, Parnelli, 14, 18, 28, 30, 32, 38, 40-41, 45, 48-54, 58-61, 63, 64-71, 73, 79, 94-97, 108, 111-113, 119, 124-125, 136, 139, 153, 155, 214, 216, 225.
Jorgensen, Bill, 213.

K

Kaiser, 179.
Kansas City, MO, 136.
Karelas, Nick, 167-168.
Katzenjammer Kids, 35, 80, 171-2, 175, 178, 223.
Keck, Howard, 154.
Keller, Al, 14.
Kelly, Art, 167.
Kemerly Chevy and Olds Special, 100.
Kemerly, Richard, 100.
Kenyon, Mel, 148.
Kimberly-Clark Corp., 18.
Kimberly, Jim, 17-18, 22, 31, 33.
Kladis, Danny, 170-172, 175, 221, 225.
Klingbeil, Gus, 165.
Knepper, Arnie, 123.
Knoxville Nationals, 136.
Kokomo, IN, 166.
Konstant Hot Special, 27, 63, 66.
Kouba, Earl, 199.
Krueger, Armin, 52, 124.
Kurtis Bardahl Special, 15.
Kurtis chassis, 34, 53, 126.
Kurtis, Frank, 1-2, 24-26, 35, 223.
Kurtis-Kraft, 24, 25-26, 28-29, 33-34, 36, 44-46, 72, 75, 78, 85, 106, 114-115, 148, 171, 177, 205.
Kurtis-Kraft Novi, 78.
Kurtis roadster, 148.
KK500B, 175-176.
KK500F, 2, 5-6, 24-27, 37, 42, 44, 72, 131, 138, 205, 212.
KK500G, 120.
KK500K, 24, 131-134, 212,
KK2000, 174.
KK3000, 129, 175.
<u>Kurtis-Kraft Story,</u> 1, 24, 129.
Kuzma, Eddie, 57.

L

La Carrera Pan American, 27.
Langhorne, PA, 44.
Langworth, Richard, 184.
Lark, 39, 181, 189.
Larkin, Barney, 80.
Larson, Jud, 136, 227.
Las Vegas, NV, 26.
Laycock, Bob, 10.
Leader Card Special, 30, 38, 48, 51-52, 122.
Lee Elkins McNamara Special, 3.
Leighton, Chuck, 167.
LeMans, 75, 211.
LeMans 24 Hour, 73.
Leonard, Joe, 123, 155, 218.
Lexington, KY, 44.
Libby, Bill, 91, 156.
<u>Life,</u> 105.
Liggett, C. Dwight, 192-196, 201-202.
Liggett Chemical Company, 192.
Liggett, Edith, 201.
Liguori, Ralph, 7-12, 16, 57, 156, 205, 221.
Lincoln, 92.
Lincoln Capri, 28.
Linden, Andy, 177, 189.
Linkletter, Art, 197.
Lodge Spark Plugs, 18.
Loewy, Raymond, 180-181.
Lola, 126.
Lola Ford, 145.
London, England, 145.
Lorenz, Harold, 175, 193-194.
Lorenz, John, 175.
Lorenzen, Freddie, 130, 218.
Los Angeles, CA, 56, 122, 165, 179, 182.
Los Angeles Coliseum, 165.
Los Angeles International Airport, 179.
<u>Los Angeles Times</u>, 202.
Lotus, 31, 42-43, 68-69, 71, 75, 92, 98, 108, 126, 130, 138, 140, 144, 147, 150, 154.
Lotus Fords, 47-48, 57, 93-94, 96, 100, 109, 113, 118-119, 123-124, 141, 144-145.
Lotus-Ford turbo, 217, 212.
Lotus-Novi, 150.
Lotus Powered By Ford, 65, 107, 118, 125-126.
Lotus STP, 135.
LSR, 30, 76, 185-186, 190, 200, 203.
Lubbock, TX, 196.
Ludvigsen, Karl, 153.
Lund, DeWayne "Tiny," 49.
Lurani, Giovanni, 211.
Luyendyk, Arie, 38, 80, 216.
Lycoming Company, 200.

M

MacDonald, Dave, 96-97, 101-106, 109-110, 115, 122.
MacDonald, J.C., 186.
McCahill, Tom, 165.
McCluskey, Roger, 18, 44, 63, 66-67, 119, 136, 146.
McCoy, Billy, 209.
McCoy, Ernie, 221.
McCulloch Company, 179-180.
McCulloch, Robert Paxton, 179.
McCulloch supercharger, 178.
McDonough, Bob, 82.
McElreath, Jim, 28, 30, 38, 50-51, 73-74, 91-92, 94-98, 100, 102, 105-106, 109, 113, 119, 133, 136, 158, 207, 212.
McGrath, Jack, 177.
McNamara Special, 3.
McQuinn, Harry, 170, 176.
McWithey, Jim, 227.
Mad Dog IV, 45-46.
Mallory coils, 165.
Malone, Art, 45-49, 52, 55, 60-62, 64, 91-93, 98-100, 105-108, 110, 113-114, 116, 119-120, 130-131, 136, 158, 205, 215, 218, 228.
Marcenac, Jean, 2, 5-6, 16, 19, 32, 35, 37, 50-51, 55-56, 90, 115, 153,162, 209, 215, 222, 225.
Marchese, Carl, 27.
Marmon, 83, 183.
Marmor, Gene, 168.
Marshman, Bobby, 30, 44, 48, 50-51, 74-75, 78, 91-93, 97, 101, 109, 113.
Marston Excelcior, 89.
Martin, Jack, 219.
Martin, Mark, 44.
Marvel, Bill, 10, 44, 96.
Marvin, Bobby, 45, 47, 228.
Maserati, 123, 173.
Mates White Front, 58.
Mathouser, Bob, 105, 122-123, 153.
Mays, Rex, 82, 84, 211, 227.
Maxwell, 183.
Mechanix Illustrated, 165.
Mecom, John, Jr., 145.
Mehl, Leo, 74.
Melbourne, FL, 169.
Memorial Day, 34, 58, 170.
Menard, John, 218.
Mercedes, 84, 154.
Mercedes-Benz, 153, 201, 214.
Mercury, 164-165, 173, 175.
Merzney, Fred, 82.
Meskowski, Wally, 96.
Metal-Cal Special, 28. 33.

Methodist Hospital, 8, 173.
Mexico, 27, 56.
Meyer, Louie, 38-39, 50, 139, 186, 219, 222.
Meyer, Zeke, 86.
MG Liquid Suspension Special, 77-78.
Miami, FL, 130, 169.
Michel Vaillant Comic Series, 213.
Michels, Gilbert "Skippy," 167.
Miller, Al, 47, 57, 69, 83, 125.
Miller, Ak, 120.
Miller, Chet, 12, 46, 69, 122-123, 125, 148, 153, 161, 170, 189, 205, 208, 210-211, 215, 227.
Miller Dynasty, 211.
Miller-Ford, 170-174, 186, 205, 230.
Miller-Ford chassis, 204.
Miller-Gulf car, 83, 148.
Miller, Harry, 82-83.
Miller, Robin, 70, 226.
Miller V-8, 82.
Miller, Zeke, 83, 185.
Millers, 82-83, 206.
Mills Novelty Company, 193.
Milwaukee 100, 119.
Milwaukee 200, 91.
Milwaukee Mile, 28, 120-121, 127.
Milwaukee, WI, 111, 166.
Miracle Power, 193-194.
Mitchell, Walter, 86.
Mobil Gas Special, 96, 127.
Mobil Oil, 64.
Mobiloil, 194.
Modesto, CA, 176.
Monaco, 14.
Monocoque chassis, 42.
Monroe shocks, 199.
Monza, Italy, 5, 12, 74, 137, 153, 157, 205, 221.
Moog Special, 127-128.
Moore, George, 9, 36, 50, 139, 141, 147, 220.
Moore, Lou, 38, 153, 175.
Mormon Meteor, 191.
Morrison, Jim, 167.
Moss, Stirling, 72-74.
Motoring News, 73.
Motor Racing Developments, 21.
Mr. Ed, 197.
MRRC Company, 213.
Muncie, IN, 167.
Murat Temple, 69.
Muroc Dry Lake, 165, 188.
Murphy, Paula L., 76-77, 182.
Murray, Jim, 94.
Mustang, 101.
Mutual Racing Assoc., 166-167.

N

Nalon, Duke, 15, 50-51, 84, 128, 153, 162, 165, 175, 177, 189, 205, 209-211, 213-216, 220-221, 226-227, 229.
NASCAR, 3-4, 8, 16, 43-46, 49, 53-54, 71, 125, 130, 137, 143, 146, 211, 218-219, 225.
Nash, 183.
National Championship Series, 111, 118.
National Driving Championship, 27.
National Hot Rod Assoc., 46.
National Midget Champion, 15.
National Speed Sport News, 44, 69, 146, 220, 222-223.
Navarro, Barney, 174.
Navarro heads and manifold, 174.
Neely, William, 95.
Nelson, Norm, 130, 167.
New Castle, IN, 167.
New York City, NY, 182, 184.
New Zealand, 72.
Newport Beach, CA, 27.
Niagara Falls, NY, 34.
Nieland, Barbara, 182.
Noc-Out Hose Clamp Special, 161, 172.
Norden steering, 165.
Norquest, C. Lee, 74, 79, 90.
North Electric Special, 9.
North Tonawanda, NY, 119.
Nothing Special, 100.
Novi 4WD, 84, 153, 157.
"Novi Europ," 212.
Novi-Ferguson, 75, 77, 80-81, 88, 92, 103, 112, 207.
Novi Gas Treatment Special, 124.
Novi Governor Special, 37, 84, 171, 220.
Novi Grooved Piston Ring Special, 205, 210, 214-215.
Novi, MI, 157, 206, 214-215.
Novi Mobil Special, 46.
Novi Motorsports Museum and Hall of Fame of America, 207, 215.
Novi Purelube Special, 210, 229.
Novi Special, 212, 218.
Novi STP, 55.
Novi V-8, 85, 88, 111, 128-129, 137, 139-141, 147-148, 154, 182, 215, 228.
Nu-Chem, 192.
Nye, Doug, 43.

O

Oakes, Danny, 36, 144.
Ocala, FL, 120.
O'Connor, Pat, 4.
Odo, Larry, 167.

Offenhauser/Offy, 1-3, 5, 17, 19, 21-22, 24-26, 28, 30-31, 36, 39, 41-42, 47-48, 50-51, 53, 65, 78, 81, 83-84, 90, 95-96, 98, 100, 109-110, 113, 117, 119, 123, 125-126, 128-129, 137, 139, 144-149, 151, 153-154, 161-162, 173-175, 189, 199, 206, 217.
Oklahoma City, OK, 199.
"Old Calhoun," 54, 94.
Olsen, Norm, 173.
Olson, Les, 167.
Onan, CO, 182.
Ongais, Danny, 120.
Ontario (CA) Speedway, 91.
Orange County CA Drag Strip, 169.
Orfe, John, 210.
O'Rourke, Cowboy, 221.
Osborn, Myron, 39.
Osiecki, Bob, 45-46.
Oulton Park, 72-73.
Oulton Park Gold Cup, 72, 74.
Oursler, Bill, 69.
Over Hill & Dale Studios, 210.
Over Time Machines, 209.

P

Packard, 181, 191.
Palermo, Italy, 164.
Pan American Road Race, 27.
Panch, Marvin, 16.
Paoli, Bessie, 27, 220.
Parks, Wally, 46, 219.
Parnelli, 91, 156.
Parsons, Johnnie, 165, 176.
Pat Clancy Special, 77.
Pate, Lee, 194.
Patrick, Pat, 217.
Patton, W. Blaine, 171.
Paxton, 140, 149, 156, 160, 223.
Paxton-Novi, 17, 20, 111.
Paxton Products Company, 2, 4-5, 23, 39, 73, 85, 180, 182, 189-190, 202, 217, 224.
Paxton Products Supercharged V-8, 2.
Paxton Special, 5, 7, 12, 15-16.
Paxton Studebaker Corp., 73.
Paxton STP, 135.
Paxton supercharger, 1, 40, 76, 179-182, 202.
Peck, Ray L., 184.
Pennzoil, 186, 218.
Penske car, 153.
Perfect Circle Piston Ring, 97, 199.
Periat, Marcel, 35.
Pete Schmidt Special, 9.

Peters, Bruce, 210.
Petrasek, Steve, 73.
Petty, Kyle, 218.
Petty, Lee, 130.
Petty Racing Enterprise, 218.
Petty, Richard, 213, 218-219.
Phillips, Jud, 27.
Phoenix, AZ, 196.
Phoenix Gazette, 137.
Phoenix (AZ) International Raceway, 77, 79, 113, 119, 136-137, 162.
Pierce Arrow Company, 188, 191.
Pike's Peak Hill Climb, 54.
Pioneer Auto Rebuilders Special, 74.
Pistone, Tom, 168.
Ploesti, Romania, 193.
Plymouth, 130.
Plymouth Fury, 180.
Plymouth Road Runner, 210.
Pole Day, 7, 49, 52, 95-96, 118.
Pollard, Art, 218.
Polsky's Auto Parts Store, 194.
Pony Express, 192.
Porsche, 31, 42-43, 84, 96.
Porsche 911, 17, 140.
Porter, Herb, 140, 145, 189.
Portland, OR, 38.
"Pots and Pans Special," 3.
Pouelsen, Johnny, 50, 52, 95.
Prather, Ollie, 28, 91.
Pratt & Whitney engine, 154.
Precision Miniatures, 213.
President, 184, 186-188.
President 8, 185.
Pueblo, CO, 199.
Pure Firebird Special, 143.
Purelube Special, 209, 229.
Pure Oil Company, 218.
Pure Oil Firebird Special, 96, 107.
Puslio, John Marco, 36.
Putnam, Al, 171.
Puyallup, WA, 15.

Q

Quadcam Ford V-8, 78, 110, 140, 148, 151-152, 161, 165, 170.
Quinn, Richard, 188.

R

Race of Two Worlds, 74.
Racing Association Special, 117.
Railton Mobil Special, 190.
Rathmann, Dick, 2-8, 10-11, 13-16, 19-20, 27, 36-38, 48-49, 56, 166-167.
Rathmann, Jim, 7, 14, 18, 31, 33, 143, 157, 167-169, 174-178, 189.
Raybestos linings, 85.
RCA Dome, 227.
Red Cross Pharmacy, 194.
Redkey, Harry, 137.
Reece, Jimmy, 199.
Renner, Red, 167.
Reo trucks, 196.
Reynolds, James A., 44.
Rickenbacker, Eddie, 219.
Rigling, Herman, 187.
Riverside, CA, 130, 180, 218.
Riverside Raceway, 180.
Robbins, Jim, 3, 7, 14, 34, 92, 98-99, 137, 167-168.
Robbins Special, 7, 36, 98, 137.
Roberts, Fireball, 130.
Robson, George, 125, 172.
Rodee, Chuck, 56, 127, 141.
Rodriguez, Pedro, 47, 57.
Rogers, Bob, 223-224.
Rogers, Lois, 223.
"Roller Skate," 42, 47, 97, 102-103.
Rolt, Major Tony, 73-74, 89, 92.
Romcevich, Pete, 165, 172-173, 175.
Romite Special, 186, 188.
Rooney, Mickey, 209.
Root, Chapman, 177.
Roots blower, 84, 140, 148-149, 151.
Roots Special, 45.
Rose, Ebb, 57, 116-117, 158, 228.
Rose, Mauri, 38, 87, 175.
Roseville, MI, 69.
Rosmalen, The Netherlands, 81.
Royal Oaks, MI, 7.
Ruby, Lloyd, 16-17, 65, 106, 126, 145.
Rudolph, Lewis, 194.
Rudolph, Victor, 194.
Ruiz, Ernie, 36, 176, 178.
Rupp, Mickey, 123, 125.
Rusch, Buddy, 171.
Russell Special, 186, 188.
Russo, Bob, 204.
Russo, Paul, 2, 6, 11-12, 14-16, 19, 37-39, 53, 84, 96-97, 100, 153, 176, 208-209, 215, 222, 226-228.
Rutherford, Johnny, 47, 103-106, 127-129, 136, 216, 225.
Ruttman, Troy, 15, 28, 31, 57, 177, 188-189, 222.

S

Sabourin, Dr. Raymond N., 175.
Sachs, Eddie. 14-15, 18-19, 22, 31, 33, 38, 48, 58, 65, 67, 69, 76, 96, 102-106, 109, 115.
Saint Joseph Gazette, 201.
Saint Joseph, MO, 182, 190, 192, 194-197, 201-202, 219.
Saint Louis, MO, 196.
Sakkis, Tony, 156.
Salemi, Pete, 128.
Salt Flats, 152, 191, 199-200.
Salt Lake City, UT, 184, 199-200.
Salvino, Ralph, 219, 221.
San Antonio, TX, 119.
San Francisco, CA, 184.
Santa Fe, NM, 195.
Santa Monica, CA, 1-3, 16, 26-27, 32, 75, 111, 162, 180, 190, 206, 217, 223-224.
Sat. Evening Post, 197.
Savage, David "Swede," 217.
Savage, Tom, 221.
Schneider, Louis, 187.
Schrader, Gus, 82.
Schroeder, Gordon, 84, 122.
Schulz Fueling Equipment Special, 28.
Scientifically Treated Petroleum, 189, 192.
Scott, Bob, 178.
Seal Line Special, 27.
Sears Allstate Special, 77, 97, 102-103, 106.
Sears tires, 100, 182.
Seattle, WA, 15.
Sessions, Sammy, 128.
Seymour, Johnny, 83.
Shaw, Wilbur, 26, 220.
Shepard, A.J., 17, 18.
Shepard, Don, 147.
Sheraton Thompson Special, 57, 108, 118, 123, 128, 141.
Shrike chassis, 106.
Silent Sam, 154.
Simoniz Special, 14, 33.
Simplex, 183.
Singer, Al, 171.
Singer Special, 171.
Sirois, "Frenchy," 14.
Skinner, Sam, 167.
Smith, Clay, 28.
Smith's rev counter, 89.
Smithy mufflers, 165.
Sneva, Tom, 218.
Snider, George, 123, 141.
Snowberger, Russ, 186-188.
Snyder, Jimmy, 57, 170.

Society of Rear Engine Racers, 206.
Soldier Field, 165-168.
Sommers, Richard, 67, 93, 119-120.
Soule, Charles, 199.
Sounders, George, 146.
South Bend IN, 28, 39, 114, 183-187, 190, 201-202.
Southern California Timing Association, 165.
Sparks, Art, 150-151, 165.
Sparks-Weirick engine, 151, 165.
Speed Age, 210.
Speedway, 1-2, 5, 7-9, 12-13, 18-19, 20-21, 26, 30, 32, 34, 36-37, 39-40, 42, 44, 51, 53, 55- 59, 65, 71, 73, 76-78, 80, 89, 91, 93, 95-97, 99, 110, 113-114, 119, 129, 138-141, 143, 152, 155, 157, 160-161, 170, 172, 175, 177, 185, 187-189, 208, 215, 217-224, 227.
Spijker brothers, 81.
Spike Jones Special, 84, 172.
Spiker, Jacobus, 82.
Sports Car Club of America (SCCA), 18, 77.
Sports Illustrated, 67.
Springfield, IL, 71, 166.
Springfield Welding Special, 28.
Spyker Company, 81.
Spyker 4WD, 82.
Stay Tuned for the Greatest Spectacle in Racing, 37.
Stearly Motor Freight Special, 11.
Stein, Al, 140.
Sterling Plumbing Special, 53.
Stern, Bill, 197.
Sternquist, Willie, 167.
Stevens, Harry, 177.
Stevenson, Chuck, 26-29, 31-36, 105-106, 223.
Stewart, Jim, 77, 145-146.
Stewart, Tony, 218.
Stover, Ralph "Smokey, 167.
STP, 55-56, 75, 89, 91-95, 98, 100, 102, 112, 114-116, 118-121, 124, 126, 137-138, 140, 147, 155, 157, 160, 162, 177, 180, 190, 193-197, 199-202, 205, 212, 214, 218-219, 222, 226-227.
STP Double Oil Filter Special Offy, 217.
STP Gasoline Treatment Special, 114, 141, 144, 146, 216.
STP Lotus, 146.
STP Novi, 100.
STP Oil Treatment Special, 114, 117, 137, 144, 155, 212.
STP Products, 46, 218.
STP Special, 44, 47, 62, 111, 126, 143, 156, 217.
STP Special 500F, 44.
STP Studebaker Corp., 135.
STP Studebaker Division, 86, 110.
STP Studebaker Special, 75-76, 85, 91-92, 97, 107, 135.

STP Tombstone Life Special, 123, 221.
Stroppe, Bill, 28, 71.
Stubblefield, Stubby, 141.
Studebaker, 39, 76-77, 114, 135, 157, 171, 181-182, 184, 189, 190, 219.
Studebaker, Clement, 184.
Studebaker Company, 44, 73, 75, 86, 114, 118, 160, 182-184, 186, 189, 191-192, 201-202, 217.
Studebaker, Henry, 184.
Studebaker, John M., 184.
Studebaker-Packard Corp., 180, 201.
Studebaker-STP, 76.
Stuttgart, Germany, 43.
Stutz, 183.
Sullivan, Danny, 218.
Sumar Special, 177.
Sun City Special, 4.
Sun Valley Speedway, 91.
Sutton, Len, 38, 50, 125, 216.
Sweeney, Al, 165.
Sweeney, Gilbert, 51.
Sweikert, Bob, 226.
Swenson, Allen, 167-168.

T

Talladega, AL, 205, 215, 218.
Talladega International Motorsports Hall of Fame and Museum, 205, 215, 218-219.
Tampa, FL, 45.
Tasman Series, 72.
Teague, Marshall, 130.
Templeman, Shorty, 13, 28.
Ternalloy, 24.
Terra Haute, IN, 169.
Texaco Company, 164.
Theme Lotus, 1956-1986, 43.
They Call Me Mr. 500, 8, 136, 178, 226.
Thompson cars, 100, 109.
Thompson/Crostwaite chassis, 39.
Thompson, Mickey, 1, 30-32, 34, 38-39, 42-43, 47, 57, 74, 93, 97, 102-103, 109,120, 122-123, 153, 225.
Thompson Special, 33, 93.
Thone, "Marblehead," 168.
Thunderbird, 183.
Thunder In The Dome, 227.
Tichenor, George, 165.
Tici, Rudy, 168.
Tingelstad, Bud, 108, 127-128.
"Tinley Park Express," 12.
Tinley Park, IL, 11.
Tire Wars, Racing With Goodyear, 95.

"Tired Iron", 55, 72, 120.
Tombstone Life Insurance, 120.
Tombstone Life Special, 93, 118, 102.
Tombstone-STP Special, 121.
Torrance Torpedo, 65.
Torsen Gleason, 81.
Trackburner, 31-32, 129.
Traction Avant, 21.
Travelon Trailer Special, 5, 36, 57, 176.
Trenton, NJ, 111, 119.
Trevis, Floyd, 108.
Truitt, Ken, 58.
Tucker, Preston, 83.
Tucker Torpedo, 83.
Tucson, AZ, 27.
Tulsa, OK, 129, 193, 197, 199.
Tune Up Master, 207.
Turner, "Cactus" Jack, 15, 18, 24, 49, 219.
Turner, Curtis, 47, 49.
Twyford car, 81.
Twyford, Robert, 81.
Tyrell P34, 77.

U

Union Carbide Corp., 219.
UNOCAL, 215, 218.
Unser, Al, 95, 123, 125, 138, 144, 146, 154, 218, 227.
Unser, Bobby, 47, 53-57, 61-64, 78-79, 85-86, 90-93, 95-98, 100, 102-107, 113-119, 121, 123-125, 127-128, 130-131, 133-135, 155, 158, 207, 212-213, 215-216, 218, 220, 228.
Unser, Jerry, Sr., 54.
Unser, Louie, 54.
USAC, 7, 10, 12, 15-18, 40, 44, 46, 53, 58, 64-67, 69, 76-77, 100, 106-107, 110, 113,115, 117-119, 126-127, 129-130, 136-137, 151, 155, 167, 181, 204.
USAC National Champion Series, 111.
U.S. Congress, 43.
U.S. Fuel Champion, 46.
Utah Salt Flats, 30.
Utzman, Willy, 189.

V

V-8 Club, 47.
Vaillant cars, 211.
Vaillant, Henri, 211.
Vaillant, Michel, 211.
Valvoline Co., 99, 218.
Valvoline Ford Special, 44.
Valvoline Oil, 44, 160.
Valvoline Special, 44.

Van Acker, Charlie, 171.
Vandewater, Bill, 178.
Van Liew, Gordon, 54, 127.
Vanwall, 211.
Vasser, Jimmy, 218.
Veith, Bob, 9, 31, 105, 221, 227.
Victory Banquet, 69.
Victory Lane, 152, 155, 217.
Vidan, Pat, 65.
Vita Fresh Orange Juice Special, 54, 68, 107, 127-128, 144.
Voelker engine, 171.
Voigt, Robert. 93, 119, 171.
Vukovich, Billy, 175-176, 215.
VW Beetle, 17.

W

Wade's Indian Grill Restaurant, 192.
Wall Street Journal, 200-201.
Walsh, Ed, 177.
Ward, Rodger, 2, 4, 14, 18, 30, 38, 50-51, 68-69, 96-97, 108-109, 122, 128, 141, 216, 219, 225-226.
Warson, Steve, 211.
WA State Midget champ, 15.
Watson, A.J., 3, 33, 38, 69, 96, 100, 122, 126, 166, 174, 189.
Watson chassis, 11.
Watson-Offy, 144, 147.
"Way of a Champion," 108.
Weatherly, Joe, 130.
Webb, Travis "Spider," 174-175.
Weber carb, 57.
Weiand heads, 166.
Weidel, Conrad "Connie" Special, 173.
Weinberger Homes Special, 125.
Weir, Wally, 96, 127.
Weirick, Paul, 126, 150, 165.
Welch, Lewis, 1-2, 23-24, 27-28, 37, 45, 47, 53, 56, 71, 90, 109, 151-153, 156, 158, 161, 170, 173, 175, 187-188, 191, 204-206, 215.
Weld, Greg, 127, 136-146.
Wendover, UT, 184, 190.
Wente, Bob, 47, 100, 105.
Weyant, Chuck, 10.
Wheeler, Floyd, 5-6.
Whitt, Rick, 209.
Whittaker, Leo, 141.
Whittier, CA, 182.
"Whoosmobile," 154.
Wilcox, Howard S., 176.
Wilcox, Howdy, 176, 187.
Wilke, Bob, 4, 30, 38, 109.

Willard Battery Special, 14, 28, 52, 65, 70, 73.
Williams, AZ, 181.
Williams, Carl, 141, 199.
Williamsport, PA, 200.
Willman, Tony, 82, 170.
Wilson, Dempsey, 53, 57, 68.
Wilson, Jim, 226.
Winchester, IN, 210-211.
Winchester Old Timers Club, 210-211.
Winfield, Bud, 84, 152, 165, 170, 187, 225.
Winfield cams, 41.
Winfield carb, 187, 205.
Winfield, Ed, 152, 165, 170, 187, 215.
Winkley, Frank, 165.
Winn, Billy, 185.
Winston Cup, 44.
Wood, Glen, 130.
Wood, Leonard, 130.
Woodburn, IN, 167.
Woodward, Don, 179.
World's Fair, 164.
Worth, Sussex, England, 33.
Worthington Corp., 217.
Worthington-Studebaker, 217.
Wright, Dale, 210.
Wright, Larry, 210, 220.
Wynn's Friction Proofing Oil, 122, 177, 193.

X

X-Trac, 81.

Y

Yamaha Bardahl Gurney Eagle, 145.
Yamaha Special, 118.
Yarbrough, Lee Roy, 143.
Yarborough, Cale, 137.
Yates, Brock, 210.
Young, Allen, 197.
Young, Eoin, 72.
Yunick, Smokey, 33, 49, 150, 225.

Z

Zandvoort, 31, 42.
Zink, John, 30-32, 129, 199.
Zink Special, 15, 199.
Zink Urschel Track Burner Special, 113.
Zurich, Switzerland, 202.

ABOUT THE AUTHORS

Henri Greuter is a native of Edan, The Netherlands. His interest in motor racing begin with Formula One and sport cars when he was nine years old. Several years later he learned of the Indianapolis 500 Mile Race and the famed Novi. In time he came to realize that what he had been reading in Jean Graton comic books about both Indy and the Novis was based on the existence of an actual track and cars.

By this time his knowledge of English was sufficient that he began to collect books about the Indianapolis 500 and Indy cars. He attended his first Indianapolis race in 1988. Since that time he has witnessed five more 500s including the victory achieved by fellow countryman Arie Luyendyk in 1990.

His first publication was Novi, The Legendary Indianapolis Race Car, Volume I in which he served as a co-author. The study won first place in the book category in the 1991 STP - American Auto Racing Writers and Broadcasters Association (AARWBA) competition. Greuter was one of the first Europeans to join the National Indianapolis Collectors Club 500. Since the publication of Volume I, Henri has penned a number of articles for the Dutch automotive magazine, Gran Turismo. The articles relate to the historical background of motorsports.

Still following Formula One and Indy cars and several other forms of racing, Greuter continues to reside in The Netherlands. He works as a Research-Technician at the laboratories of the Nuclear Medicine Department of the Free University Academic Hospital in Amsterdam.

Greuter's latest visit to the Speedway had him in attendance for his first NASCAR contest: the 1996 Brickyard 400.

Dr. George Peters has followed auto racing since its resumption at the close of World War II. He witnessed his first Indianapolis 500 Mile Race in 1948 as Mauri Rose captured his third victory at the famed oval. In the ensuing years George has missed only four of the 500s.

Living in suburban Chicago during the 1940s and early 1950s he also witnessed top A.A.A. drivers compete at Soldier Field in midgets during the glory years. Additionally, he witnessed hot rod and stock car shows at the facility under the auspices of the Chicago Auto Racing Association. The Granatelli brothers became heavily involved in that organization. Other Chicagoland tracks were also frequently visited.

Moving from the role of spectator, Peters began a study of early racing. In time he started writing articles for several national magazines. Further, he penned a column for the now defunct Illustrated Speedway News. At the present time he writes a contemporary column for Hawkeye Racing News as well as the "Old Timers Pit Stop" column for National Speed Sport News.

As a racing historian and author, George has served on the nominating and/or selection committees for the Indianapolis Motor Speedway Hall of Fame, the International Motorsports Hall of Fame, the Novi Motorsports Hall of Fame and Museum of America and the National Sprint Car Hall of Fame and Museum.

He is a long-standing member of A.A.R.W.B.A. and has served as secretary for a number of years. He is a lifetime member of the Indianapolis 500 Oldtimers Club.

George has played a role in the completion of several racing books beyond the Novi volumes. These include Dick Wallen's definitive study, The Fabulous 50s, and Art Bagnall's illuminating study Roy Richter, Striving For Excellence. Research has also been provided for others seeking racing information for various projects. His passion for the sport crosses boundaries as the interest includes midgets, sprint cars, stock cars and championship cars.